JACK LORD

Jack Lord
An Acting Life

Sylvia D. Lynch

McFarland & Company, Inc., Publishers
Jefferson, North Carolina

LIBRARY OF CONGRESS CATALOGUING-IN-PUBLICATION DATA

Names: Lynch, Sylvia D., author.
Title: Jack Lord : an acting life / Sylvia D. Lynch.
Description: Jefferson, North Carolina : McFarland & Company, Inc., Publishers, 2018 | Includes bibliographical references and index.
Identifiers: LCCN 2018003923 | ISBN 9781476666273 (softcover : acid free paper) ∞
Subjects: LCSH: Lord, Jack. | Television actors and actresses—United States—Biography. | Motion picture actors and actresses—United States—Biography. | Hawaii Five-O (Television program : 1968–1980)
Classification: LCC PN2287.L638 L96 2018 | DDC 791.4502/8092 [B]—dc23
LC record available at https://lccn.loc.gov/2018003923

BRITISH LIBRARY CATALOGUING DATA ARE AVAILABLE

ISBN (print) 978-1-4766-6627-3
ISBN (ebook) 978-1-4766-3175-2

© 2018 Sylvia D. Lynch. All rights reserved

No part of this book may be reproduced or transmitted in any form or by any means, electronic or mechanical, including photocopying or recording, or by any information storage and retrieval system, without permission in writing from the publisher.

Front cover: Jack Lord, circa 1957 (MGM/Photofest)

Printed in the United States of America

McFarland & Company, Inc., Publishers
Box 611, Jefferson, North Carolina 28640
www.mcfarlandpub.com

For Faye—
I am pretty sure she knows why

Table of Contents

Acknowledgments — ix
Introduction: Steve McGarrett Aside — 1

One • A Good Irish Boy — 7
Two • Motive, Method and Means — 26
Three • The Road Rises Up — 35
Four • Making History — 57
Five • The Fate We Make for Ourselves — 74
Six • Low Aim Is Crime — 93
Seven • The Standard by Which All Others Are Measured — 105
Eight • The Most Successful Flop in History — 112
Nine • The Work Praises the Man — 131
Ten • "I *Am* Home" — 144
Eleven • Forgiving Poe — 171
Twelve • An Indelible Mark — 179

Filmography: Television and Film Roles — 191
Chapter Notes — 199
Bibliography — 209
Index — 213

Acknowledgments

A familiar maxim declares it takes a village to raise a child, and I think the same applies to writing a book. I am deeply grateful for so many remarkable people who have helped me along the way.

The fruits of my visits to the University of Southern California's Cinematic Arts Library extend well beyond the incredible material I found there and the importance of it to the work. Jack Lord gave not only his papers to the collection, but he began contributing all his *Hawaii Five-O* scripts, call sheets, and sketches to the library in the early 1970s. It was as if he knew very early on the work was going to make history. The above and beyond efforts of the staff gave me much needed validation to move forward, and they never wavered in their support and encouragement. In truth, it was Bree Russell who led me to the heart and soul of this book. Her diligence, her extraordinary kindness, and her gracious hospitality went well beyond the call of duty. I am so grateful to her for being as excited as I was with the treasures we found. Ned Comstock's kind encouragement, patience, and uncanny knack for finding lots and lots of great material were critical to the work. Truthfully, this book would never have happened without these two wonderful people. Special thanks to assistant director Dr. Sandra Garcia-Myers for staying the course and for putting up with me long after I am confident I had more than worn out my welcome.

I owe a huge debt of gratitude to some wonderful people at Lincoln Memorial University. First of all, to Michelle Ganz, a remarkable and creative archivist, who achieved the impossible over and over. She managed to get me where I needed to be, especially during the launch phase of the research. Thanks also to Janice McDonnell, interlibrary loan librarian, a very patient and inventive lady who I am sure spent more time with me than she had to spare. Much appreciation to Dr. Charles Hubbard, a Lincoln scholar, who stepped out of his comfort zone to help me with Lord's very complicated military record. Many thanks to my colleagues at my day job in the School of Education for helping me find the time to do this, for being excited and interested in the work, and for pushing me forward every time I stalled. Thanks to Dr. Teresa Bicknell for the proofreading help. Very special thanks to Trent Clagg and my brother Jay Sulfridge for their unfailing patience in fixing my recurring technology crises.

To Mr. Carl Childs, deputy director, John D. Rockefeller, Jr. Library, Archives and Records, Colonial Williamsburg Foundation, and to the remarkable staff, for allowing me access to an amazing collection and for leading me to the next book. I am deeply grateful for Jenna Anne Simpson's outstanding scholarship in her 2006 master's thesis, *Screening the Revolution*, a great history and political analysis of *The Story of a Patriot*.

I am grateful to the wonderful staff at the Margaret Herrick Library at the Academy of Motion Picture Arts and Sciences for their assistance and hospitality; also to Mark Quigley, access archivist and manager at the UCLA Research and Study Center's Film and Television Archive, a very patient and helpful person who made it possible for me to see some great film from Jack Lord's early career. Deepest appreciation to Martin Gostanian at the Paley Center in Los Angeles for his kindness and enthusiasm about my project and for the opportunity to see some great rare film. Many thanks to Kapena Shim, librarian, Hawaiian Collection at the University of Hawaii, for a wealth of material, and to Deborah Shapiro at New York University for her diligence in helping me get a much-needed jump-start when I was stalled in the biography chapter. Thank you, Emme Tomimbang, in Hawaii for some great material and for kind words of encouragement.

I am grateful to the helpful people at Photofest and to Dana at the Westwood Gallery in New York for her help with the remarkable photos and for her role in confirming Lord's Actors Studio timeline. Many thanks to Vakil Smallen and the staff in special collections at George Washington University, and to the very helpful staff at the Library of Congress.

Much love to my family for doing what they always do—climbing on board, standing ready to help, and giving me permission to go just a little crazy one more time.

Finally, I am very grateful to Mr. Jack Lord. I am one of those to whom he said his work brought an "awful lot of joy." To say a look at his career was an interesting study doesn't even begin to describe it. I certainly don't claim to have found all the answers; but I can say with confidence I have seen more than enough to validate that he was one of the most interesting, most productive, and most passionately complex people ever. This was such fun.

"We're cops.
We're not built to stand still."
—Steve McGarrett,
Hawaii Five-O, CBS, Season 5, Episode 6
(Airdate October 17, 1972)

Introduction: Steve McGarrett Aside

There is delicious irony in how well modern technology facilitates nostalgia. The Internet may have ushered in the future, but the capability it offers to return to the past has proven to be one of its greatest appeals. A few years ago, a new Netflix subscription and a much-needed commitment to the treadmill brought me back to a favorite television series with characters who were as real to me as the people I encountered every day.

September 20, 2018, marks the fiftieth anniversary of the premiere of Leonard Freeman's innovative police series, *Hawaii Five-O*. The show hit the fall lineup in 1968 at the start of my ninth-grade year, and it launched me on a long running obsession. Filmed entirely on location in Hawaii, Freeman's twist on the standard cop show captured a good audience for the highly publicized pilot. Our black-and-white set could not dim the lure of the inviting teasers—fast moving scenes set in a landscape so far removed from my own geography it might as well have been filmed on the moon. Promotional spots promised drama that could happen only in Hawaii, a place where "the mysterious blends dangerously with the beautiful," and introduced the dynamic lead, Steve McGarrett, "a man on the move—tough, shrewd—a cop who cares." The enticement of non-stop action, striking scenery, and a theme song that instantly embedded itself in my brain ensured that come 8 p.m. on Friday, September 13, I would be planted directly in front of the television set. By the time the two-hour pilot ended, I had pledged to be forever faithful to McGarrett's soon-to-be famous mandate that followed the preview of the next week's episode: "Be here."

As addictive as the show's glamorous setting and engaging storylines were, there is no doubt that a significant factor in a fourteen-year-old girl's unwavering devotion to the newest addition to the CBS line up that fall was Steve McGarrett. From the very first time he spun around and flashed a crooked grin from the top of the Ilikai Hotel, I joined thousands of female viewers all over the country who had suddenly found a new infatuation.

Even though the pilot episode was a certified hit, Freeman and the cast likely never imagined that when it was all said and done, there would be a history-making twelve seasons and millions of devoted fans all over the world who would stand by McGarrett and the Five-O team for decades after the series ended. For 35 years, *Hawaii Five-O* held the top spot as the longest running crime show on television until Dick Wolf's *Law & Order* finally captured the position in 2003. Then, exactly 42 years to the day after the first season aired, the show garnered what is in the entertainment business the ultimate tribute. McGarrett and his team were resurrected in 2010 with the launch of a successful reboot, an enterprise that led a whole new generation to discover the original show and the compelling actor who was the driving force behind it.

While the appeal of the enigmatic lead character and the innovative location for the show are important dynamics behind the resilience of the original *Hawaii Five-O*, it is also the ongoing attraction of series star Jack Lord that continues to fuel the franchise. Old and new fans alike ardently search for information about the famously private star, but the real Jack Lord remains a mystery. He left behind very few breadcrumbs to follow for those who want to know more about his life away from work. Even during the pinnacle of his success, his determined reluctance to share personal information makes it very hard to get at the real truth about him. Ironically, almost forty years after he left the business for good and two decades after his death, the scarcity of reliable biographical material still feeds the ongoing fascination with him.

Reports of biographies in the works continue to surface, and a well-documented one that moves beyond tabloid journalism in favor of good, primary source material would be most welcome. Thanks to the ongoing popularity of the show and the ease of Internet research, credible biographical information is slowly beginning to surface on a number of blogs and websites dedicated to Lord. Most notable is work by long-time Jack Lord researcher Virginia Tolles. The well-documented information from her website, rememberingjacklord.com, is an excellent depository of authenticated information about his life, much of it supported by surviving family members. Mike Quigley's *Hawaii Five-O* website, http://www.mjq.net/fiveo/, is another longstanding and well-done source with extensive information about the series and biographical information about Mr. Lord.

Although this study is not a biography in the traditional sense, it is still very much about Jack Lord the man. His deliberate and methodical preparation as an actor, his insistence that he maintain privacy in a business that demands a public persona, and his tenacious commitment to maintain control over his work substantiate the fact that it is his work that truly defines him. That is the focus of this study. The noticeable omission of an extensive treatment of *Hawaii Five-O* is in no way intended to minimize the fact that it was undoubtedly the role for which he will always be remembered. A remarkable twelve seasons and a dedicated audience for worldwide syndication certainly cannot be minimized in the consideration of his relative success as an actor. Author Karen Rhodes' *Booking Hawaii-Five-O* (1997, McFarland) is a well-done, well-documented comprehensive study, meticulously detailing each episode from all twelve seasons. The primary focus here is an account of the deliberate evolution of John Joseph Patrick Ryan into Jack Lord and a look at Lord's work aside from his successful run as Steve McGarrett. It is undeniable that his maverick approach to handling his own business affairs and his insistence upon creative control throughout his career contributed to his reputation as a difficult and conceited star. Review of his complete filmography and an extensive study of his business papers and personal correspondence shed light on his true intentions in the way he ran his own affairs. Research for this study showed that when it came to his work, Lord was a very complicated visionary who didn't hesitate to tune out his critics and move forward as he thought best for what he wanted to achieve.

Although he continues to elude absolute truth, one fact about him is indisputable. Jack Lord the actor was a very busy, very driven man from the beginning of his career. His dogged determination to be successful and his long tenure in the business confirm that once he decided to pursue acting, he was methodically and deliberately honing his skills long before Steve McGarrett first sprinted down the steps of the Iolani Palace and jumped into his waiting car. He was a hard-working and productive actor who left behind a significant body of work. His filmography is testimony to an impressive career that spanned three decades, during which time he crossed virtually every genre in the business. When he stepped out in earnest to pursue acting, he stayed the course and he worked very hard at it. For a man who became world famous for a single role, a look at his entire career shows that despite what his critics say, Lord was a diverse actor, garnering more than 80 television and film roles in twenty years of steady work before *Hawaii Five-O* hit the airwaves. During a 1966 guest appearance on *The Tonight Show*, host Johnny Carson introduced the segment with Lord by expressing his surprise at how prolific the actor's professional career had been.

This study documents his deliberate development as a serious actor who did not, as some of his critics have said, simply put on Steve McGarrett for every role he played.

For those who first encountered Jack Lord in *Hawaii Five-O*, it does take considerable effort to close the door on Steve McGarrett while watching his work in the years before he stepped into his career-defining role. Fragments of the legendary cop undeniably show up in some of Lord's earlier roles. Instead of writing it off to his playing the same character in every role, however, and in light of the fact that he was a busy actor playing diverse roles long before *Hawaii Five-O*, he is at least entitled to the assumption that as he worked at his craft, he deliberately took his characters unto himself. Perhaps it was some Jack Lord, rather than some Steve McGarrett, that seeped into them. Some validation for that theory may be found in the discussion that follows about his training under Sandy Meisner and the basic concepts of the Stanislavski method. A close look at the extended career of any prolific actor reveals repeating characteristics that cannot be equated solely to a lack of "acting." Even legendary screen stars agree it is hard to totally abandon oneself, no matter how far removed the role might be from the essence of the actor playing the role. In a 1974 BBC interview, Gregory Peck said, "I think in the long run what the audience enjoys is to see someone being themselves and being allowed to look inside someone. And I think the secret to film acting is complete candor with the audience or when you let them see the real you." When asked about the patent similarity in all his characters, John Wayne responded, "I play John Wayne in every picture regardless of the character, and I've been doing all right, haven't I?"[1]

In order to achieve a clean look at Lord's development as an actor, it is necessary to engage that willing suspension of disbelief and look at his portrayal of each role in the context of the story itself. Setting aside Steve McGarrett is a tough task, but it is the only way to be fair to what he brought to the table before *Hawaii Five-O*. Revisiting all twelve seasons of *Hawaii Five-O* reminded me that I had seen Jack Lord in a number of frequently watched shows from my childhood, and I reviewed as many as I could find. That, set alongside a chronological review of his earlier work in television and movies, clearly showed his development as an actor. In spite of a recurring theme among his critics about his lack of range, I was struck by his versatility, and I realized this was a study worth pursuing. Yes, he was always Jack Lord; but for his fans that was okay.

An often-cited quote from Lord is instructive in validating an actor's allowing some of himself to creep into roles he plays. "What you have, what you are—your looks, your personality, your way of thinking—is unique," he said. "No one in the world is like you. So capitalize on it." And capitalize on it he did. Lord's distinctive physical appearance might very well have been the key to his winning the role of Steve McGarrett. He definitely looked the part. While his stature, his famous square-jaw and steely gaze undoubtedly helped him secure the large number of tough guy parts he played for years before McGarrett, his looks were also a quality that sometimes kept him from roles. In 1956, as Lord was pushing hard to get in front of a camera, director Joshua Logan turned him down for the role of the innocuous Beauregard Decker in the hit film *Bus Stop*, where he would have played opposite Meisner classmate Marilyn Monroe. "You can't play a virgin," Logan told the eager young actor. "Your face looks lived in."[2] Don Murray, another newcomer to Hollywood at the time, won the role and garnered an Oscar nomination for best supporting actor. It was the first of several near misses for Lord. He would later call such disappointments "punches to the gut." In spite of the setbacks, however, he held fast to his determined approach and to his commitment to maintain control of his career.

While Jack Lord may never be counted among those screen actors critics consider the greatest of all time, he achieved exactly what he wanted to do—he provided hours and hours of good entertainment to millions of fans. "There is nothing really wrong with what I do," he told Dwight Whitney in a 1971 interview for *TV Guide*. "I act. I create a character. And I bring an awful lot of people an awful lot of joy."[3] The article translated into what Lord would later call a hatchet job and became an exhibit in his growing distrust of many of the journalists who requested interviews with him during the heyday of *Five-O*. Lord saved a clipping of a November 23, 1971, article from an interview with *The Oregon Journal*. He mentioned Whitney's *TV Guide* story. "I was warned the man was a poison pen in the first place and he wasn't allowed on the set."[4]

The resilience of his work is good testimony to the impact of his career. When Jack Lord died in 1998, he did not go away. In fact, thanks to modern technology and easy access to classic film and television programming, he is to some degree present now more than ever.

Throughout the extensive research for the book, every effort was made to utilize material from primary sources, including archival collections of Lord's personal correspondence, interviews, manuscripts, official records, and business documents. The reward from extensive work in the massive collection of his personal papers at the University of Southern California's Cinematic Arts Library was great, largely thanks to his meticulous recordkeeping and prolific letter writing. It appears Lord was an emotional hoarder, and the items he chose to save say much about him. His papers are testimony to his firm hand when it came to having his way on the job. Also evident, however, is his faithful commitment to his fans and what he felt they wanted from him in his work. He sometimes sent handwritten letters if he couldn't remember signing a typed response to a fan, fearing he may have neglected to reply to requests or questions. The items he chose to save also reveal a man of great passion with an obsessive commitment not only to his work, but to an impressive variety of charitable causes he supported both publicly and privately as well. He was an avid newspaper reader and frequently clipped articles, sometimes taping the masthead to them to identify the paper where they appeared. He and his wife regularly clipped and saved listings of his television appearances from *TV Guide*.

There is considerable evidence of his tenacious sense of purpose and his resolute separation of his private and public lives. To the frustration of the press and the public, he saw no reason to share his personal life with the world and he made no apologies for it. Much can be learned about the real Jack Lord, however, in his day-to-day work. The variety of artifacts from his business and his personal lives is remarkable, and his complex character is revealed in the selection of things he chose to save. Correspondence from United States congressmen is filed alongside saved Christmas cards from friends and letters from little girls who were in love with Steve McGarrett—all of whom got thoughtful and personal responses.

When secondary sources were included in the research for this work, they are clearly identified and cited as such. The nature of Lord's job in the entertainment business made him a frequent subject in Hollywood gossip magazines and other similar publications. Lord was certainly not the only celebrity to have spoken out against the misinformation peddled by some columnists and fan publications. *Weekly Variety* ran a story in the July 15, 1959, edition reporting the motion picture industry was having serious doubts about the true benefit of syndicated newspaper columnists in the promotion of films. In addition to a lack of confidence in any impact they had on the promotion, there was serious concern about the "unchecking, uncaring" way many popular columnists collected information and wrote their stories. The indictment culminated with the observation that much of what was printed in such columns was often simply fabricated and many times were the result of a columnist's "feud" with a celebrity.[5] Jack Lord would level the same accusation repeatedly throughout his professional life. In some instances, journalists' interview notes found in various collections offered more reliability than the resulting published articles.

Lord was patently outspoken about his distaste for fan magazines and yellow journalism. He expressed his frustration in an August 1, 1969, letter to journalist Jane Kesner Ardmore, who wrote several stories on him. Ardmore had written to one of Lord's staff members, asking to set up an interview with both Jack and his wife, Marie, when she came to Hawaii the following month on vacation. Ardmore had been commissioned to write two stories about him for *Photoplay*. Lord personally responded to her letter. "As an old and respected friend I must tell you that because of the cheap, distorted and shoddy practices of practically all of the so-called fan magazines, I have long ago given up any association with them. In fact I am presently in the process of exploring a damage suit against one of them who recently printed an 'interview' with me that had the audacity to put quotes around sentences and phrases I never spoke."[6] He told her he would love to do a story with her for a publication like *Family Circle* or other "good magazines," such as the kind that were customarily circulated through supermarkets or chain stores.

It is duly noted here when relevant information drawn from sources whose credibility he questioned could not be validated through traditional fact-finding efforts in primary source materials. Verifying air dates and content for some of his early television work proved difficult at times. Every effort was made to correctly document such information, but there were some inconsistencies among sources. Additionally, because so many projects and events of his life overlapped and intertwined, it was not possible to stay with a strictly chronological approach.

Lord certainly didn't inclusively shun the press, however. In fact, he established lasting friendships with several prominent journalists. It was a surprise to find he maintained an ongoing and rich personal correspondence with Hollywood gossip columnist Hedda Hopper, for example. Hopper saved Lord's letters and the frequent postcards he and his wife sent her from their travels all over the world. He also developed a lasting friendship with *Washington Post* radio and TV critic Lawrence Laurent and had ongoing correspondence with Jane Ardmore, and they too saved many of Lord's letters. The Lords also maintained a close personal relationship with Hawaii journalist Ella Chun.

An old Irish proverb says, "The work praises the man." It is a philosophy that is reminiscent of something Lord said in a 1963 interview. "I think your work speaks for itself," he said. "Or it should speak for itself."[7] Perhaps part of the reason he worked so hard at keeping the real Jack Lord hidden is because he wanted his legacy to be more about what *he did* than *who he was*. He was quiet about his philanthropy and he was quiet about his upbringing and his life at home with his beloved wife. Perhaps he would be pleased that to millions of people he is, and always will be, Steve McGarrett, Stoney Burke, or any one of the many other characters he played that some fan somewhere can't forget. I think he would be fine with that.

ONE

A Good Irish Boy

Long Island, New York, is geographically about as far from Hollywood as one can get without leaving the country. For a very determined young man from the Richmond Hill community, however, the distance is relatively short when set within the context of his entire journey. John Joseph Patrick Ryan had experienced life well beyond his years before he was old enough to vote, but finding his true calling was a long time coming. When at last he set down permanent roots some 5,000 miles from where he started, he had reached a level of success that would rival some of the most celebrated stars in Hollywood. By the end of his career, he had acquired the paradoxical reputation both as a self-centered egoist and as one of the most generous celebrity philanthropists in history. He diligently plugged along for more than twenty-five years, and it was his final role that gave him the recognition he so desperately sought as an actor. In 2007, he came full circle when his name appeared on the roster of Richmond Hill's most notable citizens.

Jack Lord made a deliberate commitment to a very public vocation, but he drew a hard line when it came to his private life. Verifying even the most basic biographical truths about him is no easy task. He routinely went home at the end of a grueling, self-imposed fourteen-hour workday and closed the door. His persistent refusal to share details about his private life was irresistible fodder for Hollywood journalists, fueling lurid teasers splashed across the covers of fan magazines. He was well aware that no one in Hollywood is exempt from the prying eyes of the press, but he never got past his ire at fabricated stories and garish sensationalism, particularly when it was aimed at his personal life. In the early days, as he looked to find his niche in show business, he sometimes told journalists neither he nor his wife, Marie, had any family, possibly an attempt to lure them away from the subject. When he did consent to talk about his life, he spoke fondly of his parents, his siblings, and his upbringing, but there were topics that remained strictly off limits and he staunchly held his ground, refusing to address them. "Just because people want to know all about a person's private life doesn't mean I have to spill my guts to the press…. There is nothing positive in talking about old hurts. It … only opens old scars."[1]

Two decades after his death, there are those who have finally achieved a level of success, nailing down solid truths about Lord's ancestry and his early life. Due in part to the growing interest in genealogical research and easier access to public records, more biographical facts about the famously private actor can now be confirmed. His tenacious protection of his personal life will no doubt continue to create gaps in his story, but validated truths of his upbringing and early life continue to surface.

Jack Lord was born John Joseph Patrick Ryan on December 30, 1920, to William Lawrence and Ellen Josephine O'Brien Ryan. On his application to the Merchant Marines in June of 1937 he reported that he was born in New York City. He was routinely slammed in the tabloids for being ambiguous about his birthdate, due in part to the fact that he frequently gave inconsistent answers to direct questions about his birthdate. Even during the heyday of *Hawaii Five-O,* he sometimes shaved years off his age or refused to verify it. Press releases frequently reported him to be ten years younger than he was, and the misinformation became the standard. In 1980 a fan wrote to the *Los Angeles Times* asking for confirmation that Lord was 60 years old at the time, and, based on standard biographies released to the press, the paper responded he would in fact turn 50 on December 30 of that year.[2] He suffered more backlash than most for his attempts to hide his true age, when it was not that uncommon for celebrities to conceal it. At the time he was getting started, Hollywood looked for their leading men to be in their thirties, and Lord had gotten a bit of a late start after his military service and his delayed training at the Actors Studio.

In December of 1975, Lord was summoned to testify in an $18 million dollar lawsuit over disputed rights to produce shirts with the *Hawaii Five-O* logo. Plaintiffs in the case were Great Ideas, Inc., and Grover Kam, who claimed they had paid Viacom $2,500 for a license to use the *Five-O* logo. They testified the only approval needed for sample items was Viacom's. Jack Lord rejected the samples, and Viacom told the plaintiffs his approval was also required. He was subsequently charged with interfering with the contractual relations between the two parties. Lord told Todd Mason, "Everyone seemed to forget I had rights to all approvals."[3]

The plaintiff's attorney began his interrogation by grilling Lord about the wide discrepancies in his reports of his age. He addressed the witness as "Mr. Ryan" and Lord promptly requested that he be addressed as "Mr. Lord." The attorney eventually agreed, but only after insisting he admit under oath that he had never legally changed his name. He repeatedly asked Lord to state his age for the court. "Everyone knows that I'm over 45," he replied. The attorney read Lord's biographical entry in *Who's Who in America* into the court record. He worked the math aloud, saying if the information in that profile was correct, Lord would have been seven years old when he graduated from high school. Although the obvious intent to agitate him was successful, he stayed true to form, dug in his heels, and adamantly declined to state his true age for the record.[4] Lord was on the stand for three days of the eleven-day trial, and he was not happy about the loss of time.

During a press conference for the launch of *Hawaii Five-O*, a reporter asked him how old he was. He diverted the focus, took the high road, and quoted Hollywood journalist and friend Hedda Hopper. "[She] said that a girl who would tell her age would tell anything. That goes for a man too."[5] The distraction tactic worked and the interview moved on. Official academic and military records verify his true birthdate as December 30, 1920.

In a 1986 letter to a fan that sold on eBay Lord said his mother had five children— "all successful." Lord had one older brother, William Lawrence Ryan, Jr., one younger sister, Josephine, and two younger brothers, Thomas H. and Robert G. Ryan. Citing census records and information provided by surviving relatives, Lord researcher Virginia Tolles confirms Lord's assessment of his siblings—they were all successful professionals. William was a noted artist and head art director at a New York agency. Josephine taught at a teachers' college in Connecticut. Thomas Ryan studied law at New York University, and had a diverse and distinguished professional life that included service as New York assistant attorney general, television co-producer, and entertainment attorney. Robert also completed legal studies at New York University and went on to practice immigration law.

Jack Lord described his mother as a strong woman whose family emigrated from Tipperary, Ireland, and settled on a farm in the Hudson Valley area of New York. He attributed his skill as an accomplished horseman to the significant amount of time he spent as a youngster on his grandparents' farm. He often said he remembered his grandfather picking him up by the scruff of the neck and dropping him on the back of their old plow horse, Appetite. Lord's lifelong comfort level with horses would become an asset that served him well in the many western roles he logged throughout his career. He proudly said he learned to ride horses the same way he learned to act—he climbed right on and gave it all he had.

The Ryans raised their children in Richmond Hill, a picturesque village in New York State that dates to 1868. Originally conceived as a planned community and nestled in lush rolling hills near the ocean, Richmond Hill was well within reasonable traveling distance to the city. It was a desirable location for those who worked in metropolitan New York, yet wanted to maintain a quiet family life outside the bustling city atmosphere. Enticing advertisements for the new community touted lush green lawns, gardens and parks, picturesque affordable cottages, and an established school and church. In 1836, railroad connection between Brooklyn and the area facilitated rapid settlement and by 1894, Richmond Hill further grew as it absorbed the nearby communities of Morris Park and Clarenceville. The village lifestyle and strong sense of community continued until 1898, when the greater New York City area began to absorb the quiet village.[6]

While most early settlers in the area were Protestants, the population also included a small group of Catholics. There was no established church for them within the community at the time, so they were forced to travel to other areas to attend Mass. As the Catholic population continued to grow, a group eventually petitioned the Bishop of Brooklyn for a parish in the community, and their request was granted in July of 1892. The new parish was placed under the protection of Saint Benedict Joseph Labre, and the cornerstone for a new wooden church was laid on November 6, 1892. As the congregation continued to grow, a new brick church was constructed in 1916 and the old wooden structure was designated as a school annex. The first group of children graduated from Saint Benedict's that same year.[7] The Ryans sent all five of their children to the school for their elementary education.

Lord recalled his boyhood as a time when he felt blessed with parents who guided him and his siblings with love. The Ryan children learned the importance of self-responsibility through designated chores paired with earned privileges. He was grateful for the clear guidance from his parents, as he learned to distinguish right from wrong and the value of knowing that the freedom of choice to do the right thing was something that could not be taken away from him.⁸ Lord was very much aware of the lasting and positive impact of the abundantly diverse opportunities he experienced as a child. A keen sense of self-awareness was evident in his extraordinary attention to detail and in his heightened visual sensitivity. Both qualities were foundational to his famous insistence on perfection in his work, and he always came out of the gate with high expectations. It was a practice he applied to himself and to those around him.

He developed an avid interest in visual art very early in his life. Among his personal papers at the University of Southern California's Cinematic Arts Library is a worn copy of a 1978 issue of the *Saturday Evening Post*. "See page 5" is scrawled across the cover in his distinctive handwriting. The notation references an elaborate tribute to Norman Rockwell on his 84th birthday. Lord's name appears on a list of distinguished well-wishers in the article that includes Ronald Reagan, John Wayne, Bob Hope, and Pearl Bailey. He describes the excitement he felt as a young boy, delivering the *Post* in his neighborhood. He remembered eagerly opening the bundles to study the new Rockwell art on the covers. "When I grew up, I went to college and majored in art," he wrote. "I realized what a master painter of Americana we had in this distinguished man." He was clearly grateful for that early opportunity to study Rockwell's work.⁹

Lord did two extensive phone interviews with Todd Mason, one in 1972 and a second in 1976. Mason was an actor who sometimes used the name Todd Howland. He did several small television roles, was a journalist who interviewed celebrities for magazines and newspapers, and at times worked as a personal assistant to actors. Mason was a close acquaintance of Mike Connors, who was best known for his starring role in *Mannix*, a popular CBS detective series that ran from 1967 to 1975. During the interviews, Lord talked at length about his family, his beliefs about religion and marriage, and his famous work ethic. Mason routinely taped all his phone calls, sometimes without telling his subjects they were being recorded, and his phone conversations with Jack Lord offer a rare opportunity to hear him speak candidly and naturally.

Mason later penned an article from his Hawaii interview sessions. Publication of the article could not be confirmed, but a November 30, 1972, letter to Lord from long-time CBS press agent Betty Lamm confirms that Mason had finished his extensive story and indicated Lord should be receiving a copy of it for his review in the very near future.¹⁰ Although it appears he never published the article in the existing format, some of Lord's comments from the tapes and the written version frequently show up almost verbatim in other interviews—oftentimes as standard answers to questions he frequently fielded from reporters.

The tapes are delightful because the real Jack Lord comes through as he settles into an extended conversation with Mason, who later worked as Lord's stand-in for some episodes of *Hawaii Five-O*. He was clearly comfortable with him and the dialogue is spontaneous and natural. He periodically prefaces remarks with "This is off the record, okay?"¹¹ One such incident was when Lord was telling Mason about his being encouraged by some locals to run for governor of Hawaii. Lord said when he discussed it with Marie, her response was an emphatic, "Absolutely not." It was not uncommon for those who spoke one on one with Lord for the first time to express surprise at his soft-spoken and easy manner, qualities that are very evident in the Mason tapes. It is not the impatient, tyrannical and temperamental image often promoted by his critics.

In the manuscript, Mason relates Lord's reflection on the influence of his family and his growing up years in what he termed a strict, middle-class, Irish Catholic background. He remembered his parents as a good match, a couple that complimented each other—"he, the high seas, daring, adventerous [sic], and she from the farm—mother earth, roots, three squares a day, mustard plasters when we had a chest cold." He described his busy father as a strong, dominant figure who, like his mother, always made time for him and his siblings and made them feel loved and cared for.[12]

Lord frequently referred to his mother as an "Irish matriarch" and praised her role as a good homemaker who ran a beautiful home—a quality he considered to be important in a successful marriage, and one he often attributed to his wife. He considered Marie's meticulous housekeeping and her talents in the kitchen as important elements in his eventual success. He frequently talked about the importance of her steadfast support as he struggled in the early days to find work as an actor. "My wonderful wife and I decided long ago that my career was *our* business—and it really takes two. She's not only cook and housekeeper, she's secretary and hostess and valet. She's always with me in selecting my clothes and keeps them in order so that they are all ready for any emergency. I can ask a producer or a talent scout or a fellow actor home any time and know that our apartment will be clean and sparkling and that Marie will be a charming hostess."[13] The Lords would later become well known for their hospitality. Journalist Bessie Little did an article on Lord for a teen fan magazine in the early days of *Stoney Burke*. She reported that she had been a guest on several occasions in their New York apartment and praised him for his gracious treatment of their guests. "They hosted the greatest parties I'd ever attended.... Jack has a way of keeping guests entertained as no other host I know. He has the art ... of steering the conversations into channels in which everybody present can add to the subject at hand."[14]

William Ryan's influence on his son was also evident. Most sources say he was a successful ship surveyor, a shrewd businessman who owned five ships, all named for angels. Lord told journalist and celebrity ghost biographer Jane Ardmore his father was an "executive of a steamship company ... [who] was a genius with ships," declaring he moved ships around the way most men move automobiles.[15] Ryan built his own company from the ground up, routinely sailing between Singapore and Hong Kong and along the China coast. Lord said his father made over a million dollars during the first five years he was in the shipping business, lost it all during the Depression, and then made it back.[16] Ardmore interviewed Lord on several occasions and the two became friends. Her notes from a 1970 interview with him include a statement that his father made his millions when he "cornered the pepper market," lost it, and made it back when he sold out about 1939.[17] While a variety of versions of his father's business successes and failures exist, one thing is certain. William Ryan's dogged determination in overcoming setbacks showed up in his second son's famously exasperating persistence.

Jack Lord was not blind to his quick Irish temper and a tendency as a young man to settle things with his fists. "I could fight like a steer. I started off in the Police Athletic League and we learned really to use our mitts."[18] He said his father accepted his sons' brawling as a part of growing up, and it was a reflex action he carried with him into adulthood. He admitted he once physically threw a customer out of a car dealership showroom where he worked because the man asked him to hold his cane. As he got older, however, he realized the fallacy of punching first and asking questions later. He consistently credited his wife with helping him to overcome what he called his "flash temper." With her guidance, he eventually came to realize that a raging temper is synonymous with self-will, part of a driven intent to get his way, regardless of the effect it had on other people. He began consciously to work on it when he came to understand how important it was to him that he do everything in his power to be the kind of person his wife thought he was.[19]

Lord said his last fight was an altercation with a cabdriver who bumped into him in the middle of New York's Broadway and 42nd Street at high noon. He approached the open window of the cab and as he leaned in to talk, the driver promptly punched him in the face. He dragged the man out through the open window and the fight was on, right on the street. When he was forced to give a full accounting of the incident to Marie to explain the bumps and bruises he had suffered during the brawl, she was not pleased. He wound up paying the cabbie's doctor bills to avoid formal charges and to appease his angry wife.

Even though his father was frequently away from home on business, Lord credited both his parents with instilling a solid work ethic and a bent toward persistence and goal setting in all their children. Once he achieved solid success as an actor, he often spoke of the physical, mental, and emotional stamina the job required and the toll it took on his confidence and on his resolve. He was grateful for his parents' insistence their children learn responsibility and the value of a hard day's work, and he carried that work ethic with him throughout his life.

Good scholarship, a thirst for knowledge, and a love of literature was standard for all the Ryan children. Lord described his father as an avid bibliophile who taught him to read when he was four years old. William Ryan paid him and his siblings a penny a line to memorize poetry, and it was a practice Jack Lord continued throughout his life. He called it an exercise in "mental gymnastics," acknowledging it was good training for his future work when he had to memorize script, especially when he was given a very short time to get it done. He was known as a stickler for actors' coming to the set fully prepared, as he applied the elevated bar he set for himself to everyone else. He had no tolerance for wasted time on the job and it earned him the reputation as a tough taskmaster.

Reading was a passion he carried with him throughout his life. He frequently spoke of his siblings' eager attention to their father's daily after-supper readings from Dickens and other classics. Saturday outings with his father and his older brother to New York's 14th Street neighborhood, an area he remembered as a rich haven of good bookstores, were an especially fond memory for him. He said his father always stood ready to buy treasured finds for them. Lord continued to be a voracious and eclectic reader throughout his life and he maintained a huge personal library, numbering somewhere around 6,000 books at one time. While he was particularly fond of history and art subjects, he had a healthy list of favorite fiction writers as well, and he carried out prolific correspondence with some of the authors whose books he loved, including John MacDonald. Some of MacDonald's books auctioned during the Lords' estate sale included lengthy personal notes written to the Lords. As soon as he finished reading it, he called a friend at 3 a.m. to praise MacDonald's book on the Coppolino murder case.[20] He and Marie were also collectors of cookbooks and he said they read them the way most people read novels.

He occasionally purged his constantly growing library, donating them to universities and other charitable causes. While working on *Hawaii Five-O*, he gave 3,000 books from his personal library to the University of California at Los Angeles. He was delighted to learn each one bore a bookplate with his and his wife's names. He lamented the cost of transporting his large collection of books when he and Marie were moving during his early days of trying to find work as an actor. He said in a 1962 interview it cost twenty cents a pound to move the half van full of books when they moved from New York to Los Angeles. A massive personal library, cancelled checks for significant amounts to bookstores, and letters of inquiry to dealers all over the country as he sought out rare books were among the hundreds of items from the Lords' estate sale following Marie's death in 2005.

Lord developed an early and avid interest in the American Civil War, and it was a passion he maintained the rest of his life.[21] In 1964, he registered a script about the assassination of President Abraham Lincoln with the Writers Guild of the American West with a working title of *Five in a Box*. In a story for the *Washington Post* that same year, journalist and long-time friend Lawrence Laurent, reported Lord had spent more than two hours at the Ford's Theatre Museum during a recent trip to the nation's capital. He told Laurent that he was working on a play in which he would draw a parallel between the Lincoln and Kennedy assassinations.[22] A handwritten, unfinished draft of the play and a collection of reproductions of Civil War era newspapers by the *New York Times* are filed among his papers. A worn copy of the 1866 French book *Confession de John Wilkes Booth* is included. Lord had the book translated into English in 1963, and a note written in red ink and attached to the translation reads, "Love to you both, Sido." Lord had made a paper cover for the fragile copy of the book, and he had already penned the dedication for the unfinished script. "To the wife of my youth who abides with me still this play is lovingly dedicated."[23] The quote is derived from Civil War General Lew Wallace who wrote, "To the wife of my youth who still abides with me" as the dedication for his classic novel, *Ben Hur*.

Lord had fond memories of visiting friends in Macon, Georgia, as a youngster, saying he spent Thanksgivings with the Joe Hall family, close friends of his parents. He got his first single-shot shotgun while there and remembered he loved the rabbit and quail hunting on his visits. "I remember the massive doors to the home had a Crusader cross across them. And smack in the middle was the heel print of a Union solider implanted there during the Civil War. It seems he became angry and attempted to kick door down, but was unsuccessful."[24]

When it came time for young John Ryan to begin his secondary education, he followed older brother Bill to John Adams High School in the Ozone Park neighborhood of Queens. Adams is alma mater for several other celebrities, including Jackie Gleason, Bernadette Peters, fellow *Dr. No* actor Joseph Wiseman, and Pulitzer Prize winning New York columnist Jimmy Breslin. Lord's sister and two younger brothers also attended. Principal William A. Clarke penned a farewell message to the graduates in Lord's senior yearbook, alerting them to the demands they would face as they made their way in the world. Most of the members of the Class of 1938 declared an intention to begin college in the fall, and Mr. Clarke wanted them to understand why the next level of their education would be critical to their success. "The career that we hope to make our life work will largely dictate our choice of subjects.... We must learn to live as well as to make a living," he told them. "No planning can mean more for the present and future happiness of our students than such clearness of vision, generosity of impulse and firmness of purpose."[25] John Ryan heeded his principal's advice, carrying that firmness of purpose with him as he went off to college, intent on pursuing a career that revolved around his love of visual art. Ironically, his resolute approach to his work as an actor was a quality that brought him much criticism from the press and from many who worked with him on a daily basis.

In stark contrast to the famously assertive man he would become, John Ryan the teenager was known as a quiet, polite loner. His senior profile reported a diverse list of accomplishments from his busy high school years: "Bronze, Silver "A's"; Honor, Meritorious, Distinguished Service Certificates; Senior Life Saving; Major "A"; Intramurals: P.S.A.L. Pins; Varsity Football Team; Dean's Squad; Art Editor "Campus"; "Clipper" Art Staff; Art Office; Key of Courtesy, President, Student Supervisor Arts and Crafts, Secretary, Newman, Etching, Young Scientists Clubs."[26] In addition to his notoriety as a talented athlete, he also put his artistic bent to work as art editor for his senior yearbook. In contrast to his future reputation as a self-absorbed egoist, he selected none of his own work to include among the many illustrations that were created by his classmates. He and his older brother Bill gained recognition very early for their artistic talent. Lord developed a great passion for collecting fine works of art, many of which he eventually gave to museums all over the country.

Lord's reluctance to talk extensively about his early life necessitates considering information found in sources that he would eventually come to disdain. While popular fan magazines of his day were not known for prioritizing accuracy, verifiable facts do sometimes arise from some of their stories about him. More than thirty years after he graduated from high school and two years into his career-making role as Steve McGarrett, a reporter for a popular fan magazine discovered that a friend of hers was a classmate of Lord's at John Adams High School. She suggested the reporter visit the Richmond Hill area, interview some of his classmates and teachers, and write an article about the "real" Jack Lord. The article provides some verifiable information about his early life.

Her research confirmed the Ryan brothers' early reputation as gifted artists, and classmates vividly remembered John's paintings were frequently displayed in the hallways of the school. Football coach Peter Troyano, who still worked at the school at the time of the interviews, said he remembered John Ryan as "the essence of courtesy" and he commented on his always appearing younger than his chronological age. It was a quality that

John Joseph Patrick Ryan's 1938 senior photograph from John Adams High School, Queens, New York. Lord, his sister, and his brothers all attended the school (*Clipper* 1938 yearbook; author's collection).

came in handy later when he began to shave years off his age in his professional biographies. "I don't recall he dated much," his coach said. "I got the impression he was much too serious about his schoolwork … [He] always behaved like a young man with a purpose."[27]

The coach's observation that he didn't date much may have been accurate, but it appears his lack of an active social life with the girls was not because of a lack of interest on their part. Classmate George Norwig penned a lengthy narrative poem about the graduates for the senior yearbook in which he reported, "Ryan is femme-surrounded/And keeps the girls a-sighin'!"[28] Norwig was surprised to learn from the reporter that his classmate John Ryan and "Steve McGarrett" were one and the same, and he was not the only '38 alumnus who did not know what had eventually become of the quiet, courteous John P. Ryan.

One person who had kept up with him as he evolved into Jack Lord was Principal Clarke. In a 1963 letter to Lord, written on school stationery, he indicated that he received frequent correspondence from his former pupil. Following the greeting "Dear John" Clark explained that he could not address him by any name except the one he knew him by. He assured him that he had missed very few of his television appearances throughout his career, and he told Lord how proud he was of him for his work on *Stoney Burke* and the good critical reviews it was receiving. He told him that all five of the Ryan children still stood out vividly in his memory and he was very proud of their individual successes as adults. He wanted Lord to know that the yearbook advisor had made a copy of his senior annual available to a reporter from *Movie Life* magazine. He assured Lord that he had made it very clear any material about him had to be approved in advance.[29]

Principal Clarke was retired at the time of the interview and he told the eager reporter that he would not talk extensively about his famous former student unless he received written permission from Jack Lord to do so. He called him a "splendid boy and a natural leader," and praised the well-known integrity of the Ryan family in the community. The same reporter also approached Lord's sister Josephine. She politely responded she would comply with her famous brother's request to his family; she would not discuss him without prior written consent from him.[30]

Lord's tenacious protection of his privacy, aggressively supported by those who knew him best, was already in full force early in his career. He frequently told reporters that he had lost contact with his family years before he gained fame as an actor. Other stories said he lost contact with them in the 1960s. The break may not have been as definitive as he implied or as reported, however. A 1969 story in a San Antonio paper announced that Lord would be a visitor in town for the Thanksgiving holidays. "He's visiting a sister here but wants to keep it all quiet," the story reported.[31] Such betrayals by the press likely had much to do with Lord's reluctance to talk to reporters about things he wished to keep private. He also told a reporter for *Aloha* magazine in 1980 that his mother was then 81 years old and that she had gone back to the farm after his father died. He said he "occasionally" saw her. He admitted that he was not close with his family, saying they had all gone their own ways. "All the rest of the family is on the Eastern seaboard so it's easier for them."[32]

In addition to an artistic bent, John Ryan shared another activity with his older brother, and it was one that would prove to be an unexpected stepping-stone in the journey to his life's work. He said when he turned 14, he joined his brother and began spending his summers working on seafaring freighters. The work gave him the opportunity for adventure and carried him to exotic landscapes that profoundly inspired his art. He never took for granted the lasting impact of traveling the world as a teenager. "I wanted to go to sea as a cadet," he said, "which is a very posh job on the bridge, but my dad said no. 'No, if you are going to sea, son, you're going in on the forecastle.'"[33] Lord said his father wanted him to work his way up, just as he himself had done. William Ryan's mandate that his sons pull their load was yet another building block in the driven man John Ryan would become. Lord was known as a tough taskmaster by those who worked with him throughout his career as an actor, but few would deny he unfailingly pushed himself at least as hard as he pushed everyone else.

The time he spent traveling the world on freighters agreed with him. On June 19, 1937, the summer between his junior and senior years in high school, John Ryan filed an application for service as Ordinary Seaman with the shipping section of United States Department of Commerce's Bureau of Marine Inspection and Navigation. His responses to the questions on the application form are neatly printed in perfectly symmetrical, heavy lettering—a distinctive and strong penmanship that graced his paperwork throughout his life. He gave his address as 9528 125th Street in Richmond Hill, the house in which he grew up. The photo attached to the application shows a solemn, dark-skinned, thin-faced young man, with very curly hair cropped close to his head. He looks much younger than his seventeen years. His application was approved the same day.

Certificates of service dated July 7, 1938, with endorsements for the engine department, as well as proof of his rating to serve as a food handler, with further endorsements as messman, cabin steward and utilityman on U.S. Merchant vessels are included in his record. Work with the Merchant Marines also certified seamen for work on cruise ships, a qualification that later put him in place for a life-changing event and one of the most elusive stories from his biography.[34] He attended Fort Trumball Academy at New London, Connecticut, after high school.

Sometime during Lord's maritime service, he reportedly was on a liberty ship that was torpedoed and the crew was forced into lifeboats. Printed versions of the story either vary greatly as to when it happened or avoid assigning a definitive date to the incident. As with many other events in his life, the exact details are hard to pin down and a variety of versions appeared in fan magazines over a period of several years. None of the ships listed in his service record show up on the Merchant Marine roster of damaged and sunken ships, which is not to say it didn't happen, especially considering that his time at sea spanned his teenage years and continued through World War II. After his success in *Hawaii Five-O*, a Hollywood fan magazine ran a lengthy account of the event, but the story contains several facts unrelated to the incident that can be confirmed as incorrect. Some of the statements have been repeated in other publications.[35]

Lord shared a story with Jane Ardmore about an experience that occurred as he sailed on a liberty ship named the *Kelly Hall*. Several versions of the story have appeared in a number of sources. He told Ardmore that he was still in his teens at the time, but it is unclear when the event occurred. He had terms of service that began in 1937 and ran past the end of World War II. Even looking at his full military record, it is difficult to confirm specific dates for his terms of service and to definitively place events in chronological order. His service on a ship named the *Hall J. Kelly* in 1944 is documented in his record, but there is no *Kelly Hall* listed. He freely admitted that even as a teenager, he had become a tough customer. Fueled by his hot Irish temper, he was already eager to settle things with his fists. According to Lord, the ship was sailing down the east coast of Africa, when the refrigeration system failed and all the meat on board quickly turned putrid in the hot temperatures. At the same time, weevils infested all the dry supplies and the crew found themselves totally without food. The ship's captain refused to put into port to buy fresh supplies and insisted the spoiled fare would suffice until they reached their destination. The ship was scheduled to make a stop in Mozambique, and the crew conspired to throw all the supplies overboard before their arrival to ensure they would have to take on fresh goods while they were in port.

The captain was infuriated by the conspiracy. He wired the American consulate and reported mutiny on board. When they arrived at port, the entire crew was taken to jail at gunpoint and formally charged with mutiny. Young John Ryan was terrified. He recalled the thing he feared most about the incident was the knowledge he would have to face his father with no acceptable explanation for his insubordination. He sat in jail for three days, dreading the time he would stand before his father to explain his actions much more than he feared standing before the judge in his upcoming court appearance. When the men were finally taken to trial, most of them were sentenced to six months hard labor. John Ryan was miraculously released.

As it turned out, this was not the last time he would face a potential court-martial during his years of maritime service. On July 10, 1944, while docked in domestic port, he missed returning to the *George H. Williams*, and he was formally charged with failure to join. His record shows a revocation or suspension of his seaman's license dated July 21, 1944. The suspension was for one month, with a six months' probation to follow. A second memorandum filed November 7, 1944, indicates a rehearing and decision for probation to terminate November 2, 1944.

When he told Ardmore about the failure to board incident, he said he had fortunately done very well in a crap game the previous night, managing to wipe out the financial resources of most of the crew. When they docked, he had over $2,000 in his pocket and he loaned the men's money back to them so they could go ashore. One of the men owed him $600 and stepped up on the young seaman's behalf, testifying that he most assuredly would not intentionally miss the ship. The witness pointed out that with so much cash loaned out to other seamen, he would not have deliberately stayed ashore. It could be his shipmate's testimony led to the rehearing and termination of his probation slightly earlier than the scheduled reinstatement date.

Lord applied for his license as third mate of ocean steam and motor vessels. A March 9, 1945, letter indicated his character review was such that he was considered eligible, but he that he lacked 12 days sea service meeting the required 14 months required for enrolling in the U.S. Maritime Service Officers Training School.

John Joseph Ryan was honorably discharged from the U.S. Coast Guard on August 15, 1945. He had earned a certificate of proficiency issued June 5, 1945, from the Navy Department, certifying him for wartime merchant ship communications completed at Fort Trumball. Documenting dates of Lord's attendance at Fort Trumball is difficult. Some accounts say he attended right out of high school, other sources say it was during the war years. The officers' training program at Fort Trumball graduated more than 15,000 officers between 1939 and the transfer of the program to the U.S. Merchant Marine Academy occurred in 1946.

After completing his high school years, John Ryan followed through with the plan he reported in his senior yearbook and enrolled at New York University. He frequently included in professional profiles that he was the only art major in the university's history to attend NYU on a football scholarship. Alumni archives confirm his position on the football team, where he played tackle and right tackle. His presence on the freshman squad in the fall of 1938 is good validation he was good at it and he certainly could have been there on a football scholarship. He had a spot on the primary team in 1939 and was listed again, wearing the number 43 jersey in the University's 1940 *Football Facts* booklet. His stats, just like his Merchant Marines records, report his height at six feet. Throughout his career as an actor, tabloids and disgruntled coworkers frequently accused him of wearing lifts in his shoes to appear taller than he actually was. He routinely reported his height as six feet two inches.

Lord reportedly had his nose broken twice while he played football for NYU. The first time was when he ran into a steel yard marker, and it was broken again in a scrimmage. In 1969, Lord sat for an interview with a large group of reporters in Chicago while on a junket to promote his new show, *Hawaii Five-O*. He told the photographers that he could only be photographed from "certain angles and with certain lights. There are limitations to my face." He said he had a deviated septum from an old football injury. *Chicago Tribune* journalist Harriet Choice was at the junket and she echoed the sentiments of hundreds of female fans: "How he looked to us: Good from any angle."[36]

When he began his college education, he adhered to Principal Clarke's admonition to the graduates to go forth with a "clearness of vision." He stayed true to his intent to major in art education and he stayed busy. In 1939 and 1940, he appears with the editorial staff of the *Education Violets*, the yearbook for NYU's School of Education. A 1940 Bureau of Public Information blurb about John J. Ryan lists him as a School of Education major who hoped to be an art teacher. The short bio entry reports he was actively involved in campus publications, serving as business manager of *Trek: Caravan of Student Thought*, an all-university literary journal. Much of the art in the journal is credited to his brother, William Lawrence Ryan, who was managing art editor for the publication. John J. Ryan is listed with the art editorial staff. The same university public information source confirms the Ryan brothers were owners and instructors of art courses at the Village Academy of Arts on MacDougal Street in Greenwich Village. John Ryan included in his profile he "spends summer vacations on world-wide trips, working on tramp steamers and freighters."[37] Lord told Hal Humphrey in 1963 that he earned his pilot's license during his sophomore year at NYU. His summer experiences would later provide fuel for his work when he began writing screenplays and concepts for television series pilots. After he was an established actor, he often said he never considered his college education as a waste of time, crediting the experience with sparking his interest in travel, the arts, and business.

John J. Ryan crossed into a gray area sometime during his senior year at NYU. His brother William graduated from the university's school of education with a bachelor of science degree in June of 1941. Lord again played for the NYU football team in the fall of 1941, the first half of his senior year, but he drops off the archival record at the university by the second half of the academic year. He is not listed on the roster of graduates for the 1942 spring commencement, and there is no record at the university confirming he completed his degree. He told Jane Ardmore that he completed his degree after the war. The commencement roster for 1954 lists a John J. Ryan as receiving a bachelor of science degree in industrial relations, but a photo from the school yearbook confirms it is not Jack Lord.

Set against world events at the time, Jack Lord's military records may stand as an explanation of his whereabouts when he left NYU before the 1942 spring semester. *American Biography Online* reports he left college before graduating to join the Merchant Marines. In March of his senior year in high school, Japan's invasion of China initiated the genesis of the Second World War, and when Germany attacked Poland in September of 1939, the memory of World War I was still painfully fresh, and international concern for the rapid escalation of hostilities increased. On October 30, 1940, while campaigning for reelection in Boston, President Franklin Roosevelt offered steadfast assurance to Americans that they would be safe from involvement in the conflict. "I have said this before, but I shall say it again and again," he assured the frightened public. "Your boys are not going to be sent into any foreign wars."[38] Roosevelt's confident declaration offered no comfort thirteen months later, however, in the aftermath of events that took place over United States territory at 7:48 a.m. on December 7, 1941. The futility of FDR's promise was undeniable when 353 Japanese planes hit the U.S. Pacific Fleet at Pearl Harbor in a surprise attack, resulting in the death of more than 2,000 Americans and inflicting massive damage or destruction of all ships, planes, and facilities on the site.

Interpreting the chronology of Lord's years in the military is difficult. His file is massive, and spans a period from his high school years through an extended time after the end of World War II. The record shows multiple entries of time served in the Merchant Marines and the Coast Guard, and the exact dates of service are very hard to determine. His complicated and extensive military record is further evidence of his industry and dogged determination to stay busy.

A press release announcing the cast for the 1950 Edward Leven production of *Cry Murder* has Jack Lord signing on with the U.S. Engineering Department at the outbreak of the war, where he was assigned to work on building supply roads to Russia from the Gulf to the Caspian Sea. That same press release reports he joined the Merchant Marines in 1943, and served four and one-half years before he was discharged. Those dates don't match entries in his military papers, however.

Lord filed an application for a certificate of efficiency as lifeboatman with the United States Coast Guard, Port of Baltimore, Maryland, on August 21, 1943. His paperwork includes a photo of a very different John Joseph Ryan than the young man pictured in his earlier Merchant Marine file. Looking much more like Jack Lord—thick, wavy hair, piercing eyes and square jaw—John Ryan clearly had become an adult. He had seen tough times and his face shows it. "I was never colder in my whole life than when standing watch for the Coast Guard," he would later say. "[W]hen our ship pulled into Boston Harbor it struck me as the coldest place in the world."[39]

His application lists the six certificates he earned during his service with the Merchant Marines in 1937, and his signature on the oath of service form attached to the application verifies his graduation from the Maritime Commission School Ship. On the official application, his birth date is recorded as December 30, 1922, two years later than his actual date of birth. It is possible the error could have been typographical. It occurs again on a handwritten copy of the efficiency certificate for lifeboatman issued August 21, 1942, the same month and day as his application, but a year earlier. His record of certificate of service issued April 7, 1944, shows that after he graduated from MCTS and clocking three months service at sea, he was rated as able seaman.

Ryan's service record includes seven Department of Commerce discharge certificates for foreign voyage assignments issued by the Bureau of Marine Inspection and Navigation, all aboard steamship class vessels. Between September 16, 1943, and March 9, 1944, he served aboard the *Richard Henry Dana* and was discharged at Baltimore. He shipped out again on April 14 aboard the *George H. Williams* and was discharged at New York on June 24, leaving four days once again on the *George H. Williams* and returning to New York July 10. Four days later he left New York on the SS *Hall J. Kelley* and was discharged October 12 in Philadelphia. He boarded the *Marine Eagle* on December 8 with a deck maintenance rating and arrived back in New York on January 23, 1945. His certificate of release from active duty has a separation date of August 15, 1945, with an honorable discharge due to "an end of hostilities." At the time of his discharge, he reported a mailing address in Watseka, Illinois. The honorable discharge certificate shows service between December 7, 1941, the date of the attack on Pearl Harbor, and December 31, 1946.

His next voyage was from New York on July 14. He boarded the SS *Robin Sherwood* with a junior third officer rating and he returned on August 24. His last discharge certificate records his longest term of service. He left Philadelphia with a third mate's rating aboard the *Mingo Seam* on December 4, 1945, and returned to the same port on January 16, 1946, logging almost a full year of continuous service.

Jack Lord said he caught the acting bug after the war when he was assigned to illustrate Navy textbooks while in Washington, D.C. He told Jack Hirshberg in 1958 that he had a tendency to whistle while he worked and it was the catalyst for his being noticed as a good prospect for an assignment that would ultimately lead him to his life's work. He said someone heard him whistling as he worked with other artists on training manuals, walked over and asked him if he would like to act in a Navy training film. He instantly agreed. The experience put him in front of a camera for the first time when he was asked to step in during the production of Navy training films. He took to the work right off and credited the experience he gained from his work on 51 films for the Navy as the genesis of his desire to become an actor.[40]

The most resilient roadblock to verifying complete biographical information about Jack Lord lies with the story of his first marriage and a son. Primary sources on the subject have eluded researchers for years, and most of what is commonly held up as fact is little more than recycled material drawn from fan magazines. A biographical article by Brett Bolton for *TV Radio Mirror* says the story of Lord's first marriage was printed in only one publication prior to 1970. The December issue of *Inside TV* that year credits the release of the "official" story to Jerry Asher, a noted fan magazine writer and MGM publicist. Asher said his version was printed "just as Lord himself" told it to him. It is interesting that Lord would voluntarily give the story to Asher, considering it was a part of his life he worked very hard to keep private. Fan magazine editor and publisher Lawrence Quirk said Jerry Asher "had the biggest mouth in town [and] gossiped like crazy."[41] *Inside TV* claimed Asher got the story because of his well-known "skill and compassionate heart," and his friendship with Jack Lord. Asher said Lord decided to tell the story because he had come to realize that with fame came the inevitable demand from the public and the press for information about his private life. *Inside TV*'s reprint of Asher's version added Lord decided to go public with it only after he talked it over with Marie. While it is a plausible theory that Lord may have given Asher the story, trusting him to tell the truth of the matter, settling it once and for all, and finally drawing attention away from something he did not want to talk about, it does not fit with his tenacious separation of his private and public lives.

Dwight Whitney's extensive September 4, 1971, *TV Guide* article included the story of his first marriage and the death of his son. Although it appears the topic was a part of the interview with Lord he did for the article, much of the content is drawn from fan magazines. It is highly doubtful Lord would have openly discussed it.

The consensus of stories about Lord's first marriage has the young seaman meeting and instantly falling in love with a beautiful young woman during a term of duty aboard a cruise ship. Ann Cecily Willard was born December 15, 1921, in Paris, France. At the time of her birth, her father listed his occupation as a civil engineer, born in Brooklyn, New York. Willard's mother was born in Nice, France, and became a naturalized citizen of the U.S. when she married her husband.[42]

Some sources say the ship's captain married the couple in 1944, and, at the end of the voyage, he was called back to duty and had to be away from his new wife. Asher's version reports they were married when he was nineteen years old, which would mean the year was 1939. Although Lord was enrolled at NYU at that time and was spending his summers at sea, sometimes working on cruise ships, that scenario seems unlikely in the light of what is now known about the birth of their son.

Some sources say Lord's first marriage was in 1942, which is a more plausible theory. The couple reportedly enjoyed a five-week honeymoon. The bride returned to school when Lord rejoined his ship and went back to work. A few months later, he received a cable from her with the news that he was going to be a father and that she planned stay with her parents until after the baby was born. It has been confirmed their son was born December 1, 1942. Asher says Lord rented a house for them on the Chesapeake Bay during his next leave and he wrote to tell her the good news of their new home. Attempts to find evidence of this scenario were unsuccessful.

There are a variety of versions of the eventual outcome of the marriage. Lord's steadfast refusal to talk about it for the rest of his life makes verifying the details difficult at best. Asher's version says the answer to his letter about their new home was his wife's announcement that she would not allow their child to be raised in America. Many sources say her father was an Argentinian diplomat, giving rise to theories that her parents may have had some objections to their daughter and grandchild living out of the country. That seems unlikely, however, since it has been confirmed Lord's son was living in Connecticut at the time of his death. Several sources say that he never saw his son. Asher says Lord saw him once, during a leave when the baby was born, which also has Lord's young wife holding firm to her plan to get a divorce and raise the child alone.

Many speculate that Lord lost track of them, saying his letters to her were returned unopened. An article published in *People* magazine the month after Lord died said he told the story to a *Motion Picture Magazine* reporter in 1964 that he was back at sea when she wrote to tell him she was expecting and that she wanted a divorce because she didn't want to live in the U.S.[43]

There are two widely held theories about what ultimately happened to Lord's son. One theory is that the boy died at an early age from illness, while another attributes his death to a drowning accident which happened when he was a teenager. Lord reportedly told Asher the boy was killed in an accident when he was thirteen, and he learned of his son's passing when he received a death certificate in the mail with no letter.

It is now known that Lord's son was living in Greenwich Riverside in Fairfield County, Connecticut, when he died of virus hepatitis, on August 24, 1955, barely three months before his thirteenth birthday. A possible explanation for discrepancies surrounding the cause of the child's death may be explained by events which occurred in the area around the time he died. The convergence of two hurricanes in the region surrounding Stamford, Connecticut, caused extensive flooding and resulted in the death of about 100 people.[44]

In the late summer of 1955, the hurricanes hit the area very close together, one on August 11 and the other on August 13, followed by several days of rain on the already water-soaked communities. Area papers reported that over 14 inches of rain fell during a 36-hour period, on August 18 and 19. Massive flooding led to nearly 100 deaths in the area and millions of dollars in property damage.[45] It may be the theories of illness and accident as cause of death for young John Ryan arose from the events in the area at the time.

The boy was under a doctor's care for ten days, and hospitalized for five days before his death. It is widely known hepatitis can result from bad drinking water, and it is possible some of the theories about an accidental death could have come from suppositions of contamination of the water in the area at the time, or a drowning accident in light of the expansive flooding in the region. The death certificate confirms the onset of the hepatitis was three weeks prior to his passing, however, which would have been the week before the hurricanes hit. There is an antecedent cause of death coded as 092 listed on the certificate. An antecedent cause refers to a condition that led to or precipitated death. CDC Code 092 refers to cardiorespiratory failure.[46] In essence, cardiorespiratory failure as the precipitating factor in a death simply means a patient's heart stops beating. Ann Willard Ryan is listed as the informant on the death certificate.[47] She reportedly later remarried and continued to live in the United States until her death.

A 1976 article in a Hartford, Connecticut, newspaper contradicts the belief that Lord completely cut ties with his family. In April, during "one of their four-times-a-year visits" to "his onetime home town," he talked with the paper about his frustration with losing their studio space back in Hawaii. While the majority of the article is about the successes and struggles of his nearly ten years with *Hawaii Five-O*, the reference to his frequent visits questions the validity of the theory that he had no contact with family back on the Mainland.[48]

Tabloids freely wove the scant verifiable information and Lord's refusal to answer questions about his first marriage into sensational stories, many accusing him of negligence in his responsibility as a husband and a father. Except for his reported conversations with Asher, he never addressed it publicly. Whether he chose to keep that door closed to shield his first wife from public scrutiny or, in keeping with his ardent protection of his privacy in general, he didn't feel the need to share something that had no relevance to his work cannot be determined. The fact remains that it was a chapter of his life that he did not feel he was obliged to share. Reporters who asked Lord's family members about his first marriage were told he had explicitly asked them not to talk about it and they honored his request.

In 1963, Jane Ardmore interviewed Lord for an article with the working title, "Jack of All or Many Trades." Her notes contain his response to her question about how he met his wife, Marie. "There's an area of public life and an area of private life," he told her. "I'm not willing to pay that price."[49] Lord did open up later, however, about how he found the love of his life, and the story is great testimony to his strong determination to get what he wanted.

Ruth Bowser penned an extensive story for the February 1964 issue of *Motion Picture* magazine, indicating hers was an exclusive and that Lord himself provided the details. While on leave in 1946, he was visiting his brother in upstate New York. An avid photographer, he took his camera and went for a walk, but that quiet stroll in the woods netted more than some good photos. It led him to the one person who could wrangle his Irish temper and soften his tough shell. She captured his undying devotion for the rest of his life.

Marie DeNarde was born August 16, 1905, in St. Louis, Missouri, to Gerard DeNarde and Elise Defranze DeNarde. She became a successful fashion designer and was an independently wealthy businesswoman. She had an apartment in the city and she owned a house in the Woodstock area. Like many significant events in his private life, there are a number of versions of how Jack Lord met Marie. During an interview when he was still a relatively unknown actor, Marie offered the most credible story.

Lord was in Virginia in May of 1956, working on a film for the Colonial Williamsburg Historical Site's new visitors center. Reporters from several area papers were frequent visitors to the set, providing day-to-day coverage of the filming. Lord never traveled without Marie, and she was on location with him for the duration of the filming. A recurring clause in his contractual agreements stipulated that accommodations for any location work had to include his wife. Sunday editions of both *The Norfolk Pilot* and the *Portsmouth Star* on May 27 carried the story of an interview journalist Robert Smith conducted with Marie Lord in which she told how she met her husband.

Marie told Smith she had built an L-shaped stone house for herself in upper New York State. She said she came home from work one evening to find a letter with an offer from a man to buy the house. The offer he made was "ridiculously low," so she threw the note in the trash and forgot about it. Marie also maintained an apartment in Manhattan where she often stayed during work, and she said shortly after she received the letter, she started getting phone calls at the apartment, which she also ignored. She would later learn that Lord had stopped at a local market and it just so happened the proprietor had done some work for her and he had given the young man her phone number.

Eventually, DeNarde received a message with a phone number and a plea that she please return the call. She finally relented and called the persistent caller back. She

Marie DeNarde, circa 1947. Photograph believed to be have been taken by Jack Lord near the stone house she owned in upstate New York (author's collection).

plainly told the man that she had received the letter with his lowball offer to purchase her stone house and that she had no intention of selling. "Well, madam, I'm a sailor," the man said. "I have never written any letter, but I have spent all of my leave trying to reach you." She suddenly realized there were two men interested in buying her lovely stone house. The young man on the phone told her he had gone for a walk while in the area visiting his brother. An avid photographer at the time, he was taking photos of the countryside when he came upon the house and was immediately taken with it. True to form, he did not relent in spite of a number of unreturned phone calls. He persisted until he finally got to speak to her. Marie said she felt guilty that she had caused him to waste all his leave time, and although she no intention of selling her stone house, she agreed to have him come and meet with her to talk about her house. She told Smith she was very surprised when she opened the door and saw "that handsome sight" standing there.[50] Over the years she would tell reporters they talked five hours on that first visit and she confessed she was instantly smitten with the young sailor, saying he reminded her of a Wonder Bread commercial—broad chested and strikingly handsome.

Her relationship with John Ryan was a unique pairing. Marie DeNarde was fifteen years older than her young suitor, and she was financially independent with a successful career as a fashion designer. The courtship was a fast one, and Lord evidently knew he had found his soul mate. Included in his papers is a clipping from the November 18, 1963, issue of *Woman's Day* with the story of his proposal. He was to meet her for dinner at El Farro's, a Spanish restaurant in Greenwich Village, where he planned to propose. He sat at the bar, ordered a martini, and waited for her. When she arrived and they were seated at their table, he had just begun his proposal when actor Jack Elam walked up, slapped Jack on the back and struck up a conversation. Marie told Elam that she was planning a trip to Spain. When they were alone again, Lord told her he was leaving New York to move to the West Coast. He asked her to go with him. When she asked him if he was offering a marriage proposal, he said he was. She instantly replied, "Then I accept."[51] Biographer Virginia Tolles says they were married January 17, 1949, and the couple moved into her New York apartment at 145 East 49th Street the same week they were married, and lived there until 1957. Some sources say the couple wed in 1948, but Tolles' timeline seems more likely. Lord would later say they never celebrated their wedding anniversary, but chose to commemorate the day they met instead.

Marie literally devoted her life to taking care of her husband. Cast members from *Hawaii Five-O* often talked about how she mothered him, describing her as a gracious lady. Throughout his very public life, mention of their devotion to each other was a recurring part of news items about him. When the couple appeared in public, they were always holding hands. Lord loved talking about his wife, frequently boasting about her nineteen-inch waist, her exemplary cooking skills, and her meticulous housekeeping. He freely credited his wife with helping him to learn to control his temper, and with her guidance, he was able to break his habit of settling everything with his fists. Jack Lord often said that Marie was the only thing in the world he really cared anything about and that he wouldn't walk around the corner without her. She was his constant companion, his sounding board, and the only person in the world who really knew him. "Meeting her made all the difference. I might have sailed on merchant ships for the rest of my life. She gave my life a purpose, [he said]."[52] Once he became successful, he often credited his wife with keeping him focused and he never forgot that she gave up her own career to devote all of her time to helping him with his. He knew he was pursuing a tough business, and her constant support and encouragement was vital to his staying the course in the rough years. "I think my whole life has been an effort to become the man she thought I was," he said.[53]

Lord loved children and he showed a gentle side when they were around. Kam Fong, who worked alongside Lord in *Hawaii Five-O* for ten years in the role of Chin Ho Kelly, fondly remembered how the stern, aloof Jack Lord he worked with every day became someone altogether different when children appeared near the set where they were working. Fong commented on how his face softened, clear evidence he was as drawn to them as they were to him. Jack and Marie had agreed early in their marriage they would not have children as they committed all their energy to launching Jack's career. They worked toward that goal in perfect tandem. As they began to see that Jack's career was taking off, they talked about children again. It was not to be, however, and although they were disappointed, they moved forward. Some sources say Marie had a miscarriage at some point. In a devoted commitment to the famous resolve of her husband, Marie joined him in focusing on his work. Jack Lord wanted to be an actor and his wife gave him the green light." "Go," she told him. When they set out together in earnest to pursue his new life as actor, however, they soon discovered it would be a long, hard road and that soon to be famous Jack Lord resolve would be tested.

Two

Motive, Method and Means

While there are stories of aspiring actors who are pulled out of their everyday lives and hustled directly onto a movie set, it is not the norm. Jack Lord certainly didn't have a fairy tale start to his acting career, and to say it was a rough road is putting it mildly. When they married, his wife left behind a good career, and he continued to insist she not return to work as they struggled in those early years. He had to keep his day job as a car salesman to pay the bills for a period of time, and by all accounts, he was very good at it. He was in a holding pattern as he figured out how to get himself in front of the camera, but he was certainly not standing still.

John Ryan the car salesman held fast to the same punishing work ethic that would later become a hallmark of Jack Lord the actor. Like so many other events in his life story, sources disagree about the exact date he started work at Ralph Horgan's Ford dealership on Columbus Circle in New York. Lord said it was 1949, but Horgan later recalled hiring the eager young salesman the previous year. In 1958, Lord told a reporter for *TV Headliner* magazine he was down to his last $3 when he walked into Horgan's dealership and asked for a job. He said at the time he was living in a dingy, $50 a month apartment on 47th Street, and that he had just earned $50 for a one-week run in summer stock work in Pawling, New York.[1] The accuracy of some of the material in the article is questionable, however, as there is information included that has since been proven to be incorrect. Comments from a former high school classmate of Lord's in 1970 suggested he might not have been as destitute at the time as has been implied. William Meyerriecks said the John Ryan he knew and his older brother William came out of the Merchant Marines with a nice nest egg, partially from the bonuses they had earned for their dangerous assignments in the service, boosted by income from an investment John Ryan had made in radio equipment after the war. Meyerriecks contended any successes his famous classmate had were strictly the result of his work ethic and his perseverance.[2]

Ralph Horgan described John Ryan as a "damn good salesman," vividly recalling his disappointment when he left the business in 1949 to go to work for the Cadillac Motor Car Division at 1775 Broadway. The money in the new job was better, and he was eventually earning in the neighborhood of $16,000 to $18,000 a year. Horgan said his star salesman was making a respectable salary of $10,000 a year selling Fords, and despite the demands of his day job, he was finding small parts in local theatre and taking acting lessons at night. In 1969, Lord told a New England journalist he did some work in little theatres in Marblehead and Boston.[3]

After Jack Lord achieved star status, Mr. Horgan granted an interview with a fan magazine, where he commended his young employee for always coming to work impeccably dressed. Horgan said he looked more like a stockbroker than a car salesman. "John never wasted time kidding around," he said. "He was there to work and he did very well. He made friends, everyone liked him, but he didn't talk about himself."[4] Lord's close-mouthed tendencies in sharing about his private life would later cause him much grief, but he was also often indicted as an insufferable egoist.

Horgan was very much aware of the fact that money was tight for young Ryan and his wife. Even though he was making a good salary at his day job, tuition for his acting lessons and other expenses associated with his training cut into their budget. In a May 27, 1956, interview with *The Portsmouth Star* during filming for *The Story of a Patriot*, Marie told reporter Robert C. Smith, "There were many times when Jack could have let me work and help support him while he was struggling to become an actor. But he never did. He always told me if I could struggle with him, he would rather I didn't work."

In an interview with Jack Hirshberg, Lord described Marie's critical role in his early transformation into an actor and beyond. "She feeds me like a gourmet, watches my weight, goes with me to my tailor. She's secretary, business manager and makes my linen leisure jackets herself. She can darn a sock or discuss Stanislavsky or the Giants' batting averages."[5] Even though they saw hard times in those early years, Marie complied with his preference that she stay home. They continued to devote their united efforts and finances to launching his acting career, and their commitment and sacrifice eventually paid off.

Horgan said he always knew John Ryan would make it. Running a business so near the theatre district in New York, Ralph Horgan had seen a lot of aspiring actors come and go and he had also seen the business end of it. He had worked for a short time as a manager for popular bandleader Fred Waring, and he had a daughter who was a professional ballerina. He was impressed that he continued to receive frequent greeting cards and personal correspondence from Lord for many years after he became a successful actor. A prolific letter writer, Lord treasured correspondence from friends and fans and he saved many of the cards and letters he received. Despite his reputation for being standoffish and cold, the Lords' reputation for adhering to the social graces is solidly documented in his papers and in their reputation for frequently entertaining in their home.

Among Lord's papers is a handwritten letter from Joseph Corker, a former salesman at the Cadillac dealership where Lord worked. He wrote to offer his congratulations to Lord on his eleventh season of *Hawaii Five-O* and to tell him that even though he was now 80 years old, he still vividly recalled the young car salesman's aspirations to be an actor. "You have come a long way, Jack, and you deserve it all. If you ever see this little note, drop me a line." Lord answered his letter six months later, on February 8, 1979.[6]

Fellow salesmen at the Cadillac dealership remembered him as the same quiet, impeccably dressed and driven young man Horgan described. One of his fellow salesmen remembered how driven and serious he was, saying he always thought it odd Lord never drank at social events. Throughout his life, a good deal of ink was devoted to whether

Jack Lord drank or smoked and whether he did either to excess. There are several versions of how he did or did not conquer those two vices. In a 1963 interview for *The Western Horseman* about his successful run on *Stoney Burke*, Lord talked about his decision to stop drinking. He admitted he drank during his years in the Merchant Marines and that he drank socially for years. "My reasons for not drinking are based on a long, hard look at the problems caused by alcohol in the schools I attended, at sea, as a steelworker in Iran, on the sets of television and motion pictures in which I worked, and in the social life of my community. What I have seen I do not like."[7]

In 1969, Lord told a reporter his version of why he stopped smoking. "'I quit eight years ago and I have to thank my wife for that. One day she told me she wanted a present. Visions of a Rolls-Royce floated before my eyes, but she said, 'I want you to quit smoking.' I said, 'You've got it.'" He talked about the "diabolical" effect tobacco has on the human system, but said he had no objection to actors smoking on the *Hawaii Five-O* set.[8] He did, however, frequently encourage others to quit. A note from actor Ted Hamilton, who did a 1979 guest star appearance on an episode of *Five-O*, expressed his appreciation to Lord for "giving him a shot." He offered his regrets that he had to cancel doing a second episode, and added a postscript. "You also encouraged me to quit smoking—now that's a 'biggie!'"[9] Lord also kept a letter he received from an elementary school teacher in 1975, thanking him for getting in a "no smoking" comment in an episode of *Hawaii Five-O*. She asked if he would send her a quote of the statement with his autograph, thinking it would make an impression on her young students and help her campaign against smoking.

When he began his job at Cadillac, he made up for lost time when he was on the job by devoting even more time to his training. He attended classes on alternate days, worked on his acting at night, and, according to Marie, worked with Sanford Meisner two nights a week from seven until midnight. On his nights off he rehearsed scenes. Meisner gave the determined young actor a scholarship for his second and third years. In 1970, he told Jane Ardmore he was earning $18,000 a year when he left the Cadillac dealership; his earnings for his first year as a full-time actor were $2,200.[10] Ardmore said he finally resigned his sales career in the spring of 1952. From then on, he relied completely on acting for his livelihood.[11]

The young actor had a memorable encounter with a customer during his time at Cadillac that became one his favorite stories. Lord's idol, actor Gary Cooper, walked into the dealership to look at an old Duesenberg he had once owned. Lord wound up with an invitation to lunch at Schrafft's and an opportunity to talk shop with Cooper, and it was an experience he never forgot. Sources disagree about the continuing friendship of the two men; for the rest of his life Jack Lord was very open about Gary Cooper's influence as a role model.

One constant in his dependency on outside influences to see him through the tough times was his complete and utter devotion to Marie. Co-workers at both dealerships vividly remembered his "lovely, sweet wife," commenting on the couple's complete devotion to each other. His exclusive relationship with his wife, paired with his reluctance to talk about other events in his private life, became another target when fan magazines, always on the lookout for sensationalism, began to take an interest in him during those early years.

Jack Lord had been a successful car salesman, and he wanted that same level of success as an actor. When the time came to make it a priority, he was willing to sacrifice whatever was necessary to make it happen. "Dreams have a way of disappearing if you don't move fast," he said.[12] Before he made what he knew to be a lifelong commitment, however, he first did what he always did when there were important decisions to make. He talked it over with his wife. He fully understood it was going to be a rough road, and he had no intention of setting off on such a journey without the full support of Marie. Her response to him was simple: "Go." Once the decision was made, he wasted no time taking definitive action in his preparation for becoming an actor.

He credited getting his feet on the ground to his decision to study under Sanford Meisner. He said when he and Marie resolved he should move ahead, he met with Meisner and was surprised when, after a three or four-hour examination, he questioned the eager young man about his intentions. "He asked very probing questions, why I wanted to be a stage actor, why I wanted to be in the theatre, and he was as interested in the why as he was the where I was going."[13]

"Meisner really opened me up," he frequently said throughout his career. The precise timeframe for the events that occurred during his training, like so many other events in his story, is hard to pin down. Some sources say he quit his job at Ford in the fall of 1949, took the job at Cadillac, and began to devote more time to his training. If he and Marie were in fact wed in January of that year, that scenario is plausible. Some sources say he immediately got a role on Ralph Bellamy's *Man Against Crime*, but contracts for his work on the series show he wasn't signed for the part until January of 1953. Lord often said Meisner told him it would take 20 years to become an actor, and rather than becoming discouraged by Meisner's reality check, he moved forward, more determined than ever. Although the timeframe is sketchy, it is known Lord enrolled at the Actors Studio, apparently at first attending classes a couple of nights a week, while he kept his day job with Cadillac before he eventually made the difficult decision to quit his day job and concentrate full time on his acting. Lord said that even though the training took a financial toll on him and Marie, he still refused to let her work.

He was in good company at the time he was at the Actors Studio. Paul Newman, James Dean, and Marilyn Monroe were among the future superstars who were classmates. Although it is still unclear when he started his formal training, it has been confirmed that he was definitely at the Actors Studio in 1955. Photographs in the collection at New York's Westwood Gallery include candid shots taken by Roy Schatt of Lord with Monroe and other celebrities who were at the studio in 1955. Schatt was invited to be an observer at the Actors Studio by Lee Strasberg. Strasberg was so impressed with the photos, he named him official photographer for The Actors Studio. Schatt photographed actors, writers, directors and playwrights associated with The Actors Studio as well as many other images of personalities active in the New York theatrical community from the 1950s and '60s.[14] Westwood Gallery in New York City is the exclusive representative of Schatt's estate. While inquiries about alumni records at the Studio were unsuccessful, as they were undergoing digitizing at the time, archival material for the Schatt collection at Westwood Gallery confirms Schatt photographed Lord and Marilyn Monroe in 1955. Lord often said he spent three years at the Studio.

He had definitely chosen the right path if he wanted to work with the best and if

Jack Lord and Marilyn Monroe in New York City. Lord and Monroe were at the Actor's Studio in 1955 when legendary celebrity photographer Roy Schatt invited him to visit the Studio to take some candid photographs. New York's Westwood Gallery is the exclusive representative of Schatt's estate (© 1955 Estate of Roy Schatt, courtesy Westwood Gallery NYC).

he wanted to see and be seen, and he learned much during his time with the Studio. Meisner, along with fellow actors Lee Strasberg, Stella Adler and others were the founders of the Group Theatre, a company originally committed to Russian actor and director Konstantin Stanislavsky's method acting approach. The Neighborhood Playhouse closed twelve years after its 1915 start, but it reopened in 1928. Meisner came on board in 1935, bringing change to traditional method acting techniques. That year Meisner, Adler, Lee Strasberg and others from the Group Theatre joined the faculty of the Neighborhood Playhouse. The Playhouse was one of the first Off-Broadway theatres with a strong commitment to bringing theatre to the community, and was a successful enterprise that eventually moved toward expanding the original mission to focus on the training of actors.

In essence, the Meisner Method has at its foundation the principle that actors create from within and the performance comes from affective memory. "Meisner believed that the study of the actor's craft was rooted in acquiring a solid organic acting technique. It was a cornerstone of his teaching that this learning process occur not in a theoretical, abstract manner, but in the practical give and take of the classroom, where as he once

Lord is in good company for lunch in this 1955 Roy Schatt photograph. From left: actor/playwright Michael Gazzo, author of *A Hatful of Rain* (when Ben Gazzara got a part in the production, Lord stepped into his role as Brick in *Cat on a Hot Tin* Roof); actress Shelly Winters; Lord; and actor/director Frank Corsaro, who was head of the Actor's Studio in 1988. Schatt captioned the photograph: "After the Acting Class: The real discussion takes place at the corner lunch room" (© 1955 Estate of Roy Schatt, courtesy Westwood Gallery NYC).

said, 'the students struggled to learn what I struggled to teach.' Through that struggle the gifted student, over time gradually begins to emerge solidly in his or her work."[15] Meisner believed reactions should be impulsive and natural, not artificial reproductions. He called it a process of living truthfully under imaginary circumstances. "What about talent?" he asked. "That is the real, inexorable primary tool. Either there is an actor or there isn't. Continuous and deepening psychological insight into self as life goes on is one of the characteristics of talent."[16]

Meisner instructed his pupils to live truthfully. A primary part of their tutelage involved improvisation exercises with a partner, when they work from the stimulus of their reaction to what is being said and done by their partner rather than from scripted lines. Lord often said that Meisner "opened him up," crediting him for getting him past his tendencies toward being an introvert. He recounted his first day of class when Meisner asked him to leave the room and come back in as a "ham Shakespearean actor." Lord admitted he was terrified and stood outside the door for fifteen minutes as he struggled with how he might bring that character to life. He said he was suddenly struck with some lines he had learned to earn pennies from his father, slung his overcoat around his body like a cloak and burst through door, ready to go.[17] Lord would later say winning a part in *The Traveling Lady* and his work at the Neighborhood Playhouse were catalysts for his break, and he was confident Eli Kazan's choosing him to replace Ben Gazarra for the role of Brick in *Cat on a Hot Tin Roof* was the due to what he had seen of his work at the Playhouse.

Lord's evasiveness in revealing his true age and the fact that many of the anecdotes he shared years after they happened create issues when trying to nail down a definite timeline for the genesis and progression of his early successes and failures. Interviews he did after his success often have contradictory timelines. Even in the early years of his career and with the first of what would become many gray areas in his closely guarded private life, the tabloids gave considerable ink to a long running debate about his age. He shaved ten years off his age in early biographies that went out as part of his introduction to the professional community. It was a decision that would come back to bite him for the rest of his life. Adjusting one's age up or down, however, was not an uncommon practice for aspiring actors, especially in the Hollywood of the 1940s and '50s when Lord was first coming on the scene.

Lord said at some point, likely early 1950, he and Marie bought a second-hand Cadillac and headed off to Hollywood, where he got an offer from MGM for a seven-year option at $350 a week. He knew of another actor who was given the same option for $500 a week. He determined his three years' work with Meisner and his two years at the Actors Studio was worth more, so he turned it down. Throughout his career he was often criticized for being too picky as he frequently turned down roles in spite of the fact he needed work. A few years down the road, he would take a very public stand against accepting work in which he was cast as the "heavy," or the bad guy. He felt he was being typecast, and he longed for an opportunity to show what he could do if given the chance to step out a bit. He told Johnny Carson in a 1967 interview, "When you strike an A, you should get an A back. You should get what you want and it takes time."

After two months in Hollywood without a nibble, Lord said they sold the car and went back to New York. He later recounted he had heard Alan Mowbry was doing *Flame Out*, so he went to his hotel to ask for a part. Even though he did get a role, it was not a bright spot on his resume. The play was a flop. Again, pinning down the timeline is a problem. *Flame Out* was a 1953 production, and his role in *The Traveling Lady* was in 1954. He was known to have been at the Actors Studio in 1955, so it is difficult to determine exactly where he was when during those years. He would later say when he went to Hollywood to do the sound looping for *Story of a Patriot*, he and Marie stayed 11 months, during which time he was signed for roles in five pilots and three movies, but attempts to confirm his activities at the time were unsuccessful.

Lord never forgot Sanford Meisner's admonition that he should be prepared to give it twenty years. "He means [to become] an actor—not a personality. He means men like Lee J. Cobb or Marlon Brando—the giants in our business. And that's what I'm striking for. I don't want to be just a personality who works. I want to be able to characterize what the author puts on paper.... Technique is how to use yourself and I think that's very important, especially in the demands of television today."[18]

Once Lord had formally put boots on the ground in the pursuit of his new life, the next order of business was to give himself a new name. Adopting a screen name is a common practice for actors as they develop their professional personae, and many legendary actors were not known by their given names. After all, *Marion Morrison* splashed across a sprawling western backdrop on the big screen clearly does not have the same effect as *John Wayne*. Jack Lord was criticized more than most throughout his career, however, for his choice of a professional name, specifically in his decision to adopt *Lord* as a surname. His critics frequently gave his choice of a stage name as evidence of an inflated ego. Lord said on several occasions the name was one he drew from his family's ancestry, and he had little else to say about it. He attributed his decision to forego using his given name professionally solely to the fact that there was already an actor named John Ryan registered with the Screen Actors Guild. He also said his real name sounded too much like an Irish policeman.

Lord was also accused of changing his name in an effort to mask his Irish Catholic heritage, when in fact he was publicly very proud of his birthright. He told Jane Ardmore his fellow shipmates during his early days at sea called him "Mick," a slur to his Irish heritage. Ardmore said his wife still called him Mick on occasion.[19] Todd Mason's collected notes as he prepared to conduct interviews with Jack Lord during the heyday of *Hawaii Five-O* included the question, "Why does [Marie] call him Mick?" Lord often said it was Marie who taught him to cool his quick Irish temper and helped him understand that settling things with his fists was not the first option in a difficult situation.

In a September 8, 1970, letter to Ella Chun, Marie Lord responded to Chun's request to talk to her on the record about Jack for the Hawaiian newspaper *Star Advertiser*. She spoke fondly of his talents and accomplishments, his dogged determination when it seemed everything was going wrong, and of his devotion to her. "He's reserved by nature, but he's also Irish and that means explosive. His reactions are immediate, strong and to the point. You know exactly how he feels, where he stands and where you stand, and then it's all over as far as he's concerned. He's not devious or even diplomatic, but he doesn't hold grudges and he doesn't hate anyone."[20]

As it turned out, Jack Lord's timing in kicking off his career was both prophetic and poetic. Even though he longed to find a niche in live theatre and movie work, his true legacy, and much of his income even in the early years, came from his history-making work on the small screen, and it was a good manifestation of his innate good business sense. He was astutely aware of the importance of being at the right place at the right time and his creative edge helped him recognize opportunity when it presented itself. History has a way of inflicting itself on humanity; in the end, and no doubt totally unexpected to Jack Lord, it was television that made him a very famous, very wealthy man.

RCA president David Sarnoff formally introduced the television at the 1939 World's Fair by broadcasting the opening events of the fair, highlighted by an address by President Franklin Roosevelt. The lure of the limitless possibilities of the revolutionary new technology immediately captivated the public. Everyone who attended the RCA exhibit left with a card from RCA that read, "We hope you have enjoyed your tour through our World's Fair Exhibit, and that when you return home you will have a new understanding of what RCA is doing in the vast field of radio, television and recorded music.... We hope that you will tell your friends about what you have seen, and pass on to them some of your enthusiasm."[21]

And tell their friends they did. By the late 1940s and early '50s, Americans were caught up in a full-blown love affair with television that has continued to grow exponentially.

For many aspiring actors of the time, live television shows, such as the popular *Playhouse 90*, were the best of both worlds. It felt like theatre, it was a chance to show what one could do, it was an opportunity to hone the skills, and, best of all, it had a paycheck attached.

When the Federal Communications Commission licensed the first two television stations for commercial broadcasting on July 1, 1941, young John Ryan was likely at sea, traveling the world on ships, and preparing for his coming final year at NYU. He had no idea the impact this new industry would have on his own life, and he certainly could not have known the extent to which it would change the world.

Three

The Road Rises Up

By mid–April of 1949, *John Ryan* was *Jack Lord*, and he was at work on his first big screen role. *Project X*, also known as *Red Bait*, was filmed entirely on location in New York, and it was the first of several opportunities he would have to work with producer/director Edward Montagne in the early years of his career. When the film premiered on October 14, Lord shared star billing with former model Rita Colton and Keith Andes. Even though the two leading men were the same age and shared several common life experiences, Andes came to the set with the advantage of more time in front of a camera. Andes got his first role at twelve years old. When he was cast in *Project X*, he had already logged a respectable number of radio programs, two minor movie roles, and some television work. Like Lord, Andes was an education major who had served in the armed forces during World War II and earned a Theatre World Award early in his career. *Project X* was Rita Colton's first and last movie role. She did a handful of television guest star spots before retiring completely from the business in the mid-1950s.

Project X hit theatres two years after a group of ten prominent film producers, directors, and screenwriters publicly denounced an investigation by the Un-American Activities Committee of the House of an alleged Communist influence infiltrating the movie industry. The "Hollywood Ten" each received a one-year prison sentence for suspected Communist activities, and their names were placed on a rapidly expanding blacklist of suspected activists banned from working with major studios. The list held strong for thirteen years. The committee's indictment of the movie industry as a vehicle for spreading Communist propaganda to an unaware public had a debilitating impact on the business of Hollywood. In addition to facing the lingering effects in the American workforce of the Great Depression, struggling actors, producers, and directors had difficulty finding work of any kind as studios continued to suffer close scrutiny under the spreading Red Scare. Some of the biggest names in Hollywood were unemployed because studios did not want to risk being tied to suspected Communists.

Fortunately, a clearly articulated anti–Communist theme made *Project X* a safe enterprise during the Red Scare. The sixty-five-minute documentary-styled film is set shortly after the end of World War II and deals with the intrinsic danger of suspected Communist infiltration into American colleges and universities. Andes was cast in the role of Steve Monahan as a physicist working on a project to create nuclear energy without using uranium. In his very first feature film, Lord came out of the gate playing the

Rita Colton and Jack Lord in Lord's first movie role. *Project X* was released October 14, 1949. The film was an anti–Communist propaganda film meant to raise public awareness of Communist activity on American college campuses (Film Classics/Photofest).

heavy, a trend that would later become a source of great frustration for him. His character is John Bates, Monahan's college classmate and an active member of the Communist party. He pressures his old friend to share details of his secret research and threatens to out Monahan as a former Communist if he doesn't comply.

Lord got a nod for his work on the film from journalist Bob Considine. In his syndicated column, Considine calls him an "up and coming screen fellow," thankfully avoiding a concentrated focus on the disappointing film. He tactfully chose to direct his comments about the emerging young actor to New York sports fans, calling Lord "one of the best tackles ever turned out by Dr. Mal Stevens ... at N.Y.U." Considine lists Lord's accomplishments outside show business, mentioning his pilot's license and the art school he and his brother founded in Greenwich Village, praising his "artistic knighthood." He said Lord had turned down quick-paying offers from the Philadelphia Eagles and the Cleveland Rams pro teams in exchange for a new racket in the movies.[1]

Daily Variety was not so gracious, however. The film got a scathing review as a clumsily made melodrama that reflected little of the fundamentals of sound motion picture production, evidenced by a plodding cast, uninspired direction, attempted leads and "inept, amateurish values, including lensing and editing."[2] Jack Lord apparently agreed with *Variety*'s opinion about his screen debut. Five years later, soon after he had finished *The Vagabond King*, he told publicist Jack Hirshberg that he had three New York films to his credit—all stinkers. "One was titled 'Project X' and that is what it turned out to be—an X-budget, X-quality epic," he said. "Another like it and I'd be on the way to working as an insurance salesman." He admitted his experience with New York filmmaking had nonetheless taught him a valuable lesson. "Make movies in Hollywood where they know how, and not in the east," he said.[3] Hirshberg's interview notes for the story include a reminder to himself that Lord had asked that he please not print the names of the three films. When the article was published, however, the "stinker" list was prominently included in the story.

If life experience truly has anything to do with a believable performance, Lord's second foray into New York filmmaking was a part he could certainly pull off. *Cry Murder!* was released on January 6, 1950, by Film Classics, Inc. The storyline was based on *Lost and Found*, a play by A.B. Shiffrin. This was Lord's second time working with producer Edward Leven, and he had star billing alongside Carol Matthews and Howard Smith. Lord plays Tommy Warren, an intelligent and rugged artist—a role he could certainly pull off. Warren is a scheming alcoholic who gets hold of some letters belonging to a newlywed young actress. The letters have information that if misinterpreted would seriously damage her reputation. When she tries to pay off the blackmailing artist, she is knocked unconscious and awakens to find herself a suspect in a murder investigation.

Jack Lord and Tom Pedi in *Cry Murder!* Released January 6, 1959, Lord played blackmailing artist Tommy Warren (Film Classics/Photofest).

In addition to his starring role, Jack Lord was able to add an associate producer credit to his resume for the film.

Variety dealt *Cry Murder!* a hard hand in its weekly edition, citing an implausible plot, stilted dialog, a "talky" script, static direction, and poor photography. While the review offered some mercy to two of the actors who had minor roles, leads Mathews and Smith were soundly blasted. The weekly edition, however, credited Carole Mathews as the only stand-up actor in the whole production. While Lord escaped printed indictment in the review, the ink he got for his effort was scarcely worth clipping the article for his scrapbook: "Jack Lord is okay as the artist."[4] The February 7 daily edition of *Variety* agreed with Lord's perception of New York filmmaking. "Filmed in NY, *Cry Murder!* lacks all the Hollywood knowhow of picture making. Any bids the film makes towards realism through excessive use of exteriors and cheap interiors are swiftly overcome by amateurish direction and performances."[5] The *Los Angeles Times* deemed it a "mild melodrama, filmed in New York, and wordy."[6]

In April, *Screenland* magazine printed a full-page story about *Cry Murder!* with three small stills and a cutout from the film featuring Jack Lord spread across the page. Focusing on the likelihood of female fans' attraction to his impressive six-foot stature, brawn, and brains, the story talked mostly about his accomplishments as an artist and star football player for NYU. An unidentified press release for *Cry Murder!* in Lord's biography file at the Margaret Herrick Library includes a statement that stands in stark contrast to future criticism about Lord's demeanor on the job. "One of Jack's best attributes is that he is extremely easy to work with."[7]

He was back on screen a month later working again with Montagne on *The Tattooed Stranger*, released by RKO Pictures on February 9, 1950. The film noir, or "black film," genre was popular in the mid 1940s as producers, directors, actors, and adult audiences were looking for a departure from the standard Hollywood fare of the time. Popular screenplays were dark crime stories, populated with cynical, hardened characters and storylines focusing on the underbelly of human nature. The characteristic violence and grit of film noir later became a trademark of the modern detective story, so Lord was getting some valuable experience in a genre that would eventually become his bread and butter.

The Tattooed Stranger follows a group of New York City detectives as they unravel the identity of a young woman found dead in a stolen car in Central Park. The only clue is a mysterious Marine tattoo on her wrist. The cast is replete with cynical career cops who take every opportunity to swap cavalier quips as they go about the grisly business of connecting the dots in a very tangled investigation. Screenplay writer Phil Reisman, Jr., integrated a romantic sub-plot, as the rookie detective assigned to help with the investigation falls for a beautiful botanist who ultimately holds the key to solving the complicated case.

Weekly Variety called the film a solid program with a fast-moving screenplay and "adequate" performances, predicting it could hold its own against other crime movies due to hit theatres that week. Filming in the streets of New York gave the film an element of reality, and helped set a precedent that would carry over to the crime genre in period television.

Jack Lord's appearance in the film was minimal. As Detective Deke Del Vecchio, he appears in three brief scenes for a total on-screen time of less than three minutes. He has a couple of lines in his first scene, and when the credits roll at the end his part is uncredited. There are instances when he appears to be studying the other actors, watching them intently as they run their lines.

Even though his third film appearance wasn't a stellar experience, he stayed the course, taking full advantage of every opportunity to watch, to learn, and to get face time with key people in Hollywood. Money was tight and he and Marie continued to see some lean times during that period. He couldn't afford to be too exclusive as he pounded the pavement and waited for his big break.

Lord kept his role models always before him as he persevered in those early years. Legendary actor Walter Huston died suddenly of an aortic aneurysm on April 7, 1950. Lord penned a heartfelt sympathy letter to his son, John Huston, the following day. Huston's achievements as an accomplished actor, screenwriter, and director, whose body of work include some of the most enduring films in movie history, had inspired the young actor, and he wanted to pay homage to his career and to his influence. "He was my ideal," Lord wrote, "and in humble tribute to a great artist I am attaching this little clipping from the press book of a recent B picture I made."[8] Early in his career, Lord frequently told reporters that he would consider himself an accomplished actor only when he could make people feel the way he felt after seeing Walter Huston perform. Throughout his career, he often acknowledged role models in his life, and it was a practice that sometimes translated in the press as evidence of an inflated ego.

After *The Tattooed Stranger*, Lord hit a debilitating dry spell, and it was two years before he was seen on television again. He finally landed a role on an episode of the first season of Edward Montagne's *The Hunter*. The CBS series followed the adventures of undercover spy Bart Adams who posed as a businessman while traveling the globe to fight the spread of Communism. Like so many other television series at the time, the show's development followed a complex journey. Sponsor R.J. Reynolds had put it up as a summer replacement for *Man Against Crime*, maintaining Montagne and series writer Phil Reisman for the new series. *The Hunter* fared relatively well despite having a time slot opposite some stiff competition, but CBS made the decision to cancel it at the end of the first season, even though an additional 13 episodes had been filmed with another star playing the lead. In 1954, they sold the first season episodes to NBC as a summer replacement option. They later bought the additional unaired episodes as well. Even though the series was eventually syndicated, it faltered and disappeared.[9] On July 2, 1952, Lord appeared in an episode titled "The Puzzle of Pier 90," the story of an attempt to smuggle a Communist imposter into nuclear labs at Oak Ridge, Tennessee.

An unidentified clipping in Lord's papers from the third season of *Five-O* lists a starring role for him in *Mr. and Mrs. North*, a series about a married couple who enjoyed working as amateur detectives. The show aired on CBS from 1952 to 1953, then moved to NBC for its final year. It was in fact Richard Denning, who would later play McGarrett's boss in Five-O, who had the role.

The following year Jack Lord captured a place in a project that would make history in more ways than one. *Man Against Crime* creator Lawrence Klee was the brain behind an innovative genre that fit neatly into the up and coming medium of television and introduced a format that became Lord's hallmark. The series premiered in 1949 with

Ralph Bellamy in the lead role as private eye Mike Barnett, and it is often credited as the prototype for the modern detective show. The popular series ran for about five years and early on it was broadcast live, seen simultaneously on NBC, CBS and DuMont Television Networks during its last season from 1953 to 1954. It was later syndicated as *Follow that Man*.

Montagne's series followed the then popular production trend of location filming and the utilization of actors outside mainstream Hollywood offerings. Lord may very well have put some of the lessons he learned during his experience with location shooting to good use later as he worked in the streets of Hawaii on his landmark role as Steve McGarrett.

In January of 1953, Lord signed a day player agreement with the William Esty Company. He was paid $85 a day for three days work on an episode set for the fourth season of *Man Against Crime*.[10] In a self-authored article for *Mr. Magazine* in 1957 Lord wrote that he was paid $100 a day for his work, but when filming for the episode wrapped on January 9, he had actually earned a total of $255 for his work.[11] "The Midnight Express" aired on February 18, 1953. The primary action in the episode depicts a scowling Lord tailing costar Audrey Meadows back and forth through the narrow corridors of a moving train as hard-boiled Ralph Bellamy, in the role of Detective Mike Barnett, tails both of them. Lord's character is later revealed to be an undercover treasury department agent in pursuit of a ring of counterfeiters. After the reveal, he quickly transitions from a dark, scowling suspect to an affable, dedicated lawman.

Filed among Lord's papers is a framed, autographed photo of actor Basil Rathbone. On the back Lord has written, "Did my first live T.V. show in Criminal at Large by Edgar Wallace, starring Basil Rathbone." He listed the eight other cast members and noted the dates of the work as "Mon. Thru Fri. Feb 2nd–6th 1953."[12] "Criminal at Large" was an episode of the second season of the *Broadway Television Theatre*, a popular series that featured adaptations of Broadway shows. Some sources list the airdate of the episode with Rathbone and Lord as February 2, 1953.

Jack Lord finally made it to the New York stage later that year when an English version of French playwright Andre Roussin's comedy, *La Pettite Hutte*, or *The Little Hut*, opened at the Coronet Theatre on October 7, 1953. The "Broadway Showlog" section of the October 7 *Billboard* reported 21 performances were set to run through October 24. *The Little Hut* is the lighthearted tale of a man, his wife, and her lover, who find themselves shipwrecked together on a tropical island. The trio decides to take the high road and deal with the potentially awkward situation of one woman and two men by agreeing the two men will equally share the attention of the woman.

Author Nancy Mitford had translated the play into English and it enjoyed a long and very successful run in Paris. When it opened in London's West End Lyric Theatre in August of 1950, it was a smash hit with English audiences, playing to rave reviews for more than 1,200 performances over three seasons. When *The Little Hut* opened America, again under the direction of Peter Brook, it did not garner the same praise it had received abroad. The reviews were less than kind, and critics expressed surprise that the much-anticipated European hit had flopped so miserably with New York audiences. Brooks Atkinson's October 8 review in the *New York Times* proposed it was the English actors who had put the spark in the story when it played abroad. He called out American cast members Anne Vernon and Colin Gordon for their "literal" interpretation, saying they acted as though they only half believed what they were saying. "*The Little Hut*," he said, "cannot survive honest playing." Maybe it was just as well that Jack Lord's small role as a loincloth-wearing native was an uncredited one, and that his name did not appear in the playbill. The tall, fit young actor should have at the very least received some credit for wearing the costume well. Perhaps *The Little Hut* had simply run its course by the time it reached the U.S. Even a distinguished cast headed up by Ava Gardner and David Niven couldn't save a 1957 MGM movie version of the comedy.

Lord told *Daily Variety* in 1972 that he was paid $100 a week for his role in *The Little Hut* at Marblehead, Massachusetts; Marie Wilson was paid $6,000 for her starring role.[13] He resolved early on that one day it would be Jack Lord earning the big paychecks. In spite of the epic fail of *The Little Hut*, he was not completely deterred from a desire to try his hand at comedy again. Twenty-five years later, he mentioned his one comedy experience with *Hut*, remembering it as a time he got to "stretch muscles ... never used."[14]

Some sources indicate *The Little Hut* was not his first turn in the theatre, reporting Lord had a bit part in a Plymouth Theatre production of Robert Sherwood's *Abe Lincoln in Illinois*, which ran from October 15, 1938, until November 25, 1939. The play won the Pulitzer Prize for drama in 1939, and the *Playbill* cover for the original production features a classic rendering of the young Lincoln by Lord's hero, Norman Rockwell. Although the coming together of a couple of Lord's loves makes for a nice anecdote, it is very likely not true. John J. Ryan was 18 years old when the play opened, and his name does not appear in the cast or in the ensemble listings in the *Playbill*. While it is possible he may have had an uncredited role in one or more performances, it is more likely that over time he has been confused with fellow John Adams High School graduate Joseph Wiseman. Wiseman graduated from Lord's alma mater in 1935 and started his acting career in summer stock as a teenager. He made his Broadway debut in 1938 with a bit part in the Lincoln play. He and Lord did share a landmark intersection in their respective careers later however. Wiseman is better known as the first actor to play a featured villain in a James Bond film. Cast as the evil Dr. No in the James Bond film by the same title, he worked alongside John Adams High classmate Jack Lord in his role as Felix Leitner.

Always in onward and upward mode, Lord moved on after his disappointing stage experience. On October 31, 1953, *Billboard* announced the cast for a new play bound for Broadway in December. The production would include three promising new actors in top roles. Harry Carey, Jr., Jack Lord, and Phillip Kenneally would share the spotlight in *Flame-Out*, a unique comedy-drama written and directed by renowned stage, screen, and television actor Alan Mowbray. The play was set to open in Hartford, Connecticut, on November 12, 1953, and other performances were scheduled for Philadelphia on November 16 and Washington, D.C., on November 30.[15]

As a founding member of the Screen Actors Guild who had made a significant financial contribution to the guild's incorporation, Mowbray was a heavy-hitter. Always aware of the importance of being seen by the right people, Lord no doubt appreciated the chance to work alongside some well-established actors and with someone of Mowbray's status. In the 1957 article for *Mr.* magazine, Lord said that after only five days of rehearsal for *Flame-Out*, his role was elevated to the lead. Confident the play would make it to Broadway, he believed he was finally off and running.

Flame-Out was set during the Korean War era and was publicized as a possible successor to other recent successful offerings from the First and Second World Wars. It is the story of a pilot who is held responsible for the death of a comrade shot down during combat. The pilot is exonerated in the end when it is discovered he had intentionally put himself in the line of fire after learning he had a terminal disease. His motive was to secure a pension for his widow and to gain hero status in the eyes of his son. Lord worked alongside Harry Carey, Jr., son of the legendary Harry Carey, a prolific and versatile stage and screen actor, stunt man, and writer who worked with all the greats in western film. Harry Carey, Jr., followed in his father's footsteps, accumulating an impressive filmography throughout his long career, including several classic John Ford westerns. Lord would work again with Carey in December of 1957 in an episode of *Playhouse 90*.

Flame-Out proved to be yet another disappointment. The show's reviews in early press coverage from the Hartford run were brutal. Lord recalled there was a two-week break for the cast and crew in Philadelphia for rewrites and then more rehearsals before they opened on November 30 for a two-week run at the Sam S. Shubert Theatre in Washington, D.C. The hope was *Flame-Out* would be next in a series of recent plays that had been well received by Washington audiences and then moved on to find certain success on the Broadway stage. It was not meant to be.

The program cover for the Shubert performances indicates the play would have a one-week run in the capital, even though text inside the program promised a two-week run. Lord later attributed the failure of the play to the presence of a large number of Air Force brass in the audience and their reaction to a storyline set in the Korean War with a cast of Air Force fighter pilots. The war had ended less than five months earlier and the wounds were still raw. The dishonorable actions of the dead pilot likely didn't endear the story to the military presence. Whatever the reason for the fail, Lord was out of work again.

As he faced yet another disappointment, he would not be dissuaded. He picked himself up and moved on. He continued to get some work on television and some scattered live theatre work, but the pay was not what he needed to adequately support himself and his wife. There are some discrepancies in reports of the exact date Lord gave up his salesman job to devote himself full time to acting. The reality of their financial situation was surely bleak at this point. He said on several occasions his annual income from his acting at this time was around $2,200, a huge step down from what he was earning as a car salesman. He was determined to make a go of it and, with the ever-devoted Marie's full support, he stayed the course.

Some sources say Jack Lord's next turn on the stage was in a production of Sol Stein's first play, *Napoleon*, also known as *The Illegitimist*. Stein, along with Tennessee Williams, and Robert Anderson, was a founding member of the Playwrights Group of the Actors Studio. The verse drama was written while Stein was under a fellowship at Yaddo, a prestigious artists' colony in New York State, and was named the best full-length play by the Dramatists Alliance in 1953. It played for the first time at New York's American National Theatre and Academy in 1953. A role in *The Illegitimist* customarily appears on a list of Lord's theatrical experience in his biographical information. Attempts to find his name tied to any production of the play in either California or New York venues were unsuccessful. It is possible he may have had an uncredited role and was not listed in playbills, or he could have appeared in a workshop production of the play somewhere.

Lord signed on for another episode of Bellamy's *Man Against Crime* in February of 1954. He earned $75 per day for three days' work February 9–11 in "The Chinese Dolls." On his file copy of the contract, he penciled in all the deductions from his earnings: "Gross 225.00; SS 4.50; Ins. .30; WT 33.60." He also noted a 10 percent payout to Max Richard, possibly referring to the Max Richard Booking Agency operating in New York City at that time. His net pay for the job came to $164.10.[16] "The Chinese Dolls" aired two months later, on April 11, 1954. Lord's contract called for compensation ranging from 50 percent of his salary to 25 percent for repeated runs from the third through the sixth and additional runs. It was not exactly the kind of payday he was looking for, but he was taking work whenever and wherever he could get it.

Jack Lord clearly had a propensity toward steady vigilance for the "next big thing." Even though he had expressed frustration with the New York film scene, he was fortunate to be living in the center of what was becoming a rapidly growing phenomenon as he endured a constant struggle to stay the course. By the late 1940s and early '50s, it was a common practice for high profile stage actors to take television roles. The new medium was beginning to take off, especially as versions of popular radio shows of the time were showing up on the small screen and more and more Americans were buying TV sets. Television work was an opportunity for a paycheck and for exposure before a national audience—a benefit the theatre could not offer. The studio system was failing, and as actors were being released from their contracts, many began to look for work wherever they could find it. Hollywood was seeing an exodus of many of its major stars. With the oppressive political and economic atmosphere of Hollywood threatening their livelihood, big screen actors began showing up in New York. The rapidly growing popularity of live television, especially for audience favorites like westerns and anthologies, was a good fallback and kept the paychecks coming. Even after the unions got involved and the pay for television work improved, many actors were still forced to hold down second jobs just to survive.[17]

As New York suddenly became the place to be for actors, writers, and directors, Jack Lord's geography was ideal for the next big thing and, being the proactive person he was, he took full advantage of the new market. He desperately wanted live theatre time, but when he couldn't find it, live television drama was the next best thing and he took every opportunity to work. He soon got a small part in another popular New York–like live television program. *The Web* was an anthology series produced by Mark Goodman and Bill Todman that ran on CBS for four seasons from 1950 to 1954. The scripts were adaptations of stories written by members of the Mystery Writers of America and the series was popular fare at the time. Lord had a small part in "Grand Finale." The episode aired May 2, 1954, and it is the tale of an aging, paranoid opera star who suspects his younger wife is romantically involved with one his young protégés, played by Lord. Frustrated with the faltering, second-rate opera company in which he finds himself, the Maestro fears he will lose his status as a premier performer. Lord's character has a sword fight scene in a play with the aging Maestro, and the old man removes the adhesive gum from the tip of the stage prop sword, killing the young performer on stage as he feigns a tragic accident.

In the meantime, the Maestro has taken fledgling singer Miss Garvey under his wing, offering to tutor her at night. He later suspects she knows the death of the young actor was intentional when she finds the discarded gum from the sword. Eventually the Maestro's wife tells her husband the young man was secretly helping her raise money to invest in a reputable opera company worthy of her husband's grand stature in the opera world. The Maestro reacts to the news with a grandiose wailing fit, suitable for a production of *King Lear*.

While Lord's part was critical to the plot, his performance, consisting of one-line, is forgettable. He is on screen for a total time of less than 59 seconds, and his name does not appear in the credits. The murder scene occurs off camera, and in the long run it hardly seems worth the effort of his putting on the elaborate costume he wears. In the opening segment, however, series host Jonathan Blake introduces Lord as a "promising up and coming new actor" and the experience at least adds another credit to his resume.

Carroll Baker, another up and comer, appeared in the same episode, and she later attributed her big break to that small role. "'On a TV show, 'The Web,' Jack Lord was cast opposite me,' she said. 'The night it aired, George Stevens caught the show, and asked to screen test me for the part of Luz in *Giant*.'"[18] Baker went on to have a long and highly successful career, working with some of the biggest names in Hollywood. She won the Golden Globe in 1957 as New Star of the Year for her part in *Baby Doll* and went on to garner future Oscar and the Golden Globe nominations.

Television audiences had an opportunity to see Lord again on June 22 in an episode of the CBS series *Suspense*. Another live show, it was based on a 1942 radio series by the same name, and many of the stories for both the radio and the television versions of the show were drawn from classic literature. Lord had a part in "String," the true story of a group of men who are captured and tortured for espionage during World War II. The series had a brief return on NBC in 1957, but he did not appear in any additional episodes.

The year was not all about bad news and disappointments, however. Lord got an opportunity for some serious acting in early September when he was cast in the role of Slim Murray for thirty performances of Horton Foote's classic work *The Traveling Lady*.[19] The show opened on October 27, 1954, at The Playhouse on West 48th Street, and it was Foote's last full-length play produced on Broadway until *The Young Man from Atlanta* in 1995. Reviews were mixed, but for the most part members of the cast were praised for good, genuine performances. In the starring role, Kim Stanley was the standout player and virtually every review praised her performance and confirmed her guaranteed soon-to-be-a-star status. *The New York Times* reported the play had made the Theatre Guild subscription list, but the October 28 *Daily Variety* expressed serious doubts it would move to the commercial market, even though it was due a measure of respect as a good drama. The review said it was not "theatrical" enough. The *Playbill* highlights Lord's significant work on television to date and mentions his previous stage appearances in *The Little Hut* and *Flame-Out*. Most of the biographical information is about his diverse experiences as a Merchant Marine and his achievements as an artist.

Slim Murray is a tragic soul struggling to recover from his late wife's painful indifference to his affection. He quickly falls for Stanley's character, Georgette Thomas, and seeks to rescue her and her young daughter from her no-good husband, who has just been released from prison. Hobe's October 28 review in *Daily Variety* declared that Stan-

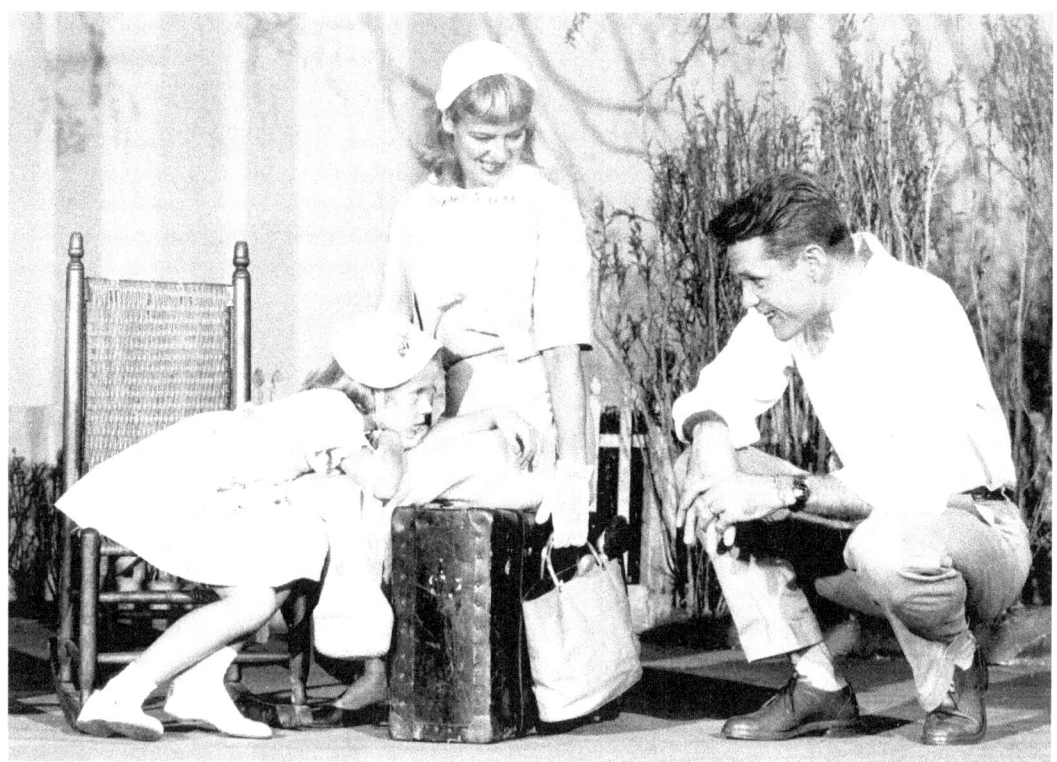

From left: Brook Seawell, Kim Stanley, and Jack Lord in a 1954 Broadway production of Horton Foote's *The Traveling Lady* (Photofest).

ley put forth "easily the best performance of her young career," deeming it tender, sensitive, unashamedly honest and undeniably touching. Dampening the praise heaped on the leading lady, however, the review went on to say it was difficult to be excited by the performances overall. "It's likely to be a hard show to sell the public." *New York Times*' critic Brooks Atkinson did not agree, declaring Stanley's performance head and shoulders above the rest of the cast. Lord got what may have been a backhanded compliment. "Jack Lord's man in the house, taciturn in manner, has a fervent sincerity that is overwhelming in the last scene."[20]

Lonny Chapman filled the role of Stanley's husband in the play, and he later recalled her stinging indictment of Lord's work, saying she "disdained" him as an actor. "'Out of town, you couldn't unwind after the show, so we'd go to the bar and talk about the theatre," he said. "[Kim] loved to do that, except with Jack Lord. She thought he was stiff as an actor. She said no matter what she did on stage, even if she stood on her head, he'd still do the same thing."[21]

New York Times critic Fitzroy Davis put forth what may have been the most creative indictment of the two male leads' performances. He declared that while their delivery may have been appropriate for film, it did not resonate with a live theatre audience. "The performances given by Jack Lord ... and Lonny Chapman ... might have been accurate to type and quite moving if they had been seen at close range by a camera, but they failed to project as theatre performances, especially in terms of vocal eloquence."[22] Davis went on to conclude that due to the "tameness and lameness" in the leading men, Stanley had to work "like an entire Trojan army" to project the center of the play.

It was a good thing the Theatre World Awards Committee for the 1954–55 Season did not concur with the lukewarm reviews or with Kim Stanley's opinion of Lord's ability to carry a part. When it was all said and done, he emerged triumphant. The Theatre World Awards, given at the end of each theatrical season for an actor's successful debut performance, stand as the oldest recognition given to new actors as "the most promising personalities of the Broadway stage." The intention is to encourage promising new talent to continue their work in the theatre. When the awards for the season were announced, Lord was counted among those whose work had earned a place on the list, and he found himself in good company at the ceremony. Fellow recipients for the season included Anthony Perkins, Christopher Plummer, and Julie Andrews. Foote later adapted *The Traveling Lady* for a *Studio One* episode that aired on April 27, 1957. Although Kim Stanley reprised her role as Georgette, actor Stephen Hill replaced Jack Lord as Slim. Hill is best known for his ten-year run as District Attorney Adam Schiff on the first season of the original *Law and Order*.

From left: Jack Lord, Eva Marie Saint, and David Daniels at the 1955 Theatre World Awards ceremony. Lord received a Promising Personality recognition for his work on *The Traveling Lady* (Louis Melancon; author's collection).

Lord signed a minimum freelance contract with the Screen Actors Guild on December 16, 1954, for a part in Paramount's musical *The Vagabond King*. Production was set to begin on December 27, and Lord was promised a minimum of six weeks work at $700.00 per week.[23] The numbers on his contracts were coming up. Keeping Lord's whereabouts in chronological order for 1955 and 1956 is a challenge. He was suddenly very busy, and it seemed as soon as he had something in the can and ready for release, he was already at work on multiple other projects. His activity makes for a tough timeline.

As 1955 got under way, he continued to rack up appearances in several popular television series on all three networks. On March 29, he was seen in "Season for Murder," an episode from the last season of *Danger*, another CBS live drama offering. The following week he appeared on NBC's *Armstrong Circle Theatre* in an episode titled "Buckskin" in which he played Clay Cochran, an ironically unarmed gunslinger. He was back on CBS less than a week later, working alongside Actors Studio classmate, Paul Newman. "Five in Judgment," the second episode from the premiere season of *Appointment with Adventure*, aired April 10, 1955. Patricia Breslin, who would later guest star alongside Lord in *Stoney Burke*, was also part of the cast.

The episode is the story of a tragic case of mistaken identity. Lord's character is a hot-tempered, apron clad cook at the Paradise Diner where an odd mix of characters take refuge during a horrible windstorm. As a radio in the background blasts updates on the intense investigation of a local murder case, those gathered in the diner collectively decide the perpetrators are among the customers. Lord puts forth his best effort in the bad guy role, and he holds his own alongside a young Paul Newman.

"Five in Judgment" was reviewed well in the *New York Times*. The first episode of the new series had aired the previous week and it had not fared so well in the reviews. *Times* critic J.P. Shanley, however, held out hope for show based on the success of the second episode. He judged the performances to be expert and praised the tense excitement of the plot, holding out hope the second start "provided reason for optimism" for the new series.[24]

Whether intentional or incidental, Lord is noticeably breathing hard throughout the episode. A self-confessed heavy smoker at the time of the filming, Lord sometimes said he quit his habit as a birthday gift for Marie. An often-repeated story about his eventual success in stopping smoking has him going into a church with a friend, kneeling on the altar and vowing to God that he would not smoke again. The church declaration version comes from Lawrence Laurent. Laurent's papers at George Washington University document a long-term friendship and trust between them, and the two men carried on extensive correspondence for years. It is likely that it was Lord who shared this version with him.

After the *Appointment with Adventure* episode, fans would not have to wait long to see Jack Lord on the small screen again. Two months later he appeared in the first season of *The Elgin Hour*, yet another live TV offering, airing every other week from New York. "Combat Medics," the last of nineteen episodes for the series, was broadcast June 14, 1955, and it put Lord in a role he could certainly do. He plays Lieutenant Davis, a tough Korean War army lieutenant who is hunkered down under heavy fire with a group of medics in a bombed out building. John Kerr stars and the supporting cast includes Brian

Keith and John Cassavetes. Lord got a "with" billing for his part. Five years later, Lord and Brian Keith would share a near-miss experience for a place in what would become a film classic. Both men were considered for the role of Sam Loomis, Marion's lover in Alfred Hitchcock's *Psycho*, but the part ultimately went to John Gavin. Gavin beat out Lord yet again in the late 1960s for the lead in *Cutter's Trail*, an unsuccessful pilot for a new western series that aired as a TV movie.

In spite of the setback things were beginning to look up. On June 17, Lord signed a free-lance contract with United States Pictures to fill the role of Zachary Lansdowne for *The Court-Martial of Billy Mitchell*. He was guaranteed no less than two weeks' work at $1,250, beginning June 23. Travel and room and board expenses were added to the package as he commuted from New York for location filming. Even though Marie customarily traveled with him, there is no mention of expenses for his wife.

True to his man of many parts personae and still struggling financially, Lord continued to seek out every opportunity he could to capture a paycheck. The June 21 edition of *Daily Variety* reported that Cornell Wilde had hired him to write the lyrics for Elmer Bernstein's ballad melody from his new movie. Released on February 1, 1956, United Artists' *Storm Fear* is the tale of a group of criminals who wind up hiding out after a deadly robbery in an isolated mountain cabin that is home to the brother of one of the gang. Based on a screenplay by Horton Foote, the action centers on a continuum of surprising reveals about virtually every member of the cast. The twists, turns and surprise connections keep the conflict going and make for several effective technical climaxes in the story.

In addition to his starring role, Wilde served as director and his independent film company, Theodora Productions, handled the production of *Storm Fear*. Jean Wallace, his wife and partner in Theodora, costarred. Apparently, the deal between Lord and Wilde for a musical collaboration failed to come to fruition. Lord would later become known for sticking to his guns when it came to business deals and something apparently went wrong during negotiations with Wilde. *Variety* reported on August 3 that Jack Brook, best known for his classic song, "That's Amore," would do the lyrics for the release of the theme song, "Why Try Again."

While Lord was relatively successful finding a respectable amount of television and movie work, the theatre continued to hold a special appeal for him in his resolve to be recognized as a serious actor. Punishing schedules and a self-imposed quest for perfection fit well with the challenges faced by those whose primary medium was live theatre. Keeping it fresh for every performance was a challenge, especially in a long run. Building on the premise there is really no such thing as a "method" actor, but rather only good or bad actors, *The Anonymous Method* blog effectively clarifies the critical distinction between the necessary tools for stage acting and those required of a film actor. Good actors are the ones who can experience and re-experience, and that is the goal of their training. A film actor has the opportunity to do it until it's right, and that sought after, perfect re-experiencing can be put down for good. The stage actor does not have that advantage. He must constantly re-experience for every performance and it must look as though he is doing it for the first time.[25] The nature of Lord's work ethic and his famous perfectionist tendencies were good evidence that he relished the challenge of the theatre and the necessity of doing it right the first time and every time thereafter.

Even after *The Traveling Lady* closed following 30 performances, Lord continued to reap career-advancing benefits from the experience. Hollywood director Michael Curtiz had seen Lord's performance in the play and subsequently signed him in January for the role of Ferrebouc, King Louis' captain, in *The Vagabond King*. Otto Preminger would be directing. Even though the film featured a number of elaborate musical scenes, Lord expressed his disappointment to Jack Hirshberg that he would not be singing in his role. Familiar with Lord's resolve, Hirshberg told his readers that even though the part would not offer Lord an opportunity to show off his musical ability, he assured them Lord would not give up. "In view of his dedication to purpose, it's not too much to assume he'll probably start taking lessons soon from [opera stars] Jan Peerce or Robert Merrill."[26] While Jack Lord did not precisely fulfill Hirshburg's prophecy, he did subsequently pursue singing lessons for another landmark role he would capture a few years down the road.

Paramount's *The Vagabond King* was a remake of a 1930s film by the same name, derived from a 1925 operetta based on a play that dated back to 1901. It was the first of two projects he would work on with actress Kathryn Grayson. Even though the storyline of an attempted overthrow of King Louis XI in 15th century France had enjoyed longevity, the outcome was not as lucrative as the creator of the film version had hoped. Lord's part was not a prominent one, but in the midst of the experience, his luck was rapidly changing, and while he was at work on it other opportunities were in the works. July 7, 1955, was a red-letter day for Jack Lord. Things were finally coming together at the speed he preferred.

On October 5, 1954, *The Hallmark Hall of Fame* ran a radio episode narrated by Lionel Barrymore dramatizing the true story of Colonel Billy Mitchell's fight with Army and Navy superiors over their refusal to supply adequate air support for the United States Armed Forces. Eight months later, on June 7, 1955, Otto Preminger began screen tests for his upcoming Warner Bros. film, *The Court-Martial of Billy Mitchell*. Lord at first was inclined to turn the part down because of the brief screen time it afforded. Fortunately, Preminger put it in perspective for him. "My boy, it's a picture in color with Gary Cooper. Think of it as a screen test with the greatest actor in the world."[27]

The announcement came on July 7 that Jack Lord would be included in the cast. By the end of the month, the *New York Times* reported he would be replacing Ben Gazzara in the role of Brick for Tennessee Williams' *Cat on a Hot Tin Roof*.[28] Sol Stein and Elia Kazan had served as production observers for the play. If Lord did in fact have a part in Stein's *Napoleon*, their familiarity with his work may have been a contributing factor to his being chosen to step into Gazarra's place when he began work on *A Hatful of Rain*. *American National Biography Online*, however, says it was Meisner who recommended Lord. The *New York Times* ran a nice headshot of Lord over the caption "Receives Major Role" on August 29, the same day of Lord's first performance in "Cat."[29]

With two significant opportunities running concurrently with his work on *Vagabond*, timing was critical. Fortunately, he was finishing up *Vagabond* June 18, which was the date *Billy Mitchell* was scheduled to begin shooting. Lord was set to complete his work on that role by July 18, and that would give him three weeks' rehearsal time before he stepped onto the stage in the role of Brick. He was off and running, blissfully busy and optimistic that things were at last turning around with rapid speed. Otto Preminger

Burl Ives, left, as Big Daddy and Lord as Brick in a 1955 production of Tennessee Williams' classic *Cat on a Hot Tin Roof* (Photofest).

wrapped filming on *Billy Mitchell* on Saturday, August 13. Lord was running in high gear, and it was the way he liked to work.

It was almost a year after *The Vagabond King* wrapped before audiences saw the final product. With a huge cast, over-the-top musical numbers, and elaborate costumes, it has the feel of a big studio Hollywood production. The street mob scene in the final ten minutes of the film was impressively intense for its day, as 200 extras were crammed together in a small space, most of them thrashing about madly and armed with a variety of weapons. The Screen Actors Guild ruled that the scene was so realistically dangerous, all the extras should be classified as stunt workers. Paramount was forced to increase their daily pay from the customary rate of $19.48 a day to $70.00. The Guild's concerns were apparently warranted. Nancy Baker incurred a bite on her shoulder inflicted by a goose and received three stitches as a memento of her role. Former boxer-turned-actor Nobel "Kid" Chisael, who had an uncredited role in the film, was struck on the nose by a flying object.

Other hurdles made for a rough experience for everyone involved with the film. There were issues with illness from the beginning. Producer Pat Duggan was down with the flu just days before January filming was set to begin, and it apparently hit the two leads as well. Kathryn Grayson caught the bug and had difficulty getting her vocals completed and Oreste Kirkop was reported to have had voice issues as well. The overhead for the project ran $25,000 a day and the recurring delays were certainly hard on the overall production budget. It appears that Jack Lord avoided both illness and injury, however.

As Ferrebouc, King Louis' Captain, Lord has several scenes, but very few spoken lines. He is visible throughout the film, decked out in some of the flashiest costumes of his career. The menagerie of brightly colored clothing, elaborate headgear and complicated choreography give the production a *Wizard of Oz* feel. Most of Lord's scenes have him in a cumbersome metal helmet and his soon-to-be-famous perfectly coiffed hairstyle is visible in only one scene. A single curl falls across his forehead in place of the customary bangs that would be later become his trademark. He neither sings nor dances in any of the musical numbers. He does have an imposing presence as he stands on the sidelines as the steely captain of the guard—in spite of the pastel tights he wears.

The Hollywood release for *Vagabond* was set for the 1956 Labor Day weekend, almost a year after filming was completed. Jack Lord entertained a cadre of correspondents who were in town to cover the opening by personally cooking up a batch of roast beef for them, but his efforts didn't help the eventual poor reviews. The initial expectation for a successful project diminished with each week's reports. The film came to the East Coast a couple of weeks later and did "fairly well" at first, but faded fast. Grayson had told *Daily Variety* in January before the release in September that she had initially planned to retire after *Vagabond* was complete. She indicated she was "surprised" by herself and the experience in general had made her resolve to begin reading scripts. She would later refute her own validation of the quality of the film, however.

The initial reviews were mixed, but in the long run *The Vagabond King* was deemed a disappointment. In spite of the confirmed talents and star power of Grayson and Oreste, both of whom carried the leads well, the movie did not get the kind of kudos nor the box office receipts Paramount had hoped to harvest. Some felt there was not enough well-known talent in the cast to lure audiences in and to strengthen the film as a whole. Other reviewers singled out Grayson and Oreste, and some of the actors in more minor parts, for a job well done. Lord got a nod in the September 5 *Variety* as having made his "bit stand up" in his role as the loyal officer. The September 13 review by the *New York Times* focused on this being the third rendition of the story and noted that while the old songs had withstood the test of time, overall it had not aged well. Lord got no mention.

Hollywood columnist Hedda Hopper set off a bit of a firestorm when she quoted a catty remark from Grayson about the final product. Grayson said she had not worked since the film and Hopper reported her saying, "The other day I ran into Rudolf Friml (composer of the original operetta), and we both hung our heads in shame." *Variety* soundly reprimanded both women—Grayson for what they deemed a "cheap shot" and Hopper for putting it in print.[30] Grayson did continue to do some television spots, including a later appearance with Jack Lord on *Playhouse 90* a year after *Vagabond*, but she did no further movie work.

Tennessee Williams' classic *Cat on a Hot Tin Roof* premiered at the Morosco Theatre on March 24, 1955. Barbara Bell Geddes and Burl Ives headed up the stellar cast, and with Elia Kazan added to the mix as director, it looked as though the show couldn't miss. Kazan and Williams had chosen Ben Gazzara for the role of Brick. Five months into the run, however, Gazzara left the cast to fill the lead role of morphine addict Johnny

Pope in the stage production of Michael V. Gazzo's groundbreaking drama *A Hat Full of Rain*. Gazzara received a Tony Best Actor nomination for the role, so the choice to pass off the role of Brick was not a bad move for him. It certainly turned out to be a fortuitous turn of events for Jack Lord.

On October 28, 1955, Bob Kass of New York's WFUV reviewed the play. Overall, Kass' review was an indictment of the problems inherent in the work itself and a "contrived plot," particularly in what he determined to be a disconnect between Brick's self-image and the second plot line of the imminent death of Big Daddy. Kass had done his homework; he read the play before he saw it. He was up front about how unimpressed he was with Gazazza's interpretation of Brick, saying he found the actor's impassivity "most disconcerting." Kass felt he had presented Brick with such coldness it was hard to have any concern about what happened to him.

Brick was a role Lord could get his teeth into, one that promised steady work for a while and he rose to the occasion. It turned out Kass had seen Jack Lord earlier in *The Traveling Lady* and when he got word Lord had been tapped to take Gazarra's place, he saw the play again. He could not say enough about the high quality of Lord's performance. "Mr. Lord is an actor who plays almost entirely from within, but with enormous warmth and feeling. There were many moments in the play when [his] acting made me really believe in Brick as a character and, more important, as a man at war with himself. But [he] has captured perfectly the feeling of emotion choked down, striving with a kind of ferocious intensity to keep it from spilling over. There is compassion and understanding in [his] interpretation—qualities which even Mr. Williams has not given to the character."[31]

In addition to evening performances, matinees were scheduled each Wednesday and Saturday. It was a grueling schedule for Lord as he continued to aggressively seek work in other venues. In his bio for the *Cat* playbill, Lord listed television appearances for *Omnibus*, *You Are There* and *Circle Theatre*. Although his appearance on two episodes of *Omnibus* have been confirmed, attempts to verify appearances on the other two programs were unsuccessful.

After coming on board with *Cat* near the end of August 1955, Lord stayed the course, giving Brick his best effort until he handed off the role to Alex Nicol at the end of October.[32] A year later, in August of 1956, *Variety* ran an announcement that Lord's name had inadvertently been left out of the publication as Gazarra's replacement in the role of Brick. Since he had been out of the cast for several months by that time, it was an understandable oversight. In spite of his good work in the role, when *Cat on Hot Tin Roof* went to Hollywood in 1958, it was Paul Newman who brought Brick to the screen. Gazzara was offered the role, but turned it down, and no evidence that Lord was considered has surfaced. Although the film was highly successful and still stands as a classic to this day, it won none of the six Oscars for which it was nominated.

Jack Lord did eventually pay it forward to Gazarra, however. He penned a thoughtful letter to the *New York Times* drama editor, praising Gazzara's work in *Hatful of Rain*. He directed his comments to theatregoers who were "inclined to shy away from plays that are morbid and depressing." He admitted he felt compelled to go since it was originally an Actors Studio project. His final verdict was that it was one of the most enjoyable theatre experiences he had seen in years. "Instead of morbidity and depression, I found tingling excitement, pathos, humor, brilliant playwriting, and a deeply moving performance by Ben Gazzara and the rest of the cast."[33]

By mid–July Jack Lord had finished location work in Washington, D.C., on *The Court-Martial of Billy Mitchell*. The screenplay by Emmett Lavery and Milton Sperling is based on the true story of United States Army General William L. Mitchell and his campaign to convince the armed forces of the value of increasing the nation's air power. He persistently and publicly called out the brass for their responsibility in the loss of military life due to their continued refusal to provide funding for an inadequate air force. His indictment of his superiors cost him his brigadier general rank, and he was demoted to colonel. He intensified his campaign after the fatal crash of the Shenandoah airship and was eventually court-martialed for insubordination.

Gary Cooper was cast in the lead as Colonel Mitchell. There was some criticism of the choice, including objections from Mitchell's family that Cooper was not a good fit for the part. Mitchell was short of stature and many felt casting the towering Cooper was inappropriate. Mitchell was also a famously fiery presence, but Cooper played the role as a determinedly cool advocate for his position. *The New York Times* praised Cooper's performance, however. Jack Lord certainly did not criticize the choice of Cooper for the lead. He was delighted to find himself working alongside his role model.

Lord had made no secret of the fact that he idolized Gary Cooper and he frequently got flak in the press for his expressed admiration of Cooper. The November 17, 1962, edition of *TV Guide* featured Lord on the cover in his role as rodeo rider Stoney Burke. The article quoted an unnamed actor who reportedly had worked with him. "I feel sorry for Jack.... He could be good if he wanted to portray a real person instead of a great big star. He wants to be Gary Cooper."[34] Lord sometimes said he wanted to be like Cooper, and the distortions of his remark were often used as evidence of an inflated ego. When he showed up for work on *Billy Mitchell*, Lord asked Cooper if he remembered him, referring to their meeting during his days as a car salesman. "Yeah, you're the guy that likes Duesenbergs," Cooper responded. The story became a favorite anecdote of Lord's and it appears in a number of published interviews.

Otto Preminger completed work on *Billy Mitchell* on Saturday, August 13, and went straight to work on to his next project, *The Man with the Golden Arm* with Frank Sinatra in the starring role. The official release date for *Billy Mitchell* was not until December 31, 1955, but the world premier of the film was held December 14 in Zanesville, Ohio. Residents would get the first look as a reward to Muskingum County for being first in the country for the number of Christmas Seals sold. Ironically, Zanesville is only about 45 minutes from the primary crash site of the ill-fated Shenandoah in Caldwell, Ohio. Fred Clark, who played Colonel Moreland, was the only cast member present for the Ohio world premier. Tab Hunter, Natalie Wood, and Rosanna Rory were among the Hollywood celebrities in attendance for the event, although none of them were in the film's cast. Gary Cooper and fellow *Billy Mitchell* cast member Rod Steiger recreated a scene from the film on *The Ed Sullivan Show*. The performance was Cooper's first live television acting experience.

For the most part, reviews were lukewarm as far as overall performance was concerned. The *New York Times* called the film "a competent but not distinguished exercise in sentimental recollection of a military figure ... [that] legend has idolized."[35] The

From left: Jack Lord, Gary Cooper, and Elizabeth Montgomery in Warner Bros.' 1955 film *The Court Martial of Billy Mitchell*. Lord loved the idea of working with his idol, Gary Cooper (Warner Bros./Photofest).

strength of the writing, the production and direction were lauded, and there was little doubt the film would generate much talk. Whether it came from Oscar Wilde or P.T. Barnum, there is much truth to the old adage about the value of publicity of any kind. The documentary style treatment of a thirty-year-old case was sure to push some political buttons. As predicted, there were those who called out Paramount for the film's clear implication that Mitchell was justified in using his court-martial as a means to the end of getting a platform for his position. Critics also felt the film version planted a seed that Mitchell was unsuccessful at his trial due largely to the cunning techniques of the prosecuting attorney.

Los Angeles Times' critic Edwin Schallert, however, could not say enough good about it. He praised the film's realism and accuracy, declaring it adhered so closely to actual events, it could have taken place yesterday rather than thirty years prior. "[E]ach acting performance seems to add material impact.... James Daly, Jack Lord, Peter Graves and Darren McGavin are prominent."[36] Most of the reviews did include kudos for the trial scenes. *Daily Variety*'s December 9 review called it a "writer's picture, rather than an actor's"—an accurate observation.

Although the death of Lord's character Zachary Lansdowne was ultimately the catalyst for setting the whole process in motion, he got no significant press from the role. Elizabeth Montgomery portrayed his widow, and even though she too had very little screen time, her performance during the trial scene earned good reviews. Milton Sperling and Emmet Lavery received an Oscar nomination for Best Writing, Story and Screenplay. Lord would work with Montgomery again in 1962 on an episode of the CBS series *Checkmate* and with Lavery the following year when he worked on a career landmark piece set during a much earlier war.

The Court-Martial of Billy Mitchell was Lord's last movie job for the year, but he wasted no time getting back to work early in 1956. On January 15 television audiences saw him on NBC in an episode from the eighth and final season of another popular live TV series, *The Philco Television Playhouse*. "This Land is Mine" had Lord working alongside Pat Hingle, who would go on to make three guest appearances on *Hawaii Five-O* in the recurring role of contentious scientist Grant Ormsbee.

In February, Lord stepped into a role that proved to be a dress rehearsal of sorts for what would turn out to be an extraordinary landmark in his career. *Omnibus*, hosted by Alistar Cooke, was live TV with a very unique format. The show had the feel of both a documentary and a live theatre performance. Lord was cast in two episodes, and the nature of both scripts undoubtedly appealed to the history buff in him. Both episodes were also closely tied to future projects in his filmography.

"One Nation" dramatizes the debate for the ratification of the United States Constitution by the Virginia Convention. In the opening sequence, Lord marches into the hall with the other delegates and takes a seat in the back. As House of Delegates member and Federalist Party leader John Marshall, he has a prominent scene in which he makes an impassioned plea for ratification. In a convincing Virginia drawl, he outlines the benefits of the federal jurisdiction system proposed in the new Constitution. In another scene, he positions himself firmly in Patrick Henry's face while the narrator explains the rationale behind the debate on the floor. Lord looks very much like John Fry, his *Story of a Patriot* character from the Colonial Williamsburg visitors center film that deals with the same historical event. His name appears last in the closing credits of the *Omnibus* episode.

On April 11, Lord appeared in a second episode of *Omnibus*, based on yet another event from American History with which he was very familiar. Four months prior, the film version of *The Court-Martial of Billy Mitchell* had Lord in a relatively small role, but for the *Omnibus* episode he got the unique opportunity to do a repeat performance of sorts from a different point of view and this time he had a featured role. The episode put Lord in the role filled by Rod Steiger in the film version of the Mitchell event. "Trial by General Court-Martial: Colonel William Mitchell, Air Service" aired April 1, 1956. Lord has three relatively brief scenes, and he nails his part as Major Allen Gullion, the army's chief prosecuting attorney. His presence is a strong one as he mercilessly grills Mitchell in the trial scene. As would become the modus operandi of Steve McGarrett, he throws hard punches and still maintains control as he ruthlessly questions Mitchell. He props his foot on the witness platform, positions himself directly in Mitchell's face and slaps his notes, mercilessly demanding that Mitchell answer his questions.

Unlike the film about the same event, the *Omnibus* episode is historically correct, providing Lord another chance to indulge his love of history. All the dialogue is drawn word for word directly from the actual trial transcript, and it marked the first time the public had an opportunity to hear the contents of the actual proceedings as they occurred in October of 1925.

The Wednesday, March 14, 1956, "Television Chatter" column in *Weekly Variety* announced that Jack Lord would have an upcoming role on NBC's *Justice*, a series about cases from the files of legal aid society lawyers. The show was on the air from April 1954 until March 25, 1956. Attempts to find Lord's name on a guest star list were unsuccessful. Since the series ended slightly more than a week after the notice appeared in *Variety* it is possible filming was not completed, or the episode may have been filmed but not aired.

At the end of April that year, his name appeared in press releases across the country with the news he would have the lead in one of the most unique and enduring roles of his life. He and Marie were set to travel to Williamsburg, Virginia, the first week of May where Lord would spend 16 days on location for a film that would put his face before millions of people and assure a place for him in movie history.

Four

Making History

By the spring of 1956, Jack Lord was seven years into the business. With sixteen television appearances, five movies, and a couple of Broadway plays under his belt he had added some respectable credits to his resume. Although his part in *The Court-Martial of Billy Mitchell* was a small one, it gave him the opportunity to work with his idol, Gary Cooper. An Oscar nomination for screenwriters Milton Sperling and Emmet Lavery brought widespread attention to the film. Lord's next job put him in the right place at the right time for what would become the most unique and enduring role of his career.

The project originated not in the back lots of Hollywood, but in the quiet streets of one of the oldest towns in the nation. In the late seventeenth century, Williamsburg, Virginia, was the center of pivotal events in American history. As the colonial capital, it was the meeting place for the House of Burgesses during the debates that preceded American independence and was frequented by iconic figures such as Thomas Jefferson, George Washington, and Patrick Henry. The transfer of the capital to Richmond in 1780 marked the onset of a decline in Williamsburg's fortunes, and its historic buildings eventually fell into disrepair. In the 1920s, W.A.R. Goodwin, rector for the Bruton Parish Church, recognized the importance of ensuring that future generations would know the critical role Williamsburg played in the founding of America. He set out to find a way to preserve its remarkable structures.

Goodwin knew the renovation project would call for significant financial support. In 1926, he made a successful appeal to philanthropist John D. Rockefeller, Jr., and the long-term restoration of the village was set into motion. By 1949, the elder Rockefeller was less involved in the ongoing work and his son moved into a key role. The vision of the younger Rockefeller called for a significant expansion of the original plan for the popular tourist site. He wanted to carry its historical message and significance to an international audience, and over the next few years, the strategic plan was expanded.

The renovation included a new Information Center, complete with a dedicated audio-visual department, a motion picture production unit, and two state-of-the art theatres. The $7,000,000 structure would be situated outside the immediate area of the original buildings. The site had earned widespread critical acclaim for its meticulous attention to historical accuracy in their educational films about the American Revolution. In 1951, they debuted *Williamsburg Restored,* an orientation film for visitors to the site.

Officials knew they would need to upgrade the film to match the modern facilities and to achieve the sophisticated impact they wanted. The two theatres would be central to the visitors' overall experience, setting the tone for what they would see once they entered the restored area.

Because Colonial Williamsburg officials envisioned a production worthy of the extraordinary venue, they made the decision to outsource the primary production roles of screenwriter, producer, and director. They wanted a production staff with boots-on-the-ground experience in making quality films. As they began their search in Hollywood for the right screenwriter for their project, a top priority was to find a writer with a firm commitment to historical truth. They soon discovered it was a much more difficult task than they thought.

With a tentative list of eight hopefuls in hand, project director John Goodbody flew to the West Coast to find a screenwriter, preferably one with historical feature film credits and the professional credentials to match the quality product they envisioned. The final budgeted cost for the screenplay, including treatments and writer's expenses, was $20,000. Goodbody talked to 15 noted screenwriters. In spite of a healthy budget and the exemplary credentials of the prospects he interviewed, he returned home with no signed contract. What he did bring back, however, was report of widespread and enthusiastic interest in Hollywood for their unique project.

In 1954, Goodbody returned to Hollywood, this time with a delegation from Williamsburg. They were determined to find the right people to advise them on best practices for their ambitious undertaking and to fill the positions with the best available talent. They met with representatives from the top studios—Paramount, Universal, Disney, MGM, Warner Bros. and 20th Century–Fox. At the time, the West Coast was still dealing with fallout from the Hollywood Ten investigation and the lingering effects of the Red Scare. Williamsburg officials were well aware of the political atmosphere and how it was reflected in Hollywood. The foundation was carefully considerate of the conservative nature of the Rockefeller family and they wanted assurance that the screenwriter they hired would not bring controversy to the project. Goodbody reported the delegation had sought advice about their concerns from studio officials. "We were generally advised that we are safe if we employ someone who has had continuing recent employment with major studios," he said. "On the other hand, if we select someone who has been barred from work since the trial of 'the Hollywood Ten,' we might be asking for trouble or embarrassment for this or other Rockefeller interests."[1]

As it turned out officials at Williamsburg were not completely exclusive in their search for a "safe" production staff. Of the fifteen potential screenwriters who had made the list for consideration, acclaimed author—and noted liberal—James Agee was at the top of the list. Sarah Rouse Sheehan noted in her master's thesis about the film that Agee had been openly critical of Colonial Williamsburg more than a decade earlier, criticizing the foundation as "politically and ethically reprehensible" and calling the historical interpretation work at the site "nationalist propaganda."[2] Widely lauded as a journalist, a film critic, and a novelist, Agee's talent as a screenwriter was well validated in 1952 when he and John Huston received an Academy Award for Best Adapted Screenplay nomination for *The African Queen*. Agee biographer Laurence Bergreen said his agreement to take the job on the Williamsburg project was partly motivated by "a sense of nostalgia" on the part of the writer, and that Agee saw the restoration at Williamsburg as a "shrine of civic religion" worth preserving.[3]

Goodbody reported Agee's fee was $1,000 plus $300 per week for the duration of the work. The total amount budgeted for the script included the cost of treatments and the writer's expenses, and Goodbody hoped Agee could get the first draft of the screenplay completed by the fall of 1954. He effectively convinced foundation officials at the December board meeting that he had found the right man for the job when he showed them Agee's masterful contribution to a series of *Omnibus* episodes about Abraham Lincoln. The Ford Foundation had loaned a copy to Goodbody in November for viewing at a board meeting; they loved it. They were optimistic Agee had mellowed in his liberal take on the Revolution, and it was clearly evident that his work was first rate.

Goodbody made arrangements for Agee to come to Williamsburg after Christmas, but the writer postponed three times. He eventually shared details with Goodbody of his rapidly failing health and his struggle to complete the project. In addition to his illness, he began to have doubts that he could accurately capture the historical period to the extent the foundation wanted. He wondered if he might function better as a consultant rather than as screenplay writer for the project. Goodbody told him about the board's praise for the *Omnibus* series, and their confidence that he was the right one for the job. Agee relented and continued the work.

The ailing writer finally visited Williamsburg for two days in mid–January, and it looked as though they were at last off and running. Agee's proposal was to create a "day in the life" scenario, set during a single day before the Revolution. His idea was to choose a day that was not focused on any significant event, but one that had inherent "ferment." He proposed no famous men from the period appear in the film, particularly advocating the absence of the founding fathers, and he envisioned an "intellectual planter" as the main character. Williamsburg officials were satisfied with the concept and all agreed to press on.

Agee's health, however, continued to deteriorate and the work seriously stalled again. He had not signed the contract for the treatment and Goodbody was concerned that Agee may have been wavering again on his ability to complete the work to the satisfaction of the foundation. When he finally signed the contract and returned it to Williamsburg, the foundation prepared a press release, announcing James Agee as the screenwriter for the new visitor center film. The release was set to go out May 17, 1955. James Agee died of a heart attack while riding in a taxicab in New York City on May 16. Goodbody quickly traveled to New York and collected the incomplete film treatment from Agee's apartment, the last page of which was still in his typewriter. After much effort, Williamsburg officials could not reach a consensus on Agee's treatment. Some thought it was "extremely impressive" and others indicated they did not like the "slice of life" concept after all. They decided to shelve it and start over.

Goodbody went back to the drawing board, revisiting the list of potential writers. In August, MGM Studios recommended a writer, and the foundation signed him. A press release sent out by Colonial Williamsburg on Friday, January 13, 1956, announced Emmet Lavery, writer for *The Court-Martial of Billy Mitchell*, was at work on the screenplay. Lavery's specialty was historical drama, and he brought to the table the level of recognition and respect the foundation sought in their screenwriter. He was a past president of the Screenwriters Guild from 1945 to 1947, a member of the board and former vice president of the Academy of Motion Picture Arts and Sciences. Lavery had also been the recipient of two Rockefeller grants—one for work at Vassar and the second as a playwright in residence for a year at Smith. A final asset for Lavery was the fact he had never been on any political blacklists in Hollywood.

The transition in screenwriters was completed as quickly as possible. A January 10, 1956, foundation expenditure report shows Agee had been paid $2,500 for his work during that fiscal period. Lavery's pay, $3,448.33, appears on the same report.[4] Agee's social-history take on the film was set aside in favor of a more patriotic theme, and the intellectual planter character Agee envisioned became the central character for the film. Young John Fry would be portrayed as a man who was "transformed through a series of historical events and attitudes by the burgess who join in the final unanimous vote for independence on May 15, 1776."[5]

The foundation was just as successful in securing exemplary talent in their choice of a director for the film. They spent a significant amount time and effort looking closely at bids from MGM and from Dudley Pictures Corporation, but the decision was made to go with Paramount Studios and with George Seaton as director. Seaton was a two-time Oscar winner, former president of the Screen Writers Guild, and president of the Academy of Motion Picture Arts and Sciences. At the time he accepted the agreement, he was at work on *The Proud and the Profane* and he agreed to come to Williamsburg in April as soon as the film wrapped. Seaton would bring with him a distinguished production crew, including Academy Award winning cinematographer Loyal Griggs and producer Mel Epstein. Seaton's office and his affiliation with Paramount helped the board make their final decision. The studio reported he had "an excellent working relationship with the various technicians and department heads."[6]

A definite asset in Seaton's qualifications was the cinematography he could bring to the project. On January 10, he met with Williamsburg representatives in New York where he gave an outstanding presentation of the physical logistics and the results of using double-frame VistaVision in the new theatres. The image on screen would be an impressive 46 feet in width and they would use six-channel sound. It was just the kind of impact they were hoping to make with the new facilities.[7]

Goodbody notified the other studios under consideration of the foundation's final decision, and he explained the reason for their choice. They had been urged by the Executive Committee to work in association with a major studio: "I think you will understand why an organization like ours, somewhat remote from such projects as a major film, would move in this direction." Carl Dudley sent regrets that his company had lost the bid to produce the film, but he confirmed that having Paramount on board was evidence of the kind of quality they sought for the project. He recognized the significance of winning Paramount. It was a departure from the norm for the studio to associate themselves with this kind of project. Howard Strickling, Director of Studio Publicity at MGM, agreed with Dudley that the foundation had made a wise choice. He told them in a January 26 memo, "You are in good hands. As much as we would have liked to have you here at M-G-M, we most certainly agree that working with Seaton and using double-frame VistaVision you should be at Paramount. For your sake am glad you decided to use VistaVision."[8] *Story of a Patriot* is the only film ever to be shot entirely in VistaVision.

Things were quickly coming together, but the venture was not without occasional backsets. On February 21, Colonial Williamsburg Executive Vice President Carlisle Humelsine received word from CBS Television they had decided against releasing Epstein from his duties to produce the Williamsburg film. CBS executive Alfred J. Scalpone acknowledged the value of the Williamsburg project and explained the motive behind their decision. "The very reasons why you would want Mr. Epstein to produce your film make him necessarily very valuable to us."[9] It proved to be a temporary setback, however. Seven days after Epstein pulled out, *The Hollywood Reporter* announced that William H. Wright would be the producer for the film. With fifteen films to his credit, Wright was a well-respected producer and writer for MGM films. Once again, the Foundation moved forward.

Goodbody had been in possession of Lavery's treatment since January 17. In what would later prove to be of financial benefit to Jack Lord, Lavery's version included the much-debated use of a narrator. It was a reversal of an earlier decision against using a narrator for fear it would stifle the innovative nature of the film. They wanted to stay as far away as possible from anything that would recall a typical visitors center orientation film. In a January 11 letter, Seaton communicated to Goodbody that he felt unless they employed the narrator technique, the film as they envisioned it was doomed to fail.

After preliminary meetings with Goodbody, Seaton began to fear that effectively producing the film represented in the outlines would require a full two-hour entertainment-type format. He questioned whether it could be done in the required twenty-nine-minute timeframe. "If our inexperienced actor has to play a scene of any consequence at the end of an intricate camera maneuver—if he is in effect the anchor man on the relay team—here is a great chance it will have to be done over and over again. If, however, the narrator takes care of most of the content of the scene and we only have to depend upon the actor for a line or two, I promise you the task will be simpler all around."[10]

When casting for the film began in early April, the "inexperienced actor" who won the role was deemed willing and able to provide the narration, and to effectively carry the on-screen work. The final decision was to complete any necessary bridging of the story through voice-overs to be accomplished as John Fry wrote detailed letters to his wife about events he witnessed. Thad Tate was assigned as special research assistant, and his job was to ensure absolute historic accuracy in events, people, and wardrobe in the film.

Once again, Lord's residency in New York proved to be an asset rather than a hindrance to finding work. Williamsburg officials and casting personnel agreed early on that they would look to New York, not to Hollywood, for the actors. They definitely wanted professionals and they would give priority to competent actors not readily recognized by the public to the degree major stars that had appeared in several motion pictures would have been. A willing suspension of disbelief for viewers of the film would not apply here. They would not risk audiences becoming distracted from the historical accuracy of the film by the recognition of an actor who would be instantly connected to a prior role. To ensure their lead character would have the everyman quality they wanted, the foundation decided to seek out an unknown actor for the role of planter John Fry.

The *Virginia Gazette* reported on Friday, April 27, 1956, the cast of 17 professionals, all experienced stage television and film performers, had been finalized the previous week. Papers across the country touted the wisdom of the selection of an unknown,

Lord works on getting his colonial hosiery in place during make-up before filming for *Story of a Patriot*. Filming began on May 7, 1956, and wrapped on May 24. George Seaton was director for the unique project that brought Hollywood to Colonial Williamsburg (Colonial Williamsburg Foundation).

"square-jawed individual with blue eyes and a shock of brown hair" in the lead role. The *Reporter*'s Radie Harris praised the wisdom of choosing Lord as the leading man for the upcoming Williamsburg project. "Jack Lord, who gave such a good account of himself when he followed Ben Gazzara in 'Cat on a Hot Tin Roof,' and Leora Dana, Ty Power's favorite actress, draw the only two fictional leads as husband and wife."[11] The press prophetically predicted he would be seen by more movie-goers than any star in history— "long after Gable and Brando have been forgotten."[12] Lavery was of course acquainted with Lord's work on *Billy Mitchell*.

Filming was set to begin May 1, but cameras didn't roll until Monday, May 7. The schedule called for an intensive 16 days of shooting. It was good practice for Lord's soon-to-be famous tolerance for a grueling schedule. Throughout his twelve years on *Hawaii Five-O*, his days would begin at 4:30 a.m. Call sheets from the Williamsburg production show Lord was to be picked up by private car at the hotel most days "having had breakfast." Depending on locations, he was scheduled to be in makeup between 6:15 and 7:00 a.m. and was on the set by 7:30 or 8:30 each day. It was an early start to his day, but Lord was up to the task. Costumer designer Kate Lawson, who was responsible for the 800 costumes needed for the film, said Jack Lord had 14 costume changes, three of which were added at the last minute. Lord would also provide the voice-overs, an additional bit of work that would extend his time on the payroll.

While it is true Jack Lord may have fit the bill as a relative unknown at the time, decades later visitors to the site frequently shout "Steve McGarrett!" when the "anonymous young burgess" first appears on screen. Lord continued to receive letters throughout his career from fans reporting their delightful surprise at seeing him in the film during a visit to the site, and he saved many of them. He may have been an unknown at the time in the eyes of those responsible for casting *Story of a Patriot*, but he wasn't a newcomer to entertainment press. A journalist for *The Hollywood Reporter* who was part of a junket that included a viewing of Seaton's recent work, *The Proud and the Profane*, reported the group got an added bonus. They were also invited to a viewing of the film at Williamsburg and the review included a comment on the "anonymous" star of the film. "Incidentally, the cast for "The Williamsburg Story" were all unknowns to George [Seaton] and producer Bill Wright, because they were not familiar movie faces in these historical roles, but they were all recognizable to us Broadwayites, who have often applauded Clarence Derwent, Francis Compton, Leora Dana, Jack Lord, Fred Warriner, et al., in the *theatah*."[13]

The Williamsburg project put Jack Lord in front of some distinguished Hollywood people and gave him an opportunity to showcase his professionalism and his talent. He fully realized the value of the experience at the time, and he never forgot it. "I was a young actor under contract to Paramount in 1953 when I did the picture," Lord told Vernon Scott in 1977. "I was paid guild minimum scale and we shot it in Williamsburg, in and around those wonderful old buildings."[14] Screen Actors Guild scale pay for an actor appearing in television motion pictures in 1955 was $80 per day. The Williamsburg project was to be shown free to visitors to the site, so he likely earned somewhere in the neighborhood of $1,280, plus expenses, for the sixteen days work.[15]

Never one to shy away from thinking outside the box, when it was all said and done Jack Lord carried with him some the unique experiences from the Williamsburg project throughout his career. More than a decade later in his defining role as Steve McGarrett, many of the production issues of the groundbreaking television series' location filming were no doubt reminiscent of things he learned during his earlier work filming in the streets of New York, in his role in the *Patriot* film, and later in the significant amount of location work he did on *Stoney Burke*. Lord and the *Five-O* production crew got significant press coverage about the blessings and the curses of utilizing a large number of extras drawn from area citizens and the extent to which they had to work with and around the normal activity of diverse filming locations. Thankfully, Williamsburg area schools did approve the occasional release of students from classes to fill in the needed

Virginia House of Burgesses delegate John Fry greets his son Robert, played by Richard Stryker (Colonial Williamsburg Foundation).

children's roles. Depending on who is doing the talking, Lord has been portrayed both as a kind and patient teacher for untrained extras and as a cruel tyrant, taking out his frustrations by yelling at nonprofessionals when they didn't perform up to his expectations. Conscious of the expense of wasted time on the set, he no doubt did understand the high cost of repeated takes and interruptions during filming, but that in itself is not a fair measure of his demeanor in general.

An incident from a May 25, 1956, Williamsburg press release reported a recurring difficulty many of the extras had complying with the high demand for adherence to period authenticity. Lord said the biggest challenge faced by the amateurs on the set was how they frequently forgot to take off modern eyeglasses during shooting. "One day Lord was disconcerted to have a courtly colonial gentleman bow to open air instead of to him. 'Would you mind telling me whom you're greeting?' director George Seaton called out. 'He must have moved,' the sheepish thespian explained. 'You said to take off my glasses and I can't see a darn thing.'"[16]

Seaton's ire at such costly issues associated with location filming was often tempered with humor, however. One day a young newsboy suddenly rode his bicycle directly into the middle of a scene during shooting—a $2,000 an hour operation. He tossed the paper onto a porch and rode on. Seaton called to the boy, asking sarcastically if it was okay to continue shooting. The young man nonchalantly waved a "go ahead" signal and rode away. "That's the most expensive paper in Virginia," he remarked. A reshoot was also called for when a young boy popped his bubble gum while cameras were rolling. Extras in the film would later say Seaton sometimes displayed "a little temper" if things didn't go to suit him, but quickly added that it was "always controlled." In a 1982 article in Colonial Williamsburg's newsletter marking the up-coming twenty-fifth anniversary of the film, Thad Tate remembered Seaton as a "remarkably humane, even gentle man, but one who knew what he wanted in his work. If necessary, he achieved this by successive retakes of a scene or by improvising on the set, but never by demeaning an actor or member of the technical and advisory crew."[17]

The demand for absolute historical accuracy led to some interruptions in the lives of local residents during filming. Key players in the production were diligent in acknowledging the valuable contribution Williamsburg residents made to the success of the project. Goodbody sent a note of appreciation to the Rev. James Brown at the Methodist Church, thanking him for silencing the traditional five o'clock chimes at the church while the filming was going on. He freely acknowledged the impact the absence of the chimes had on virtually everyone in Williamsburg. He had also managed to arrange for a halt to all fly-overs in the area for the duration of the 16-day filming schedule. The halt included planes from the naval base in Norfolk, Langley Field, and Piedmont Airlines. Only planes whose altitude was high enough to render them soundless on the ground were permitted in the airspace during filming.[18]

Shooting on location in Williamsburg, Virginia, was a very different environment from the location sites Lord would encounter later in *Hawaii Five-O*, however. Project planners anticipated about 300 extras would be needed and finding enough, especially the number of adult men needed, was difficult. Most local men had full-time jobs and could not take time away from work during the day to meet the demand. Although Lord would have a good pool of locals to work with in Hawaii, finding enough in Williamsburg called for a good measure of resourceful thinking.

They decided to utilize the availability of a pool of locals who just happened to have their days free and who would no doubt welcome a diversion from their day-to-day lives. Eastern State Mental Hospital was located very near the location. A large group of patients were hired to fill the roles of non-speaking extras, particularly those needed in the scenes involving delegates to the House of Burgesses. The role was simple. They need only to sit in costume and appear to listen attentively. The doctor at the hospital felt the activity was not only appropriate, but the experience would also be a beneficial activity for the patients. The patients who participated were paid the same as other extras working on the film. The money they earned was deposited to their individual spending accounts at the hospital, and for many, it was the first time their accounts showed available dollars in years. The special group of extras was praised for their work. Project Director John Goodbody sent kudos to Hospital Superintendent Dr. Granville Jones. "This group was the most reliable we had, and there was much evidence of real talent."[19]

The work appealed to Lord and his papers reflect the pride he felt in being chosen for the part. The John Fry character gave him a starring role in a very unique motion picture, and the production's meticulous adherence to actual historical events was an added bonus for the self-confessed history buff. While he was chosen for the role because of his lack of exposure in Hollywood, ironically the Williamsburg film put him in front of some of the biggest names in the business at the time. It was an opportunity for him to showcase what he could do.

Jack Lord was clearly the star on the project. In what would become standard procedure when booking him, his contract with the Williamsburg Foundation stipulated travel and accommodations were also required for Marie. During shooting, the Lords stayed at the lovely Williamsburg Lodge, situated very near the heart of the historical area. Location meal allowance vouchers indicate a daily allowance of $5.00 or $6.00 for most of the cast and for key production personnel. Leora Dana in the role of Fry's wife in the film had a $6.00 daily allowance. Jack Lord's daily meal allowance was $25, which likely was intended to cover expenses for his wife as well. Marie Lord was a constant presence on the set and for other events during the 16 days of filming. She was frequently seen chatting with the wives of cast and crew and was often present on the sidelines while Lord was working. She appeared in some press release photos dressed in period clothes, giving interviews to local papers. Many remembered her as a very gracious and charming presence, clearly devoted to her husband.

When filming wrapped on Thursday, May 24, Lord penned a note on Lodge stationary and left it in their room upon checking out the next day. He expressed his and Marie's gratitude for the hospitality they had enjoyed during their time at Williamsburg. The brief text, penned with his customary thick line marker, covers three pages of the small hotel tablet paper. "We cannot leave ... without telling you how very much we enjoyed your warm welcome and generous hospitality. The picnic you gave for us in Jamestown last Sunday was such a delight that we shall never forget it."[20] A heartfelt expression of their appreciation for kindnesses shown by others was a familiar tradition for the Lords. They were well known for their adherence to the social graces and often sent personal notes for even very small acts of kindness shown to them.

Lord was elated with the experience, declaring the film to be just what he needed. "The picture has helped my career already," he said, as soon as the work wrapped. "After we finished shooting, Mr. Seaton called me to Hollywood to do the narration. That was six months ago. I only expected to stay six days. Now I've got a good role in MGM's *Tip on a Dead Jockey* and a lot of television work lined up."[21] *Jockey* was released six months after the March 31 premiere of the Williamsburg film. The General Operations Plan for the premier contains no evidence the Lords were in attendance at the Williamsburg release event.

His extraordinary work ethic and the customary handling of his own affairs were finally paying off for the driven actor. After Jack and Marie were back home in New York, Lord did due diligence when it came to helping with promotion of the Williams-

As was customary, Marie Lord was on location with her husband during the filming. She was on set for most of the filming and the Lords enjoyed the hospitality events, including a cookout, throughout the sixteen days of work (Colonial Williamsburg Foundation).

burg film. Three months after the production wrapped, Lord wrote to the foundation, asking for photos depicting him in his role in the film. The photo lab had the pictures on their way to him within the week.[22] A large number of photographs were taken during the filming and by October, the audio-visual department was dealing with questions about usage rights to them. They determined that the payroll vouchers signed by all the extras included blanket permissions to use them without further permission or compensation. The provisions of individual SAG contracts, however, would determine use of photos that included images of the actors.

Archival records at Williamsburg include copies of letters Lord wrote to the site with contacts for press releases and other story placements about the movie and the new visitors center. An August 15 letter from Williamsburg's Press Bureau Editorial Assistant Alice Sircom detailed his commitment to getting the word out about the upcoming premier. "It seems as though you and Marie will soon have to be added to our staff as special agents for boosting Williamsburg," she wrote. "When I stopped in to see an old friend, Jack Danby, editor of *Redbook*, a month ago in New York there was little left for me to tell ... he had been so well briefed by both of you the day before at a cocktail party."[23]

Even in those early years, the businessman side of Jack Lord was evident, and he was always thinking outside the box when it came to finding opportunities for the next paycheck. In July after *Patriot* was finished, he contacted officials at Colonial Williamsburg with a suggestion they consider holding an international film festival at the site. He was clearly taken with the restoration work in the village and the beauty of the area, and he proposed it to be an ideal location to host such an event. He highlighted the advantage of the two state-of-the-art theatres. "This would be a natural projection of the first theatre of the 18th Century brought up to date and physically the accommodations set-up would be fine in an off season," he said. His idea was to promote the event as a United States Film Festival, designed more or less along the lines of those typically held at Cannes, Edinburgh, and Venice. He said he had gotten the idea from a clipping in which George Murphy, a fellow actor who was also director of public relations for MGM, urged the American motion picture business to hold an international film festival in this country. Murphy said, "They should sit down with other industry representatives soon to pool their thoughts and to evaluate the whole subject of a United States Film Festival." He had attended the Cannes Festival as a special representative for the Department of State. The idea was broached in a meeting where Humlesine and Seaton were present. Humlesine was very interested and found the idea to be an intriguing proposal. George Seaton quickly burst their bubble, however, when he told them countries hosting festivals underwrote the entire financial backing—typically to the tune of $100,000.[24]

Journalist Vernon Scott's comment that Lord's performance in *Story of a Patriot* would be long remembered after other actors were forgotten was verified in a special ceremony at Colonial Williamsburg in May of 1970. English teacher Jean Eberline and her army husband Carl were enjoying their first visit to the site when George Seaton, then on the Board of Trustees at the foundation, and actress Helen Hayes, stopped her. They asked her to pose for a picture and told her that she was the 10 millionth person to see *Story of a Patriot* since its 1957 debut. Hayes had recently appeared in Seaton's film, *Airport*, and he had asked her to accompany him on a visit to the site. She presented Mrs. Eberline an engraved pewter bowl to commemorate the occasion. David Brinkley was also in Williamsburg that weekend as a specially invited guest of Seaton.[25] Hayes was the adopted mother of James MacArthur, who filled of the role of Danny Williams on *Hawaii Five-O* for most of the series' run.

At the time of filming for *Story of a Patriot*, Bonnie Brown was an employee at the historical site, working at a loom in the Spinning and Weaving Shop, and she was chosen as an extra on the film. Sixteen years after the making of the movie, she vividly recalled encountering Jack Lord in a dressing room during makeup. She said he passed by her with a "curt nod and a half smile" as she entered the room. "He was big, handsome and aloof," she said. She also commented that Lord was just recently married and was "very in love, so much so, that in one scene which touched on the bedroom he couldn't remember his lines, and in desperation they were finally deleted altogether."[26] Jack and Marie Lord had been married seven years at the time of the filming. Decades later it was not unusual for people to comment on the couple's devotion to one another.

Jack Lord fondly remembered the Williamsburg project for the rest of his life, and he stayed in touch with the Foundation for years. An October 6, 1975, memo originating in the Department of Defense reported a 5:45 p.m. phone call from George Seaton. Jack Lord had phoned Seaton early that morning to report he and Marie had been to dinner the prior evening with Admiral and Mrs. Noel Gayler, commander-in-chief for the Pacific Fleet. Mrs. Gayler shared with the Lords that she had just returned from a trip to Williamsburg and she had been so impressed with *Story of a Patriot*, the Admiral decided he wanted the film to be made available on board every ship in the fleet. He felt the servicemen needed to know the history of events depicted in the film. With the Bicentennial coming up the following year, Gayler felt the timing was perfect.

Lord wasted no time getting the ball rolling. He offered to pay for "a film" if there was a charge. Seaton did not know how to make it happen, so he passed the request on to Williamsburg officials. Two days later, Ray Martin, the Foundation's audiovisual manager, called the Department of Defense. He followed up with a letter that same day, reporting that the DOD had in fact purchased 596 prints of the film back in 1959. He wondered if those copies might be located and supplied to the Fleet. If they were not found, Martin suggested they might consider buying prints.[27] Attempts to find evidence that the project was completed were unsuccessful.

In January of 1967, the Foundation made plans to offer a unique souvenir item for the gift shop. They proposed the creation of a set of paper dolls based on key characters from the film. The first step was to seek approval to replicate images of the actors. A selection of stills from the film and the resulting drawings for the doll version of John Fry was mailed to Lord for his approval. Lord responded with a handwritten letter in which he referenced a photo that had been sent to him soon after filming that he thought would be acceptable. He mentioned that he was facing left in the photo, validation of his preference about his profile.[28] After reviewing the final wash drawings, Lord signed the approval document. The Fry family paper dolls are still available from the Foundation.

In 1984, *Story of a Patriot* found another venue in addition the theatres at the historical site. Hotelvision began running the film on March 14 in 20 area hotels—more than 3,000 rooms, occupied by millions of visitors each year. Jack Lord's performance as Burgess John Fry continues to endure. Twenty years after he completed the work on his role, he still had a fondness for the experience with the Williamsburg project. On March 5, 1987, Roger Thaler had an extended phone conversation with Lord about a proposal the actor had made to Carl Humelsine regarding a cast reunion party for the 30th anniversary of the film. He indicated he didn't want to be any trouble, but he thought bringing everyone back together would be fun. Lord suggested Thaler contact actor Ed Asner, then president of the Screen Actors Guild, to help them locate everyone. Thaler told him that many of the cast members were no longer living. Asner guest-starred on *Hawaii Five-O* in 1975 and later reprised his villain role in an episode of the reboot of the series. Thaler said the foundation would prefer to host a small dinner party whenever Jack and Marie were on the East Coast. Lord insisted he did not need to be "honored," explaining that his intention was simply to gather everyone for a fun event.

Thaler's report says Lord spoke fondly of the whole experience, calling it a "labor of love." He told Thaler he believed he had done the work on the film for no pay, but he had stated in earlier interviews that he was paid scale wages for the role, and financial records at the foundation document he was compensated for his work.

As Thaler chatted with Lord about the state-of-the-art theatres, Seaton's good work on the design, and some of the prominent events that had been held at site during which the film had been presented to special groups, he mentioned that the 9th G7 Summit during Ronald Regan's administration was held at Williamsburg. Lord was pleased the president had seen the film and told Thaler he and Reagan were friends. Telegrams from Lord's estate with birthday wishes to him from Reagan were recently sold on eBay. Lord suggested if he and Marie should visit Williamsburg in the near future, it would be a good opportunity for the Foundation to get some publicity. "Maybe you don't need publicity," Lord said. Thaler suggested they plan something around an upcoming event scheduled for the following May.[29] No record of the event was found.

After his outstanding experience with the Williamsburg project, Jack Lord continued to work in a variety of roles and his growth as actor began to show. He continued to win roles in popular live television drama series, and he still relished the challenge of live action TV work. On July 23, 1956, he starred in "An Incident of Love," an episode of CBS's *Westinghouse Studio One*. The series captured 18 Emmy nominations and three wins during its ten-year run and was often praised for quality writing and innovative production.

Lord is captivating in the role of Paul Chester, a man who was blinded in an accident that took the lives of his wife and young daughter. Suffering from constant headaches, he is completely dependent on his overbearing mother. He spends his days alone in their small apartment, grieving the loss of his family, his self-sufficiency, and his freedom. Paul was a successful commercial artist before the accident, and he tells his sympathetic neighbor, Bertha "Bert" Randall, that he always wanted to be a serious painter but he couldn't make a sufficient living at it to support his family. The neighbor, played by Lois Nettleton, makes regular visits across the hall, tending to the young man while her husband and two sons are away during the day.

Paul and Bert eventually fall in love and she is conflicted by her desire to be with him and her devotion to her own family. Their situation is further complicated when a nosey older woman who lives in the same apartment building tells Paul's mother of the romantic attraction she sees developing between them. In a memorable closing scene, Bert decides she must remain with her family, and when she tells Paul the news, he clings to her, desperately pleading with her to leave her husband and marry him. She tells him she is moving away with her husband. Lord gives an impressive performance, and even though the episode has gone relatively unnoticed, it could in fact be some of the finest acting of his career. Seeing him in the role of a vulnerable person, dependent on others around him is a rare opportunity, and he pulls it off.

In August, Lord made the short list of featured newcomers in the "Stars in Their Eyes" lineup in the inaugural edition of *Hear the Voice of Hollywood*. The unique fan magazine included a perforated, playable 78 rpm record attached to the cover. His photo is a pensive headshot and he appears much younger than his 36 years. "Watch for him in romantic leads," the caption advises. "He's of the 'realism' school ... and handsome!"[30]

Lord appeared in a second episode of *Studio One* that same season. "A Day Before Battle" aired September 3, 1956, and he was cast alongside Warren Oates who would be a regular with Lord six years later in the *Stoney Burke* series. The episode tells of events in a Union Army camp on the day before the Battle of Gettysburg. The August 4 edition of the *New York Times* reported a rehearsal at the actual battlefield to help with motivation for the key players. Lord's character Matt stands as the voice of reason amid the desperate chaos in the mounting tension before the conflict.

Matt and his fellow Union Army soldiers have just been informed that their long-overdue leaves have been cancelled due to an escalation of the fighting in the area. A further complication arises when they capture a Confederate spy, played by Oates, who must be guarded in a makeshift outdoor cell until they execute him the next morning. Gerald Sarracini plays Jamie, the unlucky private who is ordered to pull guard duty over the prisoner. Jamie is desperately looking for a way to break away so he can escape with a promiscuous young woman who unabashedly throws herself at the frustrated young soldier.

Susan Oliver is cast in the role of the heartless woman, set on being a "dying vision" for the gullible Jamie. Oliver would later work with Lord on episodes of *Bonanza* and *Rawhide*. Desperate to take advantage of the opportunity he has been given to spend what may his last night on earth with a woman, Jamie rationalizes there is no harm in killing the prisoner since his number is up anyway come daylight. He loosens the lock on the door, giving the prisoner the chance to escape and providing justification to shoot him. Matt fervently pleads with Jamie to do the right thing. He explains that his scheduled furlough has been reduced and he too has lost his chance to see his wife before the looming battle. As the two men debate, the prisoner makes a run for it. Matt is forced to shoot him and he is devastated by what he has done.

Reviews for the episode were mixed. Oates's performance as the pathetic pawn was praised by some and deemed merely acceptable by others. Lord has the closing scene, and even though he aptly pulled it off as he carries the body of Oates off the field, some felt Matt's being forced to kill the pathetic prisoner was an illogical and melodramatic resolution. *Weekly Variety* praised Oates' performance, but slammed the script. "[It] failed to make full-fledged drama and the director could do nothing about it."[31] Helm's review in the September 5 edition was much the same with one exception. Susan Oliver was touted as bringing the standout performance, while Oates' and Lord's performances were judged "passably acceptable." The *New York Times* featured a nice photo of Lord and Gerry Sarracini in the September 2 edition, but gave no kudos to the actors for their performances.[32]

Before the end of the year, Lord got another good opportunity for a live performance when he was cast in an episode of *The Lux Video Theatre*. CBS debuted the show on October 2, 1950, as a companion to the highly successful *Lux Radio Theatre*, which had been on the air since 1934. The tenure of the two formats overlapped for five years. The shows drew their name from their sponsor, Lux Toilet Soap, whose unique ads featured only the most iconic Hollywood celebrities of the day. The casting of famous stage and screen actors in the new television version added to its popularity. The radio series was produced in Hollywood, but the video version was based in New York for the first three seasons as it rode the tide of the growing popularity of television. The decision was later made to move the show to the West Coast—closer to the big stars. Viewers were reminded each week that the focus was on Hollywood as the opening credits appeared after a night view of iconic scenery from Tinsel Town.

The premier television version was reviewed well. Iconic celebrities from film and stage were cast alongside aspiring and up-and-coming talent and many actors got their start on the show. Connie Billips and Arthur Pierce did an extensive study of both the radio and television versions of the Lux series in their 2012 book *Lux Presents Hollywood*. The study looks at casting and production practices and the process of translating plays into film. The writers of selected original works were generally in attendance at the rehearsals that began on Tuesdays and ran for six days. The cast did a final dress rehearsal that ended less than two hours before airtime.

In August of 1954, *Lux* moved the series to NBC, extending the 30-minute format to 60 minutes, and the scripts were generally adaptations of popular movies. The live drama concept was appealing to Lord as a young actor who still longed to get his teeth into a good Broadway role. In essence, *Lux* was a stage with a camera and the selections for stories paid tribute to some great classic films. The work put Lord in good company with some of the most popular actors of the time and he had the opportunity to work like a live stage thespian while learning the ropes of television work.

On October 30, Lord was cast alongside Charles Drake for "Jezebel," an episode based on the 1938 movie by the same title that featured Bette Davis in the lead role of Southern belle Julie Marsden. Julie was a headstrong Scarlett O'Hara type who delighted in flying in the face of propriety to get her way. Davis won the Best Actress Oscar for the film, and Faye Bainter got the best supporting actress statue. The film garnered three additional Oscar nominations. It has been compared to *Gone with the Wind* and is listed in the Library of Congress' National Film Registry. Deemed worthy a remake, *The Lux Radio Theatre* had offered up a version of "Jezebel" in 1940, with Loretta Young as Julie and Brian Donlevy in the role of Buck Cantrell, the part Lord would be signed to do fifteen years later for the TV version. Cantrell, an admirer of Julie's and an unfortunate pawn in her plot to seek vengeance on her former fiancé, winds up getting killed for his efforts on her behalf.

The *Lux* television version aired November 8. The show received lukewarm reviews, primarily based upon comparisons to the power of the original movie version. *Variety* said of Lord and three of his fellow supporting actors they had "acquitted themselves satisfactorily." While it was not exactly the sort of review for one's scrapbook, it was kinder than the blows leveled at the primary stars of the episode.

Lord was tapped November 23 to star in another *Lux* episode, in the part of Rudd Kendall for a recreation of *Old Acquaintance*, based on the 1943 Warner Bros. film by the same name. The episode aired six days later on November 29. The movie starred Bette Davis as successful writer Kit Marlowe and Gig Young in the role of Rudd, Kit's much younger boyfriend. Rudd winds up being spurned by Kit, and is caught between her and her good friend before it is over. Ellen Corby had a part in the television version. Best known as Grandma on the long running *Waltons* television show, she went on to guest star in a 1968 episode of *Hawaii Five-O*. The December 3 *Daily Variety* was another of those punches to the gut Lord endured. "[B]efore Jack Lord ... ventures before public gaze again, a rigid course of thespic polishing is recommended."[33]

The November 1956 issue of *TV Star Parade* ran a four-page spread by Westley Ryder about Lord, praising him as a versatile performer who had been compared to the likes of Marlon Brando, Jimmy Dean and Burt Lancaster. Twelve stills included with the article support his flexibility in the impressive variety of roles and genres he already had on his dossier, and credited his versatility to his complicated and adventurous life before he stepped in front of the camera. A photo included in the spread is identified as coming from an episode of the CBS live television show *The Web*. That caption says the episode is titled "A Play within a Play" with Lord in the role of a Shakespearean actor, but the photo is actually a scene from the May 2, 1954, episode, "Grande Finale." The magazine hit the stands in September, one month after the release of *The Vagabond King*. Ryder advised his readers to remember the face: "It belongs to a man on his way up."[34]

FIVE

The Fate We Make for Ourselves

By 1957, opportunities for live television drama in New York were becoming less frequent and Jack Lord was commuting more to the West Coast for work. He and Marie were still living in her apartment at 212 East 48th Street, but correspondence from his papers and notices in the Los Angeles press show he was spending more and more time in California. While he would still commute between the coasts, he would eventually find the Hollywood area was the best geography for them. Some sources say the Lords moved to Los Angeles sometime in 1957, and that is likely correct. In the early part of the year, the papers noted his comings and goings, and it was evident he was still commuting quite a bit.

Their new address was a plush apartment in the historic Voltaire building at 1424 North Crescent Heights Blvd. The location had a rich history, with a number of Hollywood personalities calling it home as far back as the early 1930s. Several celebrities and other industry notables have called the historic building home over the years, including Rock Hudson, Janet Gaynor and Ann Sothern. Marilyn Monroe moved out of the building in 1954, just before returning to New York when she was at the Actors Studio with Lord the following year.

When *Story of a Patriot* wrapped, Lord told reporters he already had a lot of television work lined up, and he was busy with filming for those roles in the early part of the year although audiences wouldn't see his work until spring. He was back in New York for filming "Pattern of Violence," an episode of ABC's anthology series *Conflict*, which would air on May 14. *Conflict* was an anthology series by writer and producer Roy Huggins. Although the series was a short-lived one, it produced two episodes that were the genesis for two successful series, *Maverick* and *77 Sunset Strip*.

By the following Saturday, he had been signed for an episode in the third season of *Climax,* a CBS series that ran for four seasons. In "Mr. Runyon of Broadway," he plays Charlie Mullaney, a promising young boxer who gets caught up in a dangerous situation when his wife pleads with him to throw an important bout. A notorious racketeer manages his opponent for the match, and his wife confesses to him she is $12,000 in debt to the man for gambling debts. *Variety* declared Lord was "good" as the honest fighter.[1]

The December 26, 1956, issue of *Daily Variety* reported filming had begun that day for *Have Gun Will Travel,* a new series in the CBS fall line-up, with Lord in a guest-starring role. While it was a one-time gig for him, it was a good addition to his resume. Richard Boone had the lead as Paladin, a suave and sophisticated gun-for-hire. Paladin's home base was a San Francisco hotel as he traveled about the county, putting his extraordinary skill with a six-shooter to good use.

The show would prove to be a highly successful venture, running seven years and consistently holding a prime spot in the Nielsen ratings. The concept was yet another contribution to the fast growing field of new television westerns at the time. While the popularity of the genre had been on the rise since the early 1950s, it was reaching its peak by the end of that decade and stretching into the early '60s. The going rate for supporting actor appearances on television westerns at the time was in the neighborhood of $750 for six long workdays with early calls. Although Lord was not always making significant money for a role, he was taking all the jobs he could find—a stark contrast to his future reputation as a picky actor.

Jack Lord stepped up, doing a good job as despicable murderer Dave Enderby. Enderby had married a prosperous rancher's daughter and, against her family's wishes, carried her away to Perdido, a dingy town in Mexico. The girl's father hired Paladin to bring her back. Paladin's first mission as a hired gun was a resounding success. He not only brought home the girl, he arrived with the rancher's son-in-law in tow, turning him over to the local authorities where he would stand trial for his part in the murders of more than twenty men.

The inaugural episode of *Have Gun Will Travel* was strong, and even though Boone had a prolific career with some of the biggest names in the business, the suave and deadly Paladin became his trademark role. John Ford western actor, Harry Carey, Jr., said the series was the "most fun to work on.... Dick Boone was a powerhouse physically, and he had extraordinary authority as to the casting and the scripts.... He wanted the people he worked with to be happy."[2] Carey later appeared in a *Playhouse 90* episode with Lord and also guest starred on an episode of *Stoney Burke. Have Gun Will Travel* still stands as a classic in the genre of television westerns and Boone, also an Actors Studio alum, enjoyed a successful six-year run as Paladin.

A decade later Richard Boone and Jack Lord would again cross paths at a critical point in Lord's career. After *Have Gun Will Travel* ended, Boone moved to Hawaii, settling on the island of Oahu. Some sources credit Boone with being the catalyst for Leonard Freeman's innovative decision to film his new cop show, *Hawaii Five-O,* completely on location in the islands. Boone had just completed and presented to CBS the pilot episode of *Kona Coast,* filmed in Hawaii. The network passed and went instead with *Hawaii Five-O.* According to some sources, Boone turned down the role of Steve McGarrett and recommended Jack Lord for the part.

Boone and Lord shared some other common interests and professional experiences. Like Lord, Boone was a liberal arts major who had a successful career as an athlete during his college years. While Lord showed his prowess on the gridiron, Boone made a name for himself as a lightweight boxer. He also served in the Navy and, while he racked up some movie roles during his career, it was television that would become his defining medium. He was once asked if he viewed television as a compromise when compared to feature films. "No way," he said. "You have to pull out a whole bunch of stops day after day to keep it fresh."[3] Jack Lord would no doubt amen Boone's take on the challenge of television work after his twelve-season run on *Five-O*. Like Lord, when Boone retired from acting he turned to his second love—painting.

The *Have Gun Will Travel* episode aired eight days after the premiere of Jack Lord's next movie role. The film's roots went back three years with the March 6, 1954, issue of *The New Yorker* magazine's publication of a new short story from noted American writer Irwin Shaw. The protagonist in "Tip on a Dead Jockey" is a World War II pilot living in Paris. A flamboyant stranger approaches him with an offer of a large sum of money to undertake a smuggling mission. Although he refuses, he later becomes involved when he learns his buddy Jimmy Richardson took the bait and has been missing for more than a month, leaving his wife and two young children to wonder what happened to him. Producer and director Dore Schary acquired the story for MGM in September of 1955 with the stipulation that it would need a significant amount of writing before it could be produced as a full-length movie. Apparently, Schary was right; the final screenplay from Tony Award winner Charles Lederer bears minimal resemblance to Shaw's original storyline.

By October of 1956, the studio was confident the film was a sure thing. It was a welcome opportunity at a time the movie industry was feeling the pressure of the rising popularity of television and studios were devoting considerable time and resources to telefilms. Orson Welles was originally slated to direct, but when casting and production began in earnest in late January of 1957 Richard Thorpe was tapped as director. Edwin Knopf would produce and it would be his last film for MGM. Robert Taylor starred as battle fatigued combat pilot Lloyd Treadman. The role would also give Taylor a rare opportunity to showcase his singing talents. The script called for a duet with Dorothy Malone, who plays his ex-wife.

Jack Lord was tested February 1 for the part of Jimmy Heldon, Lloyd's friend and fellow pilot from the war, and he arrived in Los Angeles on February 3 to begin filming.[4] Lord's character in the film is a significant departure from the original story. In Shaw's version Jimmy is an overweight, pathetic, down on his luck fellow. The role called for a charming adventurer who is a devoted husband and the father of an infant son. The primary premise of the film, Lloyd's trauma-induced fear of flying, is not included in Shaw's story. In fact, Lloyd does not take to the air at all in the original version.

Actual production on the film began with background shots in Reno on February 11, followed by two weeks' work in the studio and two weeks of exterior shooting in Spain. Shaw's story is set in Paris, but the primary action of the screen version takes place in Madrid and other exotic locations along the route of Lloyd's perilous smuggling mission to Egypt. Thorpe liked European backdrops, praising the "intangible dimensions" of authentic international settings. The cast and crew had returned to Madrid in late March for more filming and again in April for background shots, when they hit an unusual roadblock. The operators of the racetrack location denied the studio permission to use the oval for shooting unless Robert Taylor agreed to make a personal appearance. Although Taylor did not customarily do such appearances, he at last agreed to present the silver cup to the winner of the featured race of the day so filming could go on. Shooting wrapped on April 25. Robert Taylor made the return trip to the States aboard the Queen Elizabeth instead of taking a plane with the rest of the cast. His intent was to

From left: Marcel Dalio, Martin Garralaga, Jack Lord, Frankie Darro, Gia Scala, Robert Taylor, and Dorothy Malone. The 1957 film *Tip on a Dead Jockey* was Lord's first appearance with Robert Taylor (MGM/Photofest).

"rest up" before he returned to the studio to complete the remaining work. Jack Lord went back to work.

He got some good ink in the August 7 edition of the *Los Angeles Times*. "Jack Lord seems suddenly to be cutting quite a swath in Hollywood. Playing a costarring part with Betsy Palmer in *The Grasshopper* at Columbia, he has been signed for Buck, the older brother of Robert Ryan and husband of Tina Louise in *God's Little Acre*, the Anthony Mann feature with Aldo Ray, Buddy Hackett and Fay Spain."[5] *The Grasshopper* was actually a working title for Lord's next movie, *The True Story of Lynn Stuart*, set to start filming August 12, 1957. Tina Louise left the cast of the stage version of *L'il Abner* to step into her first movie role in the part of Griselda for *God's Little Acre*.

Lord rode an emotional rollercoaster as he earnestly plugged away, and the punches to the gut kept coming. When *Tip on a Dead Jockey* was finally released on September 6, 1957, the reviews were disappointing. Critics indicted the film for offering too little show and too much tell, saying there should have been more action scenes to move the story forward. An early review from the *Los Angeles Times* near the end of August called the film a "misfire," in spite of the "exceptionally good dialogue" from Lederer. Robert Taylor, Gia Scala and Martin Gable got virtually all the kudos in the review, and Lord and Joyce Jameson were soundly thumped. "Jack Lord is out of his class as Jimmy Heldon, and Joyce Jameson has little to do. Her character need not have been written into the script."[6]

The New York Times credited Taylor with effectively pulling off his role with the proper level of restraint and overwrought demeanor befitting the angst of his character. Dorothy Malone in the role of Taylor's ex-wife was judged "merely pretty and intense." As for Jack Lord, the only kudos he got for his work was that he was "earnest" in the part.[7] *Variety* called it a "solid, satisfactory action film," but found the plot of yet another "war-weary pilot" redundant and unsalvageable, particularly with the burden of the excessive dialogue. Overall, it did poorly at the box office, losing significant money, to the tune of more than $800,000. The bleak reviews certainly didn't help, but Lord would at least soon get a second opportunity to work with Robert Taylor.

Lord racked up another starring television role in 1957 when he was cast as Commander David Hurt of the ill-fated SS *Perch* on an episode of the syndicated series *The Silent Service*. The two-season show was based on true stories of the United States submarine fleet during World War II. Each episode featured actual period submarine footage, and Lord gives a strong performance as he leads his crew during the destruction of the *Perch* and his subsequent capture by the Japanese.

As he was finishing up *Have Gun Will Travel*, ongoing activity at a new production company would result in a plum role for him. In September of 1957, three brothers were successful in setting up The Mirisch Company. The brothers vowed they would have six new pictures at a cost of $8,000,000 completed for United Artists by December of the following year. Separate companies would be created for each of the projects, and top Hollywood stars would head them up.

The Mirisch enterprise on the drawing board that held particular appeal for Jack Lord was Ashton Productions and their partnership with Gary Cooper. Cooper rented his Montana ranch to them in November 1957 for a location shoot. In December, Ashton announced plans for filming Anthony Mann's new western *Man of the West*, based on Will C. Brown's 1955 Best Western Award winning novel *The Border Jumpers*. Cooper had three films on the burner at the time, but he was cast in the starring role as Link Tobin. Cooper's busy schedule necessitated a one-month delay in the filming schedule. As it turned out, he eventually stepped aside from one project, *The Sundowners*, citing health issues as the reason, and Robert Mitchum stepped into his role for that one.

Screenwriter Reginald Rose, who had earned an Academy Award nomination for *Twelve Angry Men*, was brought on board to do the script for Mann's new western. He arrived in Los Angeles on December 4 to work on final revisions for the screenplay. Production was set to begin early the following year.

Jack Lord closed out 1957 back on the small screen, appearing in two popular series, and he was getting some attention for his busy work schedule. *Variety* ran a stellar review in January of his appearance in "Lone Woman," the December 6 episode of *Playhouse 90*. Media and culture scholar Gary Edgerton acknowledged the impact of the series and others like it offered in the training of new talent. "[P]art of the golden halo drives from the astonishing artistic legacy left behind by all of the young talent who cut their teeth on these live dramas and continued making their marks afterward on stage, in theatrical films, on series TV, and in other kinds of creative venues."[8] Lord took full advantage of the training—and the paycheck—these experiences had brought to the table for him.

"Lone Woman" starred Kathryn Grayson and Scott Brady. The episode was originally intended as a pilot for *Buckskin,* a new series based on the true account of the only privately owned fort during the nineteenth century. It was Lord's first time working with Grayson since *The Vagabond King.* Costars were Vincent Price, Raymond Burr, and Harry Carey, Jr. Lord would later present a strong performance as a guest star on Burr's hit television series, *Perry Mason.*

The premise for the proposed series was an intriguing one. Brothers Charles and William Bent ran Bent's Fort in Colorado, and they were leasing it to the army and to area trappers. Internal network memos from early 1956 indicate CBS officials were comparing the concept to *Gunsmoke,* evidence they were clearly optimistic about the potential success of the series. Even though the network had scheduled filming of the pilot for April of 1956, it didn't happen. Series writer Al C. Ward had completed three scripts for the proposed show by May, but they had encountered difficulty with casting.

The decision later came down to cancel plans to produce *Buckskin,* but the concept was not completely discarded. The network looked at converting the original idea into a series under the same title as the *Playhouse 90* episode, with Kathryn Grayson maintaining her starring role. CBS moved forward with preparing scripts in October and the pilot was set go before cameras by the end of the month.

By November 1, CBS decided to depart from doing the half hour pilot film and chose instead to do it as an episode of *Playhouse 90* so they would be able to utilize audiences already in place to gage reactions to the concept. Network officials held out hope the show had promise as a marketable series. Lord's role as n'er-do-well trapper Jim Kester is at first reminiscent of one of his later roles—the soulless Coaley Tobin in *Man of the West.* As it turns out, however, Kester runs a bit deeper than the unredeemable Coaley.

The story follows a ruse by William Bent designed to ease the threat of competition in the trapping business brought on by newcomer Jesse White, who was portrayed by Price. Bent proposes marriage to a beautiful Cheyenne woman (Grayson) so he will be recognized as a blood brother who could stand as a tribal partner in the fur trade. While Bent is away on business, Kester decides to pay a visit to his lovely bride. Although his initial intentions are to do unspeakable things, Kester becomes enamored with her and ends up spending all night talking to the woman—just talking. In the meantime, Jesse White kills one of Kester's enemies and sets up Kester for the murder.

Still under the spell of the beautiful young bride, Kester won't use his all-night visit with her as an alibi, fearing no one would believe nothing happened and she would be disgraced. In the end, the woman comes forward and defends him.

Variety praised the episode and the cast for a superb performance and credits Price, Lord, and Burr with "boosting the story upward."[9] Rumors persisted there were two additional episodes of the proposed series set to air on *Playhouse 90,* "Carbine Webb and the Four Sisters" and "Without Incident," but the network would not confirm.[10]

In mid–August Lord had signed on with Desilu Studios for a guest starring spot in the premier season of *U.S. Marshal.* "Sentence of Death" aired on October 25, and he effectively carried yet another bad-guy role for the episode. Condemned cold-blooded killer Matt Bonner flees jail in a spectacular escape, running and shooting and just generally wreaking havoc. The episode was criticized for being over the top as far as believability was concerned, but Lord was praised for a noticeable performance. "[He] knows his way around television and gave the opener its high moments of melodrama."[11]

He next landed a role for the December 14 episode of *Gunsmoke*, and it was one that would allow him to stretch himself a bit as he played two parts, twins Myles and Nate Brandell. Lord sports a moustache, a bad front tooth, and a serious attitude in the role of Myles. He encounters Doc Adams on his way to treat an injured man, pulls a gun and threatens to kill Doc's horse. Before he can fire, Doc kills him. Nate, a clean-shaven, fresh-faced version of his brother, appears in Dodge, looking for justice for his brother's murder.

Since Myles had a price on his head for crimes he committed in Colorado, Nate believes Doc killed his brother for the $1,000 reward. He gets tangled up in a gunfight with the marshal and is shot. Doc saves his life and the marshal locks him up to protect Doc. Nate learns that Myles had intended to kill the man Doc was on his way to treat. When the reward money comes, Doc gives it to Nate, hoping it will serve as an incentive for him to turn from the murderous ways of his brother. Doc wants Nate to know that he will forever regret that he was put in a position that necessitated he kill a man. The penitent Nate sees the error of his ways and vows to take the money to his dead brother's wife. Lord successfully pulls off giving separate personae to the brothers as they come across as two distinct characters.

Lord was back on television again the following week, appearing January 2, 1958, in "Reunion," an episode of the second season of *Playhouse 90*. "Reunion" is based on a novel by Merle Miller and tells the story of four World War II veterans who come together and share personal failures, secrets, and crises the four men have encountered since their war days. The script is an adaption of a novel by the same title from author Merle Miller. The ending is cataclysmic with an attempted murder, a failed effort to dissolve a bad marriage, and a rejected marriage proposal.

While Lord gets mention in the January 6 *Daily Variety* for a "good portrayal" alongside his three costars, entertainment critic Jack O'Brian was not so kind. He singled out Frances Farmer as bringing the only successful performance in the episode.[12] Jack Gould of the *New York Times* attributed the show's failure to not enough time for fully developing the cadre of characters. The result was a "marathon of unconvincing emotionalism." He credits Patricia Barry with the standout performance and said of the rest of the cast, "[T]hey suffered and suffered with varying degrees of Hollywood proficiency."[13] Lawrence Laurent chastised the network for a profuse parade of commercials that debilitated the flow of what he thought was a commendable performance by the actors who, despite their "heroic efforts, were lost in the excessive advertising. "The cast merits a 'Reunion' that will allow a dramatic situation to exist for as long as 15 minutes without an interruption."[14]

Lord was never shy about weighing in with his opinion in the press if he had a stand. In January of 1958, he jumped on the train of critical pros and cons of Stanley Kubrick's *Paths of Glory*, a film starring Kirk Douglas set during World War I and loosely based on a true account of three soldiers who refuse to carry out an order that was in essence a suicide mission. *Los Angeles Times* writer Philip Scheuer did not include the film in his list of the best of 1957. The resulting backlash drew Lord out, and he expressed his opinion in the January 16 edition. Scheuer described Lord as an up and coming actor and a "pro" and published his comments. "'I must say I agree with you wholeheartedly in your criticism of 'Paths of Glory.' I, too, found it wonderfully photographed, but with absolutely no reality—even from the three principals. I didn't believe anyone—it was all surface noise—no depth—no roots in truth. The tiny moment that the German girl did was the only thing I thought came to life.'"[15] Throughout his career, Lord would often take flak for inserting his adamant opinion, but it never seemed to deter him.

In early January Lord worked alongside Peggie Castle in the pilot episode of another proposed new series from CBS. Castle would go on to costar in *Lawman* a western series that ran from 1959 until 1962, and she and Lord later shared common experience. She traveled about the country, singing and dancing at rodeos with fellow *Lawman* regular Peter Brown. After *Stoney Burke* ended, Lord had what became a very lucrative rodeo circuit career as well.

His next job was on *The Sergeant and the Lady*, a police drama produced by James Fonda about a San Diego policewoman. Lord's role as the tough, in-your-face police sergeant foreshadows Steve McGarrett. By April, Fonda had left CBS to take a position at Screen Gems. *The Sergeant and the Lady* stalled until July when it appeared on the list of ten new shows that failed to fly for the fall season, but were promised consideration for the next year. Ten days later Al Scalpone announced he had established LaMesa Productions, an independent telefilm shop, promising CBS four pilots over the coming two years. One of them was *The Sergeant and the Lady*. Near the end of July, Scalpone reported he was reworking the scripts even though CBS had already filmed the pilot.[16] The series drops off the radar after that. Even though *The Sergeant and the Lady* never made, it was another learning experience for future reference for Jack Lord. Filming was done on the streets of San Diego with full cooperation of the city's police department.

Dave Kaufman's January 24 column "On All Channels" in *Daily Variety* announced plans for the new season's lineup of *Climax!* Lord is listed in the cast for a projected May 1 airing of "They Flew with Terror," a story based on the true adventures of the crew of a jet fuel tanker in Antarctica. Among those under consideration for lead roles were Richard Burton, Trevor Howard, and Scott Brady, with Sammy Davis, Jr., and Sidney Poitier. The real-life hero of the story, Captain Sullivan, was on the list of potentials for supporting roles. Lord is listed with Al Salmi in consideration for "other parts." There is no evidence the episode ever aired or that filming was completed. Two days after Kaufmann's article, the *New York Times* featured a nice photo spread of upcoming films, leading off with a scene from *God's Little Acre*. Jack Lord is pictured in the foreground.[17]

In the meantime, the pieces were coming together for a project that would be a lasting feather in Lord's cap. Julie London was signed in January for the role of Billie Ellis for *Man of the West*. Lee J. Cobb was cast as outlaw Dock Tobin and Arthur O'Connell would play con man Sam Beasley. Filming was set to roll in Sonora, California, on February 10.

Mirisch's Ashton Productions spared no effort in ensuring the film benefited from first-rate backgrounds. A significant part of the script involved more than a dozen pages of dialogue slated for scenes set on a train, culminating in a dramatic robbery sequence which would be the catalyst for a complicated chain of events for a mixed bag of characters. The scenes were filmed onboard an actual 1870s moving train, a production decision that added realism to the work and saved some budget dollars as well. As the cast traveled to locations in Sonora and Red Rock Canyon, Cooper spent the commute time productively, teaching costar O'Connell how to play poker; *Variety* reported O'Connell was the standout financial victor in the effort.[18] Later in the month, Mirisch transported huge plaster red rocks that were used in studio filming to the canyon to facilitate continuity between studio and location scenes. The obvious rationale was that moving the plaster replicas was easier than bringing tons of boulders back to the studio.

The company was scheduled to film on a ranch in Thousand Oaks the week of February 20, but a soaking rain and persistent stormy conditions moved the work to MGM Studios. Roadways were washed away and outdoor sets suffered massive damage. That same week, Jack Lord had just finished working with Mann on *God's Little Acre* when he was signed to play the villainous Coaley Tobin for *Man of the West*. It was a rough start to the production process, as bad weather became an unfortunate trend. In March, filming was forced indoors seven times because of storms, and scheduling location work in the canyon was especially problematic.

Filming was finally nearing completion by mid–March. Bobby Troup, who was dating Julie London at the time, was signed in April to write the title song for the movie. London would lend her vocal talents to the tune, and Liberty Records planned to send

From left: Gary Cooper, director Anthony Mann, and Jack Lord in the 1958 United Artists production of *Man of the West*. Mann advises Lord before one of the more memorable scenes. It was Lord's second time to work alongside "Coop" (United Artists/Photofest).

it to a selected group of disc jockeys in April, with the understanding they would pull it back if the response was positive until the film's release. London's silky voice as she tells of the angst of loving a man she could not have would have been a good title tune, but in the end the song did not make the film.

Taking on the role of Coaley Tobin turned out to be a good opportunity for Lord to show what he could do. When it was all said and done, Coaley was a key player in two of most enduring scenes not only from *Man of the West*, but in western film history in general. In an agonizing scene when he ruthlessly forces London's character to strip while he holds a knife to Cooper's throat, the disgust for the Coaley reveling in her humiliation is powerful. In a later scene, Coaley winds up in a horrific fistfight with Link. The scene lasts almost eight minutes, and Link brutally gets the better of him. Coaley is poetically subjected to fitting retribution for his earlier cruelty to Billie. Link forces him to the ground and strips off his shirt, boots, and socks as the rest of the outlaw gang watch. The scene has become a classic and Lord still maintains recognition for it. Even by today's standards, the exquisitely done fight scene is hard to watch. Again, well-done scenes such as these no doubt helped contribute to his repeated casting as a heavy. He played it well.

Although *Man of the West* was filmed ten years before the 1968 MPAA movie rating

From left: Arthur O'Connell, Royal Dano, Jack Lord, Gary Cooper, and Julie London, during the iconic fight scene from *Man of the West* (United Artists/Photofest).

system, films released prior to that time were subject to review and censoring for content. There was some concern about both the strip scene and the brutal fight between Lord and Cooper passing censors. The Code Administration's preview at the end of July resulted in a pass for the strip scene; the fight between Coaley and Link was deemed too violent and had to be modified to bring it up to code.

Theatrical premiere for *Man of the West* was scheduled for a 700-date booking—the biggest opening in history at that time for United Artists. While the film received mixed reviews, the overall consensus was disappointing. *Variety* predicted a good box office, commending the contrast the film offered to other period big dollar westerns, particularly in its high regard for realism more than for psychology. Not surprisingly, London's strip scene and the fight between Coaley and Link were highlighted, judging them realistic enough to make the audience's skin crawl. Kudos for "striking settings" validated the effort put forth in the production decisions. Criticism was leveled at a noted delay in revealing motivation behind some of the actions of the characters early on and for an abrupt ending. Lord got a shout out for his work, as well he should have. "Jack Lord, his handsome face distorted by jealousy and malevolence, is fine in an offbeat casting."[19]

The New York Times highlighted the "expert staging," and confessed that even though it is in essence "a small picture" with a plot that offers little more than a battle of wits between Cooper's and Cobb's characters, it has a "cryptic defiance and an aura of snakelike evil that gets one ... [Cooper] mops up the prairie in one of the meanest fist-scrounging duels we've seen in years."[20] The *Los Angeles Times* said the film was "just another western, like you might find at almost any hour of the day or night on the small living room box, only longer and lots bloodier. In fact, it's one of the bloodiest old-west dramas in some time.... There's ... a slugging match between Cooper and Jack Lord which, for length and realism, rivals any seen on screen for moons."[21] *Man of the West* is still today often cited as being among the best western films ever. After it was all said and done, it was an excellent addition to Jack Lord's filmography and today stands as a classic in the genre.

While Lord was working on *Man of the West* in the early spring, his name was showing up on movie marquis when Columbia Pictures' *The True Story of Lynn Stuart* hit theatres on March 3, 1958. Betsy Palmer had the only starring role, and Lord shared a "with" billing alongside Barry Atwater. The format of the film has a documentary flavor, opening with an indictment of the growing narcotics problem by then California Attorney General Edmund G. Brown, who would go on to become a 1960 candidate for the Democratic nomination for President.

John Kneubuhl extracted the screenplay from newspaper accounts by Pat Michaels and the storyline stayed close to actual events. In spite of the risk of imminent danger, the real life housewife who is the subject of the film served as a consultant. When she appeared in public during her work on the film she covered her face with a mask. Studio promotional material provided to theatres for *The True Story of Lynn Stuart* revealed that Columbia had agreed for the protection of the woman and her family the film would never be shown in a California prison.

The film's protagonist, Phyllis Carter, volunteered to go undercover to help police cripple a notorious gang of traffickers after the drug-related death of her nephew. Lord was cast as the callous Willie Down, a key player in the gang who could lead authorities to the mastermind behind the rapidly growing trafficking operation. Carter takes on the alias Lynn Stuart and poses as a carhop at a local drive-in frequented by Down. She quickly strikes up a relationship with him and finds herself in the company of some ruthless characters. While the ploy is successful, it is not without a series of nail-biting close calls for the housewife turned undercover cop.

The story stays close to actual events, extracted primarily from period newspaper accounts, and Lord once again does a good job as the captivating bad guy. Reviews praised director Lewis Seller for pulling top performances from both Lord and Atwater. Lord brings depth to a role that could have easily come across as a stereotypical period villain. There are moments when it is hard not to root for Willie Down. While he handles Lynn Stuart with a rough hand at times, he brings an element of very believable charm to the role, effective enough to make one forget that, when it comes right down to it, Willie Down is a very bad man. Lord repeatedly expressed his frustration in those early years at being always cast as the bad guy, but when he puts heart and soul into a character like Willie Down, it's easy to see why he was so often boxed into those roles. The man

Betsy Palmer and Jack Lord in *The True Story of Lynn Stuart.* **The Columbia Pictures film recounted the true story of a woman who went undercover to expose a drug smuggling operation. The real Lynn Stuart consulted on the film and wore a mask on her face to protect her from retribution by the criminals she exposed (Columbia Pictures/Photofest).**

could pull off a dirty thug with the best of them. The film also features Gavin MacLeod who would be a recurring *Hawaii Five-O* guest star as the villain "Big Chicken."

Lord's next movie was a film that also still stands as a classic, albeit one fraught with controversy even before it went before the cameras. The genesis of United Artists' *God's Little Acre* was twenty-five years before its theatrical premiere on August 13, 1958. Like *Tobacco Road*, Erskine Caldwell's earlier novel turned stage play, *God's Little Acre* was ahead of its time, replete with sex and tragically flawed characters. The edgy theme gave Hollywood censors some significant headaches and incited protests by concerned citizens. Even planned location shooting hit some roadblocks early on during filming. A *New York Times* story said Mann had set sights on Augusta, Georgia, and reportedly had permission to film in and around an old cotton mill, a row of workers' houses, and on a local farm.

Apparently the locals took offense to the seedy theme of the story, and still smarting from the indictment they felt they had been handed from the novel, forced the production crew to make a change in plans. "Mr. Mann and Mr. Caldwell issued a statement in Hollywood saying that they were unable to film the drama in the original locale because we have been denied facilities and cooperation of the Augusta, Ga., area in what we believe [to be] a program of organized harassment."[22] Shooting was moved to an area near Stockton, California.

Some literary critics who lauded Caldwell's original story denounced the softening of the original plot by the filmmakers, calling it a dilution of otherwise brilliant and true to life people. Many felt both sides had tied the hands of legendary director John Ford when he brought *Tobacco Road* to the screen, rendering him unable to put forth a film that was worthy of the book. The same expectations vexed the proposed production of *God's Little Acre*. Director Anthony Mann consistently held that his intent was to ensure his actors remained true to Caldwell's characters and he did not anticipate trouble from the Production Code Administration. "There's an important difference between what a person will accept in the privacy of reading and what he will find tolerable in a public place like a movie theatre. Anyone making movies has to make allowance for that."[23]

Director Anthony Mann was up to the challenge, and even though some of the same issues related to *Tobacco Road* applied, he managed to do the book as much justice as the times would allow. *New York Times* reviewer A.H. Weiler concluded Mann had treated Caldwell's characters with dignity and intelligence, pronouncing the final product realistic and actually funny. "Although the starkness, tragedy, poverty, ignorance and inter-familial lusts are there, they do not appear degraded but natural to the people and their environment."[24] Bosley Crowther agreed. "There are in the sprawling complications of this turgid and trashy family, a lot of assorted low-brow humors and ribaldries good for fat guffaws. But there are, too, in Ty Ty Walden a basic dignity and humility that pop through."[25]

Lord's performance did not get the critical attention he had likely hoped for, but he does a memorable job as the pathetic Buck Walden. He is diligently compliant with the demands of his misguided father to find phantom gold on the Walden property, all the while maintaining an uneasy vigilance over his wife Griselda. Lord did get a nod in the May 9 *Daily Variety* alongside Vic Morrow for admirably capturing Caldwell's characters, saying the two men played them as both "strong and pitiful."[26] He garnered two

From left: Jack Lord, Buddy Hackett, Robert Ryan, and Tina Louise in Anthony Mann's 1958 adaptation of Erskine Caldwell's classic novel, *God's Little Acre*. The film was released to a significant amount of negative publicity for its racy content. This was Lord's first appearance with the sultry Louise (Photofest).

mentions in that edition, the second of which was a notice of a pending pilot for a new western based on a Frank Gruber novel.

The following week Caldwell was at the Los Angeles authors club to accept a Milestone award in honor of *God's Little Acre* as the "world's all-time best seller." *Hollywood Reporter* critic Jack Moffitt praised the film and credited Lord with evoking a "brooding malevolence as he shows the audience that [Griselda] is too much woman for him."[27]

God's Little Acre was Tina's Louise's debut movie. Like Lord, she is best remembered for a continuing television role, but she earned critical praise for her work on the film. Before her two and a half year run as the sultry Ginger on *Gilligan's Island*, she captured a Golden Globe as Most Promising Newcomer for her portrayal of Griselda in *God's Little Acre*. Her character is a memorable one, and she plays it well as she unintentionally torments her poor husband with her voluptuous figure and the attention she gets from every man in the room. Lord's soon to be famous McGarrett square jaw remains emphatically clinched through much of the film as he endures both the humiliation of Griselda's eventual wandering eye and the futile dreams of his father. Lord and Tina Louise would team up again with Robert Taylor later in the fall for work on *The Hangman*, Taylor's first venture after leaving his long tenure with MGM.

Although he received little recognition for it, Michael Landon made his acting debut in *God's Little Acre* as Dave Dawson, the albino Ty Ty Walden believed to have magical powers for finding hidden treasure. The two men worked together again when Lord landed a guest-starring role in the first season of *Bonanza*.

As a result of the expected controversy over the explicit content, promotion for the film was copious, and Lord was getting some great exposure as a result of it. By the end of February before the planned August premier, the cast had completed nine foreign language tapes for international promotions and Erskine Caldwell was diligently working the academic circuit in both the U.S. and in Europe, lecturing extensively about the book. Leading cast, including Lord, were set to take part in telephone interviews with 245 radio deejays from across the country in April and May before the release. The April 4 edition of *Daily Variety* reported a three-theatre world premiere scheduled for May 7 at the Iris, Rialto and Wilshire Theatres in California. While the cast was scattered about over the country for premier hype, Caldwell continued to work the academic community.

As the movie primaries did their part to get the word out about the upcoming film, Director Mann worked to keep a lid on the growing opposition of the sex theme from civic groups across the country. He strategically counteracted with the popularity of Caldwell's novel as a routine selection on American literature college reading lists across the country. United Artists released ten thousand reprints of an *Atlantic Monthly* article published in May of that same year, and taped interviews with Caldwell that went out to more than 350 radio stations owned by universities. As the massive pre-emptive damage control intensified, Jack Lord and the rest of the cast were getting some great exposure from the press coverage. If the hype following the film proved to be as good as it had been for the preview, he would surely rack up a fine credit for his resume. The *Los Angeles Times* proclaimed, "'God's Little Acre' may have been topped (or bottomed) by France or Italy, but it is certainly the bawdiest bash ever to emanate from Hollywood."[28]

Early runs of the film broke records. The buzz on university campuses was prolific as the history of the prior twenty-five years of controversy surrounding the novel was resurrected. It was a good film for a struggling actor who wanted his face in front of audiences. The casting for the film was lauded in the press, validating Lord's and the rest of the cast's expected ability to carry their roles. Writer/producer Sidney Harmon waxed eloquently in the June 27 edition of *Daily Variety* about the benefits of a producer having the final say in casting, replacing film and casting directors' involvement. He condemned traditional method of readings, saying a reading showcases an actor's voice, but tells nothing about that actor's ability to act. In Harmon's approach, "actors are given the script and minimal instructions and asked to return in two or three days with their own characterizations worked out. The producer himself ... should watch the performance and make his selections on the basis of thespic ability."[29] It was the method Harmon used for *God's Little Acre*, so Jack Lord must have put forth his best effort for his audition.

The movie hit theatres in general release August 13, and it did well. *New York Times* film critic Bosley Crowther named it as one of the Top Ten Films of 1958.[30] *God's Little*

Acre still stands strong alongside Caldwell's original literary work, and it was a good credit for Lord. He was moving forward.

The September 1958 issue of *Pageant* magazine ran a unique story about Lord that brought three of his worlds together. The publication debuted in 1944 and the unique format included the size, reminiscent of *Readers Digest*, and an offering of very diverse articles. It was a departure from other Hillman Publications that were largely true confession and crime stories. *Pageant* offered diverse, general interest features and drew a wider audience than its sister publications. *God's Little Acre* was getting abundant attention and the release date for *Man of the West* was but a month away.

The article gave Lord the opportunity to bask in the benefits of his part in *Man of the West*, not the least of which was the opportunity the film gave him to again work alongside his role model. He had already proven he could do westerns and his repertoire in the genre would continue to grow quickly. *God's Little Acre* allowed him to show his ability in another arena, and the public was about to learn his visual arts bent went beyond painting.

Lord was an avid photographer and he started early in his acting career documenting his work with a camera. Always the innovator, he was diligent in ensuring that during important times in his professional life he took what was a forerunner to the modern day "selfie." He would set the timer and dash in front of his camera to capture stills of his costumes, other cast and crewmembers, and film sets. Working alongside Gary Cooper was an experience he did not want to forget and, according to the *Pageant* article, he shot some 4,000 photos during the three months of shooting. The magazine ran two pages with selected photos taken during the filming in Sonora, California, including a shot of Lord taking a photo of a grinning Gary Cooper.

Lord was clearly grateful to those who helped him in those early days, no matter the capacity. In a December 28, 1958, *Los Angeles Times* story Hopper had selected him for her list of projected new faces headed for stardom. His photo appears alongside a sultry shot of Tina Louise. Proclaiming that the slate of newcomers for the year were "different," Hopper identified a trend toward what she termed a "more stable and spirited appeal coupled with talent and intriguing personality."[31] In Hedda Hopper's typed notes from a February 19, 1963, face-to-face interview with Lord, she recounts his reminding her of recognition she had given him five years earlier—long before the two became friends.[32] Hopper had done a phone interview with Lord on January 4, 1963, and she had asked if he would be willing to do an in-person interview. Lord was of course happy to accommodate her. He had earlier mentioned his gratitude for the shout out in a December 31, 1961, letter to Hopper.[33] He carried a copy of the article with him to the interview and handed it to Hopper when he came into the room. "I appreciated the article—you went out on a limb when no on else was willing to do it.... When nobody here knew me, you chose me ... and I appreciate it." A dedicated letter writer, Lord penned a handwritten note to Hopper four days after the interview expressing his delight at the opportunity to meet the famous journalist in person. "Now I know the legend is true! ... I guess you could call it love at first sight." Although he closed that first note to Hopper with "Sincerely, Jack Lord," future correspondence to her was consistently signed, "Love, Lord and Lady."

In the preface to his comprehensive work on unsold television pilots, Lee Goldberg defines pilots as "fresh faces and old favorites lining up for a one-night stand with the viewing public.... It's the betting stub you're left with after your horse has lost the race."[34] NBC's head of comedy development Perry Simon explained the crapshoot element to television pilots. "When pilots work, they work well. And when they flop, they thud pretty loudly. There are a thousand ways it can go wrong and only one way it will go right."[35] Before the end of the year, Jack Lord was about to see a painful illustration of Simon's thesis.

Throughout a career that spanned more than thirty-five years pulp writer Frank Gruber turned out more than sixty novels, three hundred short stories, and two hundred screenplays and scripts for television.[36] His 1957 western novel *Town Tamer* had a complicated history before the story finally hit the screen. The part of protagonist Tom Rosser seemed a good fit for Lord. Rosser was a complex man. He was a college graduate living on the frontier who just happened to have a talent for gun slinging. He also carried an innate sadness as he struggled with the death of his wife.

Producer Don Fedderson had bought the story in February of 1958 and brought Gruber on board to adapt the novel for a pilot. Originally set to go into production one month later, it was early May before casting was complete and it went before cameras. Jack Lord was tapped to play Rosser and signed a five-year contract for the projected series. The venture looked to be a long-term opportunity, and Marie left Los Angeles May 22 to join her husband in New York as he began the work.

Later that same month the title was changed to *The Quiet Man*. Don Fedderson paid a royalty to Republic Pictures to secure rights to the new title to avoid a copyright infringement with the 1952 John Ford movie starring John Wayne and Maureen O'Hara by the same name. Part of the deal gave Fedderson film rights in addition to the television series. Author Frank Gruber preferred the original title and held out hope that when the pilot was submitted it would be called *The Town Tamer*. Even though Gruber acknowledged the popularity of westerns was diminishing, he disagreed with recent scuttle that they were on their way out to be replaced by mysteries. At the time of filming for the *Town Tamer* adaptation, he had five titles on the boiler. His prediction was the western genre would continue at least three more years. The pilot episode was completed at a cost of $70,000 and Fedderson screened "Dar Stover Returns," in Los Angeles on June 2. He had earlier hired Milton Merlin to research original story lines for the new series that same week, planning to have 39 episodes ready by January.

At the time, Lord had just finished filming for an episode of Fedderson's successful series *The Millionaire* the previous Friday. Each episode chronicled the charitable acts of John Beresford Tipton, Jr., an unseen and very wealthy benefactor, who randomly gave $1,000,000 cash gifts to average people as a study in how sudden wealth affected their behavior. For the press preview of the series in January 1955, Fedderson wanted to arrange for a million dollars in cash to be on display, but he could get no takers from local banks to supply the elaborate prop.

Lord had a starring role in the fifth season. "The Lee Randolph Story" aired on November 19, and the episode has a *Twilight Zone* feel to it. It is about a mentally ill man who becomes the recipient of Tipton's latest gift. He is released from the mental hospital where he has been incarcerated and returns home to his brother. As soon as he arrives he falls victim to his brother's attempts to make him believe he is having another

Jack Lord and Eleanore Tanin in a November 19, 1958, episode of *The Millionaire*, a CBS series about how ordinary people deal with sudden and unexpected wealth (CBS/Photofest).

mental breakdown as part of a ruse to take his money. There is a delicious "McGarrett moment" in the episode when, as Lee Randolph begins to catch on to his brother's betrayal, he rapidly and loudly snaps his fingers as the pieces begin to fall into place, a mannerism very familiar to fans of the original *Hawaii Five-O*.

Don Fedderson arrived in New York Thursday, October 16, with the pilot episode of *The Quiet Man* and the intention of screening it to network executives. Lord's character, Dar Stover, has just graduated from Harvard with a law degree and he is returning to his home in a typical rough and tumble boomtown, after a five years' absence. Riley Condor, a ruthless man who is gradually taking over the town with plans to increase his fortune from the coming railroad, has murdered Stover's adopted father, Cyrus. Cyrus was a Quaker and a man of peace who grows concerned when his adopted son Dar becomes an accomplished shooter and shows a tendency toward settling things with his gun. At his father's urging Dar has put up his guns when he leaves for Harvard to study law.

Ultimately, Condor's men murder his fiancée when a bullet meant for Dar hits her. Wanda Hendrix, who was briefly married to Audie Murphy, is cast in the role of Dar's fiancée. After she dies in his arms, Dar sets off on his quest for revenge—the impetus for upcoming episodes. At the end of the pilot episode, a preview of the next episode includes a scene with a man asking Dar if he is the one who is called the "town tamer." Lord wouldn't see the verdict of the potential for *The Quiet Man* until January.

By the first week of September he was under contract for a costarring role in another project with director Michael Curtiz (*Casablanca*, *Mildred Pierce*, *White Christmas*). *The Hangman*, Paramount's newest western, was scheduled to begin shooting on Monday, September 22, just as Lord was winding up work on *The Millionaire*. The film had been on the table at Paramount since 1957 when Edward Dmytryk was set to produce and direct. Paramount had bought Luke Short's story for $25,000 earlier that year.[37] By the time it finally rolled, Curtiz was listed as director.

In mid-December Lord was signed by producer John London to a starring role in "The Marriage Crisis," an episode of *The Loretta Young Show* at NBC, set to film on December 29. Young was not scheduled to appear, but Lord's costar was Elizabeth Montgomery. It would be their first reunion since *Billy Mitchell*. The show was scheduled to air February 15, 1959.

Lord's steady work for the previous two years had given him the opportunity to work with some prominent directors and well-established actors, and he was bent on proving he had the potential to be a serious film actor. His name was showing up more and more in syndicated entertainment columns in *The New York Times* and the *Los Angeles Times* and he had repeated mentions in *Variety* for ten of the twelve months in 1958. True to form, however, he still wasn't putting all his eggs in one basket. In true Jack Lord fashion, he kept his nose to the grindstone, making good use of his time when he was not before the cameras. In December, he gladly did a favor for his "pal" Anthony Mann, standing in for Sir Laurence Olivier in a screen test for Sabine Bethman in her try-out for a role in Mann's upcoming film, *Spartacus*.[38] Lord was no doubt pleased to stand in for one of his idols. In April of that year, he had received a gracious note from Olivier on Algonquin Hotel letterhead. Olivier was responding a letter he had received from Lord in which his praised Olivier for his performance in John Osborne's stage play *The Entertainer*. He told Lord he was "grateful in the extreme" that he had taken time to pen a letter to him, promising the young actor he would make it a point to see any of his future movies when his name showed up a marquis. Lord kept the letter.[39]

Six

Low Aim Is Crime

From his large repertoire of memorized poetry, Jack Lord sometimes pulled out a familiar quote from James Russell Lowell: "Not failure, but low aim is crime." He continued to aim high, and it often came with a cost. He had gained some momentum by 1959, adding three solid film roles to his credit, but his filmography at the end of the year was sparse. He and Marie still struggled with the uncertainty of the next paycheck, but he stood by his decisions, even though they sometimes cost him a job. He was paying more attention to the business end of the work, and he was not afraid to take charge of his own affairs. The payoff was still a long way off, but his luck would radically change over next decade.

In January, he was once again in negotiations with Walter Mirisch, this time for a starring role in a proposed new British film. Writer and producer Rod Serling was at work on the screenplay based on Frederick E. Smith's 1956 novel, *633 Squadron*. The story about a group of World War II British fighter pilots would be the first color aviation film. Early on, it looked as though the deal was sealed and Lord was in.[1] The project was unexpectedly moved to the back burner, however, where it stalled for more than three years. Filming in England was finally set to begin in July of 1963 with Lord and George Chakiris slated for leading roles. James Clavell, who penned the screenplay for *Walk Like a Dragon*, and Howard Koch were on board to do the screenplay.

When the movie opened in June of 1964, Cliff Robertson, not Jack Lord, had star billing with Chakiris. The reason for Lord's being dropped from the film could not be confirmed, but it may have been that the delayed start date conflicted with his work on *Stoney Burke*. Lord was frequently criticized for refusing roles for financial reasons or in his attempt to avoid playing the heavy. He would later confess that although he stood by his commitment to wait for the opportunity to do something different, his decision had resulted in his losing out on what turned out to be profitable parts for the actors who had accepted them.

He was getting more notice, however, and his face was showing up as a "rising star" in some reviews and a variety of fan publications. He made the list of *Movie Screen* magazine's 1959 "Stars of Tomorrow" feature. The photo for the spread is a pensive young Lord, cavalierly holding a cigarette beside his face, and he appears directly above a photo of Tina Louise. Other up and comers in the article include James Darren, Darryl Hickman, Angie Dickinson, and Troy Donahue. Lord's bio for the article reports he had appeared in four plays, fifty television shows and eight movies to date, but the count of his television appearances at that time was actually about half that number.[2]

The January 22 review following the screening of the pilot episode for Fedderson's *The Quiet Man* was beyond disappointing. Internal communication proclaimed, "We considered this MCA package to be an extremely poor western—the worst you had ever seen."[3] Even though Frank Gruber's story did eventually make it to the big screen in 1965, Lord did not get to add the credit to his resume. Dana Andrews took the lead role of Tom Rosser, heading up a respectable cast that included Lon Chaney, Jr., DeForest Kelly, and Bruce Cabot. Author Frank Gruber had a small part in the film. Attempts to find an explanation of Lord's being left off the final cast was not found, but by that time he was involved in other projects.

His first appearance after the start of 1959 was the February 15 airing of an episode of the *Loretta Young Show* he had filmed at the end of the previous December.

In "Marriage Crisis," Lord plays a hot-tempered and immature husband who can't hold down a job. He worked again with Elizabeth Montgomery in the role of his frustrated wife. The *Variety* review two days after the episode aired cut to the bone. In essence the report declared the episode "boring." The review commended the network on the choice of titles, declaring *crisis* an appropriate adjective for the story line. Both Lord and Montgomery got a positive takeaway from the scalding review, however. They were commended for well-played roles in spite of the lukewarm script.[4] True to form, Lord put yet another disappointment behind him and moved on.

The prior fall he had reported to work on September 22 for his role in his next motion picture. In *The Hangman*, he had one of the four starring roles alongside Robert Taylor, Tina Louise and Fess Parker. Parker and Louise were dating while the film was in production. The storyline for *The Hangman* is drawn from a short story by popular western writer Luke Short. Paramount bought the story in 1958, and Warner Bros.' Michael Curtiz was brought on board as producer and director for the film. Mackenzie "Mac" Bovard, is a relentless lawman, known for his perfect record for capturing criminals on the run. In *The Hangman*, he has a challenging case when he encounters a bad guy who has gone straight.

Lord was cast in the role of John Butterfield, an accused killer and part of a gang who robbed a Wells Fargo stage. Butterfield slipped capture, and wound up hiding in plain sight far away from the scene of the crime. He was living a quiet life as an upright, hardworking man known to the locals as Johnny Bishop. Lord's famous dark locks were lightened for the role. When Bovard gets wind of his whereabouts he entices Butterfield's former girlfriend Selah Jennison (Louise) to travel to where Butterfield is living to make positive identification. Her payoff will be a ticket for the trip and the $500 reward on the table for Butterfield's capture.

Jennison ultimately betrays Mackenzie when she sees Butterfield and refuses to sell him out. When she realizes he has settled down, has married, and is living a clean life, she cannot bring herself to turn him in. Eventually, the loner marshal falls for Jennison and deliberately allows Butterfield to escape so he can catch up with his wife.

Paramount ran a preview of *The Hangman* at the studio on April 20, 1959, and the reviews were lukewarm. *Daily Variety* called it a "fair western ... [that] will have to rely on the merits of its cast names to take the top half of a double-bill." Director Curtiz

A light-haired Jack Lord is a wanted man hiding in plain sight in the Paramount Pictures production of *The Hangman*. Lord worked for the second time with Robert Taylor in the 1959 film directed by Michael Curtiz. Also pictured are Shirley Harner and Mickey Shaughnessy (Paramount Pictures/Photofest).

was criticized for failing to ensure motivation for his characters' actions and for including two separate gratuitous scenes of Tina Louise taking a bath. Lord did pull an indirect compliment from the devastating review: "Jack Lord is wasted in a part of no discernible depth."[5]

Though the film had been in limited release since early spring, it arrived in theatres in wide release on June 17. Some markets reported an unimpressive box office, while others thought the initial response looked positive, and American Cinema Editors, Inc. nominated the film for an editing award in late October. When it was all said and done, the overall reception for the film was poor.

Jack Lord was not the only disappointed cast member. Fess Parker didn't take the outcome well, and he decided to place the blame where he felt it lay. He put pen to paper in the July 24 issue of *Daily Variety* to vent his ire at theatre managers for their part in the general downturn of movies. He based his case on what he saw as their failure to sell the Hollywood product. He had taken to the road with tapes to promote Cascade Records, a company he co-owned, and a new release he had completed. Paramount piggybacked the tour and Parker also carried with him promotional spots for *The Hangman*. He reported he had personally contacted 150 theatre owners, offering the tapes free of charge. He was angered that not a single tape had been utilized for promotion of the film.

Parker was on the road for more than a month, and he brought back a bleak report. By the time it was over, he had talked to more than 1,000 people during his tour and he reported that very few indicated they had been to a movie in the last month. He leveled the blame at theatre owners and their lack of upkeep of their properties and their absence of any effort to promote films.[6] Jack Lord didn't weigh in on Parker's crusade.

He did maintain the momentum he had gathered in recent years in winning roles on inaugural episodes of small screen series. Television was, after all, a viable competitor for big screen audiences, and Lord would dramatically demonstrate ten years later that he was very good at thinking outside the box. On January 9 that year, CBS had launched a new western destined to become a classic. *Rawhide* was not only the vehicle that launched Clint Eastwood's stellar career. The series went on to become one of television's longest running westerns. Lord landed a part in the first episode.

Daily Variety's TV/Film Production Chart from February 20 has him in a guest-starring role alongside Gloria Talbott in "Incident of the Captive's Herd," but no episode with that title was broadcast. Lord and Talbott did appear in "Incident of the Calico Gun," however. The episode aired on April 24, 1959, the day after the disappointing early release reviews for *The Hangman*. There may have been a change in the *Rawhide* episode title after casting was done earlier in the year. Lord's filmography goes relatively quiet for the next seven months.

The August 4 edition of *Daily Variety* reported the Lords had returned to the West Coast after spending three weeks in New York.[7] They had been living in Los Angeles for two years, and it is not known when they sold Marie's New York apartment where they lived after their marriage. It is possible they could have stayed in their apartment during their extended visits back to New York. There is no evidence he was working on the east coast during that time and it is very likely he and Marie may have been taking advantage of the free time to see plays or take in other events. Lord left behind a massive collection of theatre playbills as part of his estate, and throughout his life the couple were often photographed in the theatre district. Professionally, it was one of his least productive years after he fully committed himself to an acting career. Later that month, he spent a week in San Francisco filming for a role in an episode of *The Lineup*, and while he was there, he devoted some time to public appearances on behalf of *The Hangman*.[8] He returned home from San Francisco on August 26.

The Lineup episode was for a new CBS series based on a 1950s radio show. The entire series was shot on location in San Francisco, and it was yet another opportunity for Lord to watch and learn. "The Strange Return of Army Armitage" is the story of a man serving a term in prison for a murder committed by his brother. In a macabre turn of events, shortly after his release he finds himself a suspect in yet another homicide—a murder for hire arranged by his brother. The episode was the first in the new hour-long format for the show. Early press indicated it was set to air September 30, but sources vary on the actual airdate. The October 7 edition of *Daily Variety* included a large ad printed across the bottom of two pages announcing Lord's guest starring role that night on *Lineup*, likely purchased by Lord himself.[9] Cancelled checks from his estate document occasional ad payments to prominent entertainment publications or newspapers for ads.

Lord had signed with Desilu the prior fall for a guest-starring role in an episode of *The Untouchables*. Set in 1930s Chicago, the series starred Robert Stack as real life

Marie and Jack Lord, circa 1960. Marie frequently wore hats, saying she hated to sit under the dryer and preferred covering her hair. She had the feather style hat seen here in a variety of colors, and gossip columnists often ridiculed her "feather duster" style. As a designer, she was often seen in fashion-forward dress and she designed and made clothing for her famous husband (Photofest).

federal prohibition agent Elliot Ness. Early press releases had the title as "Strange Alliance," but it aired on November 5 with "The Jake Lingle Killing" as the title. The original title was descriptive of the premise of the story; a Chicago tough guy teamed up with Ness to help bring down two gangs operating an illegal liquor trade.

Newspaper reporter Jake Lingle makes the fatal error of playing with both sides in the gang war, and he is assassinated in the subway in front of dozens of witnesses. The public is unaware that Lingle is on the take and a $25,000 reward is offered for the capture of the killer. Lord plays Bill Hagen, a slick shyster who offers Ness inside information on both gangs in return for the goods on the Lingle killing so he can collect the reward money. Lord's portrayal of Hagen offers yet another support for his recurring typecasting as the tough guy; he plays it very well. In the closing scene, Elliot Ness masterfully articulates the evidence that Lord did not play Hagan as a flat character. "Hagen was a guy who looked bad on the outside. Who knows what goes on inside." A banner across the bottom of two pages in the November 5 *Daily Variety* announced Lord's starring role in that night's episode of the show.[10] Lord also bought an ad for his appearance in the episode with *The Hollywood Reporter*.

That same fall he had another near miss on a promising movie role. Spanish screenwriter and director Luis Bunuel began casting October 21 for *The Young One*, a film about a black jazz musician who is unjustly charged with the rape of a white woman and is on the run from a lynch mob. Filming was set to begin November 15 in Mexico and Bunuel was reportedly negotiating with Jack Lord for a starring role. When the movie premiered in 1961, he was not listed in the cast.[11]

Lord continued to rack up an impressive number of small screen roles. He went to work at Paramount on October 30 guest-starring alongside Susan Oliver in "The Outcast," an episode of *Bonanza* that would air in January. Oliver plays a young woman who is shunned by the community after her father and brother were hanged for robbery. Lord is the young woman's shady fiancé, who winds up crossways with the Cartwrights when he plots to steal the area miners' payroll as it is transported across Ponderosa land. The episode aired January 1. Lord had worked with Oliver three years prior in an episode of the *Studio One in Hollywood* series, and he would work with her again two years later in his second *Rawhide* appearance.

For a story in the November 6 *Los Angeles Times* Lord reported he had turned down offers from producer/director Hal Bartlett for a costarring role in *All the Young Men* and another from Milton Sperling for a starring role in *Legs Diamond* because both parts were for heavies.[12] Not prone to sit still and wait for the career-making role to come to him, he made the decision two days later to go public with his exasperation at current casting practices in the business. The November 8 issue of the *Los Angeles Times* featured an article written by a "fine young actor" who leveled an indictment at the Hollywood system of typecasting actors. Contrasting the Hollywood trend to the more diverse practices of the British movie industry, Lord spoke out about how the system was crippling his ability to prove his range as an actor. He outlined the strategy he had undertaken to move out of the box in which he had found himself, and it was a tough one. Determined to break free of a pattern of recurring roles as the heavy, he declared he had made a conscious decision to turn down bad guy roles, and he confessed he was suffering financially because of it. He offered kudos to directors like Otto Preminger, Stanley Kramer, and Elia Kazan who were brave enough to step out and cast against type. His hope was that someone would remember his work on the New York stage and give him an opportunity to show what he could do. He said he longed to do comedy and he was confident that if he held fast to his resolution someone would one day give him that chance.[13]

Lord was looking to be heard and he succeeded, but the reaction was a mixed bag of responses. Producer/writer Charles Schnee publicly responded to Lord's article in the November 15 edition of the *Los Angeles Times*. He acknowledged the creative bent inherent in actors since the beginning of the art and the natural result of a desire to step out of the comfort zone. In essence, he challenged Lord to "be realistic" and to prove his confidence in his ability to stretch his wings professionally by taking small parts that were a divergence from his customary roles. He also recommended that Lord, and others who agreed with his position, should consider the possibility that perhaps they are typecast because they are good at what they do. Audience response to a job well done, he proposed, might very well be the reason behind the typecasting.[14]

The following day, the *Times* reported Paramount's D.A. Doran told Jack Lord he had read his article and he wanted to do something about it. Four days later Doran called him with the offer of the hero lead in James Clavell's next production, *Walk Like a Dragon*. Originally titled *East Wind West Wind*, the film was set to go into production in December and it would be in theatres the following year.[15] Lord was ecstatic. When talking with the *Los Angeles Times* about his new role he said, "And don't forget ... he's the HERO!"[16]

In an article by Lord's friend Lawrence Laurent for the *Washington Post*'s weekly TV magazine published ten years later, Laurent said Lord gave credit to Cecil Smith, television critic for the *Los Angeles Times*, for changing producers' minds about his versatility. Lord said he had "poured out his troubles" to Smith, and that it was Smith who wrote the article.[17]

Australian-born Clavell was a highly successful screenwriter, novelist, producer, and director who generated an impressively diverse body of work that includes classics like *Shogun*, *The Great Escape*, *The Fly*, and *To Sir with Love*. Paramount's *Walk Like a Dragon* was a unique offering to western film fare, examining cultural prejudice problems for the growing Chinese population on the frontier. The cast included Japanese Canadian actress Nobu McCarthy and Hawaiian born actor James Shigeta. Both later guest-starred in separate episodes of *Hawaii Five-O*.

The film was reviewed at the studio on May 23 before wide release on June 1. While the reviews after the release were not encouraging, Lord did get a nod from *Variety* when he was commended for salvaging his role in spite of the "contradictory motivation" of the characters. "Although shackled with a superficially drawn role, Lord constructs a sympathetic characterization."[18] He brought depth to the role, playing it both strong and soft as he carries out his duties as man of the house after the death of his father, while aptly showing a tender side with McCarthy. He credited Linc Bartlett as the role that finally broke his long-running streak of missing out on hero leads.

Despite recurring disappointments, Lord continued to hang tough as he entered his second decade as an actor, and it was a good thing he did; his persistence was finally about to pay off. His productivity wasn't limited to work in front of the camera as he began to put his diverse talents and solid business sense to good use. In spite of his love for the stage and for serious movie roles, he was fully aware of the potential success of a solid television pilot that would ring true with audiences. He was tired of the growing list of failed pilots on his own filmography, so he did the next logical thing—he started writing them himself.

By the early 1960s the current system that put the fate of new television series in

Jack Lord and Nobu McCathy in James Clavell's 1960 film *Walk Like a Dragon*. As Linc Bartlett, Lord becomes involved in racial prejudice on the western frontier when he falls in love with a beautiful Chinese woman (Paramount Pictures/Photofest).

the hands of networks rather than sponsors was already in place. Jack Lord saw an opportunity and he got busy. The 1961 *Catalog of Copyright Entries* shows he registered four original television plays during spring and summer of 1960. There is no evidence that three of the four concepts, *Bachelor of Art*, *Tales of the China Seas*, and *Carte Blanche*, ever made it to production. *Tramp Ship*, however, made it before cameras. Lord later said that these "lean years," when he was turning down villain roles and, as a result found himself out of work for about eight months, was the time he focused on writing, and it was the period during which he wrote *Tramp Ship*.[19]

When production for *Tramp Ship* was completed, it spent about five years making the rounds as a potential new adventure series. Lord later told Hedda Hopper that he worked on the pilot while he waited for his opportunity to win hero roles. "'I did 26 storylines and sold the series to Don Fedderson,'" he said. "Then D.A. Doran gave me my first movie lead in *Walk Like a Dragon*."[20]

Jack Lord's fingerprints are all over the details in *Tramp Ship*. The concept was based on life in a world he knew well. A tramp ship is a vessel with no fixed ports of call that takes on passengers as it travels to ports of call all over the world. The unique nature of the system offers the potential for a wide variety of characters and plot lines. As a young seaman, Lord had worked cruise ships and he had first-hand knowledge of freighters and life aboard ships. He put his experience to good use, creating a concept that had the potential to become a full-blown series with a wealth of stories.

The final pilot had the subtitle *Port of Call*, and the paper trail for the proposed series starts in earnest in 1959, with a projected production date set for February 1961. After the final script polish in January that year, the concept went into production on schedule in San Pedro one month later. Internal communication tracks the five-year progression of the concept before NBC ultimately passed on it July 13, 1964.[21]

The storyline followed the adventures of a diverse cast of characters who booked passage aboard a modern freight steamer as it traveled about the world. The pilot episode got a name change when it went into production. The original subtitle "To Catch a Tiger" was patently inserted into the dialogue of the first episode. An early long shot shows the profile of the ship with its name prominently displayed. "The Lady" was a clear derivative of Lord's production company name—Lord and Lady Productions—and Maria, the name of a featured female character, is a derivative of Lord's wife's name.

As a colorful menagerie of passengers file onto the ship, the crew, who would be the regulars on the series, reveal their own backstories. There are sufficient parallels between Brand and Lord to suggest that the role of the captain may have been written by Jack Lord with Jack Lord in mind for the part. An internal production memo to Dan Seymour has Lord's name marked through as the star, Neville Brand typed in directly after it. Although the original plan was for Lord to have the starring role, by the time filming began he had stepped aside and Brand was set to take on the role of tough, no nonsense Captain Morgan Kelly. Like Lord, Brand had his first experience in front of a camera, making military training films. Also like Lord, Brand's "lived-in face" had won him an extensive repertoire of tough guy roles throughout his long career. He was well aware that his physical appearance had facilitated his recurring bad guy roles, but unlike Lord, he embraced the hand he was dealt. "With this kisser, I knew early in the game I wasn't going to make the world forget Clark Gable," he said.[22]

The interpretation of the captain's role bears some undeniable similarity to Lord's portrayal of his iconic role on *Hawaii Five-O*. During an early scene, he engages in a McGarrett-like shutdown of his crew as they eagerly look to engage in some covert espionage spurred on by the suspicious activity of some mysterious passengers boarding the ship. "If you want to catch a tiger," he tells them, "you have to offer him live bait and we're running a ship, not hunting tigers. So forget it."

Lawrence Laurent reported in a January 11, 1964, *Washington Post* article that the script was actually based on the China Seas adventures of Lord's father, a captain in the Maritime Service. When Lord sold the series to producer Don Fedderson in August of 1960, he described it as a collection of 26 story outlines "written from the gut."[23] The pilot episode, "Catch a Tiger," was filmed at Desilu Studios under the direction of John Brahm, who brought good credentials to the project. He had directed several films in the 1930s and '40s and episodes of a number of popular television shows, including the *Twilight Zone* and *Alfred Hitchcock Presents*.

No explanation was found for Lord's decision to pass on the lead, but Laurent's *Washington Post* story said he had "resolutely declined" the role. Lord's name is also marked through as producer. Another notation on the October 14 memo says, "Tho [sic] Lord's original idea good, casting of Brand & elimination of older man weakened it. It now appears headed for syndication."[24]

Ever the hands-on businessman when it came to his intellectual property, Lord closed a deal with Don Fedderson in December 1959, indicating that he had no intention of appearing in the series. By August 18, 1960, he had sold it to Fedderson, two months before the indictment of casting Brand in the lead. In spite of the repeated lack of confidence in it, the project was set to move forward. Piloting was scheduled for November.[25]

Communication about the proposed series continued over the next four years as it bounced between ABC and NBC networks. In June of 1964 Fedderson reported that although he had a step deal with NBC, no writer had yet been assigned to a new script. A step deal allows a film producer the option to terminate a writer's services after any draft of the script. Secure with the financial agreement he had made with Fedderson in turning the concept over to him, Lord was out of the picture by then as the writer. Closing credits list Leonard Praskins and Milton Merlin as the writers for the teleplay.[26]

While *Tramp Ship* was making the rounds, Lord kept moving. In early May of 1960, he was in negotiations with French producer/director Raoul Levy for a starring role in *The Longest Day*, the story of the Normandy invasion. Levy was looking for 20 stars for leading roles for the projected $5,000,000 film.[27] When the film was released in 1962, Daryl Zanuck was the producer and Jack Lord was not among in the stellar cast. Sean Connery did have a role, and he reportedly cut it close to finish filming before going on to step into the James Bond part for *Dr. No*.

At the same time Lord was negotiating with Levy, writer/producer Robert Herridge had an innovative project stored in the vault at CBS—twenty-six plays in the can and ready to go. With his solid literary bent, Herridge was a bit of a Hollywood anomaly. A graduate of Northwestern University and the recipient of a poetry fellowship at the University of California, he applied his literary training to the new series. His intent for the *Robert Herrick Theatre* was to "take great stories they said we couldn't do on television," recreate stories by well-known classic authors, and do them as pure television. Herridge chose not to fill the casts with stand out film stars of the day. He would use only "distinguished and brilliant" television actors.[28] Jack Lord made the cut and was cast in an episode.

Herridge's "pure television" plays had been broadcast in Australia, Canada, and England where they garnered rave reviews, but American television audiences had not seen them. Herridge went on the road to promote the series, set to premier in the U.S. on October 9.[29] *The 1960 Annual Variety Review and Preview* ran an ad from CBS films announcing the availability to networks for first-run of the new series. Advanced reviews were promising, and the ad promised stories were already in the can by renowned writers such as John Steinbeck, Mark Twain, Edgar Allan Poe, and Plato.[30] Sources disagree on the original airdate of the episode starring Lord and Delores Dorn. It appears in some newspaper television listings for the week of March 20, 1961.[31] "A Song With Orange in It" is the story of a musical composer who is asked by his girlfriend to write lyrics that rhyme with orange.

Lord kept up his efforts to find a good role that would put him back on the Broadway stage. A production by A.E. Hotchner based on the works of Ernest Hemingway would go into rehearsals the week of September 12 and Lord was approached about a starring role. *Love and Death* was set to stage in January for the 1961 season, with a ten-week tour before the Broadway opening. Lauren Bacall was on the list of potential female leads.[32] By the following year, the title of the production had been changed to *A Pride of Lions* and Rod Steiger was cast in the lead. Attempts to confirm the reason for Lord's being dropped from consideration were unsuccessful. He was also later rumored to have a starring role in another Broadway production that apparently fell through. In the fall of 1963, he traveled to New York to work out a deal with Kermit Bloomgarden for a costarring role for *Side Show*, a musical production costarring Lee Remick.[33] A Tony Award winning production by that name was on Broadway in 1997. Attempts to verify an earlier version were unsuccessful.

Lord wrapped up the 1960 year in November with a guest-starring spot on the second season of Stirling Silliphant's *Naked City*. The series has a *Dragnet* feel with a documentary style format and it spawned the popular series *Route 66*. An earlier thirty-minute format of *Naked City* had been cancelled, but in late October ABC approved funding to make another run at it with some cast changes and an expanded hour-long offering. Another on-location format production, the series was filmed in New York City.

Lord did a good job in his role as Cary Glennon in "The Human Trap," airing November 30. Although it was yet another bad guy role, this one had some layers to it and he played it well. When an obnoxious small-time hood winds up dead in Glennon's ex-wife's apartment, he comes to the aid of her and their out-of-control daughter. While the main plotline is primarily working toward the reveal of the true murderer, much of the story revolves around the fractured family relationship. Glennon stoically endures the verbal abuse of his ex and her stubborn refusal to allow him to come to her aid while showing his tender side in caring for his daughter.

Even though he had no movie roles that year, Lord's filmography got a boost in 1961 when he logged guest-starring appearances on first season episodes of six new television shows. He went to work the last week of December filming an episode of *Route 66*, the *Naked City* spin-offer series. "Play It Glissando" was written by Silliphant and was set to air in January. Producer Herb Leonard cast Lord in the role of a temperamental jazz musician who holds his wife emotionally hostage with his paranoid fear of losing her. He is both pathetic and repulsive as he struggles to keep her within eyeshot.

His last television appearance for 1959 was a guest-starring role in "Father Image," an episode of *Alcoa Presents One Step Beyond*, an anthology series that ran on ABC for three years. Reminiscent of Rod Serling's *Twilight Zone*, the stories dealt with a variety of paranormal activities, all supposedly based upon actual events. Lord plays Daniel Gardner, a bitter law school student who receives an unusual inheritance from his father's estate. He finds out the old man was the owner of a burlesque theatre. When he goes to inspect the boarded-up building, he is inexplicably transported back in time. He soon learns that his father had kept some very dark secrets. Episode costar Ian Wolfe is well-qualified for the role. According to the press release for the episode, Wolfe was "considered one of the entertainment world's leading authorities on comparative religions and one of its foremost student of psychic phenomena."[34]

The episode includes a scene where Lord breaks down in tears and, as he did three years earlier in a *Studio One* episode, he does it well. Seeing him do highly emotional scenes was rare in those early days; perhaps it is because the "heavy" doesn't get many opportunities to cry. There is a memorable scene from an episode in the first season of *Hawaii Five-O* in which McGarrett breaks down following the death of his infant nephew, and Lord gives an exemplary performance.

On December 29, he signed with Producer Frank Telford to go to work on January 4 for a segment of *The Americans*, a new series set during the Civil War. It revolved around two brothers who fought on opposite sides. "Half Moon Road" would air on NBC February 27. February and March were busy months for Lord. He was at Four Stars Studios on February 1 filming an episode of ABC's *Stagecoach West*, and that same week he was in Arizona to film a second episode. The first week of March he appeared in *Outlaws*, a western series chronicling the adventures of an Oklahoma lawman. During the first season, the format was a diversion from the usual offerings in the genre. The stories were told from the point of view of the criminals. With the second season, the point of view changed and viewers saw the story through the eyes of the lawmen. In "The Bell" Lord was cast in the role of Jim Houston. Houston had just been released from prison when he encounters a deputy escorting a brutal killer to jail. He joins the two men as they try to get ahead of a coming blizzard.

Lord signed on for a second guest-starring spot on *Rawhide*, set to air on March 31. In "Incident of His Brother's Keeper," he is cast as Paul Evans, a wealthy cattle rancher who has been crippled in an accident and is confined to a wheelchair. He works again with Susan Oliver as his unfaithful wife who is plotting to run away with his brother.

The promising momentum he gained the first three months of the year abruptly slowed and it was mid-August before he picked up another job. He was signed to a guest-starring role in NBC's *Cain's Hundred*, another crime drama that lasted only one season. Peter Mark Richman, as Nicolas Cain, is a former mob lawyer turned federal agent who sets out to work his way through the list of the one hundred most wanted criminals in the country, vowing to capture them all. On November 21, Lord costarred with a young Charles Bronson in "Dead Load." When Lord was cast for the role in mid-August, the original title for the episode was "Thicker Than Water." The plot for the series followed Cain's pursuit of those responsible for brutal extortionist activities targeting longshoremen.[35]

As the Lords rang in the 1962 New Year, they could not have known the radical turn of fortune that lay before them. Before the year ended, Jack Lord would be a household name.

Seven

The Standard by Which All Others Are Measured

On New Year's Day, 1962, Jack Lord appeared in a guest-starring role for an episode of *Checkmate*, a promising new CBS series with a good Saturday night time slot. "The Star System" was filmed the prior November and he had the opportunity to work again with *Billy Mitchell* costar Elizabeth Montgomery. Cast regulars Sebastian Cabot, Anthony George and Doug McClure play private detectives who work for a San Francisco–like agency with a very unique mission—to stop crimes before they are committed. Lord plays Hollywood director Ernie Chapin, who is in a volatile relationship with a successful and self-destructive film star. The role is a good diversion from his recurring tough guy parts, and he plays it well, stoically enduring the troubled starlet's rage, her substance abuse, and her self-destructive bent.

At first glance, Lord's filmography for 1962 and '63 gives the impression he was stalled until early 1964. In fact, it was the point at which he finally reached the summit of his long climb. While it was not all good moving forward, there was a significant upswing in his career, beginning the week of October 5. The same week Jack Lord first appeared in a starring role for a brand new American television rodeo series, he also showed up on screen at the Pavilion in London appearing in the preview of a low-budget film bound for the history books.

When producer Albert "Cubby" Broccoli made the decision to bring Ian Fleming's James Bond character to the big screen, he launched an enterprise that dominated the action film market for decades. When 007 was introduced in 1953 in *Casino Royale*, the first of the Bond novels, the legendary British Secret Service agent was off and running. More than six decades later, the movies are still coming. The list of awards they have garnered and the considerable literary treatment of the Bond saga continues to grow. The tenacious success of Fleming's work supports the widespread appeal of one of the most enduring characters in modern literature, and his groundbreaking protagonist outlived him. Fleming also held the distinction of being President John F. Kennedy's favorite writer. Two of the Bond novels were published after his death, and a number of other writers picked up the character, giving rise to more 007 novels, short stories, and screenplays. Critical reactions to works beyond the originals vary, but Bond continues to thrive.

Canadian film producer Harry Saltzman had been in the business since 1945.

Although he produced several films with good literary quality, none came close to the level of financial and popular success he would realize once bitten by the Bond bug. After reading *Goldfinger*, he acquired the rights to bring 007 to film. Broccoli was also negotiating to option the Bond rights, and Saltzman joined forces with him. In 1961 the two established a holding company, Danjaq, S.A., to house the Bond copyright and Eon (*Everything or Nothing*) Productions. They endured several failed attempts to get a studio on board before United Artists President Arthur Krim agreed to a one-million-dollar budget for the film. After much debate and a complicated court battle, the decision came down that *Dr. No*, not *Casino Royale*, would be the first Bond movie.[1] *Dr. No* was published in 1958 and was actually the sixth book in the series. Despite his appearance in several of the Bond novels, the Felix Leiter character is not in the literary version of *Dr. No*. Fortunately for Jack Lord, the character was added to the film version.

Capturing the Leiter role proved to be a real feather in Lord's cap, and the timing for the Bond film couldn't have been better. A declining public affection for westerns, the genre that had comprised a significant part of Jack Lord's career up until that point, was impacting the business and a new genre was just the ticket. Paul Mavis, author of a comprehensive annotated filmography of more than 1,700 spy movies, aptly describes the shift. "An argument might be made that the spy film started to eclipse the Western in public tastes at this point; Westerns in the 1960s were increasingly bi-budget, getting away from their B-movie status. The low-budget spy film or spy spoof filled the marquees of double features and drive-ins, taking the place of the cowboy. As a result, spy films, regardless of the quality, became the defining genre of the 1960s, a position they had previously occupied during the short span of time between the two Great Wars."[2]

James Bond's first film appearance was of course not Lord's first experience with spy films. His 1949 debut movie in *Project X*, however, was a far cry from his latest spy flick. One obvious difference was the unexpected success of *Dr. No* and the cult following it spurred. It was unquestionably a qualified success. Commentary from distributors put it in perspective when the deal was struck to make the film. "All we can lose is $1 million."[3] As it turned out, loss of their initial investment would not be a concern. Domestic box office numbers hit $16,067,035, with international earnings netting $43,500,000.[4] It was a plum role for Jack Lord, and while the shoot would prove to be a tough one, there were some other unexpected benefits. *Los Angeles Times* reviewer Philip K. Scheuer made an interesting observation about Sean Connery's interpretation of 007, one that likely hit a happy chord with Lord. "Connery, as Bond, suggests a young Scotch Gary Cooper."[5]

A look at Lord's supporting character in the Bond stories shows he easily could have missed out on this pivotal role in his career. The film interpretation of Felix Leiter is a very different and fluid character from the recurring CIA agent in the Bond novels. Although Lord gets credit for originating the film version, it is Michael Pate who holds the distinction of bringing the first screen appearance of Bond's sidekick. The CBS television series *Climax Mystery Theatre* presented a one-hour interpretation of *Casino Royale* in 1954 with Pate in the Leiter role.

Dr. No would prove to be a tough gig. The Lords flew to Jamaica on January 10 to begin filming and they would be on location until March. He often talked about how difficult the work was. When they had been there about a month, he penned a four-page letter on Carib Ocho Rios Country Club stationery to Hedda Hopper, detailing the

From left: Jack Lord, Sean Connery, and John Kitzmiller (as John Kitzmuller) in a scene from *Dr. No* in 1962. Lord won kudos for his role as Felix Leiter and became the standard for future appearances of the character for the Bond franchise (United Artists/Photofest).

challenges of filming in Jamaica. "The problems of working on a location like this are endless. It is hard to believe that 600 miles from the mainland of the USA the difficulties are compounded to such an extent."[6]

He desperately missed the "clean, white catering truck" and the efficiency and quality of the food typically delivered on a Hollywood set. Food in Jamaica spoiled quickly, and it was often air-dropped onto the set by parachute. Lord confessed there were only two items that he could tolerate: "The ice cream, which I am practically living on and the beer which the crew loves."[7] When a call went out for dogs needed for a scene, there were no phone calls to trainers, who in Hollywood would have quickly delivered a variety of canines from which to choose. An advertisement of the need in the local paper for *Dr. No* produced a parade of cats, burros, sheep, and mongooses—but no dogs. An electric generator was flown in from Tampa, Florida. Broccoli had to fly the film to London to be processed, and rushes were then flown back for review. There was a lot of exasperating hurry up and wait during the production.

There were some redeeming experiences, however. The same week he penned his frustrated letter to Hopper, the philanthropist in Lord kicked in when he took part in a charitable event to benefit the locals. The prior October, the surrounding area where cast and crew were filming had been hit by Hurricane Hattie. The storm turned west before it reached Jamaica, but not before it wreaked havoc in the surrounding area, especially in Belize and British Honduras. The devastation was massive. On February 5, a benefit was held at Montego Bay to raise money to aid the victims. Lord worked the event, as did Sean Connery and Ursula Andress. In their later years, the Lords' charitable efforts were extensive, and the number of causes they supported throughout their lives and beyond is impressive.

Jack and Marie Lord were the only Americans among the cast and crew. He confessed to Hopper they were enjoying the experience very much, but he admitted the challenges they were facing made them appreciate home more. He expressed his fear if Hollywood "Union feather-bedding and waste" were not eliminated, the European studios, particularly those in Rome, stood to capture a leadership position in filmmaking. Lord closed his letter to Hopper by saying word was out that his new series, *Rodeo U.S.A.*, was sure to be a hit.

Still keeping his up his constant vigil for other opportunities, Lord made a return trip from Jamaica on February 21. Word hit the papers that he was up for a lead role in Producer Sy Bartlett's *Sergeant Banning and the Gathering of Eagles*, a film set during the Cold War. It received an Oscar-nomination when it came out the following year with a shortened title, *A Gathering of Eagles*, and Rock Hudson, not Jack Lord, was in the starring role.[8]

Most of the filming for *Dr. No* took place at an offshore location called Crab Key, and near the end of February, some of the work was at Pinewood Studios in England. Marie of course had accompanied him to Jamaica, and it seems the Lords were well thought of by the rest of the cast. Ursula Andress was virtually an unknown at the time, but she would later credit her role in *Dr. No* and the legendary white bikini she wore in her first scene as a fundamental factor in her rise to fame.

In an interview for a documentary included on a 50th anniversary DVD of the movie, Andress spoke of her memories of Jack and Marie Lord. "We were a small production and it was fabulous. It was like a family.... Jack Lord I remember with his wife he came into Jamaica—they were both there. I remember that. Always they were well, properly dressed very chic, very, very, very nice.... He was very helpful, very nice. There was no one was engaged in himself, ahead of importance, more important than the other one."[9]

Zena Marshall in the role of the double-crossing Miss Taro remembered Lord in much same way. "I was quite fond of ... Jack Lord," she said. "[He] was very, very concerned about other people. I do remember that he liked his right profile. He really liked being at an angle from the right and I thought he made his demands and I think if you look at *Dr. No*, not all but most of the shots are from the right side.... He again was very helpful ... and he was quite a friendly person."[10]

Marshall's observation that Lord favored his right side when in front of the camera was an astute one. In a 1969 letter to CBS Press Information Director Michael Buchanan Lord spelled out detailed directions regarding the use of some promotional photos for *Five-O* that had been sent for his approval. "[P]lease convey this to ... anyone who has anything to do with pictures of me—DO NOT FLIP THE NEGATIVE AND USE OPPOSITE

SIDE. [Caps in original]. Use them as they are shot—the hair is dressed to my right side when looking at them. Or, to put it another way, the part is on my left side. Again, please make this clearly understood."[11]

The following week, Lord penned another letter to Buchanan, emphatically expressing his dissatisfaction his clear directive about his profile shots had not been followed. "Mike, will you please note that some of Wynn Hammer's stuff has been mounted incorrectly. In other words, the emulsion side is not up. As explained in a previous letter my hair should always be dressed to the right side and when they flip a picture it distorts my features. I wish you would make this clear to your New York office and anyone else concerned with the project that pictures should be used as they are shot."[12]

Peter Hunt directed *On Her Majesty's Service* and later served as editor for five of the 007 films. He agreed that Jack Lord was the best choice for the role of Felix Leiter and he also spoke of his congenial presence during the shooting. "Jack Lord was a very fine supporting actor in those days. Nice man and ideal for the character he played. I'm sorry he didn't go on to play the character in other films, but by the time we were making the other film he was busy doing his own stuff and he had become too big for us."[13] Lord developed a reputation for raising his asking price, and it was a practice that sometimes cost him roles, but he held his ground in spite of the result. Director Terrence Young said although he wanted Lord, his success in the role had raised his price for future appearances. "The picture did him too much good."[14]

When it comes down to it, Lord nailed the Felix Leiter role and he held his own working alongside Sean Connery. Overall, critics liked the film, but they missed the mark in failing to project the cult classic status it would earn. *Daily Variety* got it exactly right. "As a screen hero James Bond is clearly here to stay. He will win no Oscars but a heck of a lot of enthusiastic followers."[15]

Blogger Donald W. Pfeffer's validation of Lord as the quintessential Leiter cuts to the chase. "Just look at him.... [He] has as much of a way with the ladies as Bond. Jack Lord is a fantastic actor who is a major star in his own right, so casting him as Bond's American counter-part made him stand out as something of an equal instead of the second banana he turned into in some of the later films."[16]

One of the more creative reviews of Lord's performance was written by writer/producer/filmmaker Paul "Sully" Sullivan for his blog, *Sully Baseball*. Sullivan draws a delightful parallel between hiring a baseball team manager and casting for *007*. "These two jobs seem super glamorous, don't they?" he writes. "And yet being the manager of Marlins ... or playing the part of CIA agent Felix Leiter has shockingly little job security and most people forget the parade of people who had the position." He ranks full-time Marlins managers alongside the corresponding successful portrayals of Leiter, pairing Jim Leyland and Lord in first place. "From his first appearance in the airport in *Dr. No* Lord was perfect ... [He] was handsome, tough, cool and even could exchange barbs with Connery's Bond. He truly did seem like Bond's American equal.... Not having more Connery/Lord Bond films was our loss."[17]

Lord's fan base increased substantially after *Dr. No* and the concurrent success of *Stoney Burke*. Included among Hedda Hopper's papers is a 1963 clipping of an article she wrote for the *Chicago Tribune* in which she refers to *Dr. No* as a "comedy." Attached to the clipping is a note from a reader in California who points out the inaccuracy in her article. He gives his rationale for the importance that she makes it right. If Lord is "going to play in *Goldfinger* ... naturally they want Jack Lord, she should stand corrected."[18]

Fans and critics looked forward to Lord reprising his Leiter role in future Bond films. The first week of January 1963, Lord reportedly signed a two picture deal with Broccoli and Saltzman, but it was not to be. *Goldfinger* was set to begin filming in England in the spring and plans were already on the drawing board for *Thunderball*.

Several sources indicate the reason Lord was replaced was that his in-character presence was too suave and sophisticated, so much so to raise concern he might overshadow James Bond. Others indicated his being dropped from plans for future films in the series was because he wanted more money and equal billing with Connery. Whatever the reason, he did not appear in any future 007 movies. Seven different actors have filled the role since *Dr. No*.

In the meantime, Lord was picking up some good press and he was getting the attention of some people who could do something with his potential to rise to the next level. ABC-TV President Tom Moore listed him as one of two "solid talents" who were getting attention. Moore expressed a preference for developing new talent to fill roles in upcoming series rather than turning to already well-established stars. "Television," he said, " gets its own vitality from the stars which it produces."[19]

A promotional event for the May 8 U.S. release date for *Dr. No* was held in Los Angeles mid–March and the cast, including Lord, was present. He told reporters in attendance he was planning to "summer away" from *Stoney Burke*, when he traveled to Europe to film *Goldfinger*.[20] Although his role in *Goldfinger* did not come to fruition, he was in Europe during the month of March, but he was involved in other projects. In early April, a rumor floated in the press that Lord and Chuck Connors were being considered for parts in a new Doris Day film, *Move Over Darling*. Connors made the cut, but Lord was not included in the final cast. At the end of month, the story broke that Lord had purchased the film rights to C.O. Bolton's novel *Watch Over Your Land*.

As he was enjoying the critical acclaim for the Bond film, his name appeared on a proposal for a new MGM series set to air for the 1964–65 season. Leonard Freeman was producer and writer for *Grand Hotel*, a drama based on a 1931 film by the same name. The original had a stellar cast that included Joan Crawford, John Barrymore, and Greta Garbo. The remake was set in a San Francisco hotel and arrangements were already in place to shoot in the luxurious Fairmont Hotel. Barry Sullivan was cast in the starring role for the pilot episode as the hotel manager, and Chad Everett would play his assistant. Everett later starred as dashing surgeon Dr. Joe Gannon in *Medical Center*, a CBS series that ran for seven seasons.

In December of 1963, Lord had a guest-starring role in the failed pilot, and it turned out to be a fortuitous experience in the long run. Internal communication tracks the long and winding road of the proposed new MGM series. The concept was set before NBC the prior May, and the response out of the gate was mixed. The West Coast division pronounced the idea of a show set in a luxurious San Francisco hotel "quite dull," the New York programming execs were "slightly higher" on the idea. By June, it looked as though they were close to a deal. The network made a step deal with MGM by the first of August. In a change of direction, NBC marked it dead by the end of October, but MGM and Freeman held on and it wound up back at NBC after they saw Freeman's script. Jack Lord and Gina Rowlands traveled to San Francisco for guest starring spots. The made-for-television movie did not make it past the pilot stage; by July 1964, all three networks had passed and it was officially dead.[21]

At the same time *Grand Hotel* was running the circuit, MGM was in full swing with work on several pilot episodes for the '64–65 season. One of the projects on the table was a new spy series for NBC originally billed as *Solo*. It would take advantage of the rising popularity of the spy genre, and this one would offer a futuristic twist, replete with an abundance of ahead-of-its-time gadgets and technology. Rumors floated that Jack Lord was in line for the lead. When the series launched, however, it had undergone a title change and a different leading man. Lord turned down the lead in the series, saying he thought the proposed new title, *The Man From U.N.C.L.E.*, was awful.[22] Robert Vaughn stepped into the leading role, and the series held strong for four years. Lord had a guest-starring role in a fourth season episode, however. Lord's last television appearance for 1962 before the October premier of *Stoney Burke* was a guest spot May 18 with host Art Linkletter on NBC's *Here's Hollywood*.

Eight

The Most Successful Flop in History

Before he left for Jamaica to film *Dr. No*, Jack Lord sealed an offer from Leslie Stevens for his first starring role in a television series. *Rodeo U.S.A.* was a one-hour modern day western about a bronc rider's quest for the golden buckle prize. Hedda Hopper broke the news. "When I was in New York," she wrote, "producer Cubby Broccoli told me he was going to make a picture in Jamaica the end of January called 'Doctor No.' Now he's chosen our own Jack Lord to play an American member of the C.I.D. in this spy story. When he's finished Jack will go right into a one-hour TV series by Leslie Stevens called 'Rodeo U.S.A.' ABC made the pilot and bought the package."[1]

The story led her column in papers across the country that week. As always, Lord was grateful to Hopper for the ink, and he wasted no time telling her so in a heartfelt handwritten letter. "Whenever I read a headline that has my name in it (the few times that it has happened) or a story about me, I always try to apply the advice Robert Frost gives," he wrote. He copied the full text of Frost's poem "Someone" into the body of the letter, telling Hopper he was well aware of the truth that good press was the "bricks and mortar" that led to name-value in his business. "Name-value," he said, "is the launching pad from which rockets to the stars take off. For every boulder, brick, stone or pebble that you have added to my launching pad I am grateful—very grateful indeed. You have always been a good friend, through the lean and hard years, and there have been plenty of those. I shall not forget your friendship."[2]

By the late 1950s and early '60s, television audiences had clearly expressed their desire to see something other than another western. A December 1959 Schwerin Research study showed 368 of 800 people surveyed complained that there was a saturation of westerns in TV programming.[3] Leslie Stevens, however, was banking on women viewers still showing a solid interest in the genre. He also knew that even though the appeal was declining, westerns still ranked higher overall than the general program average.

Jack Lord admitted he had grown weary of westerns, but Stoney Burke promised to be a character with conceivable depth, one that would give him the wherewithal to stretch himself as he had wanted to do for so long. Set in modern times, it was a departure from standard period western roles, and he was not only up to the task, he was clearly excited about it.

Turning down roles that later proved to be very good for the actors who took them made for a tough journey, but he stood firm on his commitment to do it his own way. He had passed on the role of Dr. Ben Casey, a career maker for Vince Edwards, and he passed on Flint McCullough in *Wagon Train*, a role Robert Horton held from 1957 until 1962. Hedda Hopper later asked Lord if he felt he had been a "bad guesser" in refusing the roles, considering those series had made the actors who took them rich and famous. Lord instantly shook his head and responded, "I was just determined to play lead roles in films.... I have no regret about 'Casey' because I couldn't work in an atmosphere of misery every day if you paid me all the money in the world."[4] His rationale for passing on the *Wagon Train* role was he felt westerns were "tired."

In an earlier letter to Hedda Hopper in which he talked at length about the production difficulties of filming for the Bond movie, he closed with a postscript. "Looks like 'Rodeo U.S.A.,' the series in which I am starred, is a hit. Since I've been down here, the rough-cut has been seen and so far I've gotten enthusiastic cable from Dan Melnick of ABC (they put up most of the dough for the pilot), Dick [illegible] of ZIV–VA (they put up the rest), and from Sam Weisbord of Wm Morris. Feels good."[5]

Back home in the states after *Dr. No*, he strapped on the spurs and climbed back in the saddle as he geared up for *Stoney Burke*. It was not the movie role he so desperately wanted, but this ride would prove to be much more than just bronc busting. He was grateful for the work, and he continued to articulate his intention to be taken as a serious and versatile actor. Lord shows up in the "Leading Men" section of the 1962 *Players Guide* directory. The entry lists him as a member of AEA, AFTRA and SAG, under exclusive management with the William Morris Agency. His profile lists only one credit: "Star of *Rodeo U.S.A.*"[6]

Lord told Hopper, "Leslie Stevens of Daystar Productions called and said he knew I didn't want a series—he'd heard it from everybody, but he wanted me to read the script.... I'd once read for one of his plays on Broadway and didn't get the part. This character is an idealistic, laconic cowboy. When I read the script my heart actually began to pound. I knew it was as close to perfection as you could get in TV. The character had all the qualities I'd outlined—strength but with gentleness—the character had a lot of range. It's a modern cowboy in a modern environment—he goes with the rodeo from town to town."[7]

He was delighted *Stoney Burke* would give him an opportunity to finally show his range as an actor, and he was philosophically and experientially a good match for the character. He believed that his unique life experiences were perfect preparation for the role, and critics later agreed. Stoney Burke had "the toughness of a sailor who has to learn how to fight, the gentleness of an artist, the naiveté of a farm boy, the integrity of country people."[8] Jack Lord's summers on his grandparents' horse farm once again proved to be a valuable asset. Even though it felt right to him on so many levels, as was his custom, he did his homework before he stepped into the role. "I visited a lot of rodeos to get the feel of the part. I learned there are about 365 rodeos held in this country every year, and that is the largest spectator sport for Americans after baseball, football, and basketball."[9]

Pitches to sponsors validated Lord's perception of the potential success of a rodeo series and they put their faith in his ability to deliver. "*Stoney Burke* comes on strong

Rodeo cowboy Stoney Burke was one of Lord's favorite characters, and when he read the proposal for *Hawaii Five-O*, he said he found the same qualities in McGarrett that he loved in Stoney Burke. Although *Stoney Burke* lasted only one season, Jack Lord's keen business sense made him a very rich man (ABC/Photofest).

with authentic rodeo sight and sound, with plenty of story muscle and with one Jack Lord in the lead. For this new talent, a meteoric rise to top TV popularity, Efrem Zimbalist and Vince Edwards fashion, is in the cards. Whatever it takes to make it big, Stoney Burke has it. Big."[10]

Howard Eaton, Vice President for Programming in the broadcasting department of Grey Advertising Agency, agreed the modern day format for the western had promise. "This next year the contemporary western will come into being. As far as television is concerned, this is a new type of show. The three new ones are *Empire*, *Stoney Burke*, and *Wide Country*. They all have considerable merit."[11] ABC Vice-President Thomas W. Moore concurred, expressing confidence in two new programs set for certain success for fall and winter. "'*The Jetsons*, slated for Sunday night viewing, and *Stoney Burke*, a Monday night entry. These are genuine sleepers,' Moore enthused."[12]

Even though the press was mostly encouraging, there were some naysayers. John Shanley reported in the *New York Times* that while ABC's latest offering might hold some fascination for those who could abide a weekly one-hour diet of broncos, steers, and riders, the appeal looked to be "narrowly limited."[13]

On the production side, the partnership between Leslie Stevens and Jack Lord just worked, and Jane Ardmore clearly saw it. "From the moment these two men met, they recognized in each other the dedication to the highest ideals of artistic integrity that makes them so alike. From their first meeting Jack Lord became Stoney Burke."[14]

Stevens just knew that in Jack Lord he had found the right fit for the complex character. He knew what Lord could do, and he knew the part was the opportunity the driven actor sought for his career. He said the words Lord had waited so long to hear from Hollywood. "Jack is an actor of extremely wide range. He's tough as horseshoe nails, a street fighter with a brooding, almost Irish-poetic quality.... But there's gentleness in him, a haunted feeling. And still, as Stoney Burke, he has broken noses all over his face."[15]

Lord quickly picked up on the starting point for developing the Stoney character as he perceived it. "I thought of [Gary Cooper] many times while I was the creating the character. Stoney had many of the qualities Coop reflected. He was honest, forthright; his work meant something, his handshake meant something. And there was great compassion in him."[16] Lord's layered interests were a good match for the character as Stevens had envisioned him, and the press picked up on it. Columnist Bob Thomas saw it first hand during an interview in Lord's dressing room. "The casual visitor would scarcely expect to see books of Renior and Van Gogh in the dressing room of Jack Lord ... but they are there."[17]

Even though he really wanted to do more movies and less television, he couldn't resist the story lines for *Stoney Burke* and the opportunity to capture a character that ran well beyond the adventures of a modern day cowboy. "We're trying to get away from the rodeo and get into good thematically solid stories," he said. He felt his and Stevens' motives were far-removed from their counterparts in television. "What we're trying to do is say something to gently lift the moral tone of society. We have a responsibility to ennoble and enlighten as well as entertain. No two people are more dedicated than we are.... I finally found what I was looking for in this series," he said.[18]

A chance for some serious artistic work was not the only windfall. The venture resulted in a dramatic change of fortune for Jack Lord—literally. The deal he landed was an early application of his soon to be famous hands-on approach to the business side of his career. It was a practice that added to his reputation as a difficult and headstrong artist, and it made him a very rich man. As a full partner in *Stoney Burke*, he earned $3,500 a week for his work. *The Hollywood Reporter* said he had also signed a three-way, five-year million-dollar contract with Daystar, Ziv-United Artists and ABC-TV.[19] Less than a month after the first episode aired, Lord told a reporter for the *New York Tribune*, "When I talked with Leslie Stevens, I told him I suffer from the disease called perfectionism. I'm not in the business just to make money."[20] It was an interesting statement, considering that time and time again, throughout the next eighteen years of his career, Jack Lord would show that while he was clearly serious about his art, he was also a shrewd businessman who did not hesitate to hold out for what he felt he deserved for his work.

Stoney Burke was a valuable experience for him as he was configuring how he would run his career moving forward. He could not have known in those early days that his legacy would ultimately be defined by a single role, and that when it was all said and done, he would be remembered for his work in television. *Stoney Burke* was perfect training ground for the rigors of *Hawaii Five-O,* and it gave him a quick education in the brutal schedule of a television series star. "I've never worked so hard," he said. "I get up at 4:30 in the morning and I work until 8:30 at night."[21] Six years after the boot camp experience of *Stoney Burke* ended, Lord kept the same grueling schedule for the entire twelve-year run of *Hawaii Five-O*. After he had been in it a few years, he frequently commented on just how exhausted he was. Robert Dowdell commented on the pressure Lord put on himself when he was working. "He is very serious, doesn't kid around too much, and is a perfectionist in seeing that things are done right in the show, beginning with his own role. He works hard to achieve that perfection, and drives himself so hard that sometimes at the end of the day you can see the fatigue written in his face."[22]

Production for *Stoney Burke* utilized extensive location work. None of the episodes were filmed in a studio, so Lord was routinely picked up at 6:45 a.m. and driven 40 or more miles for the day's work. While location shooting offers some advantages over studio filming, such as more realistic settings, it's a tough gig. "If we want a farmhouse, we find one," Lord said. Location work can be less expensive than large studio set construction, but it is not without its own unique pitfalls. Obvious downsides, such as the lack of control of environmental factors like weather and local governmental regulations, create challenges. His sustained experience with location work on *Stoney* was excellent preparation for the unique production needs of *Hawaii Five-O*.

The show began filming on June 13, 1962. "I couldn't be more enthused about *Stoney Burke*," Lord said. "It's not a routine western; I don't even carry a gun! It's a fine drama series, sensitively and lovingly written, and why shouldn't it be? Leslie Stevens ... is our producer-writer-director! Any actor would give his right arm to star [in] a series under his supervision. I consider myself mighty lucky!"[23]

He was clearly excited about his new starring role and he had good reason. This was not a "true western," and it was not the movie work he preferred, but it was a fresh subject and he was intrigued. "Rodeo competition is one part of the cowboys' life that TV has pretty much left alone," he said. "It gives us a microcosm that embodies all the hopes, fears, loves, hates, frustrations and triumphs of life itself. We can go anywhere in the country, and we can use any kind of story theme."[24]

Anticipation of success for the upcoming series was running high. Jack Lord's name was turning up in papers all over the country, and critics were predicting a hit. An added attraction for the star was the assurance that he had at long last landed a role that would get him out of the tough guy rut. *Atlanta Constitution* columnist Paul Jones said, "The name Jack Lord might be unfamiliar to those who have not seen him as a heavy in the many television shows he has appeared in. But the name likely will become familiar to millions before the next season is over.... Jack Lord's personality might be just the right thing to turn '*Stoney Burke*' into a hit show. If it isn't a hit, I will be sadly surprised — and so will lots of other people who have talked to Lord and witnessed filming of the show."[25] In August word came down that *Stoney Burke* had been bought in Canada where it would premier the same day it was set to start in the U.S.

As Jack Lord worked on evolving into Stoney Burke, he drew from his training under Meisner and from what he had learned watching method acting as applied by his idol, Gary Cooper. He told Jane Ardmore, "Talk of method—to dissolve to the essential, the ability to come alive under imaginary circumstances. Acting is behavior; how you do what you do is characterization. The way you do it. [Cooper's] instinct or sense of truth pulled him back when he might have been forced to do something he felt was not right. The qualities that Cooper had were the kind of qualities that I admire as a human being, this great combination of strength and gentleness and this kind of quality he has I saw as the qualities of Stoney Burke."[26]

An interesting aside Ardmore incorporated into her interview notes reveals Lord's reluctance to have his admiration and emulation of Cooper's style repeated in print. He suggested maybe they shouldn't continue the conversation and that his comments shouldn't be part of the article. "My friendship with Cooper has had strange repercussions and has been thrown back at me through an article in *TV Guide* where the writer I think was being rather snide."[27] He was referencing the article by Alan Gill from the November 17, 1962, issue, Lord's first *TV Guide* cover. Lord's comments that his image of "Coop," based on what he called a marvelous combination of great strength and great gentility—"tough as steel, soft

Stoney Burke gave Jack Lord his first of three *TV Guide* covers in November 1962 (*TV Guide Magazine* cover courtesy of TV Guide Magazine, LLC © 1962).

as fog," would be used over and over again for years as evidence of Jack Lord's inflated ego. Gill quoted an unnamed actor who criticized Lord for having a "Renaissance-man" complex, declaring he could be great if he would concentrate on one thing with complete honesty. While the overall focus of the article projected the promising potential that *Stoney Burke* and its star had for success, Lord was deeply offended by the attack on his personal character. It would not be the last time he would take issue with a *TV Guide* article that relied on character assassination. For the most part, however, the press about the show was good. *The Los Angeles Times* predicted that Jack Lord and *The Beverly Hillbillies* blonde star Donna Douglas were shoe-ins for "stars of tomorrow."[28]

While Lord was in Washington for an appearance as part of the press junket for the show, Lawrence Laurent once again paid homage to his friend in his *Washington Post* column on the Friday before the upcoming Monday premier. Laurent traced the roots of the series back to what he termed a "rough relationship" between Leslie Stevens and rodeo world champion Casey Tibbs. Tibbs was much more than just inspiration for the show, however. He played himself in the series, and he served another very vital function in the production.

While Jack Lord was generally able to put his horsemanship to good use in filming, Tibbs definitely had the hard part when it came to the riding sequences. Lord sat the horse in the chute and for a moment or two after the gate was opened. Then Lord came off the bronc and Tibbs got on. The horses didn't buck while Lord sat on them because they had been "flanked," or equipped with a strap that induces bucking when it is pulled tight. When his fans asked if he did all the riding in the show, as they frequently did, he told them that he was contractually forbidden from doing the dangerous stunts.

Jack Lord's climbing off the horse before the bucking began did not save him from some close calls, however. The inherent hazard in rodeo guarantees injury is likely, no matter how well choreographed the stunts or how capable the stand-ins and stunt crew. Although there are some minor discrepancies among published accounts of the incident, Lord had one particularly terrifying close call. Some versions report it happened during filming of the first episode. During a personal appearance in Independence, Missouri, more than a year after the series was off the air, Lord told his version to a local paper.

He said the incident occurred during his second rodeo scene. He mounted the bronc with no trouble, but for some reason, the horse unexpectedly began to buck in the chute, likely due to having been "stung by a bee or cinched too tight," according to Lord. The horse continued to rear, slamming him repeatedly into the side of the chute. Finally, someone thought to open the chute and the horse ran out into the arena, with Lord hanging on for dear life until he could dismount.[29] Versions of the incident in several contemporary fan magazines reported Lord was knocked unconscious as the cast and crew worked to get him off the horse and out of the chute. Whatever the level of severity of the incident, it was a disconcerting one for both him and for the witnesses, and it powerfully brought home the reality of how frequently rodeo cowboys are in harm's way.

Lord was deeply impressed with Casey Tibbs' resilience and professionalism, calling him one of the finest men he had ever met. There can be no doubt that he drew heavily from him and from the other rodeo professionals on the cast and crew for his portrayal of Stoney. In November of 1962, Tibbs was injured during a rodeo in San Francisco and Lord called him at the hospital to see how he was doing. Tibbs replied, "Oh, I'm fine.

The doctors think I have a broken back but I know I haven't because the minute they left the room I got up and walked around."[30]

Tibbs' production company did all the rodeo sequences for the series, and Lord carefully studied his speech patterns as he worked to soften his Brooklyn accent for the role of a South Dakota cowboy. In the end of the series, when Stoney has missed out on the golden buckle, he asks his friends who won the national championship. They tell him Casey Tibbs took the prize.

The cast and crew of the newest series set for ABC's fall lineup was impressive. Replete with past, present, and future legends across the board, it would, however, also prove to be a volatile mix. Stoney had three constant companions and all three roles were beautifully cast. Before production began, Leslie Stevens told Warren Oates he had a character he wanted him to play in a pilot and Oates agreed. The outrageous Vesper Painter, Stoney's sidekick, plays like a part that could have been written for Oates; in fact, it was written for him. In her comprehensive biography of Warren Oates, author Susan Compo notes that Leslie Stevens said Ves Painter was his gift for the actor, and that he had grown the character by simply emphasizing Oates' innate personality.[31] Ves Painter's antics capture attention from the very first episode and he is a consistent scene-stealer. Oates is perfect as a frustrating but irresistible foil to Stoney's impeccable morals and self-deprecating demeanor. Oates and Lord shared a common career experience. Oates got a job in 1950 at Associates Discount Corporation, a car financing company in Louisville, Kentucky. Although he did not want to make it a permanent career, apparently Oates was a good salesman. Compo says, "[Oates] had the gift of gab and apprehensive buyers were put at ease by his banter as he guided them toward payment plans."[32]

Bruce Dern was cast in the role of E.J. Stocker. Just as the part of pacifist Stoney Burke was a departure from Jack Lord's customary role as the heavy, E.J. Stocker was not Dern's standard fare. Dern claims to have played more "psychotics, freaks and dopers" than anyone, but E.J. Stocker was none of those. As an even-tempered, dutiful, and competent chute boss, Stocker was often the quiet voice of reason. Dern would later say the scripts gave him little opportunity to do anything but stand in the background, readying Stoney's ride and waiting for him to give the "Let's dance" command that would signal opening the gate. Dern later talked about his reasons for leaving the series in his memoir. "The only person I could have hated in Hollywood was Jack Lord.... I didn't hate him, but I thought he was arrogant and pretentious.... I wasn't fired, but he would've fired me, I'm sure, if he had had the chance."[33]

Even with all *Stoney Burke* had going for it, the work was not without its problems. One constant fly in the ointment was the continued palpable tension between Lord and Bruce Dern. Slightly less than two months into the show, Dave Freeman led off his column with a report of the growing animosity between the two men. "The battles between 'Stony[sic] Burke' star Jack Lord and co-featured Bruce Dern are getting longer and louder. For that matter, most of the cast and crew are unhappy with Lord's manner and attitude."[34] Freeman didn't elaborate on the specific complaints of Lord's co-workers, but some of Dern's criticisms would be echoed again and again by other actors throughout the rest of his career. *Stoney* guest star Michael Anderson, Jr., told Compo that Dern hated Lord and that he made no effort to keep it a secret.

Dern claimed Warren Oates shared his dislike for Jack Lord, but never openly expressed his opinion on the matter. Anderson said Oates "wouldn't ever dis[respect] a fellow actor. He would just stay out of the way and do his own thing." Dern, however, was very transparent with regard to his feelings. He told Compo that Lord accused both him and Oates of scene stealing, a feat Dern considered to be impossible in light of the fact that he and the other three members of Stoney's entourage had "nothing to do" on the show. "He did not like the little people," Dern said. "And to him the little people weren't just the people behind the camera. They were people who weren't stars."[35] Bruce Dern left the series after seventeen episodes.

Stoney guest star Mariette Hartley told Compo that she had a memorable run-in with Lord on the first day of filming. He sternly reprimanded her for tripping over her lines. She had just gotten the script the night before and she was very nervous. She said Jack Lord cut her absolutely no slack as she struggled to get her lines correct. "What do you do when you're on stage?" he asked her. She responded that she customarily received her scripts a month before her performance, not the night before.

Hartley's experience with Jack Lord's determination to draw nothing less than perfection from everyone on the set would be replicated many times during production of *Hawaii Five-O*. His intolerance for unprepared actors became well known and he was frequently criticized for his insistence upon quality from regulars in the cast, guest stars, and local non-professionals who appeared on the show. Longtime *Five-O* series writer Jerome Coopersmith talked about Lord's high bar with his guest stars. "He was an uncompromising perfectionist who demanded that they arrive on the set on time and be letter-perfect in their lines—as he was. Those rules were sometimes ignored by guest stars who partied nonstop from the time they arrived in the islands. If they showed up late on the set with hangovers, not knowing their lines, Jack would berate them in front of the entire cast."[36]

Years later, as *Hawaii Five-O* rose to success, Warren Oates said although he may not have liked him personally, he had learned professionalism and discipline from him.[37] It was a concession others would also make after working with Lord.

Robert Dowdell played Cody Bristol, the youngest of the four regulars. Cody got off to a bad start with Stoney in the first episode, blaming him for an accident in the chute that killed his brother. By the second episode, however, he had seen the error of his ways, and like his counterparts, he embraced Stoney's campaign to do good wherever he was. He became a constant in Burke's tight circle of friends.

Dowdell apparently got along fine with Jack Lord. In a 1963 *TV Star Parade* article, Dowdell recounts the time Lord was slammed into the chute and what a frightening close call it was. It was Leslie Stevens who encouraged Dowdell to read for *Stoney Burke*. Dowdell talked about his initial impression of Lord when they first met at Leslie Steven's house for a read through of the first episode. "He impressed me as a very capable young leading man who could probably play just about any role.... It soon became apparent that Jack was doing a terrific job as Stoney Burke. That isn't surprising when you consider what a talented actor he is."[38]

Dowdell also had a different take on Lord's reputation for being aloof and for constantly demanding special accommodations while working. He said the cast was a tight bunch and they spent down time together, but Lord was never with them. "We all like and respect Jack but he keeps to himself," he said. He mentioned the rest of cast shared a car to work each day, but Lord rode alone, and he went on to explain the reason he chose not to ride with others. "[He] studies his lines in the car on the way out and also on the way back for the next day.... He works intensely at being a star, which he is.... After all, he worked hard to attain his present position." Dowdell said for the most part, the cast and crew liked him and admired him for working as hard as a "ditch digger." It was Dowdell's opinion that Marie was the reason Jack Lord could afford to be a loner. His take on Lord's on-the-job behavior, however, would not be the standard as his career and his celebrity status continued to grow.

Stoney Burke offered up a strong cast, good production work, and well-written scripts, and the show collected an impressive list of guest stars. Virtually every week the credits featured well-established performers, such as Robert Duvall, James Coburn, Leonard Nimoy, Harry Dean Stanton, Cloris Leachman, Ed Asner, Buck Taylor and Harry Carey, Jr. Oscar winner, stuntman, and rodeo champion Ben Johnson had a guest-starring role on *Stoney* in the fourth episode. He was the voice of the rodeo announcer for the full run of the series, and he often doubled for Jack Lord. Johnson had doubled for many of the western greats—John Wayne, Jimmy Stewart, and for Lord's idol Gary Cooper.

In September of 1962, a month before the debut of *Stoney Burke*, Daystar announced four of six pilots for the following year were *Stoney Burke* spin-offs. *Kincaid* was about a police officer that worked high profile homicide cases, but winds up assigned to the juvenile division. Internal ABC/United Artists communication tracks the unsuccessful progression of Stevens' concept, beginning October 16. By January 28, Dick Clark was down as the proposed star, and the print was set to be shipped to New York on February 4. The concept was stamped dead on March 3.[39] *Border Town* was the story of an American sheriff's interaction with a Mexican police officer. *Tack Reynolds* was set in the stock car racing arena.[40] The fourth concept, *Charlie Weapon*, was a one-hour adventure series about a weapons expert. Richard Basehart was in consideration for the lead.[41]

Trouble for cowboys coming out of the chute in the rodeo arena was not exclusive to the plot lines of *Stoney Burke*. While the concept of an insider's look at the life of a rodeo cowboy was a fresh one at the time, the show had some serious competition outside the arena. NBC opened the gate on its own take with a studio-filmed series called *Wide Country*. The show premiered on September 20, 1962, with Earl Holliman starring as Mitch Guthrie and Andrew Prine in the role of Guthrie's younger brother, Andy. While Stoney worked diligently to earn the golden buckle on ABC, giving it his all along the way to right the wrongs of the numerous troubled people he encountered, over at NBC Mitch was intent on keeping brother Andy out of the dangerous work of rodeo. *Wide Country* lasted for 28 episodes, ending April 25, 1963, one month and four episodes before *Stoney Burke* went off the air.

In February of 1963, after eighteen episodes of *Stoney Burke* had aired, Jack Lord sat down with Hedda Hopper to talk about the series and his future plans. He brought Dave Foster of Foster and Ingersoll PR firm with him. It was Hopper's first face-to-face meeting with Lord, and she described him as a quiet, rather soft-spoken man, the same observation made by many people after meeting him for the first time.

In the transcript of the interview she noted that he had brought with him a copy of the December 28, 1958, story she had written for the *Los Angeles Times* in which she named Jack Lord as one of the new faces. "I've saved this," he told her, as he placed it before her. "You went out on a limb when no one else was willing to do it. This came out right after the picture 'God's Little Acre' ... People won't stick their necks out to take a chance. When no one here knew me or cared about me, you stuck your neck out to choose me as one of the new faces and I appreciate that." He also told her during the interview that he had turned down *Cain's Hundred* and *Naked City*. "I had hoped I could make it without that kind of push."[42]

When *Stoney Burke* was at the halfway point of the season, Lord was pleased with the critical reviews and with the audience reactions. Dave Foster told Hopper that Jack Lord was getting an impressive amount of fan mail. He had brought along a letter from a little girl and Hopper copied it into her transcript: "How come you never fall off the horses? I like the show better when you kiss girls. I have a cat and a turtle—they watch your show too—never take their eyes off the TV. I am 11. My cat is named Ben Casey and the turtle is Stoney Burke."[43] Lord told Hopper he read all his fan mail, and that Daystar Productions had hired three girls who stayed busy answering the 1,000 letters per week he was receiving. It was far cry from his fan mail quota in 1956 when it Marie's job to answer all the letters for him. He was most pleased that much of the mail to "Stoney" was from parents, commending him and the show's producer on the integrity of the teachings their children were drawing from the stories.

Hopper included in her notes that Lord was wearing cowboy boots with his sports jacket, matching dress shirt and tie. "Do you wear those boots all the time?" she asked.

"Yes—they're comfortable. They cost $75 a pair. I have them in brown and black. I even wear them to New York. I am allowed just one eccentricity," he said.

It looked as though Stoney was primed to go for at least three seasons. The show was getting good press and it was pulling in very good audiences in spite of the competition's hard-to-beat line up. "The ABC series has managed a respectable rating against the CBS Monday night powerhouse (Lucille Ball, Danny Thomas, and Andy Griffith) and prospects look bright for a second season," declared the press.[44]

In spite of the widespread consensus promising a bright second season, ABC pulled the plug after 32 episodes. The last installment for *Stoney Burke* was ironically titled "The Journey." It is a powerful conclusion, and the writing and the acting are first rate. Ves Painter redeems himself, stepping up to help Stoney free a herd of used-up horses headed for the slaughterhouse. Included in the herd is Stoney's nemesis Megaton, the horse that couldn't be ridden and the bronc that inflicts the injury that keeps Stoney out of the finals. The symbolism runs deep throughout the storyline. Ves is at last involved in something that is not all about his own best interests. Stoney has been held prisoner by his consuming desire for the golden buckle, and Megaton is a reminder of the difficulty he has encountered in his quest. When he sets Megaton free, in a sense Stoney frees himself.

Los Angeles Times TV Editor Hal Humphrey wrote, "The failure of 'Stoney Burke' to get renewed for a second season certainly can't be blamed on its star, Jack Lord. He did everything a good TV hero is supposed to do, from touring the 15 Nielsen cities to small-talking the wives of the sponsors."[45] Lord's earlier comment about westerns being a "tired" medium proved to be a valid concern and the unique spin on the cowboy motif offered by the series couldn't save it. The show went into reruns for 17 weeks the summer after it was cancelled, due in part to Lord's continued promotion as he was out on the road for publicity and sponsor appearances. The business side of him fully understood the benefits of the legwork, even if the artistic part of it was over. "TV is an economic tool of business.... I had a share in 'Stoney Burke,' and I'm sure my cooperating with everyone the way I did made it possible for the series to be repeated this summer. I found out that TV is an art industry, not an art form, and you can't fight the commercialism of TV."[46]

Just as he would do when *Hawaii Five-O* was at its peak, however, he refused to do sponsor commercials for the show. Considering there were 15 different sponsors involved with the series, the financial benefits could have been well worth the effort. Lord took a strong stand against having his name attached to any commercial venture, a stance he held throughout his career. The show was sold to 216 stations after it went into syndication and it was dubbed in 15 languages and seen in 27 countries.

True to form, he began to look for the next opportunity. He had done his homework about the popularity of rodeos with the public. He knew Stoney Burke had become an iconic hero, and he was not ready to lay him down. He made preparations to take his show on the road. Lord's filmography for 1963 is sparse but it is definitely not a reflection of his productivity at the time.

The year had started off well. A January 25 letter from Quigley Publishing Company notified him that he was the recipient of the Achievement Award for "Most Promising New Male Star of Tomorrow." The award was the result of a poll conducted among TV editors, critics, and columnists. The winners would be announced in a number of business periodicals. The publicity was good, and it would get his name before some significant names in the industry.[47]

He hit the ground running once again and there was significant chatter about a variety of projects on the horizon. He had signed the two-picture deal with Cubby Broccoli for *Goldfinger* and *Thunderball*, unaware at the time that his series would not last beyond its inaugural season. He planned to travel to Europe to film *Goldfinger* during his summer hiatus from *Stoney Burke*.

In April, Lord made a statement to the press that would prove to be prophetically contradictory. In his Stoney Burke personae, he had been traveling about, talking to youth groups and school assemblies, presenting lectures on a wide range of topics from Hollywood celebrities to his favorite art. "I don't go for the rodeo circuit," Lord said. "I don't want to go into an arena riding a horse and shooting a gun. That's not my cup of tea."[48] He had a tremendous respect for the character and he was leery of doing anything that may detract from the dignity of Stoney Burke. Riding and shooting may not have been his cup of tea, but he did find a medium for the sawdust arena that, *Hawaii Five-O* aside, proved to be his most lucrative experience.

Lord was also associated with a number of projects that year that were not completed. *Daily Variety* announced at the end of January he had purchased the film and television rights to "Art for Art's Sake," a short story by Arthur Warren, with plans to collaborate with the author on the screenplay and to star in the film version.[49] No evidence the project ever came to fruition was found. In early 1963, he was reportedly being considered for the role of the big Texan in MGM's 1964 *The Unsinkable Molly Brown*, but he was not in the cast when production started.

Lord gained kudos other than more roles for his good work in *Stoney Burke*. In

1963, he was the recipient of a unique recognition and it was one that Stoney would have been honored to accept. The previous year the National Cowboy and Western Heritage Museum in Oklahoma City established awards categories to recognize individuals who made outstanding creative contributions to the legacy of the American West through film, television, music and literature. The award for Fictional Television Drama for 1963 went to "The Contender" episode of *Stoney Burke*, breaking *Rawhide*'s two-year run as the winner. Lord traveled to Oklahoma City to pick up the award at the spring presentation ceremony on April 4.

Lord had planned to go to Europe for three months to paint after he finished the final three episodes of *Stoney Burke*. He was still listed for a starring role in Rod Serling's *633 Squadron* that Serling had initiated in 1959. When the film premiered the following year, however, Lord was not in the cast. That same month he had purchased film rights to *Watch Over Your Land* and planned to work on a co-production deal with Producer/Director Tony Richardson while in Europe. He spent time in Madrid, where he was involved in talks with Dino DeLaurentiis. *Watch Over Your Land* didn't make to production, but Lord did meet with DeLaurentiis and Anthony Mann about a "Bible project," in May, so it could have been the same concept. DeLaurentiis later produced *The Bible in the Beginning* in 1966, but there is no evidence Lord was involved in that film.

Although Lord's business in Europe during May and June of 1963 was primarily for a two-month promotional tour for *Dr. No*, he let no grass grow under his feet while he was there. He filmed an appearance there in May for a starring role in a BBC-TV program, *One Guinea, Two Guinea,* set to air in July.[50] While in Rome he accepted an invitation to attend the San Sebastian Film Festival in Spain during the week of June 7–16. *Daily Variety* reported that on June 17, he exhibited some of his art in Madrid. In the same news item, Universal announced it would tie in recruiting with *Gathering of Eagles* via a specially designed color poster and booklet for recruiting centers and theatres. It is not clear whether Lord worked on these materials.[51]

It was not all work as he traveled about taking care of business, however. He and Marie took time to do some sightseeing during the trip, and, as he often did, he kept Hedda Hopper updated on the places they visited. It just so happened Hopper was in Spain in late May. She attempted to catch up with Jack and Marie while there, but they were on a sightseeing trip, traveling to Florence and Venice by train, and she had left by the time they returned. The Lords loved the trip, and he talked about their experience in a long letter to Hopper. "We took that marvelous new train up to Florence and I must say it was pleasant to gaze out of a train window again and be mesmerized by the green countryside flashing by. But I couldn't help thinking of all the unmarked American graves on that little stretch of Italy."[52]

While they were in Rome, Jack Lord got a unique reminder of just how popular *Stoney Burke* was during a tour of the Colosseum in Rome. A tourist there approached him and said, "What a place to hold a rodeo, eh, Stoney?"[53] That same week American papers reported that Lord was in negotiations for a two-picture deal with Dino DeLaurentiis and director Richard Fleishcher, one of which was "Sacco and Venzetti."[54] The film would chronicle the event of two Italian immigrants who are brought up on false charges and sentenced to death because of their political beliefs. DeLaurentiis made no movie by that title but there were films released on the subject in 1971 and again in 2006.

The Lords left Rome May 31, traveled to Madrid where they spent two weeks, and then made a brief visit to Paris. Before the Lords left Madrid, they sent Hopper a picture postcard of the Jockey Restaurant, penning they had just finished a "magnificent meal," and they wished she were there with them.

Lord sent Hopper another extensive letter from Paris in mid–June, penned on stationery from the Royal Hotel. In several pages, he talked mostly about ongoing or upcoming film projects in the area, dropping names of several prominent producers he had encountered, particularly Samuel Bronston. Bronston was known for epic films with expansive and elaborate sets, many constructed in Spain. Lord had visited the set for *Fall of the Roman Empire* while there, and he commented on the splendor of it to Hopper.

He confessed he likely sounded like a press agent for Bronston. "I can't help admiring the man. He's a doer. We could stand a few more doers in Hollywood and a few less producers who keep announcing projects that never materialize."[55] Ironically, one year later, Bronston filed for bankruptcy and he would soon be in court, facing federal charges for perjury. He was found guilty, but the conviction was overturned nine years later. Lord mentioned how much he anticipated Bronston's upcoming epic, *Isabella of Spain* with Sophia Loren in the starring role, but the film was never completed. While in Paris, Lord took in the art at the Louvre and then traveled to London the following Saturday for a week. They left for home on Saturday, June 22, and Lord was back to exploring his options.

In late August Lord was meeting in New York with officials from the World's Fair where he was reportedly finalizing a deal for what was about to come the next big thing for him—his rodeo act. He was fresh off negotiations with Bronston Yordan Harmon Marton for a role in *The Thin Red Line*, a World War II movie set to be filmed in Spain and based on a novel of the same name by James Jones. The film centered on the Battle of Guadalcanal and was remade in 1998. When the movie premiered in 1964, however, Lord was not in the cast. Lord authored an article for *Movie Life* magazine in December in which he told readers he was being considered for a role in an English film called *The Devil Came from Dublin*. There was a 1955 film by that name, but Lord was not in the cast.

The first week of October the story hit the papers that Jack Lord was in New York to work out a deal for a possible Broadway stage role. Tony Award winning producer Kermit Bloomgarden was looking to cast *Sideshow*, a musical production costarring Lee Remick. Lord had been taking daily voice lessons from renowned Hollywood voice coach Lillian Goodman and he was up to the task.[56] *Sideshow* never made the stage, but Lord's efforts at honing up his singing voice were not wasted.

Stoney Burke was over, but Lord found a way to continue riding the wave of Stoney Burke's enduring popularity, and the payoff was remarkable. When he took his show on the road, his personal appearances across the country with the rodeo circuits paid off remarkably well, especially for a project that grew out of a flop. He consistently drew large crowds, and with his earnings averaging some in the neighborhood of $200,000 a year, it was good for him and it was good for the rodeos. The work largely entailed his riding into the arena, opening up with his rendition of "The Strawberry Roan," doing a few rope tricks, and singing five or six more songs. The effort was well worth his time.

On one occasion he took home $27,000 for three appearances in one week. *The Atlanta Constitution* called it right: "We should all have such flops."[57]

Jack Lord the singer got himself a backup band from Nashville, with Charlie Aldrich and Joe and Rose Lee Maphis, one of country music's most successful couples, and made his debut rodeo. The composition of his band varied throughout his tenure. In August of 1963, Doyle Holly was part of the band, but he left when he was offered a spot behind an up-and-comer country crooner. Country legend Buck Owens was just getting started and Holly was offered a spot as a "Buckeroo." When he asked Joe Maphis if he should take the job, especially since the pay was less than he was getting as Stoney's bass player, Maphis replied, "Yeah, I think Buck is gonna amount to something. It might be a good job for you."[58] A year later "Stoney" was sometimes backed up by The Wanderers, with Rue Barclay as bandleader and electric bass player, Terry Brown on the guitar and Jimmy Lawton on rhythm.

Aldrich was leading the band in April of 1964 for an appearance in Shreveport. Lord took the opportunity before the record crowd to express his gratitude to his growing fan base. "I'm so happy to see all of you. God bless you for coming. I love you—I really do."[59] He had an opportunity to display his difficult side that night, when spotlighting wasn't right and the sound system was messed up. Instead, he took the high road when he talked to the audience. "My father used to say 'keep your sense of humor and you'll never get a big head.'" Local press complimented him on being so gracious in spite of the repeated technical difficulties.

While playing an event in Sidney, Iowa, Stoney shattered the 40-year attendance record, and it quickly became a trend as he traveled the country. Virtually every arena or fairground where Stoney Burke tossed his saddle over his shoulder and cocked his hip brought in record crowds, and Lord was pulling down a more than respectable income. The philanthropist in him already budding, he frequently showed up in school gymnasiums and other venues where his younger fans got the thrill of a lifetime; his appearance still shows up in school reunions and yearbooks as fondest memory for alumni during those years. He used the opportunity to encourage his young fans to refrain from bad habits, like smoking and drinking, and he took his position as a role model very seriously. He frequently told his younger viewers to stand strong against following the crowd and to hold to their own values. He said he despised advertising campaigns directed to young people that equated bad and unhealthy habits with success and prestige. "It grieves me to see athletes and other national figures, heroes in the eyes of many boys and girls, endorsing cigarettes and liquor."[60] Lord took issue with criticism popular fan magazines were leveling at the show being "too preachy." "I feel a responsibility to kids. I feel that I've been through so much in my life—I've made all the mistakes—that if they can profit from some of my experiences, I'm more than happy to pass them on."[61]

Journalist Jim Hoffman wrote a paradoxical article for a May 1963 issue of *Motion Picture* magazine that eventually validates Lord's sincerity when it came to his responsibility to impressionable viewers and the character of Stoney Burke. As he summed up his hour-long interview with Lord, he does so in the context of the 12 points of Boy Scout law. At first, Hoffman comes across as snide as he provides tongue in cheek illustrations for each of the standards Boy Scouts are required to embrace. As the interview comes to an end, he confesses that perhaps he had gone in with a preconceived opinion and that Lord was serious about his convictions and the motivation behind his rough climb to success. "Suddenly I realized that it was I who was the fool," he said. "It was there all the time—Jack's warmth—but I had been so put off by the way Lord talked that I had failed to catch the emotion, the genuine feeling, that sometimes seeped through his weighty, self-conscious words."[62]

Stoney Burke became the biggest performer in rodeo history and Jack Lord became a wealthy man. Board games, toys, comic books, and other character merchandise offerings contributed to his income.

And as he and Marie traveled the rodeo circuit, he continued to keep his friend Hedda Hopper posted. "Dear One, California weather has Florida beat hands down. Drew largest crowds in history of Rodeo at Florida State Fair."[63] He had the same experience at the Snake River Stampede in Nampa, Idaho, the week of July 18, 1964. This time he went one better than a souvenir postcard to Hopper. He mailed her a shipment of steaks—"prime Idaho feed [sic] beef." A few days later, Hopper responded that she was "stuffed right up to the eyeballs," and expressed her delight that he had thought of her in such a creative way.[64]

"The world doesn't really end for an actor when a ... network cancels his television series. Sometimes the cancellation is a springboard to greater earnings and a fuller life. Jack Lord ... is living proof of that."[65] Journalist Lawrence Laurent's words one year after the end of *Stoney Burke* are remarkably prophetic in the context of Lord's next sixteen years' work. A cursory look at his filmography for 1964 gives the impression he was working very little that year. He logged only three paying television roles and had no film credits. Reports of several false starts and disappointments with multiple projects that never came to fruition give the impression he was struggling. In fact, the bigger question is how he managed the grueling schedule he maintained that year.

After the series ended, however, Stoney Burke was suddenly one of the hottest commodities going, and Lord had fully engaged his driven work ethic to keep up with demands on his time. Calls for personal appearances at rodeos, fairs, and other venues continued to climb. With the rodeo circuit, many of his gigs were four- or five-night bookings and "Stoney" was a guaranteed draw for record crowds turning up wherever he appeared. It was hard work, with a lot of road time and added personal appearances during the day while he waited for the evening arena performances. In the long run, the businessman in Lord knew it was well worth the effort, however. In spite of a decrease in his film and television appearances, his earnings were more than respectable, many times over what he made with his day job. Taking every available opportunity to supplement the $200,000 a year he was making for the rodeo circuit, he was also picking up between $75,000–$100,000 for other "Stoney" appearances. It was a great example of his business sense, his desire to self-manage, and his sometimes controversial bent toward thinking outside the box. He admitted that as a born and raised Brooklyn kid, he knew virtually nothing about rodeos. Once he saw it from the inside out during his brief stint with the *Stoney Burke* series, he recognized an opportunity and embraced the learning experience.

Lord shared his strategy with journalist Dave Kauufman in the spring of 1964, and, in a sense, it was a preview of coming attractions with the Jack Lord approach to his own career. Farther down the road, he would apply some of the control he maintained with the Stoney character to Steve McGarrett. Lord and his booking agent Mike North had developed a sure-fire plan for success. They wrote three scenarios for Stoney and his new gig. In the first one, Lord got a $7,500 guarantee against 60 percent of the gross over a three-year average for the events in which he appeared. That version worked well, for example, when he played the popular Sidney, Iowa, rodeo; he took home $28,500 for six days work. The second formula stipulated a $7,500 guarantee against 20 percent of the gross from all sources, and the third, written for fairs and similar venues, called for a flat $2,000 a performance.[66]

His appearances in the rodeo ring weren't his only sources of income, however. Lord enjoyed rubbing it in a bit with the network over what he considered to be a tragic mistake when the decision was made to cancel *Stoney Burke*. He owned 25 percent of the series, and it was common for local television stations to purchase the series to air in the area as soon as he was booked for appearances. Stoney was a popular guy, and long after the show was pulled, Lord continued to get thousands of fan letters a week. After *Stoney Burke*, Lord vowed he would never work another series unless he owned a piece of it, and he stayed true to his promise, even when it cost him some promising gigs.

Stoney Burke simply refused to go away. Lord and Leslie Stevens had been confident in the potential for continued success with the show, and both were committed to keep the character as he was written—upright and committed to his principles. It was a losing battle, however, when network suggestions to spice it up with more sex and more violence were rejected and the series was cancelled. Jack Lord chose to make lemonade—very lucrative lemonade. His earnings for the first year after the series was cancelled exceeded his total income for the previous nine years, and he was strategically diversifying his opportunities. A 1964 front-page story in a Missouri newspaper reported that Lord was "ramrod" over an 18,000 cattle station in Australia and that he had a smaller spread in the San Fernando Valley.[67]

The residuals of Lord's success with the defunct series just kept on coming, and a healthy income was not the only reward he was reaping. He soon discovered Stoney had some fans in high places. When he was in Independence, Missouri, in late August for a five night run with the rodeo, he and Marie took time to visit the Harry S. Truman Library and they were granted a personal audience with the former president. The meeting was highly publicized, including a front-page photo op as he presented Truman with a brand new 10x Silver Bellied Stetson hat. He also gave Truman a copy of an antique book on the Civil War from his personal library with a heartfelt inscription: "To Harry S. Truman. A great and good president. Great because he is possessed of fierce moral courage. Morally courageous because he is good. With high esteem and affection too. Marie and Jack Lord."[68] Mr. and Mrs. Harry Truman attended the Saturday night Stoney Burke appearance at the local rodeo, enduring a rainy night as they stayed through the entire performance.

Twenty-seven years after Lord visited the site, the National Park Service conducted an interview with John Martino, former custodian and driver for Truman. Martino was employed at the library from 1958 until 1972. During the interview, he shared his personal collection of photographs and other memorabilia from his tenure at the site. Even though a large number of celebrities had visited the library over the years, he recalled Jack Lord's meeting with Truman.[69]

Marie and Jack Lord visit Harry S Truman, left, at his library on August 24, 1964. Lord presented Truman with a book and a cowboy hat. In spite of a downpour that evening, the Trumans attended a performance of Stoney Burke's rodeo act (J.W. Porter, *Kansas City Star*, courtesy Harry S. Truman Library).

Lord garnered other fans at the presidential level for his work on *Stoney*. On Saturday, October 24, he and Marie were guests of Luci Banes Johnson, daughter of Lyndon Johnson, at a barbecue in Omaha, an event sponsored by the local chapter of Young Citizens for Johnson and Humphrey. After he left *Hawaii Five-O* he received periodic telegrams from Ronald and Nancy Reagan on his birthday, all of which he saved. There seemed to be a pattern with "western-minded" presidents who were Stoney Burke fans.

In 1964 TVQ did a survey for their research on the popularity of television programs. Five programs tied, showing about the same level of popularity for adult viewers: *ABC News Report*, *Dick Powell Show*, *Dick Van Dyke*, *Hootenanny*, and *Stoney Burke*.[70]

"Sure, I was hoping for three years of *Stoney Burke* but I'm not going to lose any sleep over being cancelled at the end of one," he said. "My old man used to say to me that you could look at a glass as either half empty or half full. Well, I see mine as half full."[71] From the beginning, the network had pressured Lord and Stevens to spice the series up by increasing the violence and the sex appeal to pull in even more adult viewers. Both held their ground and refused to comply, even in the face of cancellation. It was another instance of Lord's holding to his principles and his preferences, even if it meant he would be unemployed yet again.

In a 1969 interview with journalist Jack Major, Lord commented on the folly of the network's decision to cancel *Stoney Burke*. "*Stoney* was the most successful flop in television history.... As soon as it went off the network, it went into syndication. I'm still getting money from *Stoney Burke*."[72]

As disappointing as the end of *Stoney Burke* was, Lord was deeply touched by the outpouring of support he received in the aftermath of the cancellation. He penned a personal message to his fans in the December issue of *Movie Life* magazine. Beneath a bold greeting scrawled in his handwriting across the top of the page he wrote, "I want to thank every one of you who wrote to ABC protesting the dropping of *Stoney Burke*. The mail is the highest in the history of the network. It's all been delivered to me ... we've got a roomful of it! Although I can't answer each letter and ballot personally, I want you to know I'm deeply grateful."[73] Six years later Lord would still be receiving fan mail addressed to Stoney Burke, Mission Ridge, South Dakota. Among his papers are several copies of specially designed autographed cards he customarily sent to fans. He signed them all.

Fifty years after the end of *Stoney Burke*, it was released on DVD and a whole new generation of fans discovered the series and found it surprisingly engaging. Don McGregor wrote an on-line review of the show for www.comicsbulletin.com. He praises Stevens for "writing fervently and with passion." He singles out Lord's work as Stoney apart from Steve McGarrett and Felix Leiter and tells viewers they are in for a major revelation as to the range of Lord's acting skills. "For those of you who only know Lord as Steve McGarrett from *Hawaii 5-O* and as Felix Leiter in ... *Dr. No* you're in for a major revelation as to the range of acting skills Jack Lord has. Stevens gives Lord many impassioned speeches throughout the show, and Lord is up to the emotional storm, an often intense, complex mixture of reactions to the challenges he confronts." It is a review that would have pleased Jack Lord in his never-ending quest to be recognized as a diverse actor.

Lord blamed the failure of the show on Madison Avenue. "They didn't dig the show because it was allegorical. We wrote from a theme rather than from a plot standpoint."[74] In the end, Jack Lord just did what he always did. He shook the dust from his $75 boots, gathered to himself what he had learned, and he persevered. He worked hard and he diversified his experiences until the next big thing came along. And even though it was four more years down the road, the next big thing could never be labeled a flop in anyone's vocabulary.

NINE

The Work Praises the Man

Taking Stoney Burke on the road was keeping Jack Lord busy, and he was making huge strides toward recovering from the lean years he now had behind him. As far as acting gigs for 1964, his filmography was scarce, but it would be the last year of his career when that was the case. His first television appearance since *Stoney Burke* was a guest-starring role in an episode of *Dr. Kildare*. After several false starts to getting the series off the ground, Richard Chamberlain stepped into the role as the blonde, blue-eyed young intern, and the show held solid audiences for its five-season run. Derived from a series of short stories and novels by Max Brand, the James Kildare character dated back to the 1930s and the stories had spawned radio series and movies long before Chamberlain's television version debuted on NBC. It was a good opportunity for Lord to be seen in a role that was not a cowboy, a cop, or a thug.

In an episode from the third season Lord plays Dr. Frank Michaels, a brilliant and egotistical surgeon dealing with the onset of debilitating arthritis. The story focuses on Michaels' attempt to keep his condition hidden from his wife and from the hospital staff. There is a bit of irony in the part for Lord. It was rumored for years, and continues to be a frequently revisited theory, that he may have suffered from arthritis. Those who support the idea point to occurrences over the years of obvious awkward positioning and movement of his fingers. To date, there has been no substantial proof to either confirm or refute whether he actually suffered from arthritis, however. Lord has a strong presence in the episode. Forty-four years old at time, he looks appropriately mature for a well-seasoned surgeon and he exudes a confidence and a determination that fits the part.

ABC announced the previous December that Lord was set to guest star in "Man in a Hole," an episode of *Greatest Show on Earth* at Desilu, and he signed the agreement in January. The short-lived series starred Jack Palance as the manager of a circus, and it was on the air for about seven months when it fell to the popularity of the offerings on other networks during the same timeslot. "Man in a Hole" aired February 18, and was Lord's second television appearance of the new year. The following day, he was in Tampa for a Stoney Burke appearance with the Charlie Aldrich Trio at the Florida State Fair. While he was there, he took advantage of a special opportunity to talk about his second love—art. He did a guest lecture for art department students at Tampa University on "Impressionism, Post-Impressionism, and the Fauves." Lord identified with the Impressionist style in his own work, and stepping out of his cowboy personae and into the role of avid art scholar was easy for him. It was a good reminder of his diverse interests and talents. Even though he made his living from acting, he continued to paint throughout his life and he and Marie were avid collectors of fine art. In September of that year, his artwork was part of the Second Annual Goodson-Todman Art Exhibition in New York, a collection of celebrity art on display through the end of October.

On April 13, Jack Lord put on his tux and headed off to the 36th Annual Academy Awards ceremony, where he and Marie mixed and mingled with Hollywood royalty. When it came time to present the Oscar for Best Live Action Short Subject, Jack Lemon introduced Shirley McClain as presenter. She read the names of the nominees from cue cards and when the envelope was handed to her, she announced the winners. American writer Ambrose Bierce's short story, "An Occurrence at Owl Creek Bridge," set during the Civil War, is the haunting short story of the last thoughts of a condemned man. It was effectively translated without dialogue into a short film by Paul deRoubaix and Marcel Ichac. Jack Lord walked briskly to the stage. He offered a brief acceptance speech during which he indicated the winners had asked him to accept on their behalf since they were in Paris at the time. As he strode off the stage, he was causally holding the golden statue in one hand at his side.

It was early October before he appeared on television again. *The Reporter* premiered on September 25 and it was a new CBS offering about a New York newspaper journalist. Filmed in New York, the series starred Harry Guardino and featured both established and up and coming guest stars, including Lord's *Stoney* costar Warren Oates. In spite of the expected success for the show, it ended three months and 13 episodes after it premiered.

Lord continued to keep up his grueling schedule on the road with Stoney Burke, but he also managed to keep his finger in other projects. During the month of June, he worked on getting two of his self-authored pilots, *Yankee Trader* and *McAdoo*, ready for production. He announced plans to star in one of them, but did not indicate which one; neither pilot made it to production.

By July 1, he was back in the saddle and back in his bad boy clothes again when he was cast in an episode of *Wagon Train* as Lee Barton. Barton was the ruthless head of a family fleeing over miles of rugged territory after pulling off a bank robbery. Barton heartlessly sacrificed his own kin to ensure he got where he was going, and Lord played it well. The *Wagon Train* series jumped to number one in the ratings during the 1961–62 season, but its popularity had begun to decline, and it went off the air at the end of that season. "The Echo Pass Story" aired January 3, 1965, Lord's first television appearance of the new year.

As 1964 wound down, United Artists Television, Daystar, and their partner company Lord and Lady Productions were all reaping the benefits of an increase in foreign syndication of the resilient *Stoney Burke* series. Lord was definitely wise to keep his interest in the show, especially considering he maintained a share in foreign markets as well as the domestic rights. He also continued to maintain his own Lord and Lady Production Company throughout the rest of his career, and it would prove time and time again to be a wise business decision.

After his January 1965 appearance on *Wagon Train*, four months passed before he was seen on television again, but he was staying busy in the interim. Thanks to pal Casey

April 13, 1964: Jack Lord accepts the Oscar on behalf of Paul deRoubaix and Marcel Ichac for their short film adaptation of Ambrose Bierce's *An Occurrence at Owl Creek Bridge* **(copyright Academy of Motion Picture Arts and Sciences).**

Tibbs, Lord got to bring out his Stoney personae in a very unique setting to jumpstart to the new year. Tibbs gave his name to a rodeo held at the famous Rose Bowl Stadium on January 24, and for a time the grand Pasadena venue was filled with cowboys instead of quarterbacks. Grand marshals for the event were Glenn Ford and Jack Lord. They costarred with the original horses from the classic MGM film *Ben Hur*, as they were featured in a reenactment of the chariot race. While it was Stoney Burke's only performance at the Rose Bowl, rodeo events continued periodically at the stadium until the 1980s when Pasadena City Council members voted to ban rodeos and other animal events after protests from area animal rights groups.

In March, Lord was cast in an episode of *Suspense Theatre* set to air in May. In "The Long Ravine," he costars with Andrew Prine, Broderick Crawford, and Lisabeth Hush. He plays Paul Campbell, an idealistic and pitiable dreamer obsessed with making a big strike in a lost gold mine. He adamantly refuses to accept defeat, to the tragic detriment of his long-suffering wife. He wears a white panama hat for the role, a familiar look during his years in Hawaii. That same month Lord the active citizen was present on the platform for the dedication ceremony of a 2,000 feet landscaped esplanade on Lankershim Boulevard in Los Angeles donated to city by Universal Studios as part of Mrs. Lyndon Johnson's beautification project. Universal had invested $100,000 in the project as a contribution to the city.

In early June he signed to appear in the first of two guest star spots for *Twelve O'Clock High*, a series set during World War II about the United States Eighth Air Force. Lord was cast in "Big Brother," and the episode aired October 11. He played Lt. Col. Preston Gallagher, brother to series star Paul Burke's character, Colonel Joe Gallagher. "Pres" Gallagher is a troubled leader, suffering in the aftermath of a tragic loss of men under his command. At the urging of his brother, he winds up rescinding what would have turned out to be a faulty strategic decision.

Burke was new to the series at the start of the second season, replacing Robert Lansing. He took some flak from fans and critics for stepping in after studio execs made the decision to replace Lansing in favor of a younger actor for the part. Burke effectively downplayed the outcry, saying, "As for as I'm concerned, it was an open job, and some other actor would have accepted it if I had not. I'm sure Bob Lansing would have done the same."[1] Among Lord's papers are several copies of the October 11 issue of *The Hollywood Reporter* with a full-page ad for the episode featuring his photo. He wrote "page 5" across the cover of each copy.

In September, Lord's name rolled in the credits of two television series in one week. On the 22nd he appeared in "The Crime," an episode of *Bob Hope's Chrysler Theatre* on NBC based on a novel by Stephen Longstreet. It was the first of three guest-starring appearances for him on the program. As Assistant District Attorney Abe Perez, he finds himself prosecuting a former lover for a double murder. Even in reruns the following year, the episode received good reviews, praised as "an excellent drama and a "well-played story."[2]

Three days after the "The Crime" aired, he guest starred in Rod Serling's *The Loner*, a western that had a one season run. The show followed the adventures of William Colton, a Union Captain who headed west to start a new life for himself after the Civil War. Lord was cast in "The Vespers" as a gunfighter turned minister who had once saved Colton's life. Colton steps in when the minister refuses to take up his gun again to save his own life after an old enemy from his unlawful days threatens him.

He signed on in May for an October 5 episode from the fourth season of ABC's World War II series set in France. *Combat!* still stands as the longest running World War II drama on television. As Barney McClosky in "The Linesman," Lord plays a disgruntled signal corps sergeant who has an axe to grind with another officer. The unit is on a dangerous mission to lay communications wire though an active battle zone.

Jo Davidsmeyer published a comprehensive guide to the series in 2001 that included interviews with many of the cast members. Davidsmeyer reported there was extreme tension between Lord and series star Vic Morrow. "Morrow and Jack Lord were antagonistic on- and off-screen. They had clashed in the past, coming to blows during the filming of *God's Little Acre*."[3] Several blogs also indicate there was continued tension between the two actors. In 1971, Morrow was a guest star in a Season Four episode of *Hawaii Five-O*, "Two Doves and Mr. Heron." It seems odd Lord would work with Morrow as a guest star on *Five-O* if their relationship was as contentious as it was rumored to have been. Others who worked on the *Combat!* series spoke of Morrow's easy-going demeanor. Morrow was tragically killed along with two children while shooting a scene for the 1983 film *The Twilight Zone: The Movie*.

Lord snagged what looked to be a brass ring on November 4 when he signed a non-exclusive agreement with Universal Studios, and it made papers across the country. The contract had all the elements he sought as he moved forward, giving him the opportunity for both film and television work as an actor and as a director. Lord and Lady Productions was developing five of his self-authored pilots. Four of them, *McAdoo*, *The Sea Tiger*, *Ryan's Raiders* and *Yankee Trader*, had seafaring themes, and the fifth, *Clementine*, was a western comedy.

By December 2, 1966, he was back on the set with parts in two pilots up for consideration as new Universal series. "Above the Law," an episode from the first season of NBC's *Laredo*, would translate into *This Gun for Hire*, a series based on the 1942 Paramount film by the same title that was Alan Ladd's breakout role. Jack Marshall, who wrote music for a number of episodes of popular series, including *Have Gun Will Travel*, *The Virginian*, *The Munsters* and *Wagon Train*, wrote the theme music for the pilot. *Daily Variety* reported the following March that Lord was being considered as a regular.[4] The pilot never sold, but when it aired on January 13, 1966, it was intended as a spin-off for a new series.

December 13, 1965, Shirley Knight was cast to star alongside Lord in *Jigsaw*. Knight plays a barmaid who falls in love with Lord's character, a Bond-like agent, posing as an underworld killer working to gain entry into a counterfeiting gang. Production was originally set to begin on December 2 under the direction of Stuart Rosenberg, but casting was not complete in time and work did not get under way until December 15. When it aired, the title was changed to *The Faceless Man*. The concept had a complicated two-year journey. Some sources say it first aired as an episode of the *Bob Hope Presents: The Chrysler Theatre*. It was translated into a full-length film from Universal that hit theatres the last week of May in 1968, when Lord was on the job with *Hawaii Five-O*. It was one of 37 films by Universal that year, a record release year for the studio since 1956. *The Counterfeit Killer* went basically unnoticed, although *Variety* predicted its likely transition to a series, praising the potential of the main character for bringing more to the story. Lord got kudos for being "forthright and relentless" in the role.[5] *The Counterfeit Killer* was later released on video with the title *Crackshot*.

The idea of translating vidpix into theatrical presentations was catching on as a possible solution for the rapidly shrinking TV syndication market, and as usual, Lord

Lord appeared with Shirley Knight (plus *Dr. No* costar Joseph Wiseman) in the 1968 release *The Counterfeit Killer*. The film underwent several name changes as it made the rounds from a theatre production to a television movie to video (Universal Studios/Photofest).

had his eye on what had the potential to be the next big thing. Journalist Dave Kaufman reported the two-fold advantages of the initiative over standard movie making. Unsold pilots were converted into features, and once they were aired, they would be sold to foreign markets as films. The next step was to sell them as part of a package to the domestic markets in this country. The savings would be substantial compared to traditional film production. Kaufman noted, "Conversion and expansion costs are not great, while the market potential is limitless."[6]

Even though he was lining up some future work, most of Lord's television appearances for 1966 occurred during the last months of the year. September 3 he appeared in his second guest starring role for *Twelve O'Clock High*. In "Face of a Shadow" he plays the disgraced Colonel Arnold Yates, base commander near an occupied Italian village. He is romantically involved with a local baroness and he is living the high life at her villa. In protest to a reprimand he received for fouling up an earlier mission, he is basically ignoring his duties and working on being just generally obnoxious. He is good in the role, and he gets the opportunity to quote some classic poetry. In two well-played scenes when Yates is solidly drunk, he pulls it off well.

November 13, Lord appeared in Quinn Martin's highly successful series, *The F.B.I.* Based on actual cases, it starred Efrem Zimbalist, Jr., as Inspector Lewis Erskine and Philip Abbott as Special Assistant to Director J. Edgar Hoover. Hoover was a consultant for the show for eight years, but was never seen on camera. Lord played cold-blooded killer Frank Shroeder in "Collison Course." Ellen Corby, best remembered for her role in The Waltons, also appeared on the episode. She would work with Lord again as a guest star on an episode of *Hawaii Five-O*.

Two weeks later, Lord had a guest-starring role on *The Virginian*. As much as he wanted to escape the bad guy roles, he landed an excellent one. As Roy Dallman in "High Stakes," he is a man with absolutely no redeeming qualities and he plays it very well. It was another example of the blessings and the curses of the typecasting he so vehemently opposed. When he beautifully nails a pathological scoundrel as he did with Dallman, it is easy to see why he was in high demand for the bad guy roles.

Lord was surely comfortable in the setting of a December 7 episode of *Bob Hope Presents the Chrysler Theatre*. Set on a freighter carrying passengers, the plot offers a commentary on human nature in times of crisis, as the ship sails into the path of a hurricane. Once again in the role of the heavy, Lord is a both a blackmailer and a killer, and the rest of the cast offers up a true sampling of humanity—a gigolo, a desirable older woman, a voluptuous younger woman, and a fortune hunter. *Variety* praised the episode with special kudos for Lord's performance, for the producer, and for the skillful work of director Paul Bogart. "Jack Lord is excellent as the baddie with a heart of gold.... It's a sordid story, but sustains interest, mainly because of the sharp, clear cut characterizations drawn by Franklin Burton in his teleplay."[7]

Lord had been under contract with Universal since early March for a made for TV movie written by Rod Serling originally set to air on NBC in the fall. *The Doomsday Flight* was a thriller with a storyline tragically ahead of its time. Lord plays Frank Thompson, a special agent dealing with an unstable man who claims he has planted a bomb on a commercial flight. The situation is further complicated for Thompson as he realizes his wife is on the plane. Producer Frank Price's wife, Katherine Crawford, had a role in the film. Crawford said on those occasions when she found herself working for her husband or for her producer father, Roy Huggins, she generally caught more criticism than praise from them.[8]

Hopes were high for *The Doomsday Flight*, and there was much riding on the perceived success of it. Two weeks before the airdate, Universal and NBC had offered up the "world premiere" of another made for TV movie, *Fame Is the Name of the Game*. The film followed a private investigator looking into the murder of a call girl. The premiere was met with very high ratings, and network officials were happy to use the data as further validation for their contention that a made for TV movie could do as well as those that were prior theatrical release films. Naysayers denied that a realistic comparison could be drawn between the two. The first had the advantage of an extensive publicity campaign before the premier and the racy content was guaranteed right out of the gate to draw a larger audience and better critical acclaim. *Name of the Game* was broadcast on Saturday night, and *The Doomsday Flight* aired the following Tuesday. If *Doomsday* did well, the potential for a rapidly increasing television movie industry was great. The central argument about the genre was sidetracked, however, by an unexpected bit of unwelcome attention following the premier.

The New York Times ran a scathing indictment of the film in the December 16 edition, citing poor judgment on behalf of the network for putting bad ideas into potential

Jack Lord as Special Agent Frank Thompson in a NBC made-for-television movie, *The Doomsday Flight*. The storyline about a bomb on commercial airplane film created quite a stir. *The Doomsday Flight* aired December 13, 1966 (NBC/Photofest).

criminals' minds. This was long before the possibility of terrorist attacks on domestic airlines was even a thought. The repercussions of public alarm and the reality of some actual threats made to airlines afterwards caused quite a stir in the days after the film aired.

It was not widely publicized, but the Airline Pilots' Association had raised some concerns, protesting the airing of the film before it premiered. The story reported that in May of 1963, the FBI had formally asked news media not to "play up" bomb scares, but FBI representatives denied the action. Fifteen minutes before the film ended, the

Federal Aviation Agency in Washington got the first airliner bomb threat, with a total of five additional ones reported before the end. More threats to five airlines followed the day after it aired. Price told reporters that the FBI had actually assisted with some technical advising on the film and that the agency was well aware of the subject matter.

Jack Lord was a guest on *The Tonight Show* on December 12, one day before the premiere of the film. He talked briefly about it, saying in his interview that the FBI had cleared him in advance for the part. The agency later acknowledged there was a process in place to clear actors who were up for such roles. Woody Allen was also a guest on *The Tonight Show* and he suggested calling in a bomb threat would be a good way to keep a flight on the ground if there was a chance of getting to the airport too late to board. The negative response to the movie was disappointing, and Allen's inappropriately timed joke certainly didn't help the situation. The *New York Times'* take on it was clear. "Apparently this is a week for sick television values on many fronts."[9] Lord saved several newspaper clippings about the film, wrapped in brown paper and filed among his papers.

During his extended interview on the *Tonight Show*, Lord was gracious and articulate. As he introduced the segment, Carson expressed genuine surprise at just how busy and diverse Lord had been since his start in the business. "You have been on every television show I think on every network," he said. Lord talked about his work with Mesiner, what he learned about technique and the importance of that understanding in television work. "Technique is how you use yourself," he said, "and I think that is very important especially in the demands of television today.... When you strike an A, you should get an A back. You get what you want and it takes time."

On, February 14, 1967, Lord had a guest-starring role in the ABC science fiction series *The Invaders*. He plays George Vikor, a wounded Korean War veteran and successful industrial manufacturer who has fallen in with an alien conspiracy to take over the world. Sporting a familiar blue suit and crisp white shirt for the part, he projects a forceful presence. Slightly more than a year away from his landmark role in *Hawaii Five-O* at the time, he undeniably does exude Steve McGarrett in the episode.

At the end of the prior December, he had signed for a guest-starring spot on the fourth and final season of ABC's *The Fugitive*. It was the series that spawned the highly successful film with Harrison Ford in the role of Richard Kimble, a doctor on the run after being wrongly accused of his wife's murder. In "Goodbye My Love," Kimble is working as a parking attendant at an exclusive club when he encounters Alan Bartlett, an obnoxious playboy type who wants to be free of his crippled wife so he can take up with the lounge singer at his club. Bartlett was yet another bad guy role for Lord and he once again rose to occasion. As he did in *Twelve O'Clock High*, he pulled off the drunk scenes especially well. The episode aired the February 28, 1967.

In August of the prior year he had signed to do a western movie with James Farentino and Don Galloway, and the opportunity to do some comedy appealed to Lord. Some sources indicate the film was a remake of *Black Bart* a 1948 film. Initial press releases gave the title as *The Bandit*, but by early September it was changed to *The Ride to Hangman's Tree*. Melodie Johnson rounded out the final cast when cameras rolled on August 16.

A month before the film's release in May 1967, papers reported litigation by the

Jack Lord and Roy Thinnes in "Vikor," an episode of *The Invaders*, an ABC series about alien beings secretly infiltrating the human race as part of their plan to take over the earth. Lord's character is assisting the alien effort. The episode aired on Valentine's Day, 1967 (ABC/Photofest).

Writers Guild of America West over an error in writer credits included in the initial publicity. The New York Universal office had mistakenly given screenplay credit to story writers Jack Natteford and William Bowers that should have gone to Luci Ward. In spite of the legal troubles, overall reviews for the film were good. It was recommended as a good family movie, with the exception of one nude swimming scene featuring the female lead. The actors' effective playing off each other, especially in the comedy scenes, was highlighted. *Variety* said it offered a "good opportunity to showcase some of the studio's younger talent."[10] Both Farentino and Galloway were 29 at the time of the release; Lord was 47. If "younger" referred to contract tenure with the studio, not chronological age, Lord fit the bill, however. He was a little more than a year into his Universal agreement at the time of filming.

In April, Lord was signed to appear in an upcoming thriller from producers Robert Poor and Richard Todd. *Lovers in Limbo* would begin filming May 1 in Jerome, Arizona, with Swedish director, Gunar Hellstrom.[11] Sixties film writer/historian Tom Lisanti interviewed Tisha Sterling who played one of the psychotic sisters in the movie. She talked about the difficulty of filming in the extreme Arizona heat and reported the cast did not get along with Hellstrom. Sterling said it was not her first experience working with Jack Lord. "Jack was really weird but he was a terrific fellow. He lived in the same building I lived in.... Susan Strasberg was a Method actress so her technique would drive Jack crazy."[12] Since Lord also trained under Meisner, it seems odd that working with another Method actor would be problematic for him.

As it turned out, the film had a long road before it made it to theatres. During filming, Lord and Strasberg found themselves caught up in an ongoing strike against TV networks by the American Federation of TV and Radio Artists. Both actors received telegrams condemning their working on an independent production that was utilizing a non-union technical crew. Lord wasted no time contacting SAG. Both he and Strasberg were told to continue working in the light of the fact that Arizona was a right to work state, that funding for payment for the cast was already in place, and there were no legal grounds upon which the guild could refuse to okay the independent producers' using SAG members in the film.[13] Jack Lord continued to be proactive throughout the rest of his career when it came to looking out for his own best interests.

Hungarian immigrant Symcha Lipa would be one of Lord's most unusual roles. When the film debuted in May of 1968, Producer Joe Solomon had replaced Todd and the title was changed to *The Name of the Game Is Kill*. The promotional hype was reminiscent of 1950s horror features and included a mandate that moviegoers would be required to pledge not to reveal the shocking ending before purchasing a ticket. The cast

The Name of the Game Is Kill was a bizarre horror film with a *Psycho* feel that was filmed in the Arizona desert. Moviegoers had to agree not to reveal the shocking ending when they purchased tickets. As gullible Hungarian drifter Symcha Lipa, Lord (here with Susan Strasberg) was close to his career-making role as Steve McGarrett when the film was released in 1968 (Fanfare Films/Photofest).

and crew were loaded with some prominent people, including Golden Globe nominee Susan Strasberg, Collin Wilcox, who had made her film debut as Mayella Ewell in *To Kill a Mockingbird*, and actress Tisha Sterling, who would go on to appear on an episode of *Hawaii Five-O* with Lord.

Lipa winds up in a bizarre house of horrors when he catches a ride in the desert with a beautiful young woman. In the pre-release advertising the surprise reveal at the end was compared to Hitchcock's *Psycho*. The world premier was set for almost exactly a year later on May 17 in Toronto, with multiple openings on May 29 in 200 theatres across the U.S. The pre-release hype promised a sure hit. *Variety* compared it to *Whatever Happened to Baby Jane* and called it an "[o]utstanding rib of psycho dramas." The *Hollywood Report* dubbed it a "Rashomon styled" story, and *The Los Angeles Times* put it on a par with *Hurry Sundown*. Fanfair Films allocated $500,000 for co-op theatre advertising for the national release.

In the aftermath, the reviews were beyond disappointing. Pairing the film with comments on the release of *Shatterhand*, *New York Times*' critic Renata Adler was brutal: "I don't think anyone really wants to read reviews today of *Shatterhand* ... and *The Name of the Game Is Kill*.... There is nothing good in them."[14] *Hawaii Five-O* premiered two days prior to Adler's review, and Lord had already moved on in stellar fashion. It is very likely he didn't let it get him down. A *TV Guide* review of a television airing of *The Name of the Game Is Kill* put it perspective. "[At the end the movie] the lovers escape and head for California. Apparently Lord didn't stop there, as he went from this film to the set of "Hawaii Five-O."[15]

Almost fifty years later, the film is now considered a cult classic. It is sometimes billed as *The Female Trap* and it appeared under that title in a New York television program schedule listing in August of 1984. It aired at 1:00 a.m. and *Ride to Hangman's Tree* ran on another channel at 3:00 a.m. Jack Lord was a certified star by that time and some of his older work was starting to show up more on television.

In the fall before *Five-O* hit the airwaves, Lord had a guest spot on the first season of a new series starring Raymond Burr. *Ironside* was a resilient and popular series for NBC. It was set in San Francisco and followed the cases of a masterful detective confined to a wheelchair after an assassination attempt. The cast included Lord's costar from *Ride to Hangman's Tree*, Don Galloway. In the September 28 episode, "Dead Man's Tale," Lord was effective as corrupt attorney John Trask. Devious and smart as he was, however, he was no match for Ironside, and the episode ends with Trask narrowly missing a high action attempted escape on an airport runway.

Already at work on his life-changing role in Hawaii, Lord appeared on October 16 in an episode of NBC's popular spy series *The Man from U.N.C.L.E.* He was cast the prior July for a guest-starring role in a fourth season. For a while, regulars Robert Vaughn and David McCallum were two of the hottest spies on television. The series featured futuristic equipment, exotic settings, and colorful archenemies reminiscent of a Bond film. It lasted four seasons and in 1966 won the Golden Globe for the best TV show, and over its four-year run, *The Man from U.N.C.L.E.* racked up a respectable number of Emmy nominations. As Pharos Mandor, Lord put on his best suave snake in the grass personae. Originally titled "Lisbon," the episode aired as "The Master's Touch Affair."

That same month, it looked as though Lord may have another shot at a Broadway play. The *Los Angeles Times* reported, "If he can complete his role in CBS' *Hawaii Five-O* as planned, Jack Lord will start in "Avanti," an original Broadway comedy by Samuel Taylor. Richard Rodgers is producing the play later this season."[16] The show opened at the Booth Theatre on January 31, 1968, and closed after a short run on February 17. Keith Baxter had the lead. Jack Lord was not in the cast. The story came to the big screen in 1972 with Jack Lemmon stepping into Baxter's part.

Lord would have one last guest-starring role that year before settling in for the long run as Steve McGarrett. He gives a fine performance in an episode of the first season of *The High Chaparral*. "The Kinsman," aired January 28 on NBC and it would be his last villain role. As Uncle Dan Brookes, he shows up seriously wounded at the Cannon family ranch after a fifteen-year absence. Unknown to the family, he is secretly looking to escape capture by bounty hunters who have tracked him to the ranch after a robbery. In an effort to save his own hide, he goes into cahoots with bounty hunters to rob the Cannons of ranch payroll money.

As 1968 got under way, the long and winding road for Jack Lord had finally brought him to his pot of gold. He was still making money from *Stoney Burke*, but life as he knew it was about to change dramatically. Everything he and Marie had waited for was coming together at last in a paradise 2,500 miles away.

Ten

"I *Am* Home"

Leonard Freeman's twenty-three-year career in the entertainment business covered the full spectrum. He earned credits as producer, director, writer, actor, and composer of a musical soundtrack for a 1961 episode of *Route 66*. With all that experience under his belt, Freeman was not afraid to think outside the box. That quality was dramatically illustrated in 1966 when he brought a unique proposal to CBS executives that would evolve into one of the most successful television series in history.

On August 17, *Variety* announced that Freeman had been green lighted to begin stockpiling scripts for his idea for a television series to be filmed in a very ambitious location. Karen Rhodes says it was his mother-in-law who came up with the idea to film his new cop show in Hawaii. She was living there at the time, and she suggested he write something that would give her the opportunity to spend more time with the family.

In the beginning it looked as though his idea might not get off the table. He later told series writer Jerome Coopersmith that CBS executives were negative about the project from the start, with one telling him, "People who have been to Hawaii have already seen the place. And those who have never been there obviously don't care. So why should anyone watch this thing?"[1]

In a taped interview for the *Archive of American Television*, CBS Producer Perry Lafferty provides insight into the genesis of Freeman's concept. He said Freeman brought him an idea for a show about a private detective who works a chain of hotels in Waikiki. Lafferty told him he should reconsider the concept, making his lead character a state policeman to allow for more expanded storylines. Freeman was pleased to learn there was in fact no state police force in Hawaii, leaving him free reign to invent his own version. He lined up a respectable cadre of seven top-notch writers that included Jerome Coopersmith, Meyer (Mike) Dolinsky, who had written an episode of *Stoney Burke* and the script for an episode of *The Invaders* Jack Lord had appeared in. Mel Goldberg was author of the screenplay for Clint Eastwood's classic film, *Hang 'Em High* and he also penned the "Man in a Hole" episode Lord starred in for *Greatest Show on Earth*. Freeman would also write for the series.

Coopersmith later talked about the grueling schedule the writers endured from the very beginning. It was near the end of December when they were told storylines would be due by the first of the year. They were already scheduled to go to Hawaii on January 2 for research and location scouting. Early plans called for a 90-minute series, with a

Jack Lord in his career-making role as Steve McGarrett. The series ran from 1968 to 1980 and inspired a popular reboot that debuted in 2010 (CBS/Photofest).

100-minute feature as the kick off. They knew Freeman's idea to shoot the show entirely in Hawaii was going to require some creativity when it came to the production needs. The logistics of launching and sustaining a project so far away from Hollywood studios and manpower would no doubt prove to be a challenge, but Freeman was determined to make it work. He resolved early on if *Hawaii Five-O* was going to be set in Hawaii, it was going be filmed there. "We could be here five years and never use up all the landmarks and tourist attractions," he said."[2]

By the end of the first week of March 1967, CBS-TV was applauded as the first network to have its schedule for the fall season already firmed up. Expectation was high that its first pilot for the new season, *Hawaii Five-O*, would likely be in production by June, or certainly no later than Labor Day. With at least 26 projects on the board, program meetings were already under way. By early May, word was out that *Hawaii Five-O* may premiere as a theatrical release before hitting TV screens, a move that would help save on the exorbitant cost of a pilot. Other options were to air it on the network as a feature film or to present it as a two-part episode. Anticipation that Freeman likely had a winner with *Hawaii Five-O* was high, and it was getting good press even before the premiere.

In the early stages, Freeman's concept was titled *The Man*. Looking for just the right actor for the lead, he first approached his friend Richard Boone who had lived in Hawaii since 1964. Boone had recently finished *The Richard Boone Show*, a theatrical format series reminiscent of the early live television series of the 1950s. A company of eleven actors rotated roles as a new story was presented each week. Although the show lasted only one season, it was nominated for five Emmy Awards and won the Golden Globe in 1964. It is not clear if he turned down the role or if Freeman decided he was not right for the part, but Richard Boone would not be Steve McGarrett. Lord apparently didn't share the same affection for Boone as Freeman. In 1970, he bristled when a reporter mentioned his name, calling him a loser. "'Boone has a lot of gall," he said. "He used to come to Hollywood and talk about the Richard Boone Studio over here. Where is it? I've never seen it.'"[3]

Some sources say McGarrett was offered next to Gregory Peck. Freeman said when searching for a star, one always starts with Gregory Peck just on the off chance he may agree. It could not be confirmed if the role was actually offered to him or if he was just on the wish list. Freeman finally gave the part to Robert Brown, who had done guest appearances on several TV series, including multiple role on *Perry Mason*. Three days before the pilot was set to roll, Freeman decided he was not right for the part, and he was once again looking for his McGarrett. By June, he had changed the title of the series from *The Man* to *Hawaii Five-O*, a nod to Hawaii as the fiftieth state in the union.

Versions vary as to how Jack Lord was eventually chosen to head up the cast. He had just signed with CBS in September, and the network was writing a new western for him. *Cutter's Trail* was a 1970 made for TV movie and an unsuccessful pilot. Lord said the series was originally called *Slaughter's Trail*, but studio execs later changed the title to soften the connotation of excessive violence. The failed pilot would have been yet another disappointment for Lord, but it was just as well the series failed to make. The ever-vigilant business side of the determined actor had it covered this time. When he signed the contract for a starring role in the next new CBS western series, he had inserted a clause stipulating that should the show fail to make, he would have script approval of all other properties the network had on the docket. One of those scripts would evolve into *Hawaii Five-O*.[4]

That same month, Lord was also a contender for the lead in a new spy series from the Independent Television Commission, a British television production and distribution company. Dennis Spooner was a writer for *Dr. No* and one of the creators for *Man in a*

Suitcase, an English spy series that lasted only about seven months. ITC was looking to create a series that would appeal to American audiences, and they wanted an American actor in the lead. Although Jack Lord was among the contenders, Richard Bradford was cast, and as it turned out it was just as well. By the time *Man in a Suitcase* premiered on ABC in May of 1968, Jack Lord's dance card was already full.[5] *Hawaii Five-O* was moving forward, and although press releases announced Ricardo Montalban was signed that same month as the guest star for the first episode, he didn't appear until episode four.

CBS executive Paul King called Jack Lord at 7:00 a.m. and told him there was a promising project on the table he felt would be a good fit for him. He said they were moving quickly, and he wanted a response to the pilot script within two hours. Lord said by the time he was halfway through the reading, his heart began to pound. Steve McGarrett instantly rang as true to him as Stoney Burke had, and he instantly knew it was right. "This is it," he told Marie. "This is the one we've been waiting for." When he learned the project was the brainchild of Leonard Freeman, he was further convinced this was the one. Lord had been around Hollywood long enough to know that someone who could effectively fill the shoes of both producer and writer is a rare commodity, and Freeman's reputation was well known.

It had been five years since *Stoney Burke* ended, and even though he was still reaping the financial benefits from his twenty-five percent interest in the series and the nice annuity his rodeo road show had provided, he was anxious to find a role that felt as right to him as Stoney. He later said he was waiting for another character that he could love and believe in. Although at first look Stoney Burke and Steve McGarrett appear to have very little in common, Lord immediately saw the philosophical appeal in the tough cop. Like Stoney, he was a man with deeply ingrained principles and an unshakable tenacity. "He seemed an interesting, complex, complicated man who was interested in people. I saw compassion," he said.[6] He was written with some foibles, and he liked the fact that the tough cop occasionally made mistakes. McGarrett was an eclectic man, and Lord believed that as he worked to flesh out the character, he would have the opportunity to put to use his some of his own diverse life experiences.

Perry Lafferty said when they first decided on Robert Brown they had struggled to find the right actor for three months, and when Freeman dropped him Lafferty was frustrated. They had already invested a significant amount of money in the project. Lord was under contract with CBS at the time, and Lafferty thought he would be a great choice for McGarrett. Although a CBS staff member told him Leonard Freeman once said he wouldn't work with Jack Lord if he were the last actor on earth, Lafferty followed his instinct and called Freeman. The response was quick and definitive; Freeman said he wouldn't work with Jack Lord if he were the last actor in the world. Lafferty insisted he was sure he was perfect for the role, and Freeman reluctantly agreed to meet with him.

Lafferty said he didn't know what happened in that meeting, but the situation changed rapidly. Lord told him if need be, he would be willing to make the trip to Hawaii in a rowboat to get that part, and he would gladly man the oars himself. He read for it on a Wednesday, and two days later he was on his way to Hawaii, with filming set to roll the following Monday.

Although there were occasional bumps, Freeman and Lord generally worked well together artistically, and they were evenly matched when it came to handling details of the business end of the show. They each stood their ground, and most of the disagreements they had with the network involved issues related to storylines of individual episodes or disputes about the high production costs they faced with the Hawaiian location work. During the first year of the series, Lord confessed, "They [were] never exactly overjoyed to see us at CBS."[7]

Lafferty's observation about something mystical happening during the initial meeting between Lord and Freeman was an astute one. Freeman shortly changed his stand on his adamant refusal to work with Jack Lord. "He's terrific," he later said. "I'm a perfectionist and so is he. Having a star like Jack is like having money in the bank. He's always on time, no bags under his eyes, and he always knows his lines." Praising Lord's credibility, Freeman compared him to a Vince Edwards or a Jack Webb. "When he flashes his badge, people believe it."[8] Despite his initial reluctance to work with Jack Lord, he was banking on his leading man. "Lord fits the part and he seems to leap out of the pages of the script."[9]

As expected in any association that runs as long as theirs did, Lord and Freeman were not without their occasional differences. Lord's longtime secretary Margaret Doversola acknowledged there were instances of conflict. "[Jack Lord] knew that he couldn't go out painting his superiors badly in public, yet he did have strong differences with creator/producer Leonard Freeman. He was making decisions on the set and changing the script, which did not go down well with Freeman and caused major friction between them," she recalls.[10] For the most part, however, the collaboration clearly worked.

Now that CBS had their star, the next task was to find the right people to finish out the cast. Maggi Parker won the role of May, Steve McGarrett's secretary, and she filled the part for 11 episodes. Parker had worked for 18 years as a schoolteacher and administrator when she decided to lay it down to try her luck as an actress. She hoped *Hawaii Five-O* would be the launching pad that would set her on her way. Three months after the show's premier she told the press that part of her motivation for such a radical change in careers was her intent to do something for herself and *Five-O* was a start. "It's Lord's year, his show," she said early on. "So far the rest of us are pretty much part of the woodwork."[11] After Parker left the series, Peggy Ryan stepped in as McGarrett's new Girl Friday, Jenny Sherman. Ryan was married to Hawaiian journalist Eddie Sherman, who also did some guest-starring spots on the show. As Jenny, Ryan effectively and efficiently managed the driven cop's day-to-day details, dutifully keeping his ever-present coffee cup filled until 1976.

Lew Ayers appeared as the Governor of Hawaii in the pilot. By the first episode, however, Richard Denning had replaced Ayers, and he was a good choice for the part. Ayers showed up as a guest star in a sixth season episode and once again in season eight. Denning stayed for the duration of the series. In his first episode, he meets with McGarrett about the mysterious disappearance of ten wealthy women who had gone missing while visiting the islands. He expresses to McGarrett the far-reaching importance of solving this horrific crime and of doing it quickly. "Two million guests a year pass through here," he said. "We invite them and we're responsible for their safety." Later, the show would take some flak for giving the impression Hawaii was a violent and unsafe location, and there were widespread concerns about the negative impact such a perception may have on tourism. Lord told *Boston Herald* columnist Anthony La Camera they faced open antagonism at first, with most people fearing the show was going to seriously affect tourism. In the early days of the show, he remembered someone saying they were going to turn the islands in to a cesspool of crime. "'It has worked out just the opposite, however,' [he said]. 'We turned out to be a tourist attraction.'"[12]

When sixteen-year veteran police officer Kam Fong Chun was cast as Chin Ho Kelly, the network asked him to shorten his name to Kam Fong. In the pilot, Chin is initially portrayed as a light-hearted character, but by the first episode he had evolved into the more serious and experienced voice of reason on McGarrett's team. He stayed with the series for ten years, leaving when his character was killed in "A Death in the Family."

Gilbert Francis Lani Damian Kauhi, known professionally by his nickname Zulu, played Detective Kono Kalakaua in the pilot episode. He held the role until the end of the fourth season, when the change in the Kono role made for some bad press. In mid–December 1971, papers carried the story that Zulu would not be returning to *Five-O* the next season, and rumors were running rampant about the circumstances of his departure. Following a "run-in" with publicist Len Weissman, Zulu's manager said the non-renewal of his contract was expected. According to a story in the *Honolulu Advertiser*, Zulu acknowledged he made racial slurs against Weissman that were overheard by a number of other people. He was at first suspended for the final two episodes of the season, but later the decision was made not to renew his contract. Feature writer Dwight Whitney's 1971 *TV Guide* article included quoted statements from Zulu in which he revealed his frustration with the role. "'My friends think I'm a trained-animal act,' he said. 'Yes, boss; no, boss.' Well, some day this animal will be laughing all the way to the bank."[13] Zulu went on to have a successful nightclub career, adopting a respelling of his copyrighted stage name to Zoulou. Al Harrington replaced Zulu as new character Ben Kokua.

Tim O'Kelley was initially cast in the role of Danny Williams, but it turned out to be a one-time appearance. When the results of early test audience reactions to the pilot came in, most felt he was too youthful looking to be McGarrett's crucial second-hand man, and that he lacked an equally confident presence when set alongside the more seasoned cast members. The test audience's vote of no confidence on the Danny Williams role was the catalyst for bringing James MacArthur on board. Lord was pleased with the change. "It is a pleasure to have another pro like Jimmy MacArthur ... and we are fortunate to have Richard Denning to play the governor.... He adds a touch of authenticity."[14] Although Denning played a treasury agent in the sixth season episode, "Twenty-Four Carat Kill," he was McGarrett's boss for 73 episodes.

MacArthur left one year before the show ended. Some sources say he had just grown tired of the role and felt the storylines were becoming redundant after eleven years. Others indicate he wanted to return to theatre work, and he had been doing some directing in local little theatre offerings. There were indications in the press that MacArthur was not happy that Lord had the only "star" billing for the series while he and Fong and Harrington maintained "with" credits. When asked about it in a 1974 interview, Lord said he had a deal with the network going in regarding how the credits would run and there was a reason for it. He did not articulate what the reason was, but he praised MacArthur as a "marvelous" actor. "'Stardom is something you earn,' he said. 'The two shows I starred in.... I helped sell them on Madison Avenue. So, you may call it ego. I call it good business sense."¹⁵ There were reports that Lord was not happy when MacArthur had his agent notify the production office he was leaving rather than telling Lord himself. He said he was out of the country and the time, and he didn't see any problem with the way he turned in his notice.

For about five years prior to leaving the series, MacArthur had maintained a business interest in a successful Polynesian show at one of the area resort hotels. During his last season, he was also working on producing a Vegas show that would be a tribute to America's astronauts, and he had plans to travel extensively. No doubt one of the more memorable episodes for the actor was in the eighth season. "Retire in Sunny Hawaii" featured a very special guest star. MacArthur's adopted mother, legendary screen and stage actress Helen Hayes, makes an appearance as his aunt and garnered an Emmy nomination for her work on the episode.

Khigh Dhiegh, who had gotten his start as an actor when a customer in his mother's New York bookstore asked if he would like to be in a Broadway play, landed a plum part for the pilot, and he was the perfect choice. He effectively filled the role of the diabolical villain Wo Fat, McGarrett's nemesis throughout the run of series. The story goes the name "Wo Fat" came from a popular local restaurant. He slips McGarrett's grip time and time again until the final episode when the determined cop captures him at last. It was a poetic end to twelve years of their cat and mouse relationship. "'The pilot show had Wo Fat being killed,' Dhiegh said in a 1983 interview. 'They never filmed it. Lord said it was such a good character they should keep him alive and bring him back several times a year.'"¹⁶ It was a good decision.

Morton Stevens' classic musical theme for the show was perhaps as important as to the branding and the lasting legacy of the series as was choosing just the right cast. Stevens' career as a composer spanned more than forty years and his work shows up in dozens of television movies and series. He was brought on board as music supervisor for CBS in the 1960s. Freeman deemed the value of a strong musical theme inestimable, and he chose well when he asked Stevens to write it. After the CBS orchestra recorded it for the show, the Ventures later released a version, and it quickly shot to #3 on the Billboard charts. A fast-moving montage of iconic Hawaiian people and places from title designer Reza Badiyi beautifully completed the opening package. In August 1972, however, CBS censors had to change the face of the opening.

One of the images in the montage depicted a one-and-one-third-second shot of a spinning gun barrel, and censors demanded it be removed. Freeman was frustrated, saying they had never had a single complaint about the image in the four years it had appeared in the opening. "I'm fighting to stay alive and create some kind of new form while TV marches backward," he said.¹⁷ In January of that year, Lord had expressed some concern about the "Skinhead" episode. Storywriter Will Lorin penned a letter to Lord, commending him in for what he considered to be one of his "strongest performances of the season." He attached a review from a January 28, 1972, *Variety* review that confirmed Lord was "right on" in his performance.¹⁸

In addition to the unforgettable theme for *Five-O*, Stevens did some compositions for individual episodes as well. He won an Emmy for Best Musical Composition for a Single Series Program for his work on the "Hookman" episode from the sixth season. It is still one of the most memorable episodes from the series and much of the credit must go to the guest star. Lord was always on the lookout for intriguing and memorable guest stars and the choice for this first episode of the new season was a winner.

"Hookman" is about a deranged cop killer with a serious axe to grind, methodically engraving his victim's names on the rifles he uses to kill them. Guest star Jay J. Armes is masterful in his guest-starring role as Curt Stoner, a man who lost his hands when police interference led to a bomb going off in his hands during a failed robbery. Hooks have replaced Stoner's amputated hands, and watching him load rifles with perfect precision is captivating. Even though Armes was not an actor, he was the perfect choice for the role. He lost both his hands in an accident when he was twelve years old. He went on to lead a very successful life as a private investigator, overseeing a force of more than 2,000. A very diverse and driven man, his life story reads like fiction, and the variety of successes he had is amazing. He is proficient in several languages, including 33 Chinese dialects, German, Spanish, French and Italian. Lord kept an extensive clipping about Armes from the *Honolulu Advertiser* published the week he was in Hawaii for filming. Armes was just the kind of person who would have caught his attention. He was always on the lookout for good guest stars. His papers contain clippings from television program guides with handwritten notes about potential guest stars for *Five-O*.

Lord received a letter in August of 1982 from Glen Olson and Rod Baker, authors of the "Hookman" episode. They acknowledged that, while the writing credit for the script was their first, it had boosted their careers. They wanted him to know they had just discovered the episode had received a citation award from the Library of Congress in 1974. They asked Lord if he could help them obtain a copy of the citation, and they offered up their availability to write other *Five-O* episodes.[19] Lord wrote, "answered Sept. 22, 1982," on the letter, but a copy of his response was not attached.

Not all reviews of the episode were so stellar, however. A September 23, 1973, article from *Newsday* was a scalding indictment of what the reviewer deemed a endorsement of "every imaginable form of psychopathic killing in the book.... If I were active in a policemen's benevolent league, I would push CBS to have shows about a madman with a death list of TV executives who contributed to the maiming of the public with their dumb violence."[20]

From the beginning, Freeman insisted the Steve McGarrett character would have a mystique, and viewers would be offered very few details about his private life. He saw to it that McGarrett continued to exist only as a cop, and his life away from work was largely kept off limits. When Freeman died about six years in with the series, network executives began to add further dimensions to their star character. Coopersmith felt McGarrett lost some of his edge when the decision was made to allow the audience to see more of his personal life. "Leonard was right," he said. "Delving into McGarrett's psyche gave the show a soap opera tinge."[21]

Apparently, Lord agreed with Coopersmith. In a phone interview with journalist Jack Major in 1975, Lord gave his take on the wisdom of refusing to give in to recurring audience requests for a closer look at the private life of Steve McGarrett. "People want to know more about what McGarrett's home life is like.... But even if we chose to reveal that, I don't think we could match what our viewers have built up in their heads over the past seven years.... I think the enigma of McGarrett is good. It intrigues the hell out of people.'"[22]

To say Jack Lord hit the ground running from the beginning of *Five-O* is an understatement. The show operated under a punishing schedule, and he often talked about the toll it took on him, especially as the years ran on. Shortly before the pilot aired, he said he had put in 83 hours the prior week, and remarkably that would become the standard for the twelve-year run of the series. "The only thing that saves me is the Screen Actors Guild ruling that you must have a 12-hour rest period before being called back to work," he said. "I live like a monk."[23] The frantic pace that started in the very beginning showed no signs of letting up. He frequently used the monk analogy when talking about his grueling schedule, and as the series continued long past its expected life, it became apparent it was wearing on him.

After getting up at 4 or 4:30 a.m., he went for a run on the beach outside their Kahala condo while Marie prepared a large breakfast for him. He showered, ate, and ran his lines for the day's filming with her, and he was normally at the studio or on location by 6 or 6:30 a.m. His days ran until at least 6 p.m., and he said he was generally in bed by 9:00 p.m. A call sheet in Lord's papers dated May 12, 1972, for "The Diamond That Nobody Stole" episode from the fifth season, has an interesting addendum at the bottom of the page. In his distinctive handwriting is a note to Marie. "Baby—I have a 6:15 AM pick up please call me at 4:15 AM. I love you forever."[24] It is a poignant illustration of his driven work ethic, his level of commitment to his job, and his utter devotion to his wife.

As soon as *Five-O* got the green light, plans were on the table to convert a commercial building in Honolulu into a sound stage, with all the exterior filming to be done at various locations throughout the islands. As the first year got under way, Freeman expressed some regrets about his resolve to film the series so far from the mainland. "If I'd known what I know now, I might not have done a series in Hawaii.... The logistics are back-breaking. We take eight days to shoot one episode, because

Lord's second *TV Guide* cover, September 4–10, 1971. Lord took issue with Dwight Whitney's article, "Jack Lord, Superstar" (*TV Guide Magazine* cover courtesy *TV Guide Magazine*, LLC © 1971).

of all the moving we do, and there's lots of commuting between Hollywood and Honolulu," he said.[25] One year in, Lord echoed Freeman's view. "'We have to move at a slower pace because of our setups all over town. We do not have the facilities or personnel or the casting bureau available in any Hollywood lot."[26] He also lamented the difficulties associated with the flip side of Hawaii's typically lovely weather. "Just try moving heavy equipment across an open sea during the rainy season. You'll find that it is expensive."[27]

The search for a suitable facility for indoor filming was another painful reminder of the inherent challenges of being so far away from the convenience of existing studio space. For the determined production company, however, the difficulty often resulted in some very creative solutions, and they made good use of the unique geography. Although McGarrett always dashed up the steps of the iconic Ioloni Palace to go to work, the actual location for *Five-O* headquarters and the governor's office was not there. During the first season, interiors for those sites were filmed at an old warehouse in Pearl City, and it was a tough go at times. Cast members called it "Mongoose Manor" in honor of the troublesome permanent residents of the facility. There was no air conditioning, the roof leaked, and there were frequent issues with rats joining the mongooses, feasting on cables and furnishings. Rhodes wrote, "One director would fire a starter's pistol before beginning the filming of a scene in order to scare off the little animals so they wouldn't interrupt the shooting with their noisy trips across the roof."[28]

Their location for seasons two through eight was an old fort on Oahu. Fort Ruger was built in 1906 and had sat largely abandoned since 1955. While it was not ideal, it was an improvement over the previous site. It, too, was not without its pitfalls, but this time the trouble was more of a legal nature and less about wildlife issues. *Daily Variety* reported a standoff between CBS and the local neighborhood association in June of 1969. Homeowners in the area where Hawaii Studios had constructed the stage and offices on the Fort Ruger site came forward to protest CBS having permission to lease the property without first obtaining a city building permit or zoning variance. CBS countered the opposition by saying since it was state-owned land, they didn't think clearance was necessary. Lafferty told the Board of Appeals that the network had spent $2,000,000 the prior year for 26 episodes and could not afford further cost.[29] Local residents were not happy with the hustle and bustle of activity in their neighborhood and feared their property values were going to suffer. When the show became a certified hit, the brouhaha finally began to settle somewhat. Some area residents even mellowed enough to relish bragging rights for their close proximity to the studio. Even though it looked as though the hurdle was behind them, Ft. Ruger would not be their final location, and it would not be the last round of battles over studio space.

The initial intention was to air the pilot at the end of September or the first of October. The hype was already good, and by early spring the series was being touted as another *Route 66*. Filming for the pilot began on November 6, 1967, and three months and over $800,000 later it was ready to roll out. A randomly selected test audience in New York saw it first, and while the overall reaction was positive, there were some changes to bring to the table.

CBS executives followed through with their earlier idea to debut the pilot of their new show in a theatrical venue. On February 19, an invitation-only audience filled the Royal Theatre in Honolulu and the presentation opened with then CBS Programming

Executive Perry Lafferty's announcement that filming for the series was set to go in April. He took the opportunity to demonstrate the network's commitment to their intent to be a positive presence in the islands. As part of the premier event, Lafferty presented a check to the Friends of the Iolani Palace restoration group for $12,000.

Iolani Palace dates back to 1879, when it was built for King Kalaknua, the last king of Hawaii. After the overthrow of the monarchy, the grand structure served a variety of functions and eventually housed the state government. As one of his many charitable causes, Lord later became actively involved in finding further funding for the restoration project. In 1971 he reached out to his contacts at the Colonial Williamsburg Foundation to ask for guidance in identifying appropriate potential funding sources to help with the costly work. He indicated he and Marie would be at their home in Los Angeles for a month beginning the first week of February and he hoped to have an opportunity to speak to someone about where they might start. Lord told them of the importance of preserving the only royal residence on American soil. Lord wrote, "It was the building that proudly displayed the first 50-star United States flag in 1959 when Hawaii become our 50th State." He signed his letter, "Aloha and mahalo," with an asterisk after *mahalo*, explaining, "it means thank you."[30]

Carl Humelsine followed up with some suggested sources to help with the five-million-dollar project. Seven years later, he extended an invitation to Lord to join the Raleigh Tavern Society, a support group for the perpetuation of Colonial Williamsburg. Humelsine hoped Lord's celebrity status would help them to identify potential donors for the site.

Lord did his part in the fundraising effort for the Iolani Restoration Project. A letter in his papers documents a gift of artwork to the project valued at $34,775. When Steve McGarrett and his *Five-O* unit took the watch, it was designated as their headquarters and exterior shots of the structure and the wooden staircase inside were frequently utilized in filming. A photo op of Steve McGarrett's office window at the Iolani Palace is still a popular item on tour bus agendas.

With 206 CBS affiliate stations ordering the show after the pilot, it certainly looked as though Freeman had a hit on his hands. The number of affiliate buy-ins was the largest number in CBS history at that time. It was not the last time the show made television history. The *New York Times* pushed out a lukewarm review the day after the first episode aired, saying there was a "modicum" of suspense, declaring the sequence to be "slow in coming," and criticizing the ending's "stereotyped gunplay." As for the cast, Lord was deemed "stern and efficient as the head lawman, but Patricia Smith ... took what honors were available."[31] For the most part, however, most acknowledged *Five-O* had hit the ground running in spite of some major hurdles still left to jump.

Hawaii Five-O was not Jack Lord's first appearance on Hawaiian television. He just happened to be in Hawaii when *Stoney Burke* was making its debut on the Mainland. Legendary disc jockey and promoter Tom Moffatt invited him to guest star on his TV rock and roll show. Stoney showed up in full cowboy attire, complete with a saddle and a lariat. When the show was over, Moffatt offered him a ride back to Waikiki. Lord asked to be let out of the car so he could walk around and look over the island scenery. "'I'll never forget seeing him walk off down Kalakaua Avenue in his cowboy get-up, carrying a saddle on his shoulder,' Moffatt said."[32]

In what would become a recurring need, Freeman had to put on his PR hat in October after the premiere when a group of University of Hawaii students protested plans to film an episode at the campus' East-West Center. Freeman had already received permission from the chancellor to film there, but students feared what the political slant of the script would be and what effect it would have on the center for international students. Freeman reassured the students the story did not have a controversial theme, but was rather a "love story." After he rewrote some of the script, the student group voted 12–2 to allow filming in the facility. The protest was not over, however, as the minority of resisters threatened to "intimidate" the institution. The episode was eventually filmed at a Hawaiian high school and a Buddhist shrine.[33]

For all the hype and the outpouring of confidence in the potential of the new show, and in spite of coming out of the gate with such promise, *Hawaii Five-O* began to falter by the first of February. When it fell to 73rd place in the Nielsen standings, it looked as though it may become a casualty of poor ratings, and the network took action. The show initially was in the wrong time slot for the format. It first aired at 8:00 p.m. on Thursday night following *Blondie*, a family comedy show based on cartoonist Chic Young's long running comic strip. *Blondie* debuted in newspapers across the country in 1930 and has maintained its popularity, still running in more than 200 newspapers. The decision to follow a clearly family themed program with a cop show that offered up violence and adult themes was undeniably a bad call by the network.

CBS at last acknowledged their bad judgment and switched spots with *Five-O* and the *Jonathan Winters Hour* airing at 10 o'clock on Wednesday nights. Ratings quickly jumped to the top 20. Even though he initially expressed concern in a July 31 *Desert News* article they may lose viewers if they have to "hunt for" the show, Lord soon acknowledged the near miss they had with the earlier time slot and he was ultimately pleased with the change and the immediate impact it had. "Our first eight shows were an absolute disaster. We were [preempted] four of the first nine weeks.... Then on Christmas night 1968, we were switched from 8 p.m. Thursdays to 10 p.m. Wednesdays. We jumped from 64th to 35th the first week and have been gradually moving up ever since. Like Phoenix we were truly risen from the dead."[34] *Five-O* would later move to an 8:30 spot on Tuesdays, and in fact, would move several times before it ended in 1980.

As *Five-O* rose from the ashes, Jack Lord's career advanced to a sit up and take notice status. In the weeks following the premiere of *Hawaii Five-O*, many of his earlier films and television appearances were showing up in programming schedules, and continued to do so for years afterwards. In 1980, Lord received a handwritten note from Lee Paul, who did two guest-starring roles on *Five-O*. He expressed his newfound admiration of Lord's acting ability after seeing a re-run of *God's Little Acre* on television. "You were superb, as was the entire cast and film. Here's hoping we have a chance to work together in a project of such quality and significance sometime soon."[35]

The ambitious program still faced challenges. After the first 25 shows, the budget ran $500,000 over, and CBS made a push to relocate production to Hollywood. Lord adamantly refused, and thankfully it was foreign markets that bailed them out in the early days. Lord contended it takes a year to "shake down" a new show, and after that first touch and go year, they had an 80 percent share of the audience. There was no denying they were a force to be reckoned with, and by the end of 1970, *Five-O* and Jack Lord were clearly flexing their hard-earned muscles. In interviews about the show, Leonard Freeman referred to Lord as "Jack the giant killer" as he counted off the competing programs that had fallen victim to the series. Lord was right on the money with his remark to his wife when he read that first script. This was indeed the one they had waited for.

While the pilot did much to establish the flavor of the new show, by the time the first episode aired it was clear the changes in casting were prudent ones. James MacArthur had already replaced Tim O'Kelley by the first episode, and it was an effective pairing. His character is, of course, critical to one of the most enduring catch phrases in television history. McGarrett's famous "Book 'em, Danno" originated in the "Twenty-Four Karat Kill" episode from the first season. The decision to cast Denning was a good one, and he brought a consistently strong presence.

Jack Lord stepped up with his hands-on approach early in the game. Before the premier episode aired, he had already clearly established his intention to have oversight. The pilot did not air on television until September, and Lord took steps in June to head off what he felt to be a bad judgment call with regard to some pending publicity photos. When presidential candidate Robert F. Kennedy was shot on June 5 and died from his injuries the following day, the call went out to TV networks to curb televised violence in the aftermath of the event. Some series edited out violent scenes, while others reverted to reruns rather than airing new episodes that may be judged to have excessive violence. Jack Lord stopped the release of a group of *Five-O* production stills he felt inappropriate in light of recent events. As would become his practice throughout his career, he continued to maintain full approval rights for any publicity about him.[36] In July before the pilot aired, *TV Guide* offered up a brief commentary on *Five-O*, calling it yet another violent TV show. The brief article offered a color two-page spread featuring two intriguing stills of Wo Fat and Steve McGarrett with the subtitle, "It's Onward and Downward with TV Violence."[37] As the show was going into its fifth year, when Lord was asked how he felt about the violence, he said that while it is hard to do a police show without violence, he personally hated it.

Some sources say Lord was a "silent partner" in all aspects of production, but *silent* may be a misnomer. He had extensive oversight in virtually all areas of the show. His hands-on approach to the details with which most actors are not concerned is very evident throughout the twelve-season run. Again, credit must be given where credit is due. *Hawaii Five-O* was well worth his efforts. The week after the pilot aired, veteran director Seymour Robbie, who worked on four episodes of *Five-O*, offered *Variety* his take on recent press about Lord's reputation as a difficult and uncooperative actor. "I resent this very much. He's the hardest working actor I ever directed and has only the success of the series at heart. Like any other actor, all he asks is to be directed by one he respects.... No actor ever worked harder to achieve [success]."[38] Robbie's observation was echoed by guest star Jack Albertson. "[Lord] doesn't believe in wasting money. He arrives on the set early and thoroughly prepared. He's ready to work. If you're ready to work and know your lines, you have a wonderful time."[39]

Their next studio location for the show was also fraught with legal battles. The 4.8 acres set aside for the new *Five-O* studio was included in a 52-acre parcel leased to the University of Hawaii as the site for a new community college. A 1975 letter from CBS Vice President Robert Norvet to Robert Moranha, Vice President of the East Diamond

Head Association, reported CBS had promised to vacate the Fort Ruger facility prior to November 1. The governor, the president of the University of Hawaii, and the State of Hawaii Adjutant General supported the temporary use of a site currently leased to the university. Norvet proposed a phasing out of the present site, asking permission to continue to use the sound stage at the present, with a target relocation date of administration and transportation activity by May 1. Norvet further promised that use of the premises would be reduced to no more than two days a week, and all operations would cease on or before October 31. Norvet implied that denial of this time frame was going to require the "drastic actions." He made mention of the impact on local economy of the show during its seven year run there.[40]

The Association had successfully shut down Hawaii Studios where *Five-O* had operated as part of an out-of-court settlement, and the proposed new site was a half-mile away from the Hawaii Studios location. This time the association challenged the university's right to lease property that lay within the Diamond Head State Monument, an area designated for public recreational purposes only. The underlying strategy hinged on the contingency that denying the university their lease would automatically render CBS's sublease invalid. Fortunately, however, the outcome worked in favor of the network. The judge in the case ruled that the property in question was not within Diamond Head State Monument boundaries, and the argument did not hold up.[41] *Five-O* was up and running again, in spite of some area residents' continued desire to have them leave.

A hallmark of the series was the quality of its guest stars. Freeman had promised from the beginning they would be "of the heavy stripe" and for the entire twelve seasons he stayed good to his word. A guest spot on *Hawaii Five-O* was a sweet gig and they had no trouble finding "heavy stripe" takers. The accommodations were first rate and the opportunity to hang out in Hawaii on an expense account was icing on the cake. The show featured a good number of notable celebrities in guest starring roles from virtually all genres—theatre, movies, and television. Several local public figures were also recruited for guest roles, including area celebrities, news show anchors, newspaper columnists, and area political figures, such as Howard Miyaki, majority leader of the State House of Representatives.

After that demanding first year, Lord told a reporter for *The Boston Globe*, "All our shots are strictly on the Hawaiian soil. It's expensive but we feel it's worth it. We go in the hole $25,000 with each episode."[42] Four years later, he continued to echo Freeman's assessment of the downside of doing the whole series on location. "'Five-O' is the second highest budgeted show in television (behind 'Gunsmoke'). We have 40 or 50 people from Hollywood on $700 a month subsistence, in addition to their salaries. Also, we have to fly everything in—guest stars, camera parts, film, props, special vehicles, wardrobe, etc."[43] In 1970, he had reported the show cost $1,660 an hour to shoot and the budget per episode was $210,000. Even though they went over by $500,000 in the first 25 shows, he emphasized they had later made up the loss in foreign sales. Lord said, "The show is seen in 35 countries and has a 25–30 mil audience here. It was second in a recent Nielsen rating period."[44]

Issues and headaches aside, Lord frequently acknowledged the benefits of filming in the islands, including the artistic and technical advantages of the pure, clear air, and the intense light. He and Freeman stood steadfastly by their decision, and ultimately they earned bragging rights for their ambitious design. They quickly learned to be creative and flexible and they made good use of the resources they had available to them.

Even though utilizing non-professionals in small parts and as extras was aesthetically and financially advantageous, some curses came with the blessings. It was easy at times to forget they were not professionals and some needed a lot of help and coaching. Kam Fong said Lord did sometimes lose his cool with the extras pulled from the public, but he was of the opinion he was only trying to help them be better. Lord frequently said he appreciated having the opportunity to work with local people. In an early morning phone interview in Waikiki on March 3, 1972, he told Todd Mason the beauty of their location was that the land in Hawaii had not been "exploited" by the motion picture business. He said instead of the same "tired faces of extras in the background," common in Hollywood films, Hawaiian locals offered something fresh. He resented the attitude of many of the extras he had previously seen on the mainland, calling them lackadaisical and chastising them for their lack of involvement in the work they were doing. He said they are not "picture makers," but are there only to get a day's pay, spending their downtime on set playing cards or just hanging out. By contrast, with *Five-O* and its unique location, they were blessed with "lovely fresh faces—male, female, old, young—just gorgeous." He loved the mixture of cultures and the variety and realism it brought to their scenes.[45] And Jack Lord liked professionalism on all fronts.

Hawaii Five-O was a life changing experience for Lord in a number of ways, not the least of which was the decision to relocate to the islands. Although it was not their original intention, Jack and Marie Lord soon moved permanently to Hawaii, foregoing their original plan to live six months of the year in Hawaii and six months in California for as long as the series lasted. A clipping in Lord's papers from the May 3–5, 1968, *Waikiki Beach Press* includes a photograph of Jack and Marie with *Five-O* co-producer Robert Stambler. The caption reports the Lords had returned to the islands to establish permanent residence.[46] After five and half years of living in Hawaii, Lord admitted the first couple of years were tough, attributing it to the challenges of being a newcomer in an "ingrown community." He saw a culture reluctant to accept anyone or anything new, but the Lords eventually not only accepted that truth, they grew to love it.

Their first Hawaii address was a penthouse at the Illikai Hotel—the building that was the setting for *Hawaii Five-O*'s iconic opening each week. They soon purchased a 3,500 square foot condominium at 4999 Kahala Avenue with a beautiful view of the beach, located near the Kahala Hilton where guest stars for the series were sometimes housed. Lord posted his real name on Apartment #372 to protect their privacy. Sources disagree on the exact date they purchased their Kahala condo. Several say it was 1970, but he told a reporter for the *Boston Globe* in November of 1969 they had just bought the third floor condo for $200,000. The price tag was $160,000. Lord told a reporter for the *Houston Chronicle* they had bought the place "on faith." He said home had always been important to them, and even though they normally weren't ones to take chances, they loved the location and they couldn't resist it. As it turned out, they need not have worried.

By the second season, Jack Lord hit his stride with the McGarrett character, and it didn't go unnoticed by the network. He got a letter from CBS Story Editor Frank Barton that was penned the day after "A Bullet for McGarrett" aired. Barton confessed that while he had little time to write letters, he felt he must share his impression of the episode. "Your performance was outstanding ... I am a man who admires good acting and likes to think that he knows something about that profession. And I want to say that you are doing, in my opinion, week after week, the best work in series television."[47] Barton expressed confidence they would be renewed for a third season. Lord kept the letter.

Lord was set to be included in Marquis Who's Who in 1969. They sent him a draft of the biography that was to be included in the listing to review. In addition to filling in some missing dates, he also called their attention to having missed some of his more prominent achievements to date. "It seems strange to me," he noted, "that since I am noted primarily as an actor that you do not include some motion picture credits, such as GOD'S LITTLE ACRE, MAN OF THE WEST, DR. NO and WILLIAMSBURG—THE STORY OF A PATRIOT [caps in original]. The first three films are considered to be classic films and may go down in history as three of the great grossers of all time."[48] He made note in pen at the bottom of his copy of the letter that he had ordered a copy of the book on May 13, and he had included a check for $28.80.

Lord authored an article in 1971, describing how beautifully their decision to settle permanently in Hawaii fed his lifetime fascination with ships and the sea. He recalled the years he spent traveling as a teenager on tramp ships and his time with the Merchant Marines, expressing his delight with living in a place that offered him the opportunity to indulge in his passions. The article features detailed descriptions and history of some of his favorite ships, and he confesses he and Marie often stood on their lanai, looking out to sea as he tried to identify ships coming and going from Honolulu Harbor.[49] Lord reportedly owned additional apartments in the unit that he leased out to other tenants. Tolles says he also maintained a separate unit in the complex that was utilized as office space for his Lord and Lady Production Company.

After Marie passed away in 2005, the condo went on the market when the rest of their estate sold. It sat empty until the spring of 2008. Several sources indicate it was in need of extensive repairs by time it sold, and the cost of the land lease had increased sharply, making the property a hard sell. Originally listed for over $2,000,000, it eventually sold for $800,000.

When Glen Campbell filmed an episode of his *Goodtime Hour* variety show in Hawaii, Lord was a featured guest star. When it aired on October 19, 1971, audiences who had not seen Stoney Burke in the rodeo arena got the rare opportunity to hear a sample of Lord's singing voice when he offered up a rendition of "Strawberry Roan," Stoney's customary opening number in rodeo arenas. Lord saved a letter he got from a young fan soon after the episode aired. She recommended he consider doing his own specials, astutely noting that he should broadcast them from locations other than Waikiki, showing areas of the islands most people never saw. "You know cab drivers to store clerks really dig your acting," she wrote. She called out Dwight Whitney for his defamatory *TV Guide* article about Lord, saying he had the "mentality of ... a flea."[50]

A gathering of bystanders was one thing the cast and crew could count on wherever *Five-O* was filming. Large crowds showed up to watch the work early on, and local off-duty police were frequently on hand to help with crowd control, to step in as extras, or to fill bit parts as needed. As the interest and momentum grew, the show had to institute

Lord was a prolific artist whose work was acquired by museums across the country. His favorite studio was the lanai of their Kahala condominium (Photofest).

a strict policy of no visitors on the set, and Lord kept a firm hand on it. When fans gathered where they were shooting, even though he was sometimes spotted between takes, signing autographs or chatting, normally when he was working he was all business, and he insisted on the same from everyone else on set.

As he settled into the McGarrett role, he continued to garner an impressive and diverse fan base. One very notable Jack Lord enthusiast made his admiration public on January 14, 1973, when the Lords attended an Elvis Presley concert by special invitation from Presley himself. The concert in Hawaii was set to be telecast around the world by satellite, and much to their surprise, Elvis introduced Lord from the stage, calling him one of his favorite actors. They later met with Presley backstage, and they wound up entertaining Elvis at their home a few days later. Elvis brought gifts to the Lords, including a gold-plated Walther PPK handgun he gave to Jack. Some accounts say Presley gave Marie a diamond and emerald ring, and that Jack presented Presley a rare banjo, part of a collection of rare instruments the Lords owned, most of which they had donated to UCLA's Music Department.[51] Jack and Marie Lord saw Elvis in concert again in Las Vegas the following month when they were on the mainland during a break from filming.

In 1979, Lord got a letter from Marian Cocke in Memphis, Tennessee. Cocke was Presley's nurse who wrote a book about her years with Elvis. She mentioned that Presley had spoken very fondly of Lord on many occasions. She was planning a vacation in Hawaii and wondered if she would be able to meet him and perhaps get an autographed picture for Presley's grandmother, also a Jack Lord fan, and for her mother. Lord had written her mother's name and the name of Elvis' wife and daughter on the letter, along with a phone number with a Memphis area code.[52]

Just as he had done while working on *Stoney Burke*, he customarily rode alone to shooting locations, using the time to study his lines and to prepare himself for the day's work. With the fast and lucrative success of *Five-O* and the financial security he had from *Stoney*, he was now in a position to go one better, however. Since shooting locations were spread all over the islands, sometimes involving twenty or more spots for a single episode, the logistics of moving about were intense. They could be working in scenic spots for the day, or they might be parked along the street for hours. Lord's purchase of a customized portable dressing room became yet another target for his critics who held it up as further evidence of an inflated ego.

Sources vary as to the cost of his customized travel car, with estimates ranging from $35,000 to $50,000. He designed it himself, and, true to Jack Lord style, he had thoroughly done his homework. It was built on a bus chassis, and he had collected a number of school bus catalogs as he was working on the design. He wrote to several companies to determine the best option for what he envisioned. He and Marie laid out the design themselves on graph paper, beginning with the wiring schematics.

From the outside, it looked very much like a camper that might belong to tourists in the area, but the distinctive "Five-O" license plate made it difficult to hide the fact that Jack Lord was in the area. Lord said Marie had a hand in the decorating, and the color scheme with lots of greens and yellows harkened back to the décor of their Kahala apartment.

Lord sent out a memo, asking that when references were made to his portable dressing room it should be called "Jack Lord's motor home," "Jack Lord's travel home," or "Jack Lord's dressing room and travel office." Although he sometimes referred to it as his "travel car," he had learned "travel car" was a copyright protected name, and to avoid potential legal repercussions, he asked the term not be used in press releases and other published sources. Lord told the *Los Angeles Times* in August of 1968 that he and Freeman had "footed the bill" for a second portable dressing room for guest stars. "You can't bring a guest all the way over here from Hollywood and ask him to dress in the men's room," he said.[53]

The air-conditioned unit was equipped with a dressing area, hair and makeup area, and a small kitchenette, complete with a refrigerator imported from Sweden. Primary Five-O offices were located across from the studio, but he also had a small office area in the motor home, and he frequently held meetings there. When he interviewed Todd Mason about working as his stand-in he asked if it would be a problem if he were asked to remove lunch trays when meetings were scheduled around the lunch break. He told Mason he customarily got in the chuck wagon line with everyone else and picked up his own lunch tray. He said he had experienced some pushback from previous stand-ins when he asked them to clear lunch trays before meetings. He said he didn't want to offend him by asking him to do something he may consider a menial task. Mason assured him he would not be offended and he would be happy to do whatever Lord needed him to do. He had worked for Mike Connors in the same position for a long time, and he told Lord he had always been willing to do whatever Connors asked him to do. People who visited Lord in his travel car frequently commented on the eclectic library they saw there. It was a refuge for him between takes as they traveled from location to location, and he frequently hosted journalists if they had scheduled interviews while he was working.

In a lovely scene from an episode of *Emme's Island Moments*, a local TV news magazine series, Lord comes out from his travel car to distribute autographed photos to a waiting crowd of eager youngsters. He reprimands the boys for pushing to the front, telling them to stand back and allow the "ladies" to go first. When one boy asks him why, he tells him "that is just the way it is." They immediately complied.

When they had finished twenty-four shows back to back for season eight, he told Mason he was exhausted. Mason suggested he surely had four or five more years in him, and Lord told him that was not his idea of heaven. "And I have 192 scars on my body to prove it," he said. He was confident the show could run two more years, but as it turned out, he had four yet to go. Mason apologized that a lengthy story he had done about Lord three years earlier after an extensive interview had not been published. Lord said perhaps the problem was he hadn't been "snotty or evil enough."

In spite of the initial difficulties finding appropriate studio space and other out-of-the gate issues, it was obvious that Jack Lord and *Hawaii Five-O* were good for Hawaii. By 1970, the show was seen in some 25,000,000 homes in the United States and in foreign countries each week. Hawaii was now the go-to place for tourists. *Hawaii Five-O* gave people who couldn't otherwise enjoy the unique culture and extraordinary beauty of the islands the opportunity to see it for themselves. Lord racked up a number of "good citizen" recognitions that year. Sales and marketing executives in Hawaii named Jack Lord "Outstanding Salesman of the Year" for his contributions to increasing the tourist business. In February he was recognized as "Citizen of the Day" for his outstanding achievement and contribution to civic advancement and betterment of the community. The ceremony aired on Honolulu Station KGU77.

On April 17, the Hawaii State House of Representatives formally expressed their appreciation to Lord for his "outstanding contributions to the State of Hawaii" when they honored him with a formal house resolution. They credited a large part of the success of the show to his "remarkable acting ability" and to his "exceptional energy and professionalism."⁵⁴ Marie attended the ceremony with him. In his acceptance speech, Lord recalled shopping as a youngster for books with his father on 4th Avenue in New York City. He remembered finding a worn book of poetry by Hawaiian poet Don Blanding. The first poem in the book was "What Aloha Means," and he said he had memorized it, earning his customary penny per line from his father for his effort. He closed his remarks by reciting all thirteen lines.⁵⁵ He later included the poem on some of his lithographs. Lord kept a blind copy of a letter CBS Talent and Program Acquisitions Director Anne Nelson penned to Dr. Harry Wong, director of the Hawaii film office, thanking him for sending a copy of the house resolution honoring Lord.

A February 1, 1980, letter in Lord's papers documents a proposal from the Hawaii State Senate to also honor him with commending him for his contribution to the State of Hawaii after the series ended. State Senator Charles M.

Lord's third *TV Guide* cover was for a September 1973 issue. Even though Lord's image is featured on the cover, the article was about James MacArthur (*TV Guide Magazine* cover courtesy *TV Guide Magazine*, LLC © 1973).

Campbell asked Lord to confirm that he would be available to come for the presentation, asking him to send possible dates that worked with his schedule. Lord wrote a reminder across the bottom of the letter to call Campbell the second week of March to discuss it. It is unclear why he wanted to wait six weeks before responding to the letter. Attempts to confirm that he received the senatorial resolution were unsuccessful.⁵⁶

On July 23, 1970, Lord sent off a scathing memo on CBS letterhead to Leonard Freeman, Michael Buchanan, and eight others in CBS offices. "I seem to make this speech at the beginning of every season but I'd like to do it again." Unhappy about the choice of a photo that went out with a press release that showed up in the June 28 issue of the *Indianapolis Star*, he clearly expressed his disappointment. "What person who cared anything about this show would release a picture like this? ... Please, gentlemen, we've worked very hard to create an image for McGarrett. Don't let unthinking people destroy it by the total disregard of our objectives."⁵⁷ A clipping from the *Star* from the June 17, 1970, issue is included in his papers. The photo with the article is a headshot that looks like it may have been taken from a larger print.

Two years into the series, Lord was asked about his reputation as a difficult and high-strung person. His response was true to form—concise and direct. "'Everyone who's been on the show, and that includes the technical help, want to come back or stay on. Does that sound like temperament?"[58]

As the popularity of the show continued to climb, Jack Lord became one of the more popular attractions for the locals and for tourists. Any time information leaked about locations for the day's shooting, large crowds gathered. In 1970, filming was scheduled for the Punch Bowl district in Honolulu, and the crew was suddenly and unexpectedly swarmed by a large group of children. The crowd increased exponentially when a teacher released her class to go watch the action, and Lord found himself surrounded by a massive swarm of youngsters clamoring for autographs. Locals called him "Jacklord" and as the show continued to climb in popularity, wherever he was, he customarily drew a crowd, chanting "Jacklord, Jacklord." He didn't like the attention when he working, however. Early in filming for the first season, Lord was talking to a reporter in the dressing room, and when he was called to work, they went outside to find a large crowd had gathered to watch. "It's disconcerting," he said. "We're here to work. This is not a luau."[59]

It was common for as many as ten policemen from area precincts to step in to assist with keeping order during location shots. Lord said, "We try to maintain some kind of secrecy regarding our location shooting sites. Crowd control is a definite problem for us, and no matter what precautions we take, people always seem to find us. Naturally, they cause delays ... and delays are costly." Lord confessed that while he winced when they found themselves surrounded by a throng of fans and onlookers in the middle of shooting, he admitted that as "a plain old actor" he reveled in the attention.[60]

Even though his contract called for the opportunity to direct at least one episode per calendar year, it was season six when he made his directorial debut. "Death with Father" would film in September of 1973, but Lord's intense review and revision work was already in progress in early July. In August, Lord put in a rush order for a new finder from a camera shop in Hollywood for the occasion, and he was anxious to work from both sides of the camera. The experience turned out to be bittersweet. Two days before the episode aired on January 22, 1974, Leonard Freeman died after heart surgery. Karen Rhodes says Lord tried to call Freeman after his surgery to express his appreciation for his work on editing the episode, but Freeman never got the message. Jack Lord stood alone with the heavy burden of a producer. For the remainder of the series, Freeman's title, executive producer, would not be reassigned.

Lord's business-first approach to his work was a frequent source of criticism for his hard line on interruptions and waste. In August of 1974, he took extreme measures to make his point about the importance of compliance to the no visitors on set policy, and it led to an incident that wound up getting the attention of CBS President Robert Wood. Lord, director Bob Sweeney, and producer Bill Finnegan locked horns when Finnegan insisted his guests be allowed to remain on set during filming. Sweeney and Lord refused to work until the visitors were removed from the set. When Lord didn't show up to work, Finnegan still refused to remove his visitors. Eventually, adjustments to the schedule were made that presented an acceptable solution to all parties. Wood said Lord and Finnegan showed an "overwhelming spirit of professionalism" in solving the dispute and reported the situation "never reached the point where calm deliberation was lost."[61]

In a good illustration of how "the truth" often depends on who is doing the telling, the *Chicago Tribune* offered a totally different version of the outcome. Leading off with "Jack Lord, the egomaniacal actor whose age has been stuck at 42 for at least a decade," the story reported Lord "fired" Finnegan. The article further stated when CBS notified him that he did not have the authority to fire the producer Lord had initiated a boycott. Wood called the actor and "told Lord to drag his tail back to work or he'd be dumped and replaced by another chunk of cardboard." According to the *Tribune*, Lord said he came back to work only after Acting Governor Ariyoshi called and begged him to do so.[62] Earlier that month, *Daily Variety* ran a story confirming Ariyoshi did call Lord, asking him to consider the important effect the show had on the state's economy, but the details from other reports were not included in the story.[63]

There are other accounts that indicate Lord did allow exceptions to the no visitors on the set rule. His papers include several letters of appreciation from fortunate souls who were allowed to watch the *Five-O* cast and crew at work. A September 30, 1976, letter to a producer on a location shoot has Lord soundly reprimanding staff for a bad call about making him aware of a couple of visitors to the set. An elderly female fan had called requesting an opportunity to meet Lord and he agreed to meet her. When she called back to finalize the appointment, the person who took the call refused to pass her message on to him. "This is a case where someone in the office made a decision for us and it broke an old lady's heart," he said. Shortly after that, a good friend of the Lords had called while in Hawaii to arrange a visit and that message was not forwarded as well.

By 1976, the show was receiving some 5,000 fan letters a week. While he acknowledged it was a difficult chore to determine who should and should not have access, he asked that staff be informed they were not to decide which messages to withhold. "Will you please inform all secretaries ... they need not try to decide what to do about callers. Just take the name and telephone number and call my home immediately, and Marie or I will decide if the call is important or not."[64]

A Wisconsin couple requested to visit the set when they came to the islands for a two-week holiday. They got a handwritten response from Lord on plain white paper. He explains the difficulty with allowing visitors on the set since they received hundreds of requests each week. Lord consented to allow the couple to visit, however, instructing them to contact Margaret Doversola when they arrived, saying she would direct them to the shooting location for the day. Lord added a P.S. to the note. "Pardon the stationery. This is written in a car on the way to work at 6 a.m."[65] Los Angeles radio talk show host Michael Jackson and his wife were treated with a visit to the set during their Hawaiian vacation and his letter of appreciation to Lord revealed they were also entertained by Jack and Marie in their home while there.[66]

After four years in Hawaii, the Lords returned to Hollywood in January of 1972 to close on the sale of the apartment they had called home for ten years before their move to the islands. While there, they visited with many of their friends, including Marie Wilson, who starred in the production of *The Little Hut* with Lord seventeen years earlier. He returned to Los Angeles in November that same year to attend Wilson's funeral after she lost her battle with cancer. The Lords continued to keep up with old friends and with people who had helped him along the way. They customarily made visits to Los Angeles and they returned to New York when time allowed. During a two-week visit to New York City in the 1970s, Lord happily reported they had tickets to ten Broadway plays, one for each night of the ten days they would be town.

As success of the series continued to grow, demands on Lord's time increased exponentially. An item in the June 15, 1972, *Honolulu Advertiser* was a unique testimony to the far-reaching success of the show. In the "Faces Out Front" section there was a personal notice to Jack Lord from Eddie Sherman. "I received a call yesterday from Israel (first time ever from that part of the world)." Sherman said officials were requesting Lord come to Israel to participate in the 25th Anniversary of the State of Israel Celebration as their guest of honor, and they hoped he would agree to bring one of his paintings for a charity auction. By 1972, the already-tired Lord was already speaking about a possible end to the series, telling reporters he was thinking he would not renew his five-year contract. "I don't think my motor runs fast enough for TV," he told *The Atlanta Constitution*.[67] The following year, he reported that his new network contract allowed him at least two weeks off during each eight weeks of filming, but he continued to struggle with the pressure of his punishing schedule. He had asked for a yearly contract, but the studio refused, so he signed for another five years. "Acting in a series is emotionally tiring, mental work," he said in 1975. "We run up hills and drive fast cars and all of that, but the attrition really set in when you are keyed up and have to learn 10 pages of dialogue a day."[68]

When the first episode of season nine aired on September 30, 1976, McGarrett is in the middle of moving to a new office. The exterior of Ioloni Palace was totally covered with scaffolding as extensive real-life renovations were in progress, and filming in and around the building was just not feasible. The CBS lease was up on the Ft. Ruger location, so network executives had to procure an alternative site. Production went on, however, and the storyline embraced the intrusion by depicting a move for the *Five-O* team. They chose the old Territorial Building for a temporary location. Constructed in 1926, it was the former home of government offices. In the season opener, "Nine Dragons," McGarrett is complaining about the chaos of moving their headquarters as he unpacks his belongings in his new office. The temporary space depicted is the original existing office space in the building, not a production constructed set.

Some of the filming of the two-part "Nine Dragons" episode took place in Hong Kong in early May. Lord had just hired Todd Mason as his stand-in at the time, and Mason praised the strength of the episode to an acquaintance during a taped phone conversation. He indicated the script offered Lord the opportunity to show his vulnerable side and to do some "real acting," particularly during the scenes when he was tortured and helpless. Mason said he felt strongly season nine would be the last season for the series. He said Lord was showing signs of exhaustion, and the grueling six-day workweeks were wearing on him and on the crew. While the actors normally did 12 or 14-hour workdays, the crew was putting in 18-hour shifts during their eight months of filming each year. They customarily had the fourth Saturday of each month off. During that conversation, an unidentified female *Five-O* crewmember told Mason that when Lord was tired he was often difficult. Both agreed, however, much of it was because he would accept nothing less than letter perfect.[69] While in Hong Kong, *South China Morning Post* ran an extensive article on Lord and the success of the series. The reporter asked him if the stories he had heard were true, that Lord "wakes up some mornings ... as

Steve McGarrett." Lord found the remark amusing, and his answer was brief and direct. "No. Then you become psychotic."⁷⁰ He talked at length about how he had built McGarrett from his own experiences, how he had begun to make him his own over the period of six or seven weeks after receiving the first script.

"Nine Dragons" was not the only episode that took the *Five-O* cast and crew to a foreign country for filming. In April of 1978 they were on site in Singapore for three weeks for work on a season eleven episode, "The Year of the Horse." Filed with Lord's papers is a collection of photocopies of a variety of Singapore papers covering his visit and the filming for the episode. The copies have not weathered the years well, and most of them lack bibliographic information, but they are still legible and some of the articles are written in English. The stories include details about CBS executives' work to obtain legal permissions and clearances with local police, customs agents, and other "statutory bodies." There are reports of the star treatment for him and Marie from fans wherever they appeared, and details of the impressive number of social functions they were invited to attend.

The kick-off event soon after their arrival was a poolside welcome dinner with 100 invited guests at the Shangri-La Hotel on April 17. Marie was featured on the front page of one paper, in a story by Nancy Byramji. "Lord's Lady: Marie's the Only One for Jack," tells of the couple's famous devotion to each other. Lord sat for several press conferences during his time there, and he fielded a wide variety of questions, including why

McGarrett's "Book 'em, Danno" soon found its way into pop culture. Lord's shrewd business sense and his insistence upon artistic control, especially after the death of series creator Leonard Freeman, were significant factors in the highly successful twelve-year-run (CBS/Photofest).

is McGarrett such a "stone face," why does he wear that blue suit so much, and just what is that stuff McGarrett eats from a paper cup with chopsticks. Jack Lord's American audiences clearly were not the only ones who were intrigued by Steve McGarrett.

In July, Lord sent a scathing memo on network letterhead to Producer Fred Baum, expressing his disapproval of an arrangement that he made with the Ford Motor Company in Singapore for approval of their use of color photos of Lord with the cars he had used while there. "I do *not* approve of this arrangement and am incensed that it was made without my knowledge or consent. This has *never* been done before, and I assume will never be done again—by *anyone* connected with this company." He reminded Baum that he had "sacrificed hundreds of thousands of dollars" to maintain his stand on no commercials or commercial tie-ins of any kind.[71]

Lord clipped an article from the September 8, 1978, *Hollywood Reporter* about a Hollywood director who had recently misrepresented his project to officials in Singapore in order to get approvals to film there. There was considerable backlash from the incident, as filmmakers chastised the director for creating future difficulties and distrust of future Hollywood projects. Lord circled the article, noting he had written a letter to the *Los Angeles Times*, expressing his anger about the same incident. Lord's letter was an indictment of director Peter Bogdanovich's dishonest representation of a film he was shooting in Singapore at the same time the *Five-O* production was under way there. *Saint Jack* was based on Paul Thoreaux's novel about a young man who tries to open a brothel in Singapore, a concept that would not sit well with the local authorities.

Lord called out Bogdanovich for misrepresenting the story, and for withholding the truth that is was based on Thoreaux's novel. He was infuriated to learn the director had mentioned *Five-O*'s concurrent work in the city in such a way as to imply affiliation with them. "God forbid that the Singapore authorities might confuse Bogdanovich with us," he wrote. Lord had nothing but praise for the hospitality and cooperation of the local authorities.[72]

Hawaii Five-O surpassed everyone's expectations in the level of success it achieved. The grueling schedule and Lord's intense oversight beyond the front of the camera was wearing on him. His papers include extensive, typed editing notes with his changes, some with his approval written at the bottom and a request that he see the notes again with his suggestions included. By the eighth season, he was talking about looking to end the show. He frequently told friends and the press he felt they were nearing the end of the series. As it turned out, however, the weary cast and crew would pull up their bootstraps for four more seasons.

When Jack Lord was at last ready to step away from Steve McGarrett, he did not waiver in his commitment to giving it his all. "When we filmed our last show, the 284th, I strove just as much as I did on the pilot. That last show meant just as much to me as the first."[73]

CBS Press Agent Betty Lamm, who had a thirty-five-year career with the network, sent a letter to the Lords, expressing her heartfelt sadness to see the end of *Five-O*. She commended both of them for the "back-breaking schedule" they kept for the entire run of the show, crediting Lord for his part in the longevity and success of it. "It's thanks to Jack that it has maintained and held this over a decade kind of record," she wrote.[74] Lord wrote "beautiful letter" on the envelope.

McGarrett finally slams the door on his nemesis Wo Fat, played by Khigh Dhiegh, in the final episode (CBS/Photofest).

When it was all said and done, *Hawaii Five-O* had been good for Jack Lord, for CBS, and for Hawaii. Over the years, CBS spent $100,000,000 filming the show in the islands. An added benefit was not a only a significant increase in tourism, but when *Five-O* shut down, four other companies were filming there at the time. Lord was perplexed at the continued pushback he had endured, even after the show was clearly a landmark success. Crew members told him *Hawaii Five-O* had paid for their homes, sent their children to college, and taken care of their day-to-day needs for twelve years. No award from Hollywood could have better communicated to Jack Lord that his career had been a stellar success.

Eleven

Forgiving Poe

When William Shakespeare said, "One man in his time plays many parts," he was talking about the seven stages of a man's lifetime. His words are often used to describe those people who have more than their share of talents and abilities. It can be a blessing, however, that also comes with its share of curses. It is not uncommon for people with very diverse abilities to set very high standards not only for themselves, but for others as well. Jack Lord struggled with the inability to settle for anything less than perfect where his work was concerned, and he made no apologies for it. "I suffer from perfectionism," he told Todd Mason in 1972. "I realize that we go through life and we get one shot at it, and I want whatever I do to be the best possible effort. So we, Leonard Freeman and I, and the people that are close to us ... have set a standard of quality for ourselves and our crew. A guideline. We try to come up to it every moment of every day."[1] After Lord died, Kam Fong acknowledged his determination to have everyone on board with his vision. "'He was always a strict taskmaster, a perfectionist.... When we were on the set, it was strictly business; he wouldn't stand for any horseplay.'"[2]

Albert Nalick, Vice President of the National Society of Arts & Letters, offered what may be the best analogy for the slings and arrows Lord suffered throughout his career for his expectation of perfection from himself and from those around him. "We could forgive Poe for his drunkenness [sic] for what he in turn gave the world. Lord is faulted more on his personality ... than his achievements, and that should give you some idea of the caliber of his critics. Critics have always attacked the doers of the world, the ones with courage and imagination, and there's simply more to Jack Lord to attack than most men."[3] Considering the enduring nature of Lord's work, perhaps he is entitled to a pass on being a tough taskmaster.

In February of 1963, Lord told Jane Ardmore about a chance meeting he had with film icon Joan Crawford two months earlier in Memphis. Crawford's reputation for being difficult is legendary, and Lord offered up his take on it. He described Crawford as a "kind of dynamo," a woman who had ambition in its highest form. He acknowledged that an overinflated ego can be destructive, but it should never be confused with ambition. He was brought up to believe those who wanted to be successful should embrace ambition. "I don't think you can survive if you don't have ambition," he said.[4] His comments offset the criticism he suffered early in his career as he turned down role after role, waiting for the one that felt right, the one he knew he could run with. His critics wrote off his highly selective approach as evidence of his own sense of self-importance, but Lord stood firm, waiting for roles that fit. As an artist, Lord had a heightened visual acuity. In his painting and in his acting, he would not be satisfied until what he saw with his eyes matched what he saw in his head. He admitted he frequently destroyed canvases when they failed to meet his expectations.

Richard Denning worked closely with Lord for a number of years and he offered a more practical theory about the grueling demands of Lord's "tight ship" management style. Denning was adamant that Lord's motive was tied more to his diligent oversight of everyone's time. The business side of Lord had no patience with those who showed a disregard for other people's time and money. The man of many parts demanded the creative side of the job was always spot on, but he was also very attentive to the bottom line.

Working on a level that few actors do, Lord gave careful attention to virtually every aspect of the production, on and off camera, and his papers are replete with examples of just how closely he monitored the details. One good illustration is the trail of memos documenting his diligence in finding another source for a specific kind of battery they used when it became unavailable from their customary supplier. After extended research, he eventually came back with a solution that would save both time and money—they would buy them directly from the manufacturer. Shopping for batteries is a unique role for the star of a highly successful series. His critics saw these kinds of hands-on oversight as evidence of his ego. Lord saw it as protecting his interests and the interests of everyone involved with the work.

He and Marie watched every weekly episode of *Hawaii Five-O* together, and Lord carefully critiqued the creative process and the production details. After watching "Year of the Horse," the final episode of the eleventh season, he penned a memo to Tony Barr, director of Current Dramatic Programming at CBS, expressing his concern that the episode had too many commercials placed too closely together. Lord saw a distracting interruption in the flow of the story. Three days later, he got a detailed reply from Barr. "'We checked the tapes of 'Year of the Horse' for the commercial positions which concerned you. They clocked 14 minutes of commercials in the two hours, allowable in a two-hour show. If you look at the number of commercials in each position, plus the number of commercials in the allowable station break period, it is easy to understand why one would get the feeling that there were too many commercials.'"[5] Lord was satisfied with the response.

In defense of his meticulous oversight, Lord told journalist Anthony La Camera "I look upon this show as a child and, therefore, I am most solicitous of it.... Yes, I'm a perfectionist and I've been that way all my life.... We go this way only once, and we should give the most to it and get the most out of it."[6] Lord was quick to defend his child when the need arose. A stellar example occurred after an episode from the second season set off a political firestorm. "Bored, She Hung Herself" aired on January 7, 1970, and then was never seen in re-runs or syndication and was not included in DVD collections of the series. The episode has a young woman trying a yoga exercise that involves a self- hanging technique. The intent is to stop before reaching the point of passing out. When the woman is found dead, the assumption is she has accidently killed herself during the exercise. At a 1996 *Five-O* convention, Leonard Freeman's widow addressed the reason for the decision to pull the episode, explaining someone had died while duplicating the technique. The same explanation is offered in several listings of banned television episodes. Actor Joe Berliner appeared in the episode and he confirmed a viewer died after trying the exercise. In the aftermath of the event, Rhode Island Senator and Chair of the U.S. Senate Committee on Communications, John O. Pastore, singled out *Hawaii Five-O* as a prime example of the inherent dangers of "rampant television violence" at the time. Jack Lord's response was to call Pastore a "big fat windbag." It was not his first sparring match with the senator, however.

In a January 24, 1977, letter to CBS Director of Talent Administration Anne R. Nelson, Lord put on his managerial face and politely questioned the rationale behind what he felt was a case of playing favorites. His "child" had been overlooked, and he wanted to know why. Beginning his letter with "Perhaps you can enlighten me," Lord wondered why the local *TV Guide* for the week featured a full-page ad for *Kojak*, paid for by the network. "In my recollection, we have never had such support from CBS. I'm wondering why, Anne?"[7]

The April 15, 1969, issue of *Daily Variety* ran a full-page reprint of an article columnist Nicholas Von Hoffman had done for the *Washington Post*. "Where's the Real Violence on Television?" was an indictment of Pastore's proposal that the surgeon general spend a million dollars to study the connection between television and violence. Hoffman took issue with the senator's focusing solely on television programming while ignoring the violence depicted night after night on news programming and in the movies. He suggested the same microscope should also be turned on Saturday morning cartoons which were replete with violence and intended solely for children. "Juxtaposed against such a moral analysis of the causes of violence, Pastore's hectoring of the TV networks not only begins to look frivolous and eccentric but also like a positive attempt to distract us from seriously considering a problem that has become our collective, national obsession." A prominently placed line at the bottom of the page, all-caps and bold print reads, "THIS PAGE PAID FOR BY JACK LORD."[8]

When *Hawaii Five-O* wrapped after a record-breaking twelve seasons, *Variety*'s Ben Wood asked Jack Lord about the shots, cheap or otherwise, he had taken in the press for the past twelve years. "'The shots may have been deserved, some may have not," he said. "There is a phrase, 'The leader is assailed because he is the leader.' I don't sidestep any issues. I've always met them head on. You always read about the bad things.'"[9] While he freely owned the perfectionist label he had been given, he never saw himself as a bad person. He stood by his own conviction that his motives were for the good of the work.

Even though Lord generally dismissed the hits he took from the press, he was at times perplexed at being a frequent target. Nevertheless, he did not let it interfere with moving forward and doing the job in the way he felt was best for all concerned. In 1970, local journalist Ella Chun asked Marie to talk about her husband for an article for the *Waikiki Beach Press*. She responded with a long letter, expressing their gratitude for Chun's diligence in sending tear sheets for them to review and giving them opportunities for feedback before stories were printed. She talked extensively about her husband's resolve, especially in the face of adversity. "He doesn't whimper or indulge in self-pity. Just squares off his jaw and starts over again…. You know exactly how he feels, where he stands and where you stand, and then it's all over as far as he's concerned."[10]

That same year, journalist Terrence O'Flaherty said he had been a Jack Lord fan since he saw him in *Cat on a Hot Tin Roof* and *Stoney Burke*. He confessed that as a fan, he wanted to "put his arm around him and be his friend," but the "coldness" he saw made him put his hand in his pocket. O'Flaherty suggested his demeanor might be more a by-product of his theatre training than self-importance. He recognized the commitment and effort it takes to make each performance fresh, night after night. It can be difficult to hold that level of concentration for an extended period of time and still live in the real world.

He did note that the tougher the work on *Five-O* became, and the more the crew complained about Lord's demands, the more popular the show became. He suggested that the actor's refusal to hide his ego from the press could serve as proof that Jack Lord just might be the only entirely honest actor on television. "Indeed, it may be foolish to try to separate actors from their pictures on the screen," he said. "Maybe it's a mistake ever to go backstage at all."[11] It is an interesting theory, especially set alongside Lord's adamant protection of his life away from work.

For Jack Lord, careers were not made or broken backstage or off camera. He stood by his routine and his principles and his self-imposed and grueling routine. He was highly disciplined throughout his long career, and, it the end, it began to wear on him. His customary 4:30 a.m. wake up call was his way to ensure that he was fully prepared when he got to work. He frequently ate lunch alone, another habit that frequently cited as evidence that he was standoffish and unsociable. Although he did sometimes conduct business during his 30- or 45-minute lunch break, he customarily used it as a time to get away to "recharge his batteries" in preparation for the remainder of the long workday.

He frequently encountered serious pushback when he insisted that everyone come to the set fully prepared—lines for the day memorized and ready to go. He was very open about his lack of tolerance for unprepared actors on the set. When a *Los Angeles Times* reporter asked him how he felt about the criticism of his high expectations for everyone involved with the production, Lord effectively responded with an old Arab proverb. "'The dogs bark, but the caravan moves on.'"[12]

Even though he clearly received more than his share of bad press, Lord continued to maintain close, personal relationships with several journalists over the years, and he remained friends with many of them even after he left the business. While he had learned to ignore the barking dogs, the thorns in his flesh continued to occur, and he did not hesitate to call the offenders. One in particular that he could not seem to shrug off was Dwight Whitney's biting *TV Guide* article from 1971. He told Todd Mason that Whitney's published attack was the result of his refusal to meet with the journalist for an interview. He said he knew Whitney's intent was to come to Hawaii and do a "hatchet job" on him, and he refused to sit down with him. He said Whitney eventually got much of the final version of the story from a woman Lord had recently fired as a publicist and that the "interview" actually never took place. On more than one occasion, he expressed his disgust at seeing quoted words attributed to him that he had never spoken. It was a practice he seemed never to move past.

Lord also had a long-running, rocky relationship with *Hawaii Star Bulletin* journalist David Donnelly. Donnelly was also an actor and he appeared in four episodes of *Hawaii*

Five-O, but he cut Lord no slack in his reporting. He frequently described Lord as difficult, complex, and suspicious, saying the actor customarily judged those who were 98 percent for him as standing against him. Five years into the run of the show, and after an extended back and forth between the two, Lord took the high road and sent Donnelly a Christmas card, suggesting they stop all the "nonsense." Even though Donnelly agreed to the truce, taking a lighter touch most of the time afterwards, he continued to refer to Lord as "difficult."

Lord was pretty good at turning the other cheek, but he continued to take issue with out and out dishonesty and embellishment, and there are some well-documented instances that validate his frustration. A very good illustration of the burned child dreading the fire as far as his distrust of the press is very apparent in a 1975 *Chicago Tribune* story by Robert Kerwin, a West Coast free-lancer at the time. The content and tone of what appears to be a proof copy of the article filed among Lord's personal papers varies greatly from the final published version. Kerwin had a long visit with Lord on the set of *Five-O*, and it appears that their conversation covered the world during the extended session. Lord talked about his family, his training, his art, the technical and business side of producing *Hawaii Five-O*, and the rationale behind his adamant protection of his private life. He talked extensively about his bewilderment at the motives of the press in misrepresenting things he said and did. The published article, however, is replete with expletives in quoted statements, but the copy that Lord had in his files has very few. Also missing from Lord's copy is Kerwin's story that two makeup artists came into his dressing room to refresh Lord's makeup during the interview. Kerwin said Lord took up a mirror after they left and began "working on himself." He says when Lord returned to the set, he looked like a "clothing-store manikin."[13] Lord frequently recalled an incident when he went directly to a press conference as he had just left the set, still wearing make-up from the day's filming. The incident has been repeated many times as evidence that he customarily wore makeup in public.

For all his critics, he did have some staunch defenders. Actor Jack Albertson applauded Lord's commitment to professionalism on the job. "Jack is not the least bit difficult.... He doesn't believe in wasting money. He arrives on the set early and thoroughly prepared. He's ready to work. If you're ready to work and know your lines, you'll have a wonderful time." Albertson speculated that those who complained must have gone to Hawaii just for the vacation.[14] Lord spoke openly about his intention there would be no "drunks" on his set. Work was work, and he would not apologize for his commitment to seeing to it that the result of their efforts was quality.

Another hot button for Lord was the criticism he faced for his unwavering protection of his private life. From the beginning of his career, he drew a hard line when it came to allowing access to his life at home. Although the Lords were well known as very gracious and social people in the community, he saw no justification for unbridled access when it came to his life outside work. "The Cop on the Cover," a *Hawaii Five-O* episode from season ten, shows a very frustrated Steve McGarrett as he is forced by the governor to allow a female reporter working on a story about him to follow him around. McGarrett is in throes of a very difficult kidnapping case, and he resents the intrusion on his time and his concentration. McGarrett makes it very clear to the reporter that his private life is completely off limits. She is allowed to shadow him to get her story only as long as she understands he will allow nothing to interfere with his work. It is an interesting episode because viewers get a rare glimpse of McGarrett the man outside his work. Anyone with even a passing knowledge of the actor can easily see Jack Lord in the details as the woman manages to pull a small amount of information from him about his life apart from Five-O business. The plot reads a bit like Jack Lord's message to the real world about something very important to him. His wife understood that part of him and the rationale for keeping the door to his time away from work firmly closed. Her understanding of it was never more evident than it was after *Hawaii Five-O* had finished its run, and Jack Lord went home full time.

When the time came to bring an end to *Five-O*, Lord was ready to lay it down, but he was not ready to leave the work altogether. His twelve years with Steve McGarrett had been extremely successful, but they had also been extremely difficult, and he was tired. "I feel like I've been let out of prison," he said when it was over. "You don't keep a show alive for 12 years without showing the scars." Lord frequently confirmed he would never do another television series. Associated Press reporter Pierre Bowman talked to Lord in the fall of 1980, six months after *Five-O* wrapped. Bowman commented on what "great shape" Lord was in as he climbed out of his familiar white Cadillac, posed for pictures on the steps of his Diamond Head office, and then settled in to talk about laying down Steve McGarrett. He had done what few felt he could do. He had survived twelve punishing years with a weekly series. He had proven the thing Hollywood naysayers said couldn't be done, in fact, could be magnificently done.

Lord did not have to look long for the path to another paycheck. He was a very rich man when *Five-O* was over. He had been careful not put all his eggs in one basket, and his judicious investments ensured he and Marie would never have to worry about money. When word was out that the series was in its last season, he told his friend Lawrence Laurent, "We hold some AAA leases on shopping centers and supermarkets and for us it has been a bonanza."[15] The Lords had put a significant portion of their assets in real estate and they would be able to live more than comfortably even if he never worked another day in his life. They fully intended to make Hawaii their permanent home. At long last he would have time to devote to the other loves of his life—his wife and his art.

He would not sit still in his retirement, however, and he was not going to forego the chance to act again. By fall, Lord validated his intention to branch out and pursue other projects now that he had the time. He did something he had not done in seventeen years. He signed on with CAA and retained an agent, and he was exploring a number of possibilities, including some novel to film adaptations. "I don't want to just go to work. But I do want to get away from dear McGarrett."[16]

Lord was leaving *Hawaii Five-O*, but by all indications, he was not leaving the business. He frequently talked about his desire to make a motion picture, relishing the opportunity to "say some things that need to be said." True to form, he let no grass grow under his feet after putting *Five-O* to bed. A CBS memo from Robert Janes filed in Lord's papers serves as evidence that before the last episode of Hawaii Five-O aired, he was already looking ahead. Janes had written the script for what would be Lord's next project, *M Station Hawaii*—a made for television movie. The *M* in the title was for *Makai*, or "toward the sea," and the premise was about a deep-sea research and salvage company based in Honolulu.

When Janes sent the script to Lord, he admitted the first draft needed to be cut, but he was confident the characters had promise as a pilot for a series. All was generally well, except Lord took issue with the proposal the writer had made for exterior shots. Janes had suggested they utilize standing sets already available at MGM that had been used for *Ice Station Zebra* and for Universal's *Gray Lady Down*. He also mentioned they could use some of the stock footage from those productions. Lord's written reaction penciled at the bottom of the memo smacks of the kind of cut-to-the-chase oversight he had with *Five-O*. "This is crap!! The Ice Station sets are worthless and scattered all over the MGM backlot.... The stock footage ... is either non-existent or so expensive it's prohibitive to use."[17]

By the time they were ready to film, however, Lord may have had second thoughts about Janes' suggestions for sets. They built a 40-foot, scale section of a Russian sub from plywood, weighted it, and sank the $70,000 construction in 60 to 75 feet of water off the western coast of Oahu. That very night the area was hit by a major storm. The next morning when they went to check on the sub, they found a completely shattered pile of plywood. As usual, Lord would not be beaten, and they immediately began building another one. They shot 21 days on dry land and spent ten days filming underwater. To say it was a challenging venture doesn't even begin to describe it.

Word got out quickly that the tenacious Jack Lord had something in the hopper. In March of 1979, more than a year before *M Station* aired, Lord received a request from the Pacific Fleet Submarine Memorial Association in Honolulu asking if they might show the movie as a benefit for raising funds for the restoration of the USS *Bowfin* and efforts to convert it into a permanent museum. The request hit two of Lord's passions—his work and his dedicated commitment to charity. Attempts to confirm that the event took place were unsuccessful.

As *M Station* was in the works, Lord and his lady were in Los Angeles in the spring of 1980, exploring options for potential projects. They met with a number of filmmakers and entered into negotiations to acquire film rights to a novel. A memo in Lord's papers confirms that he was in talks regarding possible rights for *Mayday*, the first novel by prolific aviation author, Thomas H. Block. *Mayday* is about a missile hitting a passenger jet, killing the crew, and forcing passengers to land the plane. Proposals and cost of a made-for-television movie and for a film were included. "If a feature motion picture is produced first, [the initial $7500 one—year option] would be applied against a purchase price of $40,000 guarantee against 3–1/2% of the budget of the feature. There would be a ceiling but this would be subject to discussion." Lord wrote a note on the bottom: "Very strange deal. No one to my knowledge has ever made such a deal."[18] Jack Lord did love an out-of-the-box project.

On June 10, 1980, CBS aired what would be Lord's last work. Hope was high that *M Station: Hawaii* had the potential to grow into a series. Jack Lord was working more in the production side of the business with his Lord and Lady Production Company. He had bought *M-Station* for $1,750,000 and even though he served primarily as executive producer and director, he did a brief cameo appearance in the film—his final role. Guest stars for the pilot included Dana Wynter, who had appeared with Lord on a 1965 episode of *The Chrysler Theatre*, and Andrew Duggan, who had done seven appearances on *Hawaii Five-O*. Andrew Prine was also in the cast. Prine had two episodes of *Five-O* on his filmography, and he worked on a 1965 episode of the *Kraft Suspense Theatre*. A page torn from a 1978 issue of *TV Guide* is filed in Lord's papers. In the entry for Sunday, December 3, he circled the name of a supporting cast member for *High Ballin,'* a movie starring Peter Fonda and Jerry Reed about independent truck drivers dealing with hijackers. He wrote a note beside Helen Shaver's name–"Interesting girl for our pilot." Shaver is not listed in the final credits for *M Station*, however.

Just as he had done with *Hawaii Five-O*, Lord made good use of available local resources and settings. He received a thank you note from Helicopter Anti-Submarine Squadron Light 37 at Naval Air Station I in Hawaii. Lord had made a cash donation to the Squadron's Welfare and Recreation Fund as a good will gesture for their participation in the production.

If Lord was looking for the next big thing, *M Station* was definitely not it. The reviews were brutal, collectively saying it was obviously "stretched" so what should have been a ninety-minute film was made to fit a two-hour time slot, and as a result the quality suffered. Janes' script was judged excessively heavy on the exposition and on technical components. Although the *Los Angeles Times* said Lord's brief appearance as Admiral Henderson was "ok," reviewer Kevin Thomas thoroughly trounced his directing. "[He's] so preoccupied with making everything perfectly clear in the needlessly complicated and talky script that he has little opportunity to inject much energy into it."[19] Thomas' comments were echoed in other reviews.

As Jack Lord took one final hit for what was to be his last work, he and Marie could not have known they were about to face the battle of his life. And this was one that would not surrender to that famous squared-off-jaw determination.

Twelve

An Indelible Mark

When *Hawaii Five-O* came to an end after a record-breaking twelve seasons, Jack Lord suddenly found himself with time on his hands. It's hard to put on the brakes after running in high gear for so long, and battle-fatigued as he was, he wasted no time finding a number of ways to stay busy. There was never a question he and Marie would continue to live in Hawaii, and they stayed in their Kahala apartment for the remainder of their lives. Years before his death, Lord told Marilyn Beck, "'They'll have to carry me out of here in a koa wood box.'"[1] He and Marie were finally at a place in their lives when they could slow down and enjoy the things they cared about—their friends, the peace and quiet of their home, and each other's company. He would be able to devote time to his art and other creative outlets he had been forced to put aside during the demanding years with *Five-O*. They also stepped up their practice of giving back to the place they had called home for twelve years. "People say to me all the time, 'Do you like Hawaii?'" he said. "'And I say, 'No, I love Hawaii.' My wife and I really have a deep affection for this place.'"[2] A 1981 story in the *South China Morning Post* reported that Lord's praise for the good life in Hawaii set off an unexpected migration of Hollywood royalty to the fiftieth state. "Jack Lord ... may have unwittingly engineered the downfall of Beverly Hills.... All of a sudden, some of California's top celebrity residents are expressing boredom with the ... high taxes of [the] ... area and are setting their sights 3,000 miles out in the Pacific."[3]

Their permanent residence in the islands was not the only way Jack and Marie Lord continued to show their love for Hawaii. The couple had actively supported a number of charitable causes for years, and when Lord walked away from the *Five-O* set for the last time, they devoted a significant portion of their newfound free time to stepping up their efforts toward some of their favorite causes. They favored local children's charities, causes to support the arts in the area, organizations that provided services to people with physical disabilities, and a number of other initiatives directed toward serving the community. Lord frequently offered his celebrity status on behalf of a number of charitable organizations during the height of his career, and when he retired he became even more active in his philanthropy. He was frequently honored for his generosity and his ambassadorship for the State of Hawaii, including several recognitions that had previously been given exclusively to native Hawaiians. He was made an honorary policeman of the Honolulu Police Department, an Honorary Commodore of the U.S. Coast Guard

Auxiliary, Citizen of the Day for his outstanding civic achievements and betterment of his community, and in 1970 he was honored by the American Cancer Society and the British Variety Club for his outstanding work with underprivileged children. He was also recognized for his role in arranging free union labor and obtaining the materials for the construction of six buildings for a school for developmentally disabled children. His charitable work at this level continued throughout the rest of his life, much of it never publicized.

He served as the first statewide campaign chairman for the Hawaii Tuberculosis and Respiratory Disease Association, and he was honored in 1969 for his "immeasurable contributions." He clearly approached the support of his favorite causes with the same committed oversight with which he did with his day job. That same year, he sent a letter to talk show celebrity Mike Douglas, who had just been named National Honorary Chairman of the annual Christmas Seal Campaign, as Lord was named Hawaii's state campaign chairman. He was touching base with Douglas to see if they could coordinate something special for the Hawaii campaign. "I guess we are both in the business of peddling Christmas Seals," he wrote. Lord told Douglas that Marie was a huge fan who never missed his show, and she religiously gave him a detailed review of the entire program when he got home from work in the evenings. Attached to Lord's file copy of the letter to Douglas is a two-page scathing response Lord wrote to the Hawaii Public Relations Director for the state level organization. Apparently, the director took issue with Lord's letter to Mike Douglas, specifically his use of the words, "peddle" and "charity." Lord leveled a blast at the director in a return letter, making his opinion of the objections clearly known.

"To say the least," he wrote, "your 'comments' are pedantic." He continued with a numbered list of his own issues with the solicitation letter the director had taken the liberty of penning on Lord's behalf. "You promised me faithfully that you would never send out any release without submitting it first and waiting for my approval. This I expect you to do and if you cannot or will not honor your commitment let me know now before the announcement is made and I will gladly withdraw from any association with your organization."[4]

Lord saved a clipping from the August 29, 1970, edition of the *Honolulu Advertiser* about a sixteen-year-old wheelchair bound boy with muscular dystrophy who had come to Hawaii on vacation with his family. The boy's father had contacted the *Advertiser* to report his disappointment that they were refused service in a local restaurant and had been turned down for a Navy tour of Pearl Harbor because their son Silvio was in a wheelchair. The *Advertiser* did a story on the incident, and when Lord saw it, he immediately invited the family to the set of *Hawaii Five-O* for a visit. As it turned out, the family never missed an episode of the show, and their nine-year-old daughter was a die-hard Jack Lord fan. Lord chastised the ones responsible for the family's disappointments during their trip. "If we cannot extend the aloha spirit here and the almighty buck starts to dominate, then we have lost aloha," Lord said. Silvio's mother said she felt they had "stirred up a hornet's nest," but she was hopeful it would positively impact future handicapped visitors to the islands.[5]

In 1972, Lord manned the phones during a Muscular Dystrophy Radio-Thon, delighting donors with the opportunity to speak to him as they made their pledges.

After the sign-off, a young blind man who was a huge Jack Lord fan came to the station with a friend. He apologized for being late, but he wanted to make his $5 donation to the cause, even though Lord had already left the studio. The young man was surprised later when he received a personal thank you for his donation from the actor with an autographed photo.

The American Cancer Society's Jackie Anderson applauded Lord's faithful commitment to the causes he supported. "It's refreshing to know someone who can still be definite. He always says yes or no, never maybe. Hawaii ranked #1 in contributions per capita. I'm impressed with the fact that, unlike men with less responsibility, he makes time to help others."

In 1975, Lord received a unique proposal asking for his help in raising awareness of the horrors of child abuse. The proposal was that he agree to do an episode of *Hawaii Five-O* dealing with the issue. He explained that since the fictitious Five-O unit did not work on the precinct level of police work, "where I am afraid the crime of child battering and abuse would fall," they would not be able do such an episode, but he promised to try to interest producers and story editors. He copied his response to Finnegan, Freeman and Sweeney. In the meantime, he did what he could do to help the cause. He wrote radio and television spots about child abuse that could be aired on educational television channels.[6]

Lord saved a letter from the editor of the *Nashville Banner* in Tennessee, telling him of an elderly lady who was a devoted fan of the show and had recently lost her husband. Friends reported to the paper that her anticipation of the show had "kept her going" throughout the ordeal. Editor Charles Appleton asked Lord if he might find the time to send her an autographed photo. Lord responded five days later with a personal letter to the woman. "My spies tell me that you like our show. As you know, McGarrett has ways of finding out such things. Because I care about friends like you, I'm sending you a couple of pictures which I hope you will like.... Take good care of yourself.... We need you."[7]

Lord's papers include some of the more unique of the thousands of letters he received from fans. Contrary to persistent rumors that he was aloof and standoffish, he was impressively diligent in responding to fans' letters. During his time with *Stoney Burke*, Marie helped with reading and responding to the massive amount of fan mail he received, and even in the heyday of *Hawaii Five-O*, fans often received personal responses from him. He was customarily gracious to fans on location as long as they did not interfere with filming. When he was working, he gave it his full attention and he expected nothing less from everyone else on the job. A *Honolulu Advertiser* article that ran the day after he died reported, "By every account of autograph seekers, he was friendly and kind."[8]

He frequently heard from irate fans if their local stations preempted *Hawaii Five-O* for some special programming event. A 1972 *Honolulu Star-Bulletin* article reported a large number of *Five-O* fans lodged a protest to the local television station when the show which was scheduled to air October 24 was cancelled. A substitute program, "Wild Africa," was aired in its place. The station had made the decision to preempt *Five-O* when House of Representatives candidate Shirley Sax cried foul because her opponent, Herman Wedemeyer, made an appearance in the episode. Sax filed a complain with the

Federal Communications Commission demanding equal time as required by the FCC ruling for political candidates. The station opted to pull the episode. The outpouring of viewers' protest over the cancellation was a record for the station.

In January of 1979, an avid *Five-O* fan in Kentucky, wrote directly to Jack Lord, expressing his distress that the show had been preempted by a basketball game. He asked Lord if the episode would be aired at later date, explaining it was the only episode he had missed since the show's beginning. Lord kept the letter, but no copy of his response was attached.

Lord took a special interest in Tripler Army Medical Center in Honolulu several years before he left *Five-O*, and he continued his dedicated support after he left the show. The largest in the Asian and Pacific Rim region, Tripler's jurisdiction reportedly covers 52 percent of the earth's surface. In addition to his charitable work on its behalf, Lord was a frequent visitor to the facility and was often photographed visiting with patients. In April of 1977, he wrote a lengthy letter to baseball great Hank Aaron, in which he apologized for his lack of response to Aaron's letters on behalf of the No Greater Love, a non-profit organization which honors fallen soldiers and their families. Aaron was president of the organization and had made several appeals dating back as far as 1974, asking Lord to serve as a representative for No Greater Love in their work for Tripler. Lord said he was shocked and embarrassed that he had missed earlier letters from Aaron, saying his recent busy work schedule was no excuse for his lack of a response. "[No] response from me, no carbon copies, no thank you's for the superb job you are doing for this most worthy cause, no nothin' as Sam Goldman would say.... I must humbly apologize for not responding to your affectionate letters and this I do now. Forgive me."

The level of his involvement with Tripler is illustrated in a 1982 letter he received from the hospital's PR Director Doris Jividen, expressing her disgust at a review of the HOKU Awards, Hawaii's version of the Grammys, that ran in the *Star-Bulletin*. The event celebrated the outstanding achievements of local musicians and other performers. Jividen was offended by the reviewers' snide comments about some of the performances at the ceremony. She scolded them for their insensitivity to the fact these performers supported hundreds of charitable events in Hawaii, particularly Tripler. She wanted Lord to know she had taken action to make her opinion clearly known.[9]

Lord continued to work with Tripler on their fundraising goals for many years. His efforts were recognized with a certificate of achievement for consistent and dedicated contributions of his time and his talent to the No Greater Love program at Tripler. "The impact of the morale benefits from his generosity is incalculable for patients, staff, and hospital visitors. ... For a special star, this special award."

Another favorite cause for the Lords was their role as honorary chairmen of the Honolulu Theater for Youth's Stagehands Organization, a group that provided financial support to workshops and theatrical productions for young people in Hawaii. Lord kept a letter he had received with a donation from a seven-year-old donor. She addressed her note to "Jack and Marie," explaining that she was sending the five dollars she had received for her birthday in support of their Stagehands fundraiser. "I hope this will help you," she wrote. Lord had a special fondness for children, and he kept many letters he received from them throughout his career.

The Lords had an impressive collection of works of fine art, and they frequently donated pieces to museums and universities all over the country. In 1959, he made a significant gift of artwork to the Pioneer Museum and Haggin Galleries in Stockton, California, and he continued to add to the collection over a period of several years. In July and August of 1973, the gallery presented an exhibit of the impressive collection of prints by Chalot, Chagall, Matisse, Picasso and others that Lord had donated to the facility. Filed in his papers is his letter to the museum asking for copies of calendars the gallery had produced featuring the collection that bore his name. The collection was again exhibited for the public to view from October 2015 until January 2016.

In 1988, the Lords established the Jack and Marie Lord Fund, an umbrella that housed twelve of their favorite Hawaiian charities, and the financial support from the fund extended well beyond both their lifetimes. Lord was generous with his personal time, as well as with his money, for the causes he loved, and he frequently made personal appearances and donated personal items to help support fundraising efforts. The impressive charitable impact the Lords made during their lifetime was a small fraction of what they provided in their estate.

In addition to his efforts for charitable causes, Lord frequently spoke up in the political arena when he felt strongly about issues. He never shied away from making his opinions known in his capacity as a private citizen, but he was adamant in his repeated refusal to consider encouragement he received to run for public office. He was reportedly approached to run for governor of Hawaii on more than one occasion. He mentioned it "off the record" in the recorded interviews with Todd Mason and said when he told Marie he had been asked to consider throwing his hat in the ring, her reply was quick and definitive: "Absolutely not." Enough said.

Jack Lord was never hesitant to address his political concerns directly to those whom he felt could do something about them. In November of 1977, he received a letter from Frank R. Barnett, president of the National Strategy Information Center. Barnett was reflecting on a conversation he and Lord had at a retirement party for Admiral Noel Gaylor. During their conversation, Lord expressed his concern over the growing threats to "strategic sea-lanes." Barnett told Lord he would be in Hawaii the latter part of the month, and he welcomed further dialogue with him about the issue. He enclosed some relevant documents for Lord to review in the meantime. Although confirmation of their meeting could not be found, there is little doubt Lord followed through.[10]

He also devoted considerable effort toward improving gun control laws, and the issue was the focus of a couple of *Five-O* episodes. "And I Want Some Candy and a Gun that Shoots," an episode from the fourth season, aired on October 19, 1971. McGarrett races against time to capture a former solider turned deranged sniper who buys a rifle and goes on a shooting rampage. It turns out the clerk who sold him the weapon had failed to do a proper background check. Bob Sweeney sent a 16mm film of the episode and a copy of the script to Lawrence Laurent. Sweeney said he had just gotten off the phone with Lord. "I certainly agree with Jack that this film makes a powerful statement about one of the things that's wrong with our society. I'm sure you will agree after you view it."[11]

Lord told Lawrence Laurent in a February 3, 1976, letter, "Got a few licks in for gun legislation, though I doubt it will do much good in an election year." He attached a full page clipping from *The Tattler* newspaper with a story about Lord's advocating banning handguns.[12] In February of 1979, he made a generous donation to Handgun Control Inc. in Washington, D.C., expressing his willingness to tape radio spots for Handgun Control, Inc. The National Advisory Committee for the organization included several prominent film celebrities, including Peter Lawford, Steve Allen, Will Rogers, Hal Holbrook, as well as a number of prominent political figures, writers, and athletes. In December of that year Lord received a letter from the President of the Northern California Coalition for Handgun Control, commending him and writer Sam Roeca for their work on another episode of *Five-O* that dealt with the issue. "Use a Gun, Go to Hell," aired on November 29.[13]

Lord was widely criticized for his stand in favor of the strict enforcement of handgun laws when a license for a handgun issued to him surfaced. The license was in fact for the gold plated Walther given to him by Elvis Presley when he visited the Lords' home during his concert in Hawaii. The National Rifle Association called Lord out in their journal in March of 1980, claiming that, in spite of his outspoken stand in favor of gun control, six years earlier he had attempted to purchase a .25 caliber Browning Renaissance from a San Francisco dealer, but he had backed out when they couldn't agree on a price. The article included a quote from an interview with the *Chicago Daily News* one month later, in which Lord said all guns should be restricted to cops and the military.[14] He received a letter from U.S. Congressman Cecil Heftel of Hawaii in May of 1983, thanking him for his support of a pending bill calling for a ban on public access to armor-piercing ammunition.[15]

Lord did not restrict his political activism to gun control issues, however. A prolific letter writer, he also frequently addressed issues in the political arena and in the business of Hollywood. In 1980, he penned a letter to Spark M. Matsunaga, United States senator from Hawaii, expressing his concerns about the problems of rising inflation and the need to reduce federal government spending levels. Lord signed the letter with his birth name, as he frequently did if he felt his celebrity status may affect the response. In a two-page response dated August 20, 1980, the senator outlined some of the activities to curb federal spending that were under way at the time in Washington.[16]

In 1982, he wrote a letter to Vice President George H.W. Bush, questioning the intent of remarks Bush had made at President Marcos' inauguration in the Philippines. He signed the letter "John J. Ryan" and gave his address as the Beverly Wilshire Hotel. A copy of his original letter was not filed in his papers, but he did receive a response from the Vice President's Military Assistant/Aide.[17]

Filed with his letters to national leaders is a copy of a clipping from Marilyn Beck's column "Around Hollywood" announcing Producer Howard Koch's decision to forbid broadcasting the losers' faces during the announcement of winners at that year's Oscars ceremony. Lord wrote a note across the clipping and mailed it to Koch. "Dear Howard, Bravo! Bravo! You are a tasteful man. Thank you & God Bless. Jack."

With a newfound freedom from his punishing work schedule, Jack Lord could now devote more attention to his art and others of his creative projects. Even during those busy years keeping Steve McGarrett on the job, he managed to find time to work at honing his skills as an artist. In February of 1971, he studied lithography under Russell Davidson at the University of Hawaii, and later sent one of his original eight-color serigraphs to 100 newspaper television editors. The Lords had 120 original lithographs by famous artists as part of their extensive private art collection, and later that year they offered them for exhibit in Honolulu to help with fundraising efforts for the Iolani Palace restoration project.[18]

Lord was also an avid jewelry designer, and many of the unique pieces he and Marie wore were his original creations. After his death, his estate listed a large collection of precious stones and finished pieces he had made, and he was as meticulous in his choice of jewelry and stones for his own jewelry making as he was with the details of his day job. Among his papers is a note reprimanding an employee in the *Five-O* office for signing for a personal package containing a jade ring he had ordered that had been delivered to the studio. He was not happy with quality of the stone. "In the future please DO NOT accept anything for me, unless I specifically request it," he wrote. "It is a dangerous practice making you responsible for whatever is left there. PS. Please Xerox this note and send a copy for my file."[19]

The final outcome of one of Lord's ongoing creative projects remains a mystery. For several years, he often spoke of his plans to write a book that would be what he called his "love letter" to Hawaii. He told journalist Dick Kleiner in 1970 that he had finished *Jack Lord's Hawaii*, that he had put in an initial printing order for 500,000 copies and the release date was coming up very soon.[20] His intention was to keep the price of the book as low as possible. A clipping of an article from a September issue *California Stylist* in Lord's papers reports he had completed the project the previous year. He gives the title as *Jack Lord's Hawaii—A Trip Through the Last Eden*, and he says the book included 40 color photos he had selected from the hundreds he had taken of the area over the years. He said a primary source he had used extensively for the text of the book was *The Shoals of Time*, by University of Hawaii Professor Gavin Daws, describing it as "without a doubt, the most definitive single work on Hawaii." Two years later, Lawrence Laurent also reported completion of Lord's book, describing it a tourists' guide to the islands.

Later reports indicate that Lord had decided to do the project as a studio album. It is not clear whether he intended the album to take the place of the printed book or if it would be a supplement to the text. In April of 1981, Lord received a very detailed letter from Charles "Bud" Dant about the project. Dant was a diverse musician and composer with an impressive career that dated back to the 1940s. Dant moved to Kailua-Kona in the 1970s, where he produced an impressive body of work with Hawaiian talent. Apparently Lord had contacted him about recording an album of spoken pieces about the culture and history of Hawaii. The proposed title was *Jack Lord's Hawaii*, the same working title Lord had proposed for his book project.

Dant suggested that one track could be Lord speaking "The Meaning of Aloha" with "Aloha Oe" playing in the background. He also recommended some well-known Hawaiian legends he could read and offered to include some of his own original music he was currently composing. Dant was impressed with a proposed promotional piece Lord had designed. He told Lord it would be a very commercial cover for the album.[21]

There is no record that the project, in either format, was ever completed. When Todd Mason was preparing to come to Hawaii to work as Lord's stand in, he mentioned Lord had talked to him about some possible work as a ghost writer for a book he was working on, but attempts to find documentation of such an arrangement were unsuccessful.

What is now known about Lord's declining health in the years following his retirement may offer an explanation for the unfinished book project. By the early 1980s, rumors began to surface that Lord was suffering from declining health. He was seen out in public less often, and there were reports that he frequently appeared not to recognize people who should have been familiar to him. Locals said he often sat at the same place near a local shopping mall, and he appeared to be detached from things going on around him. When Marie was asked about his health, she adamantly denied there was anything wrong with him. Eventually reports surfaced that he at times would become disoriented when he was out by himself, and she was paying people to bring him home. She also continued to deny the truth of that as well.

In a segment for the February 25, 2006, edition of the *Today* show, Matt Lauer interviewed Andy Griffith following the death of his long-time costar Don Knotts the prior day. Griffith was clearly grieving the loss of his friend, and Lauer asked him for details about just how sick Knotts had been in the weeks before his death. Griffith made an astute observation regarding one of the downsides of being a celebrity. "I guess you know that all actors are like this," he said. "When something goes wrong with us, we don't want anybody to know." There does seem to be an expectation from the public that celebrities should somehow be exempt from human faults and shortcomings, and Jack Lord was certainly no exception. Perhaps it is simply a reluctance to see Jack Lord as anything less than Steve McGarrett.

In the last years of Lord's life, as he became more ill, Marie tenaciously clung to their privacy. She diligently shielded him from the prying press and, eventually, even from their friends. Despite harsh criticism, she consistently denied the obvious and refused to reveal just how sick he was. Her take on it was that his battle would be theirs together, and she cared for him the same way she had throughout their marriage. She stood by him, this wife of his youth, abiding with him until the very end, and she continued to adamantly safeguard his legacy for the seven years she survived him.

Although Lord was in essence out of the public eye for several years before his death, he did have a television appearance on February 27, 1984. *Bob Hope's Wicky-Wacky Special,* featuring guest stars Tom Selleck, Loni Anderson, and Mr. T., was filmed on location in Hawaii, and Hope did an extensive interview with Selleck. His series, *Magnum PI,* also filmed in Hawaii, was midway through its successful eight-year run at the time. Hope did a monologue before a large audience, during which he paid tribute to the iconic natural beauty of the islands. He mentioned he had noticed the famous gentle trade winds were not always so gentle. "The other day," he said, "the winds got so bad Jack Lord's hair almost moved. It's true. Two guys from the weather bureau follow Jack around. They see a cowlick—they call a state of emergency." The camera cut away to the Lords who were sitting in the fifth row of the outdoor stadium. Marie was dressed in a pink suit with her customary matching hat, and she was sitting very close to her husband, who appeared a bit frail. He was pale and had noticeable dark circles under his eyes. While he and his wife both smiled at Hope's comments, Marie studies Jack's face closely after each comment. Any mention of *Hawaii Five-O* or an onstage appearance by Lord is noticeably missing, which seemed odd since there were so much time given to Selleck's show.

It was widely reported that Lord suffered from Alzheimer's, but Marie continued to deny it. In his final years, he was often seen walking alone on the beach near their home, wearing his familiar panama hat. The dinner parties and other social gatherings at their home finally stopped all together. Family friend Buck Henshaw, who had worked as a set decorator on the show, talked to *TV Guide* after Lord's passing about his disappearance from any social life in those last years. "I think he wanted to stay home with Marie and rest in *their* way—quietly together and apart from the rest of the world."[22] Lord frequently said Marie was the only thing in the world he cared about, and after sharing him for so long with the world, Marie saw to it that he spent his last days exactly the way he wanted—just the two of them standing together against the toughest climb he ever faced.

Marie was by his side when he passed away at 6:09 p.m. on January 21, 1998. His death certificate indicates he suffered aspiration pneumonia for two days prior to his passing, and confirms a diagnosis of Alzheimer's disease and a stroke in 1994. The official cause of death is listed as congestive heart failure.[23] In keeping with his wishes, there was no funeral. His body was cremated on January 24, and his ashes were scattered on the water near their Kahala home with only Marie and a few very close friends present. Marie continued to live in their condo until her death on October 13, 2005, when her ashes were scattered in the same location where Jack's had been strewn more than seven years earlier. She had faithfully continued to quietly support their charitable causes, frequently donating in Jack's name. Shortly before she died, she gave money to the Hawaii Theatre restoration fund. The marquis lights were dimmed in her honor the evening after she passed away, a fitting tribute to the Lords and their love of the theatre.

Jack and Marie Lord saw to it that their dedicated charitable work continues for the causes they loved. The Lords were smart with their money, and they amassed a very large estate, with a massive portfolio of stocks, bonds and real estate investments. They created the Jack and Marie Lord Fund to house their assets and to ensure their charities would continue to benefit. The fund generates $1.6 to $2 million per year, going to 12 Hawaiian charities, including hospice centers, the Lions Eye Foundation, the Humane Society, the Association for Retarded Citizens, and arts and public television organizations. Upon Marie's death, their entire estate was auctioned on eBay, and the proceeds from the hundreds of items sold were added to the Jack and Marie Lord Fund. All their personal possessions, including clothing, jewelry, art work, photographs, and celebrity memorabilia that had been given to them—even their cancelled checks—were auctioned. All the proceeds from the eBay auction were added to the initial $40 million estate.

According to a 2007 story in the *Hollywood Reporter*, on the "Giving Back 30" ranking of celebrities who made the largest personal donations to nonprofits for the prior year, Jack and Marie Lord ranked third with a total $40,000,000 given to charities in 2006, the year after Marie's death. Oprah Winfrey was in the top spot at $58,300,000 and late designer Geoffrey Beene's $44,000,000 in contributions put him in second place.

Jack Lord always wanted his work to stand on it own merits. For all the struggles he faced during those difficult, heartbreaking early years as he worked so hard to find his niche, when he at last hit the right one, it was golden. The year 2018 marks a half-century since the premiere of *Hawaii Five-O*, and it is amazing that Jack Lord's name is even more familiar today than it was fifty years ago. His impressive fan base continues to be admirably diverse and his legacy turns up in some surprising places. The "Book 'em, Danno" catch phrase has a prominent place in pop culture and shows no signs of going away any time soon.

One of the most unique examples of the effective application of McGarrett's "Book 'em, Danno" mantra occurred in the fall of 1985 in a Hawaiian courtroom. On trial was an accomplished investment advisor, Ronald Rewald, who had swindled more than 400 unsuspecting investors out of $20.6 million in a well-executed Ponzi scheme. One of the most dramatic testimonies in the eleven-week trial came from one of his victims—Jack Lord.

When the operation began to fall, Lord was furious to find that he had been one of several celebrities whose names had been misused by Rewald to lure his victims. He was shocked to hear that employees had designated one of the offices as "Jack Lord's Office" and that his name was painted on a parking spot at the company's headquarters. He testified he had been acquainted with Rewald—they had in fact been friends—and he had critiqued some movie concepts for Rewald. He stated he had sold Rewald his mobile dressing room for $45,000 after *Five-O* ended, but he vehemently denied any foreknowledge or participation in the execution of Rewald's Ponzi scheme. "If (Rewald) had told anyone that I had occupied an office ... it would have been a damnable lie," he said. "I hate to be used.... I would have considered that being used."[24] As Lord looked directly at Rewald and shot him his best McGarrett scowl, whispers of "Book 'em, Danno" resonated throughout the courtroom.

Lord once told of a long plane ride he had during which time he sat next to a "large Texan." He said throughout the several hours of the trip, the man never acknowledged he knew who his famous seatmate was. When they landed, the man got out of his seat, slipped by Lord, stepped into the aisle, and, without making eye contact, quietly said, "Book 'em, Danno" as he moved toward the exit. Some opportunities are just too good to pass up, even for the stout-hearted.

Even though it is one of the qualities for which he is most remembered, Jack Lord never quite understood the fascination with his hair. Reams of paper have been devoted to how he managed to keep it so precisely styled, and whether it was in fact his real hair. One of the most academic and interesting treatises on the famous Jack Lord hairstyle appears in a comprehensive study on the likelihood of the origins of man evolving from ancient astronauts. According to author Lana Corrine Cantrell's hypotheses a predominant cowlick is strong evidence of the advanced state of early man and a mark of higher intel-

Jack Lord in an undated photograph (Barry Blum, Imperial Studios, 270 Park Avenue, New York 17, New York, author's collection).

ligence. She says a true cowlick curves back on the forehead. "The best example I can give," she writes, "is the most perfect one on the head of actor Jack Lord." She says his cowlick is definitely a naturally occurring characteristic, citing as proof his other facial traits and skeletal characteristics. "The 'Jack Lord Cowlick' pulls the electromagnetic fields of the head back to the skin's meridian, homeostasis at its best," she writes. Cantrell devotes several pages to Lord's physical characteristics—his neck, his earlobes, his jawline, his eye sockets, his "perfect mesocephalic face"—declaring that Lord and fellow actors Roger Moore, Charlton Heston and James Garner represent the kind of men who rarely walk the earth any more. She further advances her theory by confirming that Lord's role as Steve McGarrett, his work as a devoted advocate for charities and causes -all evidence of his "strong heart"–and the enigma he became as a "reclusive and misunderstood celebrity" prove that men like Jack Lord are a dying genotype.[25] Of all the rhetoric devoted to Jack Lord's hair, Cantrell's is without a doubt the most novel.

All good work bears repeating, and *Hawaii Five-O* has certainly not been without its share of replays and tributes. In 1996, Stephen J. Cannell wrote and produced a pilot for a new take on the *Five-O* concept. Gary Busey and Russell Wong headlined the cast, and James MacArthur returned to work as Dan Williams, Governor of Hawaii. Cannell reportedly wanted Jack Lord to have a part, but he was too ill to participate. Even though the pilot was completed, it never aired.

The *Star Bulletin* ran a story in November of 2004 that Warner Bros. was ready to make a movie version of *Hawaii Five-O*. The film would be co-produced with Warner Bros. and the projected budget was expected to run about $100,000,000. Rumors of possible leading men for the McGarrett role included George Clooney, Mel Gibson, Michael Douglas and Harrison Ford.[26] The project never came to fruition.

On September 20, 2010, McGarrett and his team were back in action on CBS in a highly successful reboot of Leonard Freeman's original series. The "O" in *Five-O* was replaced by "0," the transition of letter to numeral symbolic of the update for a current-day audience. Die-hard fans of the original who were looking for a remake were disappointed, but the new show, a tribute to the original, is written for a contemporary audience, many of whom were not even born when Jack Lord first sprinted up the steps of the Iolani Palace. The reboot served to introduce a whole new generation to Lord and his Steve McGarrett, however, and Lord and the original series has enjoyed a renewed popularity. The story of the driven cop and his top-notch team was translated into a high tech, gadget-heavy, modern day interpretation. Alex O'Loughlin's Steve McGarrett is definitely a new creation, but he runs on the same driven determination Lord brought to the original character. A 2007 *New York Times* review following the release of the original series on DVD said Lord "took to McGarrett with the intensity of a not-so-young actor who knew he had just found his career.... You watch Mr. Lord the way you listen to the show's immortal, brassy theme song, predicting every beat but caught up in the swell just the same."[27] When it is all said and done, however, Steve McGarrett belongs to Jack Lord.

Jack Lord's legacy extends well beyond the indelible mark he left on television history. A Japanese proverb says, "Fall seven times, stand up eight." He endured more than his share of falling down, but in the end, it was his persistence in standing up that counted. His true legacy lies with those who find success because they follow his example—move ahead with a clear vision, with tenacity, and a "galvanized gut."

Filmography: Television and Film Roles

Project X, released October 14, 1949, was directed by Edward Montagne, Jr., and starred Keith Andes, Jack Lord, and Rita Colton. The Edward Leven/Transcontinental Production was an anti–Communist propaganda film to raise public awareness of the impending danger of Communist activities in American universities and work places. *Project X* was Lord's first appearance on the big screen.

Cry Murder! was released on January 6, 1950, by Film Classics, Inc. Jack Lord stars as Tommy Warren, an artist who attempts to carry out a blackmailing scheme against a young actress. Lord has star billing alongside Carole Matthews and Howard Smith, and appears in the credits as associate producer.

The Tattooed Stranger from R.K.O. Pictures hit theatres on February 9, 1950, and was Lord's second time to work with director Edward Montagne. The film starred John Miles, Patricia White, Walter Kinsella, and Frank Tweddell. A forerunner to modern detective stories, the film follows a group of detectives as they solve the tangled case of a dead woman found in an abandoned car in New York's Central Park. Jack Lord had an uncredited role as Detective Deke Del Vecchio.

The Hunter was a short-lived CBS spy series from Producer Edward Montagne. Lord was cast in Episode 3, "The Puzzle of Pier 90," which aired on July 16, 1952. The episode details attempts to smuggle a Communist imposter into Oak Ridge, Tennessee. Some sources say there was an unsuccessful attempt to resurrect the series later, with additional episodes filmed but never aired.

Broadway Television Theatre, "Criminal at Large." Season 2, Episode 21, aired February 2, 1953. The story of the Lebanon family and the family matriarch's insistence her son should marry her niece to maintain the family line, but the young woman has her eye on an architect who is in charge of renovating the family castle.

Man Against Crime, "The Midnight Express" Episode 21 of Season 4, aired on CBS on February 18, 1953, and was directed by Edward Montagne. The popular television series was syndicated as *Follow that Man* and starred Ralph Bellamy as Detective Mike Barnett. Lord plays an undercover treasury agent in the episode. The show was shot on location in the streets of New York City, good training for Lord's career-defining work on *Hawaii-Five O*.

Man Against Crime, "The Chinese Dolls," Season 5, Episode 27, aired on CBS April 11, 1954. Lord earned $164.10 for his work on his second episode for the *Man Against Crime* series.

The Web, "Grand Finale" Season 4, Episode 30, aired on CBS May 2, 1954. The episode is the story of an opera star that commits a murder and later discovers he has killed a valuable ally. Jack Lord has less than a minute on camera in his uncredited role as a new opera performer. He works alongside Carroll Baker, who also appears with him in an episode of *Danger* the following year.

Suspense, "String" Season 6 episode 39 aired CBS June 22, 1954. It was set during World War II and based on the true story of a group of men arrested and tortured after being accused as spies.

Danger, "Season for Murder," Season 5, Episode 31, aired on CBS March 29, 1955. James Shigeta (*Walk Like a Dragon*) shares a two-way connection with actress Carroll Baker, Lord's co-star in this episode. Shigeta got the girl (Nobu McCarthy) from Lord in *Dragon* and in *Bridge to the Sun* Shigeta wins the girl (Carroll Baker)—again.

Armstrong Circle Theatre, Lord plays Clay Cochran, an unarmed gunslinger in "Buckskin," Episode 29 of Season 6 that aired NBC April 5, 1955.

Appointment with Adventure, "Five in Judgment," Season 1, Episode 2 aired CBS April 10, 1955, played Bill, witness to a tragic case of mistaken identity. The episode also featured fellow Actors Studio alum Paul Newman.

The Elgin Hour, "Combat Medics," Season 1, Episode 19, aired June 14, 1955, on ABC. Lord is cast as Lieutenant Davis in this episode, set during the Korean War. Brain Keith made an appearance in the episode.

The Court-Martial of Billy Mitchell is a 1955 Warner Bros. Film based on the true story of William Mitchell and his fight with military superiors for their lack of air support for troops on the ground in World War II. Lord is cast as Lt Cmdr Zachary "Zach" Lansdowne. The real Billy Mitchell's wife was an uncredited consultant on the film. Elizabeth Montgomery played Lord's wife. Lord worked with her later on an episode of *Checkmate*.

The Philco Television Playhouse was another live television drama series. "This Land Is Mine," episode 10 of Season 8, aired on NBC on January 15, 1956. Lord was busy during 1956 with a wide variety of television roles.

The Vagabond King is a 1956 film from Paramount. Lord was cast as Ferrebouc, King Louis' captain of the guard. The film is an over the top musical, with huge production numbers reminiscent of old Hollywood. Lord's role entails mostly his standing off to the side, looking stern in his colorful costume during the ensemble musical scenes.

Omnibus aired Episode 16 of Season 4 on February 5, 1956. It was the first of Lord's two appearances on the popular CBS series. "One Nation" tells the story of the ratification of the U.S. Constitution by the Virginia Convention. In a sense, it was a dress rehearsal for a later very unique role in Jack Lord's career, and it was one that put his name in the history books.

Omnibus aired "Trial by General Court-Martial Colonel William Mitchell, Air Service" on April 1, 1956. In his second appearance on the series, Lord stepped into the prosecuting attorney's role for the Billy Mitchell case. For the first time, the public heard actual court transcript of the trial. Dialogue for the script was drawn straight from the office transcript.

Westinghouse Studio One, another live television formatted series on CBS, aired Episode 44 from Season 8 on July 23, 1956. Lord is cast as Paul Chester, a young man who has been blinded in an accident that claimed the lives of his wife and child. As a vulnerable and pitiable man, Lord does an outstanding job in the episode. The part is a clear departure for the tough guy roles he best known for at that time in his career.

Westinghouse Studio One aired "A Day Before Battle" on September 3, 1956. The episode is set during the American Civil War and tells of events in a Union Army camp on the eve of the Battle of Gettysburg. Lord plays Matt, the officer who must come to terms with some desperate decisions from his men. Warren Oates, who would co-star with Lord seven years later in *Stoney Burke* has a featured role.

Lux Video Theatre aired "Jezebel" on November 8, 1956. The episode is based on a 1938 Warner Bros. movie that starred Bette Davis. The script for film was drawn from a 1933 play. Jack Lord played Buck Cantrell, the ill-fated suitor of a manipulative woman.

Lux Video Theatre featured Lord in a second episode that aired November 29, 1956. The script for "Old Acquaintance" was based on a 1943 film by the same name from Warner Bros. The plot was from a play from 1940 written by John Van Druten. Lord played Rudd Kendall, and Ellen Corby, best known for her role as Grandma in *The Waltons*, had a featured role. Corby would later guest star in an episode of

Hawaii Five-O as the landlord of a murder victim.

Conflict, another anthology series, aired "Pattern for Violence" with Lord in a guest-starring spot on ABC May 14, 1957. Filmed in New York, the series was short-lived but two of its episodes were the genesis for two popular television series—*Maverick* and *77 Sunset Strip*.

Climax! In "Mr. Runyon of Broadway," Episode 34 of Season 3, Lord was cast in the role of Charlie Mullaney, a boxer who winds up in trouble with loan sharks because of his wife's gambling problem. The episode aired on CBS June 6, 1957.

The Silent Service was a syndicated series in which Lord appeared as Commander David Hurt of the SS *Perch* submarine. The series ran for two seasons and was based on true stories of the U.S. Submarine Fleet from World War II. Episodes featured actual period submarine footage.

Have Gun Will Travel, Richard Boone's landmark role, debuted on CBS on September 14, 1957. In "Three Bells to Perdido" Lord plays Dave Enderby, Paladin's first case in the new show about a sophisticated gun for hire. Many sources say Leonard Freeman offered Boone the role of McGarrett and when he turned it down, he offered it to Lord.

Playhouse 90, Season 2 Episode 16 for the series, "Lone Woman," aired on CBS December 6, 1957. Lord was cast in the role of Jim Kester, and he worked alongside Kathryn Grayson. The episode was intended as a pilot for a new series about the only privately owned fort on the frontier, but the pilot did not make it to series status. Popular western character actor Harry Carey, Jr., also appeared in the episode. Cary's son would later appear in an episode of Stoney Burke.

Gunsmoke aired "Doc's Reward" in its third season on December 14, 1957. Lord played both roles as twin brothers Myles and Nate Brandell. He does a good job diversifying the two parts so they seem like separate characters.

Tip on a Dead Jockey is a 1957 film from MGM, starring Robert Taylor as battle fatigued combat pilot Lloyd Treadman. Lord plays his friend and fellow pilot Jimmy Heldon. The plot is based on a short story by Irwin Shaw and follows the trials of a pilot who reluctantly agrees to be a part of a smuggling operation.

Story of a Patriot debuted in 1957 as the visitors center film, produced by Paramount Studios, for Colonial Williamsburg Historical Site's new state of the art facility. Lord is cast in the role of a Virginia Burgess and gentleman planter John Fry. *Story of a Patriot* holds the distinction as the longest continuously running motion picture in history.

Playhouse 90 had Lord in the role of Homer Aswell in a second season episode. "Reunion" aired on CBS on January 2, 1958. It is the story of four World War II veterans who get together years after the war and share details about their lives.

The True Story of Lynn Stuart, a Columbia Pictures release, opened on March 3, 1958. Lord had a "with" billing as bad guy Buck Walden, a drug smuggling thug who winds up in a relationship with an undercover informant. The script is based on an actual event, and the real-life woman at the center of the story acted as a consultant on the film. Lord does a good job in the part.

God's Little Acre, based on Erskine Caldwell's classic novel, opened August 13, 1958, after an impressive amount of pre-release press. Lord has the role of Buck Walden, who toils away day after day for his father, looking for buried treasure on his family's farm. Lord's wife, played by Tina Louise, gives him cause for concern, as she is the object of every man's attention.

Man of the West was released October 1, 1958, from United Artists. Lord is cast in the role of the despicable Coaley Tobin and, once again, he pulls off the bad guy role very well. Julie London has the female lead and at the time she was dating Bobby Troup, who wrote the theme song for the film. They married the following year, and both eventually had roles on *Emergency,* a series about a fire department rescue squad.

U.S. Marshal aired "Sentenced to Death" on October 25, 1958. Lord received critical acclaim for his portrayal Matt Bonner, an escaped ruthless killer, in this third episode from the first season.

The Millionaire was a show about the reaction of everyday individuals who suddenly found themselves to be millionaires. Lord starred in a Season 5 episode. "The Lee Randolph Story" that aired November 11, 1958, on CBS.

The Loretta Young Show features Lord in a guest-starring role in Episode 20 of Season 6 Episode. "Marriage Crisis" aired on NBC, February 15, 1959. Lord works once again with Elizabeth Montgomery as he is cast as Joe, an immature husband who can't seem to hold down a job.

Rawhide featured Lord in guest-starring role during its first season on CBS. In "Incident of the Calico Gun," which aired on April 24, 1959, Lord is cast with Gloria Talbott in the role of a woman in distress, who turns out to be a ruse to get the cattle drive crew in a vulnerable position.

The Hangman was a Paramount release that hit theatres in wide release on June 17, 1959. Lord plays Johnny Bishop, a thief who has gone straight and is living a clean life when he is discovered by a determined lawman. Lord works again alongside Robert Taylor and Tina Louise.

The Lineup was a CBS television series based on a radio program. During Season 6, Lord appears in "The Strange Return of Army Armitage," which aired October 7, 1959. As Army Armitage, he falls victim to the wrong doings of his n'er do well brother.

The Untouchables was a new police series in ABC's 1959 Fall lineup. In "The Jake Lingle Killing" Lord plays Bill Hagan, a shyster who plays both ends against the middle as an FBI informant and as a noted gang member. The episode aired November 5, 1959.

Alcoa Presents: One Step Beyond aired "Father Image" on December 15, 1959, on ABC. Lord is cast in the role of Dan Gardner, Season 2 Episode 13. "Father Image" aired December 15, 1959. Dan Gardner, a law school graduate, gets a very unusual inheritance from his father.

Walk Like a Dragon was a 1960 Paramount release. Lord plays Lincoln "Linc" Bartlett, a rancher who fights against frontier cultural prejudice when he falls in love with a Chinese girl.

Bonanza featured Lord in a guest-starring role during its first season on January 1, 1960. In "The Outcast," he plays Clay Renton, who uses his fiancée, played by Susan Oliver, as a means to get his hands on a payroll wagon as it passes through Ponderosa land. Oliver had worked with Lord earlier on an episode of *Studio One* and they would be cast together two years later in Lord's second appearance on *Rawhide*.

Naked City ran an episode in Season 2 titled "The Human Trap," in which Lord had yet another bad guy role, but this one offered some layers for him to stretch his wings a bit. As thug Cary Glennon, he also shows his family man side when his ex-wife and daughter wind up involved in a murder. The episode aired on November 30, 1960.

Route 66 featured Lord in a Season 1 episode titled "Play It Glissando." It aired January 20, 1961, on CBS. Lord plays Gabe Johnson, a highstrung trumpet player who has a successful career that feeds his passion for jazz, but he holds the woman he loves prisoner out of an unfounded fear he might lose her.

The Americans was a new series for NBC set during the Civil War that first aired February 27, 1961. The show was about brothers who fought on opposite sides in the Civil War. In "Half Moon Road," Lord is cast as Charlie Goodwin.

Outlaws was an NBC series about an Oklahoma lawman, told from the point of view of the bad guys. Lord guest-starred as Jim Houston in "The Bell," which aired on March 3, 1961. Houston has just been released from prison when he encounters a deputy escorting a violent criminal to jail.

Stagecoach West featured Lord as a special guest star in Season 1. "House of Violence" is about a outlaw gang taking refuge in a relay station with hostages after they have committed a robbery and murder. The episode aired March 21, 1961, on ABC. Lord was cast in the role of Russ Dory.

Stagecoach West gave Lord a second appearance as special guest star the following week. Lord plays Johnny Kane in an episode called "The Butcher." The stagecoach crew must hold off a outlaw gang who are looking to execute a prisoner before he can be delivered to the proper authorities. It aired on March 28, 1961.

Rawhide episode from Season 3, "Incident of His Brother's Keeper," aired March 31, 1961, with Lord in the role of paralyzed cattleman

Paul Evans. Evans becomes suspicious of his friend Pete Nolan when he escorts his wife to a dance.

Cain's Hundred was a short-lived NBC series about a lawyer who is on a mission to bring the nation's top 100 wanted criminals to justice. Lord appeared in "Dead Load," airing on November 21, 1961, as Wilt Ferrell.

Checkmate featured Lord as a guest star during Season 2 on January 1, 1962, in "The Star System" as Ernie Chapman. Lord starred alongside Elizabeth Montgomery as a troubled and self-destructive actress. Morton Stevens, composer of the famous *Hawaii Five-O* theme, did the music for the episode.

Here's Hollywood, an NBC magazine style show, hosted Lord as a guest on Episode 23 of the second season airing May 18, 1962.

Stoney Burke premiered October 1, 1962, and gave Lord his first starring role in a series. It ran for 32 episodes on ABC with Lord in the starring role as a rodeo bronc rider. Even though it was cancelled after one season, *Stoney Burke* was a lucrative experience for Lord, especially as he hit the rodeo circuit after the show ended. Lord would later call it "the most successful flop in history."

Dr. No is the first James Bond film based on the Ian Fleming novels. It was released by United Artists in 1962. Lord was cast as recurring character Felix Leiter and he received good reviews for his performance.

Dr. Kildare featured Lord in a guest-starring role in Season 3. "A Willing Suspension of Disbelief" aired on January 9, 1964. Lord is cast as Dr. Frank Michaels, a talented surgeon and insufferable egoist, who tries to hide his debilitating arthritis from his fellow doctors. After his death, widespread speculation persisted that he secretly suffered from arthritis, with many noting frequent unusual positioning of his fingers.

The Greatest Show on Earth featured Lord in a guest-starring role for the first and only season of the ABC series. Lord appeared as Wally Walker in Episode 20, "Man in a Hole," which aired February 18, 1964.

36th Annual Academy Awards aired on ABC April 13, 1964, and Lord took to the stage to accept on behalf of Paul de Roubaix and Marcel Ichac for Best Short Subject, Live Action Subjects. Their dialogue-free film version of "An Occurrence at Owl Creek Bridge" was based on a short story by Ambrose Bierce.

The Reporter was a CBS series that only lasted one season. Lord appeared as Nick Castle in the third episode, "How Much for a Prince," which aired October 9, 1964.

Wagon Train featured Lord during Season 8 in "The Echo Pass Story." It aired January 3, 1965, on NBC and Lord was cast as Lee Barton. He worked alongside James Caan, whose son would go on to be a regular in the reboot of *Hawaii Five-O*. Lord is strong in lead role of the story of a desperate family trying to make it Mexico after robbing a bank to make a better life for themselves. He also works with Robert Horton, who would later appear in *Emergency* with Julie London and Bobby Troup.

Kraft Suspense Theatre aired "The Long Ravine" on NBC during Season 2 on May 6, 1965. Lord plays Paul Campbell, an obsessive dreamer who is convinced he is going to hit a hidden vein of gold. He persists with his search to the detriment of his wife and his young brother-in-law who has returned from the service.

Bob Hope Presents the Chrysler Theatre has Lord in the role of Abe Perez for a second season episode of the NBC series. "The Crime" aired September 22, 1965, on NBC and it follows the story of a lawyer who is prosecuting a former lover. His motives in his ardent quest to have her convicted are questioned.

The Loner episode, "The Vespers" was the second of the first season of a new series for CBS. Lord puts forth a strong performance as the Rev. Mr. Booker, a gunslinger turned minister who finds himself confronted with old enemies. He struggles as he tries to avoid picking up his guns again. It aired September 25, 1965.

Combat! was an ABC series about a World War II combat squad that ran five seasons on ABC. In the fourth season, Lord appeared as linesman Barney McKlosky. He is a disagreeable chap who makes their dangerous mission to lay communication lines through enemy territory even more difficult. The episode aired October 5, 1965.

Twelve O'Clock High on ABC had Lord appearing in yet another World War II series. On October 11, 1965, Lord is cast as Lt Col. Preston Gallagher, brother to series star Paul Burke's character, Colonel Joe Gallagher. Pres has issues as he struggles to cope with a bad decision that cost the lives of men under his charge.

Laredo featured Lord as Jab Harlan in "Above the Law" about a wrongly accused man and an episode intended as a spin-off from the NBC series. It aired on January 13, 1966.

Bob Hope Presents: The Chrysler Theatre aired "The Faceless Man" May 4, 1966, during its third season on NBC. It was an unsold pilot in which Lord played Don Owens. Lord received good reviews for his work on the episode. The pilot underwent several title changes, including *Jigsaw* and *Crackshot*. It was later released on video as *Crackshot*.

Twelve O'Clock High featured Lord in a second episode from the third season of the popular series. "Face of a Shadow" aired September 23, 1966, on ABC with Lord in the role of Col. Arnold Yates in "Face of a Shadow." Yates puts the men under his command in imminent danger as he pursues a relationship with an Italian countess who is suspected of spying for the enemy.

The F.B.I. was a long-running series on ABC. Lord appeared in a second season episode on November 13, 1966. He plays Frank Andreas Schroeder, a cold-blooded killer in "Collision Course."

The Virginian ran on NBC for nine seasons. Lord had a guest-starring role in Season 5. He appeared in "High Stakes" on November 16, 1966, as Roy Dallman.

Bob Hope Presents: The Chrysler Theatre featured Lord again in the next season. In "Storm Crossing," aired on NBC December 7, 1966, Lord was in the role of Harry Marcus. It follows the adventures of a group of passengers traveling on a freighter who get caught in a storm at sea.

The Tonight Show aired an episode with Lord as a guest star on December 12, 1966, on NBC. Johnny Carson commented on his surprise at the extent of Lord's prolific career and the variety of roles he had filled.

The Doomsday Flight was a made for TV movie that aired December 13, 1966, on NBC. Lord played Special Agent Frank Thompson and follows his efforts to save a plane full of passengers, including his wife, who are on a plane with a bomb on board.

Ride to Hangman's Tree opened in theatres in May of 1966. The Universal Studios lighthearted western gave Lord the opportunity to do something he had wanted to do for years—play in a comedic role. As Gary Russell, he played well with James Farentino and Don Galloway.

The Invaders featured Lord in "Vikor," a first season episode that aired February 14, 1967. Lord plays George Vikor, an industrial manufacturer who is working with aliens to effect a take over of the world. Vikor is a wounded and emotionally disturbed presidential medal of valor winner for his service during the Korean War and he has fallen in with the alien movement to fulfill his desire for power once the take over is complete.

The Fugitive episode "Goodbye My Love" aired on ABC February 28, 1967. Lord was cast as Alan Bartlett, the husband of a wealthy socialite who is confined to a wheelchair as the result of an accident. He plots with his lover, a lounge singer at his club, to kill his wife and to frame fugitive Dr. Richard Kimball for her murder. The series spawned the 1993 movie by the same name and starred Harrison Ford as Kimball.

Ironside was another series in which Lord captured a guest-starring spot during the premiere season. "Dead Man's Tale," airing on NBC September 28, 1967, has Lord in the role of unscrupulous attorney John Trask. He goes toe to toe with Chief Ironside and fails to accurately estimate the creative resourcefulness of the wheel-chair bound cop.

The Man from U.N.C.L.E. episode The Master's Touch Affair aired on NBC October 16, 1967, and features Lord as Pharos Mandor, who passes himself off as a defector from the enemy Thrush organization, but he is actually working to raise himself to a higher position.

The High Chaparral is another series in which Lord captured a guest-starring role in the inaugural season. In "The Kinsman," airing on NBC January 28, 1968, Lord plays Dan Brooks, stepbrother to John's first wife. Although he is presenting himself as a devoted relative who has run upon some bad luck, he is actually hiding out from bounty hunters who want to bring him in on murder charges.

The Name of the Game Is Kill from Fanfare Films has Lord in the role of Hungarian immigrant Symcha Lipa and was released May 1, 1968. Susan Strasberg is his costar. Not his finest role, the film has a bizarre publicity campaign whereby prospective viewers are asked to vow they will not reveal the shocking ending to the *Psycho*-ish film.

Hawaii Five-O premiered its two-part pilot on CBS September 20, 1968, with Lord in his trademark role Steve McGarrett. Twelve seasons later, the hard-nosed, complicated head of a special police force would prove to be the role that gave Jack Lord a place in the history books.

The Counterfeit Killer (aka Crackshot) was released September 23, 1968, from Universal Studios. Lord is cast as undercover agent Don Owens who is on the case of five murders and a million dollars worth of counterfeit money.

The Mike Douglas Show took on a Hawaiian flavor when Lord was a guest star on the eighth season. The show aired January 17, 1969.

The Glen Campbell Goodtime Hour was broadcast from Hawaii on October 19, 1971, on CBS. Audiences got to hear Lord sing, a talent he had previously largely used for his rodeo appearances as Stoney Burke.

Lord of the Islands was a Christmas special broadcast on Irish television on Boxing Day, Tuesday, December 26, 1973. Boxing Day is the traditional British holiday that falls on the first weekday after Christmas. Lord was filmed working in front of *Five-O* cameras and he was interviewed about his art and his life in Hawaii.

30th Annual Primetime Emmy Award features Lord as a presenter for Outstanding Lead Actress in a Limited Series. The show aired on CBS September 17, 1978.

Good Morning America hosted Lord in a guest starring spot on October 5, 1979, on ABC.

M Station: Hawaii was Lord's last on-screen role. The television movie was an unsold pilot that aired June 10, 1980. Lord has a very small role as Admiral Henderson, but he served as director and executive producer for the film under the auspices of his Lord and Lady Productions.

The Whales That Wouldn't Die was a documentary aired on KPBS September 10, 1980, Lord lends his distinctive voice as narrator to a film intended to bring attention to one of the many causes he supported as one of most prolific philanthropists in Hollywood.

Chapter Notes

Introduction

1. Louis Giannetti and Scott Eyman, *Flashback: A Brief History of Film* (Boston: Pearson, 2009), 87.
2. Leslie Raddatz, "How an Ex-Rodeo Rider Went West to Enjoy the Good Life as a Hawaiian Cop," *TV Guide*, Jan. 4, 1969, 18.
3. Dwight Whitney, "Jack Lord, Superstar," *TV Guide*, Sept. 4, 1971, 31.
4. Carol Giallaombardo, "Excuse Me if I'm Hysterical (Or Small Town Girl Meets Celebrity)," *Norwalk Reflector* (Norwalk, Ohio), Nov. 5, 1971.
5. Fred Hift, "Among Selves, Film Tradesters Gossip Re Gossip Columns," *Weekly Variety* (New York), July 15, 1959, Page 4.
6. Jack Lord, Letter to Jane Ardmore, Aug. 1, 1969, Jack Lord Collection, Cinematic Arts Library, University of Southern California.
7. Bill Tusher, "Jack Lord: He Turns the Other Cheek," *Screenland*, July 1963, 14.

Chapter One

1. Rita Witherwax, "Jack Lord: The Man Behind McGarrett," *Aloha: The Magazine of Hawaii*," October 1980, 24.
2. "Talk Back," *Los Angeles Times*, May 11, 1980, X6.
3. "Todd Mason Papers (audiotapes), 1967–1981, Collection Number PASC 363, UCLA Library Special Collections, Performing Arts.
4. "Legal Limelight Has Jack Lord Unhappy," *Los Angeles Times*, December 18, 1975, H37.
5. Harriet Choice, "A Spiffy Jack Lord Gets 'Angle' Shot, Meets a Reporter," *Chicago Tribune,* January 10, 1969, A15.
6. Carl Ballenas and Nancy Cataldi with the Richmond Hill Historical Society, *Richmond Hill* (Charleston, SC: Arcadia, 2002), e-book, Introduction; William Kroos, *A Peek at Richmond Hill through the Keyhole of Time* (New York: Woodhaven Cultural and Historical Society), n.d.
7. Richmond Hill Historical Society, http://www.richmondhillhistory.org.
8. Tex Maddox, "Vice and Virtue," *Movie Life*, July 1962, 46.
9. Jack Lord Collection, Cinematic Arts Library, University of Southern California.
10. Jack Lord, Letter to Betty Lamm, November 30, 1972, Jack Lord Collection, Cinematic Arts Library, University of Southern California.
11. Todd Mason Papers (audiotapes).
12. Todd Mason Papers, (Manuscript), 1967–1981, Collection Number PASC 363, UCLA Library Special Collections, Performing Arts, 22–23.
13. Jack Lord, "Ya Gotta Be Tough to Act!" *Mr.*, January 1957, 62.
14. Bessie Little, "Lowdown on Jack Lord," *Teen Life*, August 1963, 62.
15. Jane Ardmore, "These Things Have Changed my Life," Interview Notes, Jane Ardmore Collection, File 17.9, Margaret Herrick Library Academy of Motion Picture Arts and Sciences, no date, 1.
16. Roland Miller, "Jack Lord Talks About His Mother and Father: 'They Were Two Brutes,'" *Photoplay*, May 1971, 78.
17. Jane Ardmore, Typed Interview Notes for article, "Jack Lord Charged with Mutiny," March 1970, Jane Ardmore Collection, File 17.9, Margaret Herrick Library Academy of Motion Picture Arts and Sciences.
18. Jane Ardmore, "I Owe My Life to My Old Man," Typed draft copy with handwritten interview notes, Jane Ardmore Collection, File 17.9, Margaret Herrick Library, Academy of Motion Picture Arts and Science, no date, unnumbered pages.
19. Ardmore notes, "These Things Have Changed My Life," Jane Ardmore Collection, File 17.9, page 7.
20. Bernie McGovern, "Lord Looks to Writing to Keep Series a Hit," *Tampa Tribune* (Tampa, FL), Oct. 31, 1968, 8c.
21. Mason Papers, 22.
22. Lawrence Laurent, "Jack Lord Riding High in the Saddle," *The Washington Post and Times-Herald* (Washington, D.C.), June 11, 1964, B6.
23. Jack Lord Collection, Cinematic Arts Library, University of Southern California.
24. Paul Jones, "Jack Lord Is Macon Fan," *The Atlanta Constitution*, Aug. 8, 1969, 18A.
25. *Clipper: John Adams High School Annual,* Queens, New York, vol. 7, no. 4, 1938, 5.
26. *Clipper*, 72.
27. Brett Bolton, "You Never Read a Story about Jack Lord That Told You This," *TV Radio Mirror*, December 1970, 86.
28. *Clipper*, 84.

29. William A. Clark, Letter to John J. Ryan, March 27, 1963, Jack Lord Collection, University of Southern California Cinematic Arts Library.

30. Bolton, 88.

31. John Bustin, "Show World," *The Austin Statesman* (Austin, TX), Nov. 28, 1969, A-43.

32. Witherwax, *Aloha*.

33. Miller, *Brutes*, 101.

34. Compiled Military Record, Ryan, John Joseph, USCG Merchant Marine, June 19, 1937–August 15, 1945, copy in possession of author.

35. Lisa Reynolds, "The 16 Hours that Changed Jack Lord's Life," *Photoplay*, October 1971, 76+.

36. Harriet Choice, "A Spiffy Jack Lord Get 'Angle' Shot, Meets a Reporter."

37. New York University Archives, email message to author, Jan. 9, 2016.

38. Franklin D. Roosevelt, "Campaign Address at Boston, Massachusetts," October 30, 1940, online by Gerhard Peters and John T. Woolley, *The American Presidency Project*, http://www.presidency.ucsb.edu/ws/?pid=15887, retrieved January 21, 2016.

39. Elizabeth Sullivan, "An Early Caller," *Boston Globe*, Nov. 9, 1969, TV11.

40. Jack Hirshberg, Typed notes, *Vagabond*, 1958, 1–2, Jack Hirshberg Papers, File #5, Margaret Herrick Library, Academy of Motion Picture Arts and Sciences.

41. Val Holley, *Mike Connolly and the Manly Art of Hollywood Gossip* (Jefferson, NC: McFarland, 2003), 22.

42. Report of Birth of Children Born to American Parents for Ann Cecily Willard, 21 December 1921, American Consular Service, Paris, France, copy in possession of author.

43. Carol Day and Clark Champ, "Stanger in Paradise," *People*, Feb. 9, 1998, 60.

44. Stamford Historical Society, http://www.stamfordhistory.org/ph_1002_n3.htm.

45. Jeanne A. LeBlanc, "The Lost," *Hartford Courant* (Hartford, CT), August 18, 2005, Courant.newspapers.com.

46. The CDC, or Communicable Disease Center (now the Centers for Disease Control and Prevention), was founded in 1946.

47. Death Certificate for John Joseph Ryan, 26 August 1955, File No. 14006, Connecticut State Department of Health, certified copy in possession of author.

48. "'Hawaii Five-O'" Loses Studio," *The Hartford Courant* (Hartford, CT), April 25, 1976, 30U.

49. Jane Ardmore, Typed notes for article "Jack of All or Many Trades," February 7, 1963, Jane Ardmore Collection, File 17.9, Margaret Herrick Library, Academy of Motion Picture Arts and Sciences, 8.

50. Robert C. Smith, "Passion for Accuracy Pervades Filming of 'Williamsburg Story,'" *The Norfolk Virginian Pilot* and *The Portsmouth Star* (Portsmouth, VA), May 27, 1956.

51. "Prelude to a Proposal," *Woman's Day*, November 18, 1963, Clipping, Jack Lord Collection, University of Southern California, Cinematic Arts Library.

52. Peer J. Oppenheimer, "Jack Lord: Painting or Performing, He's a Perfectionist," *The Austin Statesman* (Austin, TX), Sept. 28, 1969, SM7.

53. Linda Elliott, "Jack Lord Tells His Wife I'm Never Going Home," Typed article draft, n.d., Jane Ardmore Collection, Margaret Herrick Library, Academy of Motion Picture Arts and Sciences.

Chapter Two

1. Paul Denis, "The Man Who Found God's Little Acre," *TV Headliner*, Dec. 30, 1958, 32.

2. Bolton, "You Never Read," 87.

3. Elizabeth Sullivan, "An Early Caller," *Boston Globe*, Nov. 9, 1969, TV 11.

4. Bolton, "You Never Read," 88.

5. Jack Hirshberg, Jack Hirshberg Papers, Undated typed interview notes, Margaret Herrick Library, Academy of Motion Picture Arts and Sciences.

6. Joseph E. Corker, Letter to Jack Lord, August 20, 1978, Jack Lord Collection, Cinematic Arts Library, University of Southern California.

7. Duane Valentry, "Stoney Burke: Television's Rodeo Cowboy," *Western Horseman*, July 1963, 50.

8. Emery Wister, *The Charlotte News* (Charlotte, NC), Sept. 13, 1969, 15c. (Clipping from The Jack Lord Collection, Cinematic Arts Library, University of Southern California.)

9. Ted Hamilton, Letter to Jack Lord, Nov. 16, 1979, The Jack Lord Collection, Cinematic Arts Library, University of Southern California.

10. Jane Ardmore, Interview notes for article, "Jack Lord Charged with Mutiny," March 1970, Margaret Herrick Library. Academy of Motion Picture Arts and Sciences Library.

11. Jack Lord Biography File, Jane Ardmore Typed Notes, Jack Lord Biography, Jan. 20, 1971, Margaret Herrick Library, Academy of Motion Picture Arts and Sciences.

12. Gene Tinker, "It Began with *Hawaii Five-O*," *Hyatt's Hawaii*, September 1984, 11.

13. Jane Ardmore, Typed Interview Notes, n.d., Jane Ardmore Collection, Margaret Herrick Library, Academy of Motion Picture Arts and Sciences, 10.

14. Westwood Gallery, 262 Bowery, New York City. Exhibit A, Roy Schatt Bio.

15. http://neighborhoodplayhouse.org/about/our-history.

16. Vera Soloviova, Stella Adler, Sanford Meisner and Paul Gray, *The Tulane Drama Review* 9, no. 1 (1964): 146.

17. Untitled typed manuscript with pencil edits, Jack Hirshburg Papers, Margaret Herrick Library, Academy of Motion Picture Arts and Sciences Library, File #5, page 1.

18. *Tonight*, 741 Sound Recording Call Number LPA 50859, Madison, LM 113, Armed Forces Radio and Television Service (March 1967), Library of Congress.

19. Jane Ardmore, "Jack Lord Charged with Mutiny," Draft Copy and Interview Notes, No date, Jane Ardmore Collection, Margaret Herrick Library Academy of Motion Picture Arts and Sciences.

20. Marie Lord, Letter to Ella Chun, Sept. 8, 1970, Jack Lord Collection, Cinematic Arts Library, University of Southern California.

21. http://www.earlytelevision.org/worlds_fair.html.

Chapter Three

1. "On the Line," Undated transcript of Bob Considine's Syndicated Column, International News Service, Jack Hirshberg Papers, File 5, Margaret Herrick Library, Academy of Motion Picture Arts and Sciences, Undated.

2. "Film Preview: *Project X*," *Daily Variety,* Nov. 1, 1949, 3.
3. Jack Hirshberg, *Vagabond* article draft, Jack Hirshberg papers, File 5, Margaret Herrick Library, Academy of Motion Picture Arts and Sciences, Undated.
4. *Weekly Variety*, Feb. 1, 1950, 20.
5. *Daily Variety*, Feb. 7, 1950, 4.
6. John L. Scott, *Los Angeles Times*, March 2, 1950, A2.
7. Jack Lord Biography, Margaret Herrick Library, Academy of Motion Picture Arts and Sciences.
8. Jack Lord, Letter to John Huston, John Huston Papers, File F.1119, Margaret Herrick Library, Academy of Motion Picture Arts and Sciences, April 8, 1950. (The clipping Lord mentions is not attached to the letter, but was likely from *Cry Murder!*)
9. http://mysteryfile.com/blog by Steve Lewis; article: "A TV Series Review by Michael Shonk: The Hunter (1952–1954)."
10. Jack Lord Collection, Cinematic Arts Library, University of Southern California.
11. Jack Lord, "Ya Gotta Be Tough to Act!"
12. Handwritten note on reverse side of Basil Rathbone Photo, Jack Lord Collection, Cinematic Arts Library, University of Southern California.
13. Army Archerd, "Just for Variety," *Daily Variety*, Jan. 6, 1972, 2.
14. Jack Lord, "Aloha 'Oe," *Holiday*, May 1977, 66.
15. Sam Zolotow, "Longacre Returns to Theatre Ranks," *New York Times*, Oct. 21, 1953, 37.
16. Jack Lord Collection, Cinematic Arts Library, University of Southern California.
17. Sandra Grabman, *No Retakes! Actors and Actresses Remember the Era of Live Television* (Albany, GA: BearManor Media, 2014), eBook.
18. "An Interview With... by Mike Fitzgerald," Western Clippings, http://www.westernclippingscom/interview/carrollbaker_interview.shtml.
19. Sam Zolotow, "Premiere in Paris for 'Blues Opera,'" *New York Times*, Sept. 3, 1954, 13.
20. Brooks Atkinson, "Theatre: Texas Drama," *New York Times*, Oct. 28, 1954, 45.
21. John Krampner, *Female Brando: The Legend of Kim Stanley* (New York: Back Stage, 2006), 87.
22. Fitzroy Davis, "Consider Your Voice," *New York Times*, Nov. 28, 1954, X1.
23. Screen Actors Guild Free Lance Contract, December 16, 1954, Jack Lord Collection, Cinematic Arts Library, University of Southern California.
24. J.P. Shanley, "Television: Coming Up," *New York Times*, April 15, 1955, 30.
25. Blog, *The Anonymous Method*, http://anonymousmethod.tumblr.com.
26. Jack Hirshberg, "Paramount/Hirshberg/Vagabond," No date, Jack Hirshberg Papers, File 5, Margaret Herrick Library Academy of Motion Pictures Arts and Sciences.
27. Wade H. Mosby, "Show Biz," *The Milwaukee Journal*, April 27, 1969.
28. Sam Zolotow, "Malden to Leave Drama on August 13," *New York Times*, July 29, 1955, 9.
29. Photo, *New York Times*, Aug. 29, 1955, 16.
30. "Inside Stuff Pictures," *Weekly Variety*, Oct. 24, 1956, 20.
31. Typed Draft, Bob Kass, *Focus: Something New in Radio* (Oct. 18, 1955), Jack Hirshberg Papers, File 5, Margaret Herrick Library Academy of Motion Pictures Arts and Sciences.
32. Arthur Gelb, "Critics Open Way for Play to Open," *New York Times*, Oct. 31, 1955, 31.
33. "Drama Mailbag," *New York Times*, Jan. 1, 1956, X3.
34. Alan Gill, "Big, Big, Big!" *TV Guide*, Nov. 17, 1962, 16.
35. Bosley Crowther, Review: *Court Martial of Billy Mitchel, New York Times*, Dec. 23, 1965.
36. Edwin Schallert, "Mitchell Feature Big in Its Impact," *Los Angeles Times*, Dec. 22, 1955, B6.

Chapter Four

1. Goodbody to Wilder, Nov. 8, 1954, *Williamsburg: The Story of a Patriot* Production Books 1.3, Media Production Archives, Colonial Williamsburg, 6. As cited in *Screening the Revolution: Williamsburg: The Story of a Patriot as Historic Artifact, History Film, and Hegemonic Struggle*, Thesis by Jenna Anne Simpson, 2006, 9.
2. "Prelude to *Patriot*: James Agee's Unfinished Script," *Colonial Williamsburg*, Autumn 1993, 57.
3. Laurence Bergreen, *James Agee: A Life* (New York: E.P. Dutton, 1984), 401.
4. W.D. Geiger, Report to Mr. Goodbody, Program Report on CW1811, January 10, 1956, Summary of all expenses, CW1811 through Jan. 10, 1956, Block 33 #6, Colonial Williamsburg Foundation Archives.
5. File memo, John C. Goodbody, Re: NICA Film, Information Center—Program, Block 33 #6, Colonial Williamsburg Foundation Archives.
6. John Goodbody, Letter to Carl Dudley, Dudley Pictures Corporation, Jan. 10, 1956, Information Center—Program Letter, Block 33 #6, Colonial Williamsburg Foundation Archives.
7. John C. Goodbody, File Copy, Report of Discussions from New York Meeting with Seaton, Jan. 16, 1956, Information Center—Program Letter, Block 33 #6, Colonial Williamsburg Archives.
8. Howard Strickling, Letter to John Goodbody, Jan. 26, 1956, Information Center—Program Letter, Block 33#6, Colonial Williamsburg Foundation Archives.
9. Alfred J. Scalpone, CBS Television, to Carlisle H. Humelsine, Feb. 21, 1956, Information Center—Program Letter, Block 33 #6, Colonial Williamsburg Foundation Archives.
10. George Seaton, Letter to John C. Goodbody, Jan. 11, 1956, Information Center—Program, Block 33 #6, Colonial Williamsburg Foundation Archives.
11. Radie Harris, "Broadway Ballyhoo," *Hollywood Daily Reporter,* April 25, 1956. (Clipping.)
12. Vernon Scott, "'Unknown's' Film to Run Forever," *Charlotte Observer* (Charlotte, NC), April 8, 1957. (Lord incorrectly gave the date as 1953; filming actually took place in 1954.)
13. Radie Harris, "Broadway Ballyhoo," *The Hollywood Reporter*, May 29, 1956, 4.
14. Scott, "'Unknown's' Film to Run Forever."
15. 1955 Television Supplement to Producer-SAG Codified Basic Agreement, July 21, 1955, Hal Roach Collection, Labor Vendor Documents, Box 1 of 2, University of Southern California, Cinematic Arts Library.
16. Press Release, Information Center—Program, Block 33#6, Colonial Williamsburg Foundation Archives.
17. Thad W. Tate, "Behind the Story of a Patriot," *Colonial Williamsburg Today*, Winter 1972, 2.

18. John C. Goodbody, Telegram to Thomas H. Davis, May 4, 1956, Block 33 #6, Information Center—Program, Colonial Williamsburg Foundation Archives.

19. John C. Goodbody, Letter to Granville Jones, June 15, 1956, Block 33 #6, Information Center—Program, Colonial Williamsburg Foundation Archives.

20. Jack Lord, Thank you note to "Friends," May 24, 1956, Information Center—Program, Block 33 #6, Colonial Williamsburg Foundation Archives.

21. Scott, "'Unknown's' Film to Run Forever."

22. Arthur L. Smith, Letter to Jack Lord, Aug. 8, 1956, Information Center—Programs, Block 33 #6, Colonial Williamsburg Foundation Archives.

23. Alice Sircom, Letter to Jack Lord, Aug. 15, 1956, General Correspondence, Colonial Williamsburg Archives.

24. Thomas B. Schlesinger, Letter to Mr. Alexander, July 2, 1956, Special Events—Film Festival—Information Center Programs, Block 33 #6, Colonial Williamsburg Foundation Archives.

25. "A Celebrity: 10 Millionth to See Film," *Richmond News Leader* (Richmond, VA), May 18, 1970.

26. Bonnie Brown, "Day They Made a Movie in Williamsburg," *The Daily Press* (New Dominion, VA), July 15, 1973.

27. Memo (no addressee, no author), October 6, 1975, Moving Pictures-Williamsburg, *The Story of a Patriot*. Also letter to Paul J. Murdoch, Oct. 8, 1975, from Ray W. Martin, Moving Pictures—Williamsburg, Block 33 #6, Colonial Williamsburg Foundation Archives.

28. Jack Lord, Letter to J. Frank Cross, March 1, 1967, Crafts—Souvenir—Dolls, Colonial Williamsburg Foundation Archives.

29. F. Roger Thaler, Memorandum to File, March 6, 1987, General Correspondence—Moving Pictures Wmsbrg, *Story of a Patriot*, Colonial Williamsburg Foundation Archives.

30. Clipping page 58, *Hear the Voice of Hollywood*, vol. 1, no. 1, Aug. 1956, Jack Hirshberg Papers, Margaret Herrick Library Academy of Motion Pictures Arts and Sciences.

31. Art, "Tele Review: 'Day Before Battle,'" *Weekly Variety*, Sept. 5, 1956, 24.

32. Warneke, "Moment of Respite from Combat," *New York Times*, Sept. 2, 1956, X9.

33. Kove, "Old Acquaintance," *Daily Variety*, Dec. 3, 1956, 8.

34. Westley Ryder, "Which Jack Lord Do You Know?" *TV Star Parade*, November 1956, 48–51.

Chapter Five

1. Daku, "Mr. Runyon of Broadway," *Daily Variety*, June 10, 1957, 9.

2. Harry Carey, Jr., *Company of Heroes* (Metuchen, NJ: Scarecrow, 1994), 162.

3. "Richard Boone, Actor, Dies at 63; Star of Have Gun Will Travel," *New York Times*, Jan. 12, 1981, Retrieved from http://www.nytimes.com/1981/01/12/obituaries.

4. Edwin Schallert, "'Twilight for Gods' Big Picture Purchase; Gia Scala to Lure Taylor," *Los Angeles Times*, Feb. 4, 1957, C9.

5. Edwin Schallert, "Kirk Douglas Seeks O'Neill Masterpiece."

6. "Melodrama Misfires," *Los Angeles Times*, Aug. 29, 1957, C11.

7. *New York Times Film Reviews, 1913–1968* (New York: New York Times/Arno, 1970), 3007.

8. Gary R. Edgerton, *The Columbia History of American Television* (New York: Columbia University Press, 2007), 194.

9. Ron, *Variety*, Jan. 1, 1958, 31.

10. "Lone Woman," TV Show Notebooks, Cinematic Arts Library, University of Southern California, March 15, 1956–January 25, 1957.

11. Helm, *Daily Variety*, Oct. 13, 1958, 14.

12. "Movie Moguls Buy Time for Oscar Awards," *St. Petersburg Times* (St. Petersburg, FL), Jan. 8, 1958, 27.

13. Jack Gould, "TV: 'Reunion' in Brief," *New York Times*, Jan. 3, 1958, 44.

14. Lawrence Laurent, "Playhouse's 90 Minutes More Pitch Than Play," *The Washington Post*, Jan. 4, 1958, A16.

15. Philip K. Scheuer, "Views Diverge on War Film: Question of Foreign Accents Raised by 'Paths of Glory,'" *Los Angeles Times*, Jan. 16, 1958, B11.

16. "Scalpone's Indie LaMesa Shop to Roll on 4 Series, *Variety*, July 23, 1958, 22.

17. Seymour Peck, "Up-and-Coming in Movies," *New York Times*, Jan. 26, 1958, SM28.

18. *Daily Variety*, Feb. 12, 1958, 2.

19. Power, "Film Review: Man of the West," *Daily Variety*, Sept. 17, 1958, 3.

20. Howard Thompson, "A New Double Bill," *New York Times*, Oct. 2, 1958.

21. John L. Scott, "'Man of the West' Proves Shock Type Western," *Los Angeles Times*, Oct. 9, 1958, B11.

22. Oscar A. Godbout, "Hollywood Seeds; Don Hartman's Design for Producing—Georgia," *New York Times*, Aug. 18, 1957, X5.

23. Richard W. Nason, "Big Stake in God's Little Acre,'" *New York Times*, May 4, 1958, X7.

24. A.H. Weiler, "Georgia Rustics; 'God's Little Acre' at Local Theatres," *New York Times*, Aug. 14, 1958.

25. Bosley Crowther, "Out of the Ordinary," *New York Times*, Aug. 24, 1958, X1.

26. Powr, *Daily Variety*, May 9, 1958, 3.

27. Jack Moffitt, "'God's Little Acre' Yields Big Crop of Sex and Laughs," *The Hollywood Reporter*, May 9, 1958, 3, Jack Poplin Papers, Folder 17, *God's Little Acre*, Margaret Herrick Library, Academy of Motion Picture Arts and Sciences.

28. Philip K. Scheuer, "'God's Little Acre' Seen as Most Daring Hollywood Film," *Los Angeles Times*, April 27, 1958, E1.

29. "Prod'rs Should Abolish Casting Depts. Cast All Roles: Harmon," *Daily Variety*, June 27, 1958, 6.

30. *The New York Times Film Reviews, 1913–1968*, 3102.

31. "Hedda Hopper Gives Her Forecast of New Faces on Film Stardom List," *Los Angeles Times*, Dec. 28, 1958, D1.

32. Hedda Hopper, Typed notes, Jack Lord Interview, Hedda Hopper Collection, Margaret Herrick Library, Motion Picture Academy Arts and Sciences, File #2144, Undated.

33. Jack Lord, Letter to Hedda Hopper, Hedda Hopper Collection, Margaret Herrick Library, Motion Picture Academy Arts and Sciences, File #2144, Dec. 31, 1961.

34. Lee Goldberg, *Unsold Television Pilots, 1955–1989* (Calabasas, CA: Adventures in Television, 2015), xxv.

35. Philip K. Scheuer, "Views Diverge on War Film."

36. "The Thrilling Detective," http://www.thrillingdetective.com/trivia/gruber.html.
37. "Must Find New Material if We Are to Stay in Business, Declares Frank Freeman," *Daily Variety*, March 3, 1957, 4.
38. Hedda Hopper, "Malden Will Costar with Van Heflin," *Los Angeles Times*, Dec. 20, 1958, B2.
39. Laurence Olivier, Letter to Jack Lord, Jack Lord Collection, Cinematic Arts Library, University of Southern California.

Chapter Six

1. "Mirisch Dickers Lord," *Daily Variety*, Jan. 12, 1959, 4.
2. "Stars of Tomorrow," *Movie Screen Yearbook*, 1959, 79.
3. TV Show Notebooks, *The Quiet Man*, Cinematic Arts Library, University of Southern California.
4. Chan, "Marriage Crisis," *Daily Variety*, Feb. 12, 1959, 14.
5. Powr, "Film Review, *The Hangman*," *Daily Variety*, April 23, 1959, 3.
6. Ron Silverman, "Exhibs Apathy in Selling Pix Hit by Parker," *Daily Variety*, July 24, 1959, 1.
7. "Who's Where," *Daily Variety*, Aug. 4, 1959, 2.
8. "Jack Lord Back After P.A. and Lineup Chores," *Daily Variety*, Aug. 26, 1959, 13.
9. "Jack Lord Stars on Lineup Tonight, 7:30," *Daily Variety*, Oct. 7, 1959, 4–5.
10. "Jack Lord Stars in 'The Untouchables' Tonight," *Daily Variety*, Nov. 5, 1959, 9–10.
11. "Bunuel Here Casting," *Daily Variety*, Oct. 21, 1959, 3.
12. "Kathryn Grayson's Return in Opera," *Los Angeles Times*, Nov. 6, 1959, C15.
13. Jack Lord, "Type Casting Steam Roller: Hollywood Crushes Actor's Versatility, Says Jack Lord," *Los Angeles Times*, Nov. 8, 1959, E7.
14. "Type-Casting Lament Unjustified-Producer," *Los Angeles Times*, Nov. 15, 1959, F2.
15. "Kathryn Grayson's Return in 'Opera,'" *Los Angeles Times*, Nov. 16, 1959, C15.
16. "Kathryn Grayson's Return," *Los Angeles Times*.
17. Lawrence Laurent, "Good Guy: John Joseph Patrick Ryan," *The Washington Post Weekly Magazine*, Dec. 28, 1969.
18. "Walk Like a Dragon" Film Review, *Variety*, Dec. 31, 1959.
19. Hank Grant, "Jack Lord a Champion in Many Varied Fields," *The Hartford Courant* (Hartford, CT), Aug. 5, 1962, 12G.
20. Hedda Hopper, "Heavies to Heroes Long Haul for Jack," *Los Angeles Times*, March 12, 1963, C10.
21. *Tramp Ship*, TV Show Notebooks, Cinematic Arts Library, University of Southern California.
22. *Fifties Westerns*, https://fiftieswesterns.wordpress.com/2015/02/10/character-actor-of-the-day-neville-brand.
23. Hedda Hopper, "Turned Down 'Casey'; Jack Lord Not Sorry," *The Hartford Courant* (Hartford, CT), March 15, 1963, 7.
24. Television Show Report Collection, Cinematic Arts Library, University of Southern California.
25. "Fedderson's 'Trampship,'" *Variety*, Sept. 28, 1960, 34.
26. *Tramp Ship: Catch A Tiger*, UCLA Film and Television Archive, Research Study Center, Powell Library.
27. "Filmland Events: 'Seven Ways' Latest Seven for Coburn," *Los Angeles Times*, May 5, 1960, C9.
28. Cecil Smith, "Couldn't Be Done," *Los Angeles Times*, May 26, 1960, A14.
29. "Herridge Hits Road," *Variety*, Oct. 5, 1960, 54.
30. *Variety Fifteenth Annual Radio-TV Review and Preview*, July 27, 1960, 58–59.
31. *Los Angeles Times* shows a March 19, 1961, airdate for the episode; The San Bernardino, CA, paper lists it for March 20, 1961.
32. "Jack Lord Up for Lead in Legitimate 'Love,'" *Daily Variety*, March 24, 1969, 2.
33. Hedda Hopper, "Jack Lord Will Do Musical 'Sideshow,'" *Los Angeles Times*, Oct. 3, 1963, C10.
34. Script, Alcoa Presents *One Step Beyond*, "Father Image," Production No. 2926, MGM Studios, Jack Lord Collection, Hawaiian Collection, University of Hawaii at Monoa.
35. "Munday in Hot Water," *Daily Variety*, Aug. 18, 1961, 12.

Chapter Seven

1. Lee Pfeiffer and Philip Lisa, *The Incredible World of 007: An Authorized Celebration of James Bond* (Secaucus, NJ: Carol, 1996), 7–9.
2. Paul Mavis, *The Espionage Filmography: United States Releases, 1898 through 1999* (Jefferson, NC: McFarland, 2001), 87.
3. *Incredible World of 007*, 12.
4. "Dr. No (1963)," accessed Sept. 7, 2015, http://www.the-numbers.com/movie/Dr.-No#tab+more.
5. Philip K. Scheuer, "Strong Drink, Weak Dames, Beautiful Isles," *Los Angeles Times*, April 28, 1963, L3.
6. Letter, Jack Lord to Hedda Hopper, Feb. 6, 1962, Hedda Hopper Papers, Margaret Herrick Library Academy of Motion Picture Arts and Sciences, File F2144.
7. Jack Lord to Hedda Hopper, Feb. 6, 1962.
8. "Jack Lord Offered a Lead in 'Eagles,'" *Daily Variety*, March 3, 1962, 2.
9. *Dr. No*, Terrence Young (1962; Beverly Hills, CA: United Artists), 2012.
10. *Dr. No*, DVD Extra Features.
11. Letter, Jack Lord to Michael Buchanan, June 10, 1969, Jack Lord Collection, Cinematic Arts Library, University of Southern California.
12. Letter, Jack Lord to Michael Buchanan, Jun 17, 1969, Jack Lord Collection, Cinematic Arts Library, University of Southern California.
13. Criterion Collection of *Dr. No*, Excerpt from Banned Commentary.
14. https://filmschoolrejects.com/39-things-we-learned-from-the-banned-dr-no-commentary-28e2a5335144#.cuiz9cuqz.
15. Rich, "Dr. No," *Daily Variety*, Oct. 17, 1962, 6.
16. Donald W. Pfeffer, "Blessed Are the Geeks," Oct. 12, 2010, https://blessedarethegeeks.blogspot.com/.
17. Paul Francis Sullivan, "The Marlins Manager-Felix Leiter Connection," Jan. 11, 2014, https://sullybaseball.wordpress.com.
18. Letter, Tom Taggart to Hedda Hopper, Undated, Hedda Hopper Papers, Margaret Herrick Library, Academy of Motion Picture Arts and Sciences, File F2144.

19. "Go for Names," *Weekly Variety*, Nov. 14, 1962, 22.
20. *Daily Variety*, March 15, 1963, 2.
21. "Grand Hotel," TV Notebooks, Cinematic Arts Library, University of Southern California.
22. Harold Stern, "Loser 'Stoney Burke' Riding High Once More," *The Hartford Courant*, July 5, 1964, 7G.

Chapter Eight

1. Hedda Hopper, "Jack Lord Will Be in Spy Movie; Also to Star in New TV Series," *Los Angeles Times*, Dec. 28, 1961, 20.
2. Jack Lord, Letter to Hedda Hopper, Hedda Hopper Collection, Margaret Herrick Library, Academy of Motion Picture Arts and Sciences, File F2144, Dec. 31, 1961.
3. "Look What's Happening to Television's Westerns," *Sponsor*, June 3, 1963, 33.
4. Hedda Hopper, "Turned Down 'Casey'; Jack Lord Not Sorry," *The Hartford Courant* (Hartford, CT), March 15, 1963, 7.
5. Jack Lord, Letter to Hedda Hopper, Hedda Hopper Collection, Margaret Herrick Library, Academy of Motion Picture Arts and Sciences, File F2144, Feb. 6, 1962.
6. *Players Guide 1962* (New York: Paul L. Ross Publisher, Sponsored by Actors' Equity Association and American Federation of Television and Radio Artists, 1962), 556.
7. Hedda Hopper, Typed Transcript, Jack Lord Interview, Hedda Hopper Collection, Margaret Herrick Library, Academy of Motion Picture Arts and Sciences, File #2144, Feb. 19, 1963, 2–3.
8. Donald Kirkley, "Former Sailor Turns Cowpoke," *The Sun* (Baltimore, MD), Nov. 18, 1962, A9.
9. Seymour Korman, "Jack Lord Wants to be a Champ," *Chicago Daily Tribune*, Dec. 1, 1962, B4.
10. "How Big is the Audience for This Kind of Excitement?" *Sponsor*, April 30, 1962, 5.
11. "A Young Man with a Plentitude of Grey Matter," *Sponsor*, May 14, 1962, 42.
12. "The Tom W. Moore Picture at ABC TV," *Sponsor*, June 4, 1962, 60.
13. John P. Shanley, "Horse Operas Discover 20th Century," *New York Times*, Oct. 3, 1962, 83.
14. Jane Ardmore, "Biography of Jack Lord," Typed draft, Jane Ardmore Collection, Margaret Herrick Library, Academy of Motion Picture Arts and Sciences, File 17.9, Undated, 7.
15. Alan Gill, "Big, Big, Big!" *TV Guide*, November 11, 1962, 15–19.
16. John C. Waugh, "How to Create a Western Legend," *The Christian Science Monitor*, August 29, 1964, 6.
17. Bob Thomas, "Jack Lord Clicks as Cowboy," *The Austin American Statesman* (Austin, TX), Feb. 10, 1963, 12.
18. Joe Hyams, "Sincerely Yours, 'Stoney,'" *New York Herald Tribune*, Oct. 14, 1962, C8A.
19. Jane Ardmore, "Jack Lord Aims High," Partial photocopy of clipping, Jane Ardmore Collection, Margaret Herrick Library, Academy of Motion Picture Arts and Sciences, File 17.9, No date.
20. Ardmore, "Jack Lord Aims High."
21. Lawrence Laurent, "Actor Jack Lord Expects Big Things from New Show," *The Washington Post and Times-Herald*, Sept. 28, 1962, B9.
22. Robert Dowdell, "The Stoney Burke I Know," *TV Star Parade*, May 1963, 76.
23. Hank Grant, "Jack Lord a Champion in Many Varied Fields," *The Hartford Courant* (Hartford, CT), Aug. 5, 1962, 12G.
24. Lawrence Laurent, "Actor Jack Lord Expects Big Things from New Show."
25. Paul Jones, "Series on Rodeos Has Big Future," *The Atlanta Constitution*, Sept. 3, 1962, 48.
26. Jane Ardmore, Jack Lord Interview Transcript, Jane Ardmore Collection, Margaret Herrick Library, Academy of Motion Picture Arts and Sciences, File 17.9, Feb. 7, 1963, 1
27. Ardmore Typed Interview Transcript.
28. Cecil Smith, "The TV Scene: Prize Right at Monte Carlo?" *Los Angeles Times*, Jan. 22, 1963.
29. Elyse Allison, "Today, We Have Stoney," *The Examiner* (Independence, MO), Aug. 26, 1964, 1–2.
30. Donald Kirkley, "Former Sailor Turns Cowpoke," *The Sun* (Baltimore, MD), Nov. 18, 1962, A9.
31. Susan Compo, *Warren Oates: A Wild Life* (Lexington: University Press of Kentucky, 2010), 105.
32. Compo, 29–30.
33. Bruce Dern, *Bruce Dern: A Memoir* (Lexington: University of Kentucky Press, 2014), eBook.
34. Dave Freeman, "TV Close Up," *The Hartford Courant* (Hartford, CT), Nov. 23, 1962, 33.
35. Freeman, "TV Close Up."
36. Jerome Coopersmith, "Book 'Em Danno! My Years Writing for *Hawaii Five-O*," *Thrilling Detective*, www.mysteryscenemag.com.
37. Freeman, "TV Close Up."
38. Dowdell, "The Stoney Burke I Know," 78.
39. *Kincaid*, TV Show Notebooks, Cinematic Arts Library, University of Southern California.
40. "Daystar Offering Six Pilots for Next Year," *Broadcasting*, September 17, 1962, 99.
41. "Spin-Offs Lead '63-'64 Program Parade," *Broadcasting*, November 5, 1962, 30.
42. Hedda Hopper, Jack Lord Interview Transcript, Hedda Hopper Collection, Margaret Herrick Library, Academy of Motion Picture Arts and Sciences, Feb. 19, 1963, File F2144, 1.
43. Hopper Interview, 3.
44. Bob Thomas, "Jack Lord Clicks as Cowboy," 12.
45. Hal Humphrey, "TV Turns Out a New Breed of Acting Talent–Touring Pitchman." *Los Angeles Times*, Aug. 28, 1963, L31.
46. Hal Humphrey, "TV Turns Out a New Breed of Acting Talent."
47. Raymond Levy, Letter to Jack Lord, Jan. 25, 1963, Jack Lord Collection, University of Southern California Cinematic Arts Library.
48. Joseph Finnigan, "Hollywood," *The Austin Statesman* (Austin, TX), April 10, 1963, 28.
49. "Jack Lord to Star Self in 'Art's Sake," *Daily Variety*, Jan. 30, 1963, 4.
50. *Daily Variety*, May 7, 1963, 9.
51. *Daily Variety*, June 17, 1963, 4.
52. Jack Lord, Letter to Hedda Hopper, Hedda Hopper Collection, Margaret Herrick Library, Academy of Motion Picture Arts and Sciences, File # 2144, May 31, 1963.
53. *Daily Variety*, May 31, 1963, 2.
54. John L. Scott, "McLaglen to Film 'Small Remnant': Marvin Cast, Wayne South; Keel in 'Crossing' Picture," *Los Angeles Times*, June 13, 1963, C9.

55. Jack Lord, Letter to Hedda Hopper, Hedda Hopper Collection, Margaret Herrick Library Academy of Motion Picture Arts and Sciences, File #F2144, June 16, 1963.
56. Hedda Hopper, "Jack Lord May Star in Broadway Musical," *Chicago Tribune*, Oct. 3, 1963, E4.
57. "That TV Flop Pays Off Now for Jack Lord," *The Atlanta Constitution*, May 11, 1964, 11A.
58. Eileen Sisk, *Buck Owens: The Biography* (Chicago: Chicago Review, 2010), 64.
59. Margaret McDonald, "'Stoney Burke' Gets Thunderous Welcome," April 3, 1964, Clipping, Jack Lord Collection, USC Cinematic Arts Library.
60. Duane Valentry, "Stoney Burke: Television's Rodeo Cowboy," *Western History*, July 1963, 50.
61. Bill Tusher, "Jack Lord: He Turns the Other Cheek," *Screenland*, July 1963, 14.
62. Jim Hoffman, "Is 'Stoney' a Phoney?" *Motion Picture*, May 1963, 49.
63. Jack Lord, Postcard to Hedda Hopper, Hedda Hopper Collection, Margaret Herrick Library, Motion Picture Academy Arts and Sciences, File # F2144, 1964, Tampa postmark faded.
64. Hedda Hopper, Letter to Jack Lord, Hedda Hopper Collection, Margaret Herrick Library, Motion Picture Academy Arts and Sciences, File # F2144, July 23, 1964.
65. Lawrence Laurent, "Jack Lord Riding Tall in the Saddle," *The Washington Post*, June 11, 1964.
66. Dave Kaufman, "Jack Lord Lassos More Loot Rodeo Circuit Than Did On TV," *Daily Variety*, April 28, 1964, 8.
67. Elyse Allison, "Today, We Have Stoney," 1.
68. Elyse Allison, "Today, We Have Stoney," 2.
69. Jim Williams. Interview #1991-13 with John Martino. Harry S Truman National Historic Site/National Park Service, July 31, 1991, Transcript of audiotape DAV-AR#4347–4348. https://www.nps.gov/hstr/learn/historyculture/upload/martino_interview.pdf.
70. *TV Media*, "TV-Q-Quiz," Feb. 17, 1964, 40.
71. Hal Humphrey, "TV Turns Out a New Breed of Acting Talent–Touring Pitchman" Hal Humphrey," *Los Angeles Times*, April 23, 1963, L31.
72. Jack Major, "Jack Lord's Fussiness About his Roles Finally Paid Off Big Time," *Providence Sunday Journal* (Providence, RI), Sept. 7, 1969, http://www.major-smolinski.com/NAMES/JACKLORD.html.
73. Jack Lord, "To the Readers of *Movie Life*," *Movie Life*, December 1963, 40.
74. Harold Stern, "Loser 'Stoney' Burke Riding High Once More," *The Hartford Courant* (Hartford, CT), July 5, 1964, 7G.

Chapter Nine

1. Dave Kaufman, "Burke's 'High' View," *Daily Variety*, Aug. 11, 1965, 9.
2. "Past Romance Plagues Murder Trial," *The Hartford Courant* (Hartford, CT), July 6, 1966, 20.
3. Jo Davidsmyer, *Combat! A Viewer's Companion to the WWII TV Series* (Tallevast, FL: Strange New Worlds, 2001).
4. *Daily Variety*, March 3, 1966, 12.
5. Gilb, "Film Review: *The Counterfeit Killer*," *Daily Variety*, May 21, 1968, 3.
6. Dave Kaufman, "Spin Off Series for Theatricals," *Weekly Variety*, May 31, 1967, 27.
7. *Daily Variety*, Dec. 9, 1966, 15.
8. Aleene MacMinn, "Show Biz Relatives No Biz Relatives for Miss Crawford," *Los Angeles Times*, Dec. 12, 1966, D27.
9. Jack Gould, "TV: A Bomb Backfires," *New York Times*, Dec. 16, 1966, 77.
10. Robe, "Film Review: *The Ride to Hangman's Tree*," *Daily Variety*, April 24, 1967, 3.
11. Betty Martin, "Movie Call Sheet: Lord in 'Lovers in Limbo,'" *Los Angeles Times*, April 17, 1967, D31.
12. Tom Lisanti, "Sixties Cinema," http://sixtiescinema.com/2012/05/14/tisha-a-go-go/.
13. "IA Protests SAG Thesps in Pic with Non-Union Lensers," *Daily Variety*, May 10, 1967, 1.
14. Renata Adler, "The Name of the Game Is Kill," *New York Times*, June 6, 1968, 54:1.
15. *The Name of the Game Is Kill*, www.TVguide.com/movies/the-name-of-the-game-is-kill/review/107220/
16. Joyce Haber, "Busy Film Future for Sylva Koscina," *Los Angeles Times*, Oct. 30, 1967, C4.

Chapter Ten

1. Jerome Coopersmith, "Book 'Em Danno! My Years Writing for *Hawaii Five-O*," *Thrilling Detective*, www.mysterysecnemag.com.
2. Jack Hellman, "Light and Airy," *Daily Variety*, June 13, 1968, 13.
3. Richard K. Shull, "'Hawaii Five-O' Turns Into Paradise for Lord,'" *Indianapolis Star*, June 17, 1970.
4. Percy Shain, "Jack Lord Loves Hawaii," *Boston Globe*, Feb. 16, 1969, B7.
5. Terrence Towles Canote, "Spy Shows of the Sixties," *A Shroud of Thoughts* (blog), January 8, 2009, Mercurie.blogspot.com.
6. Simon Cardew, "Jack Lord—The Cop that Talked," *TV Time: Hawaii's Television Magazine*, Oct. 6–12. (Clipping, Jack Lord Collection, Cinematic Arts Library, University of Southern California.)
7. Lawrence Laurent, "Good Guy: John Joseph Patrick Ryan," *The Washington Post and Times-Herald*, Dec. 28, 1969, 2.
8. Leslie Raddatz, "How Ex-Rodeo Rider Went West."
9. "Light and Airy."
10. Mufi Hannemann, "The Jack Lord Only His Secretary Knew," Midweek, http://www.midweek.com/jack-lord-secretary-knew/.
11. Marilyn Beck, "Gal Friday in Paradise," *The Sun* (Baltimore, MD), Dec. 1, 1968, TV8.
12. Anthony LaCamera, "Jack Lord, Tough Guy, Artist, Imposes Perfection on Hawaii," *Sunday Herald Advertiser* (Boston, MA), April 14, 1974, 21.
13. Whitney, *TV Guide*, 1971.
14. Slain, "Jack Lord Loves Hawaii."
15. Jerry Buck, "Jack Lord Feels He Earned 'Star,'" *The Sun* (Baltimore, MD), March 3, 1974, TV12.
16. "Khigh Dhiegh," *Variety*, Nov. 10, 1991, Retrieved from: http://variety.com/1991/more/news/khigh-dhiegh-991259221.
17. "CBS Censors Lift Spinning Gun Barrel from "Hawaii Five-O' Title," *Daily Variety*, Aug. 29, 1972, 1.
18. Will Lorin, Letter to Jack Lord, January 28, 1972, Jack Lord Collection, Cinematic Arts Library, University of Southern California.
19. Glen Olsen and Rod Baker, Letter to Jack Lord,

August 18, 1982, Jack Lord Collection, Cinematic Arts Library, University of Southern California.

20. "'Hawaii Five-O' as Educational Television," *Newsday*, September 23, 1973, A7.

21. Jerome Coopersmith, "Book 'Em Danno!"

22. Jack Major, "Name Dropping," http://www.major-smolinski.come/NAMES/JACKLORD.html.

23. "Star of 'Hawaii Five-O' Says Series Sure Bet," *Newsday*, Sept. 18, 1968, 66A.

24. Call Sheet, May 12, 1972, Jack Lord Collection, Cinematic Arts Library.

25. Hal Humphrey, "Producer Tries Island Magic," *TV Times/Los Angeles Times*, Nov. 17 to Nov. 23, 1968. 2.

26. Slain, "Jack Lord Loves Hawaii."

27. Lawrence Laurent, "Good Guy."

28. Karen Rhodes, *Booking Hawaii Five-O*, 53.

29. "CBS Threatens Exit if "Hawaii" Can't Use Facility There," *Daily Variety*, June 24, 1969, 11.

30. Jack Lord, Letter to Carl Humelsine, Feb. 1, 1971, Colonial Williamsburg Foundation Archives, Restoration—Iolani Palace.

31. Jack Gould, "TV Review," *New York Times*, Sept. 27, 1968, 95.

32. "Book 'Em Cowboy," Honolulu.com Magazine, June 1, 2010, http://www.honolulumagazine.com/.

33. "*Hawaii Five-O* Chased by Minority, Forced to Change Site," *Weekly Variety*, Oct. 30, 1968, 2.

34. *Boston Globe*, July 13, 1970.

35. Lee Paul, Letter to Jack Lord, Aug. 26, 1980, Jack Lord Collection, Cinematic Arts Library, University of Southern California.

36. "P.S. On Shrinking Violence," *Weekly Variety*, June 26, 1968, 2.

37. "He's Really Hung Up," *TV Guide*, July 13, 1968, 14–15.

38. Jack Hellman, "Light and Airy."

39. Lawrence Laurent, "Jack Lord's Ninth Year of 'Hawaii 5-O,'" *The Washington Post*, June 6, 1976, 249.

40. Robert Norvet, Letter to Robert E. Moranha, January 17, 1975, Jack Lord Collection, Cinematic Arts Library, University of Southern California.

41. Ben Wood, "Hawaii Tradewinds," *Daily Variety*, June 25, 1976, 11.

42. Elizabeth Sullivan, "Jack Lord: An Early Caller," *Boston Globe*, Nov. 9, 1969, TV11.

43. Tom Cavanaugh, "Jack Lord's Hawaii," *Mainliner*, February 1973, 13.

44. "Hawaii Five-O Star Won't Leave Island Location," *Boston Globe*, July 13, 1970, 30

45. Todd Mason Papers, University of California, Los Angeles.

46. Clipping, "Hawaii Five-O Star," *Waikiki Beach Press*, May 3–5, 1968, Jack Lord Collection, Cinematic Arts Library, University of Southern California.

47. Frank Barton, Letter to Jack Lord, Oct. 30, 1969, Jack Lord Collection, Cinematic Arts Library, University of Southern California.

48. Jack Lord, Letter to Marquis—Who's Who, Inc., May 13, 1969, Jack Lord Collection, Cinematic Arts Library, University of Southern California.

49. Jack Lord, "Jack Lord's World Seen From Boats," *The Austin Statesman* (Austin, TX), Aug. 15, 1971, 30.

50. Yoko [last name illegible], Letter to Jack Lord, n.d. Jack Lord Collection, Cinematic Arts Library, University of Southern California.

51. David Troedson, "Elvis Australia," www.elvis.com.au and www.elvispresley.com.au.

52. Marian J. Cocke, Letter to Jack Lord, Nov. 19, 1979, Jack Lord Collection, Cinematic Arts Library, University of Southern California.

53. Aleene MacMinn, "Jack Lord Finds Job in Hawaii," *Los Angeles Times*, Aug. 20, 1968.

54. House of Representatives, Fifth Legislature, State of Hawaii, Resolution #324 Honoring Jack Lord, April 17, 1970, Copy in Jack Lord Collection, Cinematic Arts Library, University of Southern California.

55. Jack Lord, Address to Hawaii State House of Representatives, April 17, 1970, Jack Lord Collection, Cinematic Arts Library, University of Southern California.

56. Charles M. Campbell, Letter to Jack Lord, Feb. 1, 1980, Jack Lord Collection, Cinematic Arts Library, University of Southern California.

57. Jack Lord, Memo to Felix Owens, et. al. July 23, 1970, Jack Lord Collection, Cinematic Arts Library, University of Southern California.

58. Shull, "'Hawaii Five-O' Turns Into Paradise for Lord."

59. Aleene MacMinn, "Jack Lord Finds Job in Hawaii."

60. "Hawaii's Pied Piper," *Boston Globe*, Nov. 15, 1970, TV9.

61. "Jack Lord Ends TV Boycott," *The Sun* (Baltimore, MD), Aug. 6, 1974, B3.

62. "Jack Lord's Coverup: A Soggy Tale of Devotion," *Chicago Tribune*, Aug. 20, 1974, A10.

63. "Hawaii Governor Acts in Settling 'Five-O' Battle," *Daily Variety*, Aug. 5, 1974, 1,3.

64. Jack Lord, Memo to Doug Green, Sept. 30, 1976, Jack Lord Collection, Cinematic Arts Library, University of Southern California.

65. Jack Lord, Letter to Edward E. Ryczek, Aug. 15, 1979, Jack Lord Collection, Cinematic Arts Library, University of Southern California.

66. Michael Jackson (talk show host), Letter to Jack and Marie Lord, Dec. 2, 1971, Jack Lord Collection, Cinematic Arts Library, University of Southern California.

67. Joan Crosby, "Lord to Wind Up Hawaii 5-O," *Atlanta Constitution*, April 15, 1972, 17T.

68. Paul Jones, "Jack Lord," *The Atlanta Constitution*, Dec. 20, 1975, 2T.

69. Todd Mason Papers 1993, Collection PASC 363, 1967–1981, Audiotapes, Box 003, Charles Young Library, Special Collections, University of California, Los Angeles.

70. Hans Ebert, "Inside Steve McGarrett—by Jack Lord," *South China Morning Post* (Hong Kong), May 16, 1976, 7.

71. Jack Lord, Memo to Fred Baum, July 6, 1978, Jack Lord Collection, Cinematic Arts Library, University of Southern California.

72. Jack Lord, "Singapore Sting," Letter to the Editor, *Los Angeles Times*, Sept. 17, 1979.

73. Rita Witherwax, "Jack Lord: The Man Behind McGarrett," *Aloha: The Magazine of Hawaii*, October 1980, 20.

74. Betty Lamm, Letter to Marie and Jack Lord, Nov. 8, 1979, Jack Lord Collection, Cinematic Arts Library, University of Southern California.

Chapter Eleven

1. Todd Mason, Untitled Manuscript, Todd Mason Papers, 1967–1981, Margaret Herrick Library, Academy of Motion Picture Arts and Sciences, PASC 363, 19.

2. Lawrie Mifflin, "Jack Lord, 77, Helped Direct and Starred in 'Hawaii Five-O,'" *The New York Times*, Jan. 23, 1998, Retrieved from: http://www.nytimes.com.

3. Mason, 7.

4. Jane Ardmore, "Jack of All or Many Trades," Typed notes from Jack Lord interview, February 7, 1963, Jane Ardmore Papers, Margaret Herrick Library, Academy of Motion Picture Arts and Sciences, File 17.9, 4.

5. Tony Barr, Memo to Jack Lord, April 8, 1979, Jack Lord Collection, Cinematic Arts Library, University of Southern California.

6. La Camera, *Boston Herald Advertiser*, 21.

7. Jack Lord, Letter to Anne R. Nelson, Jan. 24, 1977, Jack Lord Collection, Cinematic Arts Library, University of Southern California.

8. Nicholas Von Hoffman, "Where's the Real Violence on Television?" *Variety*, April 15, 1969.

9. Ben Wood, "Jack Lord Says Goodbye to 'Five-O.'"

10. Marie Lord, Letter to Ella Chun, Sept. 8, 1970, Jack Lord Collection, Cinematic Arts Library, University of Southern California.

11. Terrence O'Flaherty, "One Honest TV Performer," *The Sun* (Baltimore, MD), July 19, 1970, TW2.

12. Cecil Smith, "Jack Lord Asks: How Do You Do a Police Show without Violence?" *Los Angeles Times*, May 4, 1975, S1.

13. Robert Kerwin, "Lord of Honolulu," *Chicago Tribune*, Oct. 26, 1975.

14. Lawrence Laurent, "Endless Seasons?" *Newsday*, July 7, 1976, 58A.

15. Lawrence Laurent, "Jack Lord's Last," *Boston Globe*, Aug. 19, 1979, C18.

16. Witherwax, *Aloha*, 26.

17. Robert Janes, Memorandum to Jack Lord re "Makai Station," Dec. 14, 1978, Jack Lord Collection, Cinematic Arts Library, University of Southern California.

18. Memo to J. William Hayes from Milton Segal, Undated, Jack Lord Collection, Cinematic Arts Library, University of Southern California.

19. Kevin Thomas, "Jack Lord in M Station," *Los Angeles Times*, June 10, 1980, G7.

Chapter Twelve

1. Marilyn Beck, "Successful Jack Lord Puzzled but Unruffled by Criticism," *Sunday Herald Advertiser* (Boston, MA), February 3, 1974, 27.

2. St. Francis Healthcare System of Hawaii, "Donor Stories: Jack and Marie Lord," http://www.stfrancishawaii.org/st-francis-healthcare-foundation-of-hawaii/donor-stories.

3. "Exodus to Honolulu," *South China Morning Post*, Nov. 8, 1981, 14.

4. Jack Lord, Letter to Mr. Ned E.G. Will, Jr., Aug. 22, 1969, Jack Lord Collection, Cinematic Arts Library, University of Southern California.

5. Carole Hoyt, "Silvio Says Thanks to Everyone," *Honolulu Advertiser*, Aug. 29, 1970, Clipping, Jack Lord Collection, Cinematic Arts Library, University of Southern California.

6. Jack Lord, Letter to Drs. George and Carolyn Brown, MD, Aug. 21, 1973, Jack Lord Collection, Cinematic Arts Library, University of Southern California.

7. Jack Lord, Letter to Mrs. A.E. Hough, Feb. 5, 1977, Jack Lord Collection, Cinematic Arts Library, University of Southern California.

8. Wanda A. Adams, "Show 'Brought Hawaii to the Fore,'" *Honolulu Advertiser*, Jan. 22, 1998.

9. Jack Lord, Letter to Hank Aaron, April 4, 1977, Jack Lord Collection, Cinematic Arts Library, University of Southern California.

10. Frank R. Barnett, Letter to Jack Lord, Nov. 9, 1977, Jack Lord Collection, Cinematic Arts Library, University of Southern California.

11. Lawrence Laurent Papers, 1948–2010, MS2325. UA, Series 4: Correspondence, Special Collections Research Center, George Washington University.

12. Laurent Papers.

13. Marilyn Borovoy, Letter to Jack Lord, Dec. 1, 1979, Jack Lord Collection, Cinematic Arts Library, University of Southern California.

14. "Jack Lord: Anti-Gun Elitist?" *NRA Official Journal*, March 1980, 6.

15. Cecil Heftel, Letter to Jack Lord, May 20, 1983, Jack Lord Collection, Cinematic Arts Library, University of Southern California.

16. Spark M. Matsunaga, Letter to John J. Ryan, Aug. 20, 1980, Jack Lord Collection, Cinematic Arts Library, University of Southern California.

17. William D. Eckert, Lt. Col., USAF, Military Aide to the Vice President, Letter to Jack Lord, March 22, 1982, Jack Lord Collection, Cinematic Arts Library, University of California.

18. "Jack Lord Getting More Art Training," *Atlanta Constitution*, Feb. 27, 1971, 17R.

19. Jack Lord, Note to Pam, Sept. 5, 1979, Jack Lord Collection, Cinematic Arts Library, University of Southern California.

20. Dick Kleiner, "Lord Is Master of All He Surveys," *The Austin Statesman* (Austin, TX), Aug. 23, 1970, 15.

21. Charles Bud Dant, Letter to Jack Lord, April 10, 1981, Jack Lord Collection, Cinematic Arts Library, University of Southern California.

22. Daniel Howard Cerone, "Tribute: Jack Lord," *TV Guide*, Feb. 21–27, 1998, 7.

23. John Joseph Patrick Ryan, AKA: Jack Lord, Death Certificate no. 151 1998-000393, Filed January 23, 1998, copy in author's collection.

24. M. Allen Henderson, *Money for Nothing: Rip-Offs, Cons and Swindles* (Boulder, CO: Paladin, 1986), 150–151.

25. Lana Corrine Cantrell, *The Greatest Story Never Told* (Lakemont, GA: Biohistorical, 1988).

26. Tim Ryan, "Warner Bros. Takes on 'Hawaii Five-O' Film," *Honolulu Star-Bulletin*, Sept. 9, 2004.

27. Greg Evans, "'Dragnet' with Leis, and the Occasional Ghost," *The New York Times*, April 29, 2007.

Bibliography

Archival Collections

Colonial Williamsburg Foundation. Archives and Records Department.
Hal Roach Collection. Cinematic Arts Library, University of Southern California.
Hawaiian Collection. Jack Lord Collection, University of Hawaii at Monoa.
Hedda Hopper Collection. Margaret Herrick Library, Academy of Motion Picture Arts and Sciences.
Jack Hirshberg Papers. Margaret Herrick Library, Academy of Motion Picture Arts and Sciences.
Jack Lord Biography. Margaret Herrick Library, Academy of Motion Picture Arts and Sciences.
Jack Lord Collection. Cinematic Arts Library, University of Southern California.
Jack Poplin Papers. Margaret Herrick Library, Academy of Motion Picture Arts and Sciences.
Jane Ardmore Collection. Margaret Herrick Library, Academy of Motion Picture Arts and Sciences.
John Huston Papers. Margaret Herrick Library, Academy of Motion Picture Arts and Sciences.
Lawrence Laurent Papers, 1948–2010. MS2325.UA. Special Collections Research Center. George Washington University.
New York University Alumni Archives.
Roy Schatt Biography. Westwood Gallery, 262 Bowery, New York City. Exhibit A.
Television Show Report Collection. Cinematic Arts Library, University of Southern California.
Todd Mason Papers. Collection PASC 363, Special Collections, Performing Arts, University of Southern California at Los Angeles.
TV Show Notebooks. Cinematic Arts Library, University of Southern California.
University of California at Los Angeles Film and Television Library. Research Center, Powell Library.

Books

Ballenas, Carl, and Nancy Cataldi with the Richmond Hill Historical Society. *Richmond Hill*. Charleston, SC: Arcadia, 2002. e-book.
Bergreen, Laurence. *James Agee: A Life*. New York: E.P. Dutton, 1984.
Carey, Harry, Jr. *Company of Heroes*. Metuchen, NJ: Scarecrow, 1994.
Clipper: John Adams High School Annual. Queens, New York. Vol. 7, No. 4, 1938.
Compo, Susan. *Warren Oates: A Wild Life*. Lexington: University of Kentucky Press, 2010.
Davidsmeyer, Jo. *Combat! A Viewer's Companion to the WWII TV Series*. Tallevast, FL: Strange New Worlds, 2001.
Dern, Bruce. *Bruce Dern: A Memoir*. Lexington: University of Kentucky Press, 2014. eBook.
Edgerton, Gary R. *The Columbia History of American Television*. New York: Columbia University Press, 1970.
Giannetti, Louis, and Scott Eyman. *Flashback: A Brief History of Film*. Boston: Pearson, 2009.
Goldberg, Lee. *Unsold Television Pilots, 1955–1989*. Jefferson, NC: McFarland, 1990.
Grabman, Sandra. *No Retakes! Actors and Actresses Remember the Era of Live Television*. Albany, GA: Bear Manor, 2014. e-book.
Henderson, M. Allen. *Money for Nothing: Rip-Offs, Cons and Swindles*. Boulder, CO: Paladin, 1986.
Holley, Val. *Mike Connolly and the Manly Art of Hollywood Gossip*. Jefferson, NC: McFarland, 2003.
Krampner, John. *Female Brando: The Legend of Kim Stanley*. New York: Back Stage, 2006.
Kroos, William. *A Peek at Richmond Hill through the Keyhole of Time*. New York: Woodhaven Cultural and Historical Society, n.d.
Mavis, Paul. *The Espionage Filmography: United States Releases, 1989 through 1999*. Jefferson, NC: McFarland, 2000.
New York Times Film Reviews, 1913–1968. New York: *New York Times*/Arno, 1970.
Pfeiffer, Lee, and Lisa Philip. *The Incredible World of 007: An Authorized Celebration of James Bond*. Secaucus, NJ: Carol, 1996.
Players Guide 1962. New York: Paul L. Ross Publisher, Sponsored by Actors' Equity Association and American Federation of Television and Radio Artists, 1962.
Rhodes, Karen. *Booking Hawaii Five-O*. Jefferson, NC: McFarland, 1997.
Sisk, Eileen. *Buck Owens: The Biography*. Chicago: Chicago Review Press, 2010.

Documents

Compiled Military Record. Ryan, John Joseph. USCG Merchant Marine. June 19, 1937–August 15, 1945. Copy in possession of author.

Death Certificate for John Joseph Ryan. 26 August 1955, File 14006, Connecticut State Department of Health.
Honoring Jack Lord for Outstanding Contributions to the State of Hawaii. April 17, 1970. Copy in Jack Lord Collection, Cinematic Arts Library, University of Southern California.
House of Representatives, Fifth Legislature, State of Hawaii. Resolution # 324.
Report of Birth of Children Born to American Parents for Ann Cecily Willard. 21 December 1921. American Consular Service, Paris, France.

Periodical Articles

Bolton, Brett. "You Never Read a Story about Jack Lord That Told You This." *TV Radio Mirror*, December 1970, 37–39; 85–89.
Bowser, Ruth. "I Couldn't Even Go To My Son's Funeral." *Motion Picture*, February 1964, 53, 80–81.
Cardew, Simon. "Jack Lord: The Cop That Talked." *TV Times: Hawaii's Television Magazine*, Oct. 6–12. (Clipping. Jack Lord Collection. Cinematic Arts Library, University of Southern California.)
Cavanaugh, Tom. "Jack Lord's Hawaii." *Mainliner* (United Air Lines), February 1973, 4–5, 12–13, 22–23.
Day, Carol, and Champ Clark. "Stranger in Paradise." *People*, February 9, 1998, 59–60.
"Daystar Offering Six Pilots for Next Year." *Broadcasting*, September 17, 1962.
Denis, Paul. "The Man Who Found God's Little Acre." *TV Headliner*, December 30, 1958, 32–33, 49–50.
Dowdell, Robert. "The Stoney Burke I Know." *TV Star Parade*, May 1963, 24–25, 76–78.
Gill, Alan. "Big, Big, Big!" *TV Guide*, November 11, 1962, 15–19.
"He's Really Hung Up." *TV Guide*, July 13, 1968, 14–15.
Hoffman, Jim. "Is Stoney a Phony?" *Motion Picture*, May 1963, 49, 60–61.
"How Big Is the Audience for This Kind of Excitement?" *Sponsor*, April 30, 1962, 5.
Humphrey, Hal. "Producer Tries Island Magic." *TV Times/Los Angeles Times*, November 17–23, 1968, 2.
"Jack Lord." *NRA Official Journal*, March 1980, 6.
Little, Bessie. "Lowdown on Jack Lord." *Teen Life*, August 1963, 62.
"Look What's Happening to Television's Westerns." *Sponsor*, June 3, 1963, 33.
Lord, Jack. "Aloha 'Oe." *Holiday*, May 1977, 66.
Lord, Jack. "To the Readers of Movie Life." *Movie Life*, December 1963, 40.
Lord, Jack. "Ya Gotta Be Tough to Act!" *Mr.*, January 1957, 28–31, 60–62.
Maddox, Tex. "Vice and Virtue." *Movie Life*, July 1962, 46–49, 62.
Miller, Roland. "Jack Lord Talks About His Mother and Father: 'They Were Two Brutes.'" *Photoplay*, May 1971, 78, 80, 10, 102.
"Prelude to *Patriot*: James Agee's Unfinished Script." *Colonial Williamsburg*, Autumn 1993, 57.
Raddatz, Leslie. "How an Ex-Rodeo Rider Went West to Enjoy the Good Life as a Hawaiian Cop." *TV Guide*, January 4, 1969, 25–31.
Reynolds, Lisa. "The 16 Hours that Changed Jack Lord's Life." *Photoplay*, October 1971, 76, 124.
Ryder, Westley. "Which Jack Lord Do You Know?" *TV Star Parade*, November 1956, 48–51.
"Spin-Offs Lead '63-'64 Program Parade." *Broadcasting*, November 5, 1962.
"Star of 'Hawaii Five-O' Says Series Sure Bet." *Newsday*, September 18, 1968.
"Stars of Tomorrow." *Movie Screen Yearbook*, 1959, 79.
Tate, Thad W. "Behind the Story of a Patriot." *Colonial Williamsburg Today*, Winter 1972, 2.
Tinker, Gene. "It Began with *Hawaii Five-O*." *Hyatt's Hawaii*, September 1984, 11.
"The Tom W. Moore Picture at ABC TV." *Sponsor*, June 4, 1962, 60.
Tusher, Bill. "Jack Lord: He Turns the Other Cheek." *Screenland*, July 1963, 14–16, 46–48.
"TV-Q-Quiz." *TV Media*, February 17, 1964, 40.
Valentry, Duane. "Stoney Burke: Television's Rodeo Cowboy." *Western Horseman*, July 1963, 50.
Variety Fifteenth Annual Radio-TV Review and Preview (New York). July 27, 1960, 58–59.
Waugh, John C. "How to Create a Western Legend." *The Christian Science Monitor*, August 29, 1964, 6.
Witherwax, Rita. "Jack Lord: The Man Behind McGarrett." *Aloha: The Magazine of Hawaii*," Oct. 1980, 20–26.
Whitney, Dwight. "Jack Lord, Superstar." *TV Guide*, Sept. 4, 1971, 25–31
"A Young Man With a Plentitude of Grey Matter." *Sponsor*, May 14, 1962, 42.

Newspapers

Atlanta Constitution, 1962–1972
Austin Statesman, 1963–1972
Baltimore Sun, 1962–1974
Boston Globe, 1969–1970
Boston Herald, 1974
Charlotte News, 1969
Charlotte Observer, 1957
Chicago Daily Tribune, 1962–1969
Daily Press (New Dominion, VA), 1973
Daily Variety, 1949–1980
Examiner (Independence, MO), 1964
Hartford Courant, 1962–2005
Hollywood Daily Reporter, 1956–1958
Honolulu Advertiser 1970–1971
Indianapolis Star, 1970
Los Angeles Times, 1950–1980
Milwaukee Journal, 1969
New York Herald Tribune, 1962
New York Times, 1953–1981
Newsday, 1968
Norfolk Virginian Pilot, 1956
Norwalk Reflector, 1971
Portsmouth Star, 1956
Richmond News Leader, 1970
St. Petersburg Times, 1958
Sarasota Herald-Tribune, 1972
South China Morning Post, 1976–1981
Tampa Tribune, 1968
Washington Post, 1958–1969
Washington Post Times Herald, 1962–1969
Weekly Variety, 1950–1991

Videos

Dr. No. Terrence Young. 1962; Beverly Hills, CA: United Artists, 2012.

Dr. No. DVD. Extra Features.
Tramp Ship: Catch A Tiger. UCLA Film and Television Archive. Research Study Center. Powell Library.

Websites/Blogs

"Anonymous Method." Blog, http://anonymousmethods.tumblr.com.
Carr, Kevin. "39 Things We Learned from the Banned 'Dr. No' Commentary." Film School Rejects, https://filmschoolrejects.com/39-things-we-learned-from-the-banned-dr-no-commentary-28e2a5335144#.cuiz9cuqz.
Coopersmith, Jerome. "Book 'Em Danno! My Years Writing for Hawaii Five-O." *Thrilling Detective*, www.mysteryscenemag.com.
"Dr. No (1963)." http://www.the-numbers.com/movie/Dr.-No#tab+more.
Early Television Museum. http://www.earlytelevision.org/worlds_fair.html.
"Fifties Westerns." https://fiftieswesterns.wordpress.co/2015/02/10.character-actor-of-the-day-neville-brand.
Fitzgerald, Mike. "An Interview with…" *Western Clippings*. http://www.westernclippings.com/interview/carrollbaker_interview.shtml.
Hannemann, Mufi. October 15, 2014. "The Jack Lord Only His Secretary Knew." *Midweek.* http://www.midweek.com/jack-lord-secretary-knew/.
Lewis, Steve. "A TV Series Review by Michael Shronk: *The Hunter (1952–1954)*." http://mysteryfile.com/blog.
Lisanti, Tom. "Sixties Cinema." http://sixtiescinema.com/2012/05/14/tisha-a-go-go/.
Major, Jack. "Jack Lord's Fussiness About His Roles Finally Paid Off Big Time." *Providence Sunday Journal* (Providence, RI), September 7, 1969, as printed in "Name Dropping." http://www.major-smolinski.com?NAMES/JACKLORD.html.

The Name of the Game Is Kill. http://tvguide.com/movies/the-name-of-the-game-is-kill/review/107220/.
Neighborhood Playhouse School of the Theatre. "About Our History." http://neighborhoodplayhouse.org/about/our-history.
Perry Lafferty on Jack Lord. www.emmytvlegends.org/interviews.
Peters, Gehard, and John T. Wooley. "Franklin D. Roosevelt, Campaign Address at Boston, Massachusetts." *The American Presidency Project.* Retrieved January 21, 2016. http://www.presidency.ucsb.edu/ws?pid=15887.
Pfeffer, Donald W. Blog, "Blessed are the Geeks." October 12, 2010. https://blessedarethegeeks.blogspot.com/.
Richmond Hill Historical Society. http://www.richmondhillhistory.org.
St. Francis Healthcare System of Hawaii. "Donor Stories. Jack and Marie Lord." http://www.stfrancishawaii.org/st-francis-healthcare-foundation-of-hawaii/donor-stories.
Stamford Historical Society. http://stamfordhistory.org/ph1002_n3.htm.
Sullivan, Paul Francis. "The Marlins Manager-Felix Leiter Connection." Blog, https://sullybasevall.workpress.com.
Television Academy Foundation. Archive of American Television. Interviews. People.
The Thrilling Detective. http://www.thrillingdetective.com/.
Tonight. 741 Sound Recording Call Number LPA 50859; Madison, LM 113. Armed Forces Radio and Television Service (March 1967). Library of Congress.
Troedson, David. "Elvis Australia." www.elvis.com.au and www.elvispresley.com.au.
Williams, Jim. Interview #1991–13 with John Martino. Harry S Truman National Historic Site, National Park Service. DAV-AR#4347–4348. https://www.nps.gov/htr/learn/historyculture/upload/martino_interview.pdf.

Index

Aaron, Hank 182
Academy Awards 132, 195
Actors Studio 8, 29, 31–32, 42, 47, 52, 73, 75, 192
Adler, Stella 30
Agee, James 58–60
Airline Pilots' Association 139
Albertson, Jack 156, 175
Alcoa Presents: One Step Beyond 103, 194
Aldrich, Charlie 126, 131; *see also* Charlie Aldrich Trio
Allen, Steve 184
Allen, Woody 139
American Federation of TV and Radio Artists 141
The Americans 104, 194
Andress, Ursula 108
Andrews, Dana 94
Andrews, Julie 46
Appointment with Adventure 47, 192
Archive of American Television 144
Ardmore, Jane 5–6, 11, 16–17, 19, 23, 28, 33, 115, 117, 171
Ariyoshi, George 165
Armes, Jay J. 151
Armstrong Circle Theatre 47, 192
Asher, Jerry 20–23
Ashton Productions 78, 81
Asner, Ed 69, 121
Atwater, Barry 84–85
Avanti 143
Ayers, Lew 148

Badiyi, Reza 150
Baker, Carroll B. 44, 191–192
Baker, Nancy 50
Baker, Rod 151
Ball, Lucille 122
The Bandit 139
Barr, Tony 172
Barry, Patricia 80

Barrymore, John 110
Barrymore, Lionel 49
Bartlett, Hal 98
Bartlett, Sy 108
Barton, Frank 158, 159
Basehart, Richard 121
Baum, Fred 168
Baxter, Keith 143
Beck, Marilyn 179, 184
Beene, Geoffrey 187
Bell Geddes, Barbara 51
Bellamy, Ralph 29, 40, 43, 191
Ben Hur 13, 133
Bergreen, Lawrence 58
Berliner, Joe 173
The Beverly Hillbillies 118
Black Bart 139
Blanding, Don 163
Bob Hope Presents the Chrysler Theatre 134–135, 137, 177, 195–196
Bogdanovich, Peter 168
Bonanza 71, 88, 98, 194
Boone, Richard 75–76, 146, 193
Booth, John Wilkes 13, 143
USS *Bowfin* 177
Bowman, Pierre 176
Bradford, Richard 147
Brady, Scott 79, 81
Brand, Max 131
Brand, Neville 101, 102
Brando, Marlon 32, 62, 73
Breslin, Jimmy 13
Breslin, Patricia 47
Brinkley, David 68
Broadway Television Theatre 40, 191
Broccoli, Albert "Cubby" 105–107, 110, 112, 123
Bronson, Charles 104
Bronston, Samuel 125
Brown, Edmund G. 84
Brown, Peter 81
Brown, Robert 146–147
Brown, Terry 126

Brown, Will C. 78
Buchanan, Michael 108–109, 163
Bunuel, Luis 98
Burke, Paul 134, 196
Burr, Raymond 79, 142
Burton, Richard 81
Busey, Gary 189
Bush, George H.W. 184

Cabot, Bruce 94
Cabot, Sebastian 105
Cain's Hundred 104, 122, 195
Caldwell, Erskine 86–89, 193
Campbell, Charles M. 163
Campbell, Glen 159–160, 197
Cannell, Stephen J. 189
Cantrell, Lana Corrine 188–189
Carey, Harry, Jr. 41–42, 75, 79, 121, 193
Carson, Johnny 32, 139, 196
Cascade Records 95
Casey, Ben 113, 122
Casino Royale 105–106
Castle, Peggie 81
Cat on a Hot Tin Roof 31–32, 49–52, 62, 174
Chakiris, George 93
Chamberlain, Richard 131
Chaney, Lon, Jr. 94
Chapman, Lonny 45
Charlie Aldrich Trio 126, 131
Checkmate 55, 105, 192, 195
Christmas Seal Campaign 53, 180
The Chrysler Theatre see *Bob Hope Presents the Chrysler Theatre*
Chun, Ella 6, 33, 173
Chun, Kam Fong 25, 149, 158, 171
Clarke, William A. 13, 15, 18
Clavell, James 93, 99, 100
Climax! 74, 81, 193
Climax Mystery Theatre 106

Cobb, Lee J. 32, 81, 84
Coburn, James 121
Cocke, Marian 161
Colonial Williamsburg 23, 55, 56, 57, 58, 66–67
Combat! 134–135, 195
Committee on Un-American Activities of the House 35
Compo, Susan 119–120
Conflict 74, 193
Connery, Sean 102, 106, 108–110
Connors, Chuck 110
Connors, Mike 10, 162
Cooper, Gary 28, 49, 53–54, 57, 78, 82–84, 89, 106, 115, 117, 121
Coopersmith, Jerome 120, 144, 151
Corby, Ellen 72, 137, 192
The Counterfeit Killer see *Crackshot*
The Court-Martial of Billy Mitchell 48–49, 53–55, 57, 59, 62, 92, 105, 192
Crackshot 135, 196–197
Crawford, Broderick 134
Crawford, Joan 110, 171
Crawford, Katherine 137
Crowther, Bosley 86, 88
Cry Murder 37–38, 191
Curtiz, Michael 49, 92, 94–95
Cutter's Trail 48, 146

Daly, James 54
Dana, Leora 62–63, 66
Danger 47, 191–192
Dant, Charles "Bud" 185
Darren, James 93
Davidsmeyer, Jo 135
Davidson, Russell 184
Davis, Bette 72, 192
Davis, Sammy, Jr. 81
Day, Doris 110
Daystar Productions 113, 116, 121–122, 132
Dean, James 29, 73
DeLaurentiis, Dino 124
DeNarde, Elise Defranze 23
DeNarde, Gerard 23
DeNarde, Marie 23–24; *see also* Lord, Marie
Denning, Richard 39, 148–149, 156, 172
Dern, Bruce 119–120
Desilu Studios 79, 96, 102, 131
Dhiegh, Khigh 150, 169
Diamond Head State Monument 157
Dick Powell Show 129
Dickinson, Angie 93
Dr. Kildare 131, 195
Dr. No 13, 41, 102, 106–113, 124, 130, 146, 159, 195
Dolinsky, Meyer (Mike) 144
Donahue, Troy 93

Donlevy, Brian 72
Donnelly, David 174–175
The Doomsday Flight 137–138, 196
Doran, D.A. 99, 101
Dorn, Delores 103
Douglas, Donna 118
Douglas, Kirk 80
Douglas, Michael (actor) 189
Douglas, Mike (talk show host) 180, 197
Doversola, Margaret 165
Dowdell, Robert 116, 120–121
Drake, Charles 72
Duggan, Andrew 177
Duggan, Pat 50
Duvall, Robert 121

East Diamond Head Association 156–157
Eastwood, Clint 96–144
Eaton, Howard 115
The Ed Sullivan Show 53
Edwards, Vince 113, 115, 148
The Elgin Hour 47, 192
Emme's Island Moments 162
Emmy Awards Show 197
Empire 115
Eon Productions 106
Everett, Chad 110

Farentino, James 139, 196
Farmer, Frances 80
The F.B.I. 136, 196
Fedderson, Don 90–91, 94, 101–102
Finnegan, William (Bill) 164–165, 181
Five in a Box 13
Flameout 32, 41–42, 44
Fleming, Ian 105, 195
Florida State Fair 127, 131
Follow That Man 40, 191
Fonda, James 81
Fonda, Peter 178
Fong, Kam see Chun, Kam Fong
Foote, Horton 44–48
Ford, Glenn 133
Ford, Harrison 139, 189, 196
Ford, John 42, 75, 86, 90
Ford Foundation 59
Ford Motor Company 168
Ford's Theatre 13
Fort Ruger 153–154, 157, 166
Fort Trumball Academy 16–18
Foster, Dave 121
Foster and Ingersoll 121–122
Freeman, Dave 119
Freeman, Leonard 1, 75, 110, 181, 189, 193; challenges of location filming 152–153, 155, 157; concept for *Hawaii Five-O* 144–146; death 164; use of

guest stars 157, 161–164, 171–172; working relationship with Jack Lord 147, 148, 156, 171
The Fugitive 139, 196

Gable, Martin 77
Galloway, Don 139–140, 142
Garbo, Greta 110
Gazarra, Ben 32, 49, 52
George, Anthony 105
USS *George H. Williams* 17, 20
Gill, Alan 117–118
Gilligan's Island 87
Gleason, Jackie 13
The Glen Campbell Goodtime Hour 159, 197
God's Little Acre 77, 81–82, 86–88, 122, 135, 155, 193
Goldberg, Lee 89
Goldberg, Mel 144
Goldfinger 106, 110, 123
Good Morning America 197
Goodbody, John 58–61, 65–66
Goodson-Todman Art Exhibition 132
Goodwin, W.A.R. 57
Graves, Peter 54
Gray Lady Down 177
Grayson, Katherine 49–51, 79, 193
Greatest Show on Earth 131, 144, 195
Griffith, Andy 122, 186
Gruber, Frank 87, 90, 94
Gunsmoke 79–80, 157, 193
Guthrie, Mitch 121

Hackett, Buddy 77, 87
USS *Hall J. Kelly* 16–17
The Hangman 88, 92–96, 194
Harmon, Sidney 88
Harrington, Al 149
Hartley, Mariette 120
A Hatful of Rain 31, 49, 52
Have Gun Will Travel 75–78, 135
Hawaii Five-O 174; casting of Jack Lord 147–148; concept 144–146; end of series 176; impact on State of Hawaii 162; location shooting 152–153, 155, 157, 164, 166; Lord's oversight 162, 172–173, 174; popularity 165; violence 172–173
Hawaii Five-0 189
Hawaii State House of Representatives 162, 181
Hawaii Tuberculosis and Respiratory Disease Association 180
Hayes, Helen 68, 150
Hellstrom, Gunar 140

Henshaw, Buck 187
Here's Hollywood 111, 195
Herridge, Robert 102–103
Hickman, Darryl 93
The High Chaparral 143, 196
Hingle, Pat 55
Hirshberg, Jack 20, 27, 36–37, 49
Holbrook, Hal 184
Holliman, Earl 121
Hollywood Ten 35, 58
Honolulu Police Department 179
Honolulu Theatre for Youth Stagehands Organization 182
Hootenanny 129
Hoover, Herbert 136–137
Hope, Bob 10, 134–137, 186, 195–196
Hopper, Hedda 6, 8, 51, 89, 101, 106–109, 112–113, 121–122, 125, 127
Horgan, Ralph 26–27
Horton, Robert 113, 195
Hotchner, A.E. 103
Howard, Trevor 81
Hudson, Rock 74, 108
Huggins, Roy 74, 137
Humelsine, Carlisle (Carl) 69, 154
Humphrey, Hal 18, 122
Hunt, Peter 109
The Hunter 39, 191
Hunter, Tab 53
Hurricane Hattie 108
Hurry Sundown 142
Hush, Lisabeth 134
Huston, John 39, 58
Huston, Walter 39

Ice Station Zebra 177
Illikai 158
Independent Television Commission 146
The Invaders 139, 140, 144, 196
Iolani Palace 3, 154, 185
Ironside 142, 196
Ives, Burl 50, 51

Jack and Marie Lord Fund 183, 187
Jack Lord's Hawaii 185
Jackson, Michael (talk show host) 165
Jameson, Joyce 77–78
Janes, Robert 176
Jigsaw 135, 196
Jividen, Doris 182
John Adams High School 13–14, 41, 109
Johnson, Ben 121
Johnson, Luci Banes 129
Johnson, Mrs. Lyndon 134
Jonathan Winters Hour 155

Kahala Hilton 158
Kaufman, Dave 81, 127, 136
Kauhi, Gilbert, Francis Lani Damian (Zulu) 149
Kazan, Elia 32, 49, 51, 98
Kelly, DeForest 94
USS *Kelly Hall* 16–17
Kennedy, John F. 13, 105
Kennedy, Robert F. 156
Kerwin, Robert 175
King, Paul 147
King Kalaknua 154
Kirkop, Oreste 50–51
Kneubuhl, John 84
Knight, Shirley 135–136
Knopf, Edwin 76
Koch, Howard 93, 184
Kojak 173
Kraft Suspense Theatre 178, 195
Kramer, Stanley 98
Kubrick, Stanley 80

La Camera, Anthony 149, 172
Ladd, Alan 135
Lafferty, Perry 144, 147–148, 153–154
LaMesa Productions 81
Lamm, Betty 10, 168
Landon, Michael 88
Lansing, Robert 134
Laredo 135, 196
Lauer, Matt 186
Laurent, Lawrence 6, 13, 47, 80, 99, 102, 118, 127, 176, 183, 185–204
Lavery, Emmett 53, 55, 57, 59–62
Lawton, Jimmy 126
Leachman, Cloris 121
Leiter, Felix 106–107, 109–110, 130, 195
Lemmon, Jack 143
Leven, Edward 19, 37, 191
Lincoln, Abraham 13, 41, 59
The Lineup 96, 194
Linkletter, Art 111
Lisanti, Tom 140
The Little Hut 40–41, 165
London, John 92
London, Julie 81–84, 103, 195
The Loner 134, 195
Longstreet, Stephen 134
Lord, Marie 12–13, 32–33, 47, 66, 108, 172–207; death 33, 187; illness and death of Jack Lord 186–187; married life 10, 11, 21, 25–29, 31, 39, 69, 121, 152–154, 167, 173, 181, 183; meeting Jack Lord 23–24; move to Hawaii 158–159, 179; proposal 25
Lord and Lady Productions 101, 132, 135, 159, 177, 197
Lord of the Islands 197

Loren, Sophia 125
The Loretta Young Show 94, 194
Lorin, Will 150
Louise, Tina 77, 87–88, 93–95, 193–194
Lovers in Limbo 140
Lowell, James Russell 93
Lux Radio Theatre 71–72
Lux Video Theatre 71–72, 192

M-Station Hawaii (aka *Makai Station*) 176–178, 197
MacArthur, James 68, 149–150, 156, 163, 189
MacDonald, John 12
MacLeod, Gavin 86
Major, Jack 130, 151
Malone, Dorothy 76–78
Man Against Crime 29, 39–40, 43, 191
The Man from U.N.C.L.E. 111, 142, 196
Man in a Suitcase 146–147
Man of the West 78, 81–84, 89, 159, 193
Mann, Anthony 77–78, 82, 86–88, 92, 124
Maphis, Joe 126
Maphis, Rose 126
Marquis Who's Who 159
Marshall, Zena 108
Martin, Quinn 136
Martino, John 128
Mason, Todd 8–11, 33, 158, 162, 166, 171, 174, 183–185-207
Matsunaga, Spark M. 184
Matthews, Carol 37, 191
Mayday 177
McAdoo 132, 135
McCarthy, Nobu 99–100, 192
McClure, Doug 105
McGavin, Darren 54
Meadows, Audrey 40
Meisner, Sanford 3–4, 28–32, 49, 117, 141
Melnick, Dan 113
Merchant Marines 16, 18, 19, 26, 28
MGM Studios 20, 32, 41, 58–61, 66, 68, 76–77, 82, 88, 110–11, 123, 133, 177, 193
Michaels, Pat 84
The Mike Douglas Show 197
Miller, Merle 80
The Millionaire 90–92
USS *Mingo Seam* 20
Mitchell, William L. (Billy) 53
Mitchum, Robert 78
Miyaki, Howard 157
Moffat, Tom 154
Mongoose Manor 153
Monroe, Marilyn 4, 29–30, 74
Montagne, Edward 35, 38–40, 191

Montalban, Ricardo 147
Montgomery, Elizabeth 54–55, 92, 94, 105, 192, 194–195
Moore, Roger 189
Moore, Thomas W. (Tom) 110, 115
Moranha, Robert 156
Morrow, Vic 86, 135
Mowbry, Alan 32
The Munsters 135
Mystery Writers of America 43

Naked City 102, 122, 194
Nalick, Albert 171
The Name of the Game Is Kill 137, 141, 197
National Cowboy and Western Heritage Museum 124
National Society of Arts and Letters 171
Neighborhood Playhouse 30–31
Nelson, Anne 173
Ness, Elliott 97–98
Nettleton, Lois 70
New York University 9, 18–19, 21, 34, 38
Newman, Paul 29, 47, 52, 192
Nimoy, Leonard 121
North, Mike 128
Norvet, Robert 156–157

Oates, Warren 71, 119, 120, 132, 192
Occurrence at Owl Creek Bridge 132–133, 195
O'Connell, Arthur 81, 83
O'Flaherty, Terrance 174
O'Hara, Maureen 90
O'Kelly, Tim 149, 156
Oliver, Susan 71, 98, 104, 194
Olivier, Laurence 92
O'Loughlin, Alex 189
Olsen, Glen 151
Omnibus 52, 55, 59, 192
One Guinea, Two Guinea 124
Outlaws 104, 194

Pacific Fleet Submarine Memorial Association 177
Palmer, Betsy 77, 84, 85
Parker, Fess 94, 95, 95
Parker, Maggi 148
Pastore, John 173
Pate, Michael 106
Peck, Gregory 3, 146
Peters, Bernadette 13
The Philco Television Playhouse 55, 192
Pioneer Museum 183
Playhouse 90 51, 75, 78, 79, 80, 193
Preminger, Otto 49, 53, 98
Presley, Elvis 161, 184
Price, Frank 137, 139

Price, Vincent 79
Prine, Andrew 121, 134, 177
Project X (aka *Red Bait*) 35, 36, 37, 106, 191

The Quiet Man 90, 92, 94
Quigley Publishing Company 123
Quirk, Lawrence 21

Rawhide 71, 96, 98, 104, 124, 194
Ray, Aldo 77
Reagan, Nancy 129
Reagan, Ronald 10, 70, 129
Red Bait 35, 36, 37, 106, 191; see also *Project X*
Red Scare 35, 58
Reed, Jerry 178
Remmick, Lee 103, 125
The Reporter 132, 195
Republic Pictures 90
Rewald, Ronald 188
Rhodes, Karen 2, 144, 153, 164
Richman, Peter Mark 104
Richmond Hill 7, 9, 14, 16
The Ride to Hangman's Tree 139, 142, 196
Robertson, Cliff 93
USS *Robin Sherwood* 20
Rockefeller, John D., Jr. 57
Rockwell, Norman 10, 41
Rodeo U.S.A. 112–113
Rogers, Will 184
Rose, Reginald 78
Rose Bowl 78
Rosenberg, Stuart 135
Route 66 103, 144, 153, 194
Rowlands, Gina 111
Royal Theatre 133
Ryan, Ellen Josephine 8
Ryan, John Joseph (Lord's son) 21–22
Ryan, John Joseph Patrick (aka Jack Lord) 7–8, 14
Ryan, Josephine 9
Ryan, Peggy 148
Ryan, Robert (actor) 77, 87
Ryan, Robert J. 9
Ryan, Thomas H. 9
Ryan, William Lawrence 8
Ryan, William Lawrence, Jr. 8

Sacco and Venzetti 124
Saltzman, Harry 105–106, 110
San Sebastian Film Festival 124
Sarnoff, David 33
Sarracini, Gerry (Gerald) 71
Sax, Shirley 181–182
Scala, Gia 77
Scalpone, Al 61, 81
Schary, Dore 76
Schatt, Roy 29–31
Schnee, Charles 99

Screenwriters Guild 60
Seaton, George 60–70
Seller, Lewis 85
Serling, Rod 93, 104, 124, 134, 137
Shakespeare, William 31, 73, 171
Shatterhand 142
Shaver, Helen 178
Sherman, Eddie 148, 166
Shiffrin, A.B. 37
Shigeta, James 99
Short, Luke 92, 94
Sideshow 125–204
Silliphant, Stirling 103
Slaughter's Trail (See *Cutter's Trail*)
Smith, Cecil 99
Smith, Frederick E. 93
Smith, Howard 191
Snake River Stampede 127
Solomon, Joe 141
South China Morning Post 166, 179
Spain, Fay 77
Sperling, Milton 55–57, 98
Spooner, Dennis 146
Stack, Robert 96
Stagecoach West 104, 194
Stambler, Robert 158
Stanislavsky, Konstantin 27, 30
Stanley, Kim 44–46
Steiger, Rod 53, 55, 103
Sterling, Tisha 140, 142
Stevens, Leslie 112–120, 128
Stevens, Morton 150, 195
Stewart, Jimmy 121
Stoney Burke: cancellation 122; premiere 116; rodeo appearances 125–128; tension among cast 119–121
Story of a Patriot 27, 32, 60, 63, 68–69, 74, 159, 193–202
Strasberg, Lee 29–30
Strasberg, Susan 141–142, 197
Sullivan, Barry 110
The Sundowners 78
Suspense 44, 192
Suspense Theatre 134, 178, 195
Sweeney, Bob 164, 181, 183

Talbott, Gloria 96, 194
Tate, Thad 61, 65
The Tattooed Stranger 38, 39, 191
Taylor, Buck 121, 193
Taylor, Robert 76–78, 88, 94–95, 193, 194
Telford, Frank 104
Territorial Building 166
Theatre World Award 35, 46
The Thin Red Line 125
Thomas, Danny 122
Thomas, Kevin 178
Thoreaux, Paul 168

Thunderball 110, 123
Tibbs, Casey 118–119, 133
Tip on a Dead Jockey 66, 76, 77, 193
To Kill a Mockingbird 142
Tobacco Road 86
Todd, Richard 140–141
Tolles, Virginia 2, 9, 25, 59
The Tonight Show 3, 139, 196
Town Tamer 90
Tramp Ship 100–102
The Traveling Lady 31, 32, 44, 45, 46, 48, 52
Tripler Army Medical Center 182
Troup, Bobby 82, 193, 195
Troyano, Peter 14
The True Story of Lynn Stuart 84, 85, 193
Truman, Harry S 128–129
TV Guide 4, 5, 21, 53, 117, 118, 142, 149, 152, 156, 159, 163, 173- 174, 178, 187–210
Twelve O'Clock High 134, 136, 139, 196

University of California at Los Angeles 13, 161
University of Hawaii 155, 156–157, 184, 185
University of Southern California 10
The Unsinkable Molly Brown 123
The Untouchables 96, 194
U.S. Marshal 79, 193

The Vagabond King 36, 47, 49, 50, 51, 73, 79, 192
Vaughn, Robert 111, 142
Viacom 8
Village Academy of Arts 18
The Virginian 135, 137, 196
Von Hoffman, Nicholas 173

Wagon Train 113, 132, 135
Walk Like a Dragon 93, 99, 100, 101, 192, 194
Wallace, Lew 13
The Wanderers 126
Ward, Luci 140
Warren, Arthur 123
Wayne, John 3, 10, 33, 90, 121
The Web 43, 44, 73, 191
Wedemeyer, Herman 181
Weissman, Len 149
Welles, Orson 76
Westinghouse Studio One 70, 192
Westwood Gallery 29, 30, 31

The Whales That Wouldn't Die 197
Whatever Happened to Baby Jane 142
Whitney, Dwight 4, 21, 149, 152, 159, 174
Wide Country 115
Wilcox, Collin 142
Wilde, Cornell 48, 54
Willard, Ann Cecily 21, 22
Wilson, Marie 41
Winfrey, Oprah 187
Wiseman, Joseph 13, 41
Wolfe, Ian 104
Wong, Harry 163
Wong, Russell 189
Wood, Ben 173
Wood, Natalie 53
Wood, Robert 164
Wright, William H. 61, 63
Writers Guild of the American West 13
Wynter, Dana 177

Yankee Trader 132, 135
Young, Loretta 72, 94, 194

Zimbalist, Efrem Jr. 136
Zulu *see* Kauhi, Gilbert, Francis Lani Damian

www.ingramcontent.com/pod-product-compliance
Lightning Source LLC
Chambersburg PA
CBHW081554300426
44116CB00015B/2876